STRATFORD-UPON-AVON: PORTRAIT OF A TOWN

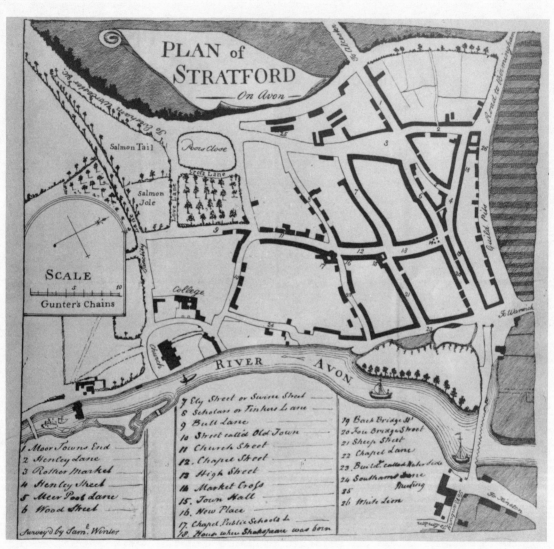

Plan of Stratford, 1759.

STRATFORD UPON AVON

PORTRAIT OF A TOWN

Nicholas Fogg

Phillimore

1986

Published by
PHILLIMORE & CO. LTD.
Shopwyke Hall, Chichester, Sussex

ISBN 0 85033 519 1

Printed and bound in Great Britain by
BIDDLES LTD.
Guildford, Surrey

Contents

List of Plates

List of Text Illustrations

Foreword

It is realised increasingly that local history represents a fascinating, invaluable and often neglected resource for the study of our past. It provides a microcosm of the life of the nation and we can find something of ourselves and our origins there. Yet the writing of it is fraught with difficulties. The inevitable unevenness of the records means that in some areas there is a welter of information, in others a sparsity. In the early centuries of this story, two facts, separated by a hundred years, may form the basis of a judgement: the unexpected discovery of a third may change the picture. In Shakespeare's time there is far more information, enabling a fuller picture of town life and personalities. Does one give greater editorial weight to this era than to the more sparsely-recorded ones which precede and follow it? The answer must be yes, for the more personalities and communities can be brought to life, the more effective the history becomes. The records the Stratfordians left behind them were not generally for posterity, but for themselves and their immediate use. Thus we deal with a partial picture. The activities of the lawbreaker, those with a grievance and the sexually indiscreet are far more likely to find a way into the record than those of the law-abiding, the content and the continent: it would, for example, be a mistake to judge the general health of the population from the notebooks of John Hall. Yet, although the glass may be misty, we frequently have no other: the distorted glimpse may be our only means of discovering anything, particularly about those the Victorians called 'the submerged one-tenth', whose impact on the records is often only through court proceedings. An occasional chance discovery can illuminate: thus the finding of the report on the apprentice pauper boys of Measham (Chapter 10) eradicated a hint that given the circumstances of the time they were probably more fortunate than most. Such illumination cannot always be found and often a statement from the records must stand alone without inclusion of the vital detail which stands behind it.

This book, like all others of its type, is thus a book of chance. What has not survived or been found could have confirmed or changed the picture. It is also, of course, dominated by the articulate. Our view of Stratford and the Stratfordians during Garrick's Jubilee comes almost entirely from witty and fastidious London scribes. It is a picture which undoubtedly differs from the one which the Stratfordians would have given, but seen in the context of the whole it is additionally valuable because it makes us realise how the people of our town appeared from a sophisticated, urban perspective. William Shakespeare, who had had a foot in both camps, appears not to have been averse to mocking, for literary purposes, the rural qualities of his townsfolk.

As I explain in the bibliography, to list all sources would be a task made excessive by the limits of time and space. I will gladly answer any specific or general queries through the publishers. I have kept original spelling wherever possible. Where it has been modernised it is sometimes for the sake of clarity and sometimes because it comes from a secondary source.

In acknowledging my debt to a large number of people, I am conscious that there are those who will be left out, but whose help was none the less appreciated. I would like to thank particularly three people: Mairi Macdonald of the Stratford Record Office read the manuscript with her usual discernment, making criticisms that were always perceptive and informed, but never destructive; Dr. Robert Bearman, senior archivist at the Record Office, has always been generous and helpful beyond the call of duty; Michael Coker, Director of Computing at Marlborough College, is truly a renaissance man of the new technology, not only explaining its mysteries, but also freely giving of his considerable scholarship in sorting out the historical *minutiae*.

I would like to thank Dr. Levi Fox, the Director of the Shakespeare Birthplace Trust, for permission to reproduce illustrative material used here, for the use of its research facilities and for his exemplary staff, who must be the envy of all such similar bodies: Eileen Alberti, Mary White, Mr. and Mrs. Roger Pringle and, during her time there, Josephine Holmes. I never got to know the staff of the Warwick County Archives so well and so can't thank them by name, but they were unfailingly courteous and helpful. The acting Headmaster of King Edward's Grammar School and the Vicar of Stratford both kindly and affably gave permission to photograph their respective buildings. Michael Payne took the photographs and I thank him for his professional expertise and enthusiasm. Edward Sturge drew the map of Shakespeare's Stratford.

In a sense, Alan Learmouth was the only begetter of the ensuing volume and I thank him for his support for the original idea, which has been taken up and nourished by Serafina Clarke, Noel Osborne and Dr. Frances Condick. Others who have contributed, sometimes inadvertently, include Ernest Thorp, Michael Davies, Dennis Flower, Dr. Richard Ough, Sidney Conway, G. Kempson, Dr. Judith Champ, David Crawford, Dr. Wilhelm Vossenkuhl, Dr. Tom Axworthy, Peter Pearce and other 'Stratford sippers'. My mother has given invaluable hospitality and support during my numerous visits to Stratford. Jean Riley, Christine Whittaker, Audrey Owen and Eileen Walmsley helped with typing. The continued interest of friends too numerous to mention has sustained my own, especially that of my wife Edwina, who has endured patiently the vagaries of the manuscript and has always made constructive and encouraging comments.

CHAPTER 1

'A Proper Little Mercat Town'

'Stratford, a proper little Mercat towne, beholden for all the beauty that it hath to two men there bred and brought up; namely *John de Stratford*, Archbishop of Canterburie, who built the church, and *Sir Hugh Clopton*, maier of London, who over *Avon* made a stone bridge . . .'

John Leland. c. 1530.

The Origins of Stratford

Stratford is not an old town by English standards. No extensive settlement existed there until the Middle Ages. Few traces of Neolithic man have been discovered, beyond a little crude pottery, implements of bone and some burnt flints. In Roman times the area was bypassed six miles to the west by Icknield Street and the Fosse Way, a similar distance to the south. The very name of the place implies that the Anglo-Saxon invaders of the sixth century found a minor Roman road linked to a river crossing, probably connecting the small garrison town of Alcester with the extensive ironworkings across the Avon. At nearby Tiddington, a Romano-British settlement flourished beyond the collapse of the Empire, demonstrating that the first English did not drive the Britons before them in an Armageddon of the Dark Ages, but settled alongside them in a process of mutual absorption. Words of Celtic origin were common in the almost-forgotten local dialect. Nearby Shottery derives its name from some 'Scot' who once lived by its brook. At Welcombe curious earthworks of obscure origin may betoken resistance to an invader, but the site would not be efficacious for military purposes.

The Anglian tribe which settled in South Warwickshire were the 'Hwiccas'; in time to be absorbed into the Saxon kingdom of Mercia. The people of the Hwiccas became Christian before the other Mercian tribes: a diocese of the Hwiccas with Bosel as its bishop was established at Worcester by 680. Like his successor, Oftfor, Bosel had been a monk at Whitby Abbey. 'Having devoted himself to reading and applying the scriptures', Bede tells us that Oftfor, 'to win greater perfection', visited Rome. On his return, he spent a long time in the province of the Hwiccas, 'preaching the word of the faith and setting an example of holy life to all who met and heard him'.[1] It was probably during this mission that a monastery was founded at Stratford. The first extant reference to it occurs when Egwin, Bishop of the Hwiccas from 693 – 717, exchanged a religious house at Fladbury for one held by the King of Mercia at *Aet-Stretford:* 'the Isle of the Ford'. Presumably this was on the site of Holy Trinity Church on the higher ground above the Avon and its river marshes. The ford which gave the place its name was probably nearby, rather than at the later road bridge further upstream.

The monks must have come south with Bosel or Oftfor and one of these bishops is the likely founder of Stratford. They were treading a land still largely heathen and kindling a light for future generations of English. The monastery was well-sited and the little community thrived. The potential for a water mill on the Avon below the Church was seen and developed. Early in the eighth century, the King of Mercia granted more lands around Shottery to the bishopric and in 781 Offa, the greatest of the Mercian kings, confirmed the right of the Bishops of

1

Worcester to 'Stretforde', an estate of 30 hides (over 3,500 acres), whose boundaries stretched to Billesley and Milcote. Another Mercian King, Bertulf, reconfirmed these privileges at a Witangemoot held on Christmas Day, 845. The land was described as sufficient to support 20 families and was free 'from all human servitude, all secular tributes and taxes'. The last recorded charter of this monastery was in 872. When, why and by whom it was dissolved is unknown. Probably it was destroyed by Danish raiders. In 1015 every religious house in Warwickshire except Polesworth was burnt down.

The Norman conquest, elsewhere a watershed of history, passed quietly at Stratford. Wulfstan, the Saxon Bishop of Worcester, acknowledged the claims of William of Normandy and retained his see. Later he prosecuted the Conqueror's wars on the Welsh Marches; perhaps some of his Stratford tenants served in his campaigns.

The Domesday survey of 1086 revealed that the Stratford estate was smaller, but wealthier than in Saxon times: some 14 hides supported 21 villeins, a priest and seven cottagers – a population of around two hundred. The tenants paid rents totalling 100s a year and had the use of 31 ploughs of which three belonged to the Bishop. The yearly cash income from the water mill, where the villagers were obliged to grind their corn, was ten shillings, but many tenants paid in kind. Each year 1,000 eels were sent to the Bishop's kitchens from his Stratford manor, from which the annual profit was a handsome twenty-five pounds.

A comprehensive feudal system with every man in his place and a place for every man developed in the manors around Stratford. In 1228 Robert de Clopton founded a long-lasting dynasty when he obtained the manor from which he took his name from Peter de Montfort. The Bishop's estates were held by knights, who were in their turn the overlords of the tenant farmers. One such tenant, Simon, was living 'bi-the-broke' in Shottery (perhaps on the later site of Anne Hathaway's cottage) in 1252. Every year on St Martin's day he paid 'wattselver' for the militia and tolls on 'each horse born to him, should it be sold within the manor, 1d . . . and for a pig over a year, 1d, and of less age 1s 2d, but it may not be a sucking pig'. Simon's lord, Thomas de Bissopedene (Bishopton), was aware of the dangers of putrifying meat, for he forbade his tenants to sell pork during the summer without permission. Simon helped brew 'Fulpthale' during the winter, but if he brewed for sale he paid a silver penny. Within the manor there was a lock-up for vagrants and other offenders where Simon took his turn at guard or from where he escorted prisoners charged with more serious offences to Warwick. He had to obtain his lord's permission for his son to leave the farm or for his daughter to marry. He worked one day a week for his lord and in summer and spring brought one of his labourers to assist him. If he harvested his corn before his lord, he owed service with one or two men 'until all be gathered in'. Even death did not end his feudal obligations, for his lord was then entitled to his best animal.

Simon's duties were the norm for the other tenants. Felice Palmeres held his land for eight shillings yearly 'as the aforesaid Simon'. Fanty the fisherman, perhaps farming eels in Shottery brook, paid 'as Simon Bythebroke' for his quarter virgate.

The society of Simon and his neighbours was one of duties, rights and labour, in which the people tilled the earth which sustained them: an unchanging world with every character fixed in place like figures in a Book of Hours. Yet in one respect life was dynamic in this corner of Warwickshire, for at the end of the 12th century a new town came into being. With its grid of wide, regular streets, Stratford has the air of a planned town, in contrast to the cramped thoroughfares of many medieval settlements. It was perhaps the building of a wooden bridge which led those responsible for diocesan finances to see the potential of the river crossing linking the rich pastures of Arden with the uplands of Cotswold and Felden, whose wool production was developing and whose barley would provide Stratford with its biggest industry of malting. In 1196 Richard I granted the right to a market every Thursday 'in perpetuity' for which the citizens paid their Bishop 16 shillings annually. The charter was witnessed by an eminent company which included the Archbishop of Canterbury, the Bishop of Normandy, William of the Church of St Mary (Warwick?) and William, son of Ralf, seneschal of Normandy. A statute of 1203 reveals a thriving town, whose planned character is demonstrated by the uniform size of tenements: three perches wide and 12 perches long and rented for 12 silver pence a year. The tradesmen included tanners, turners, mercers, whitesmiths, locksmiths, tailors, carpenters, skinners, coopers, dyers, potters, wheelwrights, ironworkers, fullers, bakers, weavers, barbers, shoemakers, butchers, salters, piebakers, chapmen, millers, fishermen, parchment-makers, curriers, cardmakers and tylers. The 'uly' or oil makers left their name in what is now Ely Street, whose alternative name was Swine Street. Other commodities were sold in 'Sheep' Street; 'Corne strete' (now Chapel Street); 'Butchers Row' (the passage through 'Middelrewe' in Bridge Street) and the great 'Rother' or cattle market. A pillory, where offenders could be pelted with the humiliating refuse of such streets, was established in 1309. The trade and prosperity of Stratford attracted immigrants. Amongst those living in the town in 1314 were John de Lapworth, John de Kynton, Hugo de Compton and Thomas de Clifford.

Fairs were a great stimulus to trade. In 1214 a fair was granted on the eve, day and morrow of the 29 October, the patronal feast of Holy Trinity. Other fairs were later granted on St Augustine's day, Ascension Day and for the Feast of the Exaltation of the Holy Cross on 23 December, the patronal festival of the Guild of that name.

The guilds of Stratford

When in 1389 the wardens of the Guild of the Holy Cross responded to a royal writ, they stated that the 'source of the Guild was from the time whereunto the memory of man reacheth not'. Certainly it existed in 1269 when the Bishop granted a charter to build a considerable complex in the town. The document implies that it was already in being but there is no mention of the Stratford guilds in a survey of the episcopal manor in 1251, so this venture was the first time any of them acquired property.

The guilds had a dual function. The members acted as guardians of those altars in Holy Trinity to which their guild had a special devotion. They were also a corporate body of Christian laity intended to protect mortal bodies and sanctify immortal souls, so they developed charitable and liturgical functions. In the second half of the 13th century there were at least three guilds in existence and perhaps others which have left no trace.

The smallest was the Guild of St John the Baptist, referred to in 1324 and in 1344, when the rental of eightpence from a messuage in Rother Street was given by William de Gorschawe to the Procters of 'the Guild of St John the Baptist and St John the Evangelist in the Church of Stratford'. The dual title perhaps signifies an earlier amalgamation. It became merged in the Mary Guild as 'The Brethren of the Blessed Mary and the Blessed John'. This Guild possessed a hall next to the church-gate, called St Mary's House. Most of the north aisle at Holy Trinity formed the Chapel of Our Lady under its guardianship. The inventories demonstrate the devotion of its brethren. Robert de Walleys endowed an annual rent charge of 12 pence to its altar; Richard Hylgar gave fourpence yearly to maintain the altar light, from 'a stall where flesh is sold'; a messuage in Henley Street was given to 'the work of the Blessed Mary' by Alice, widow of Walter Marescall. In 1313 the north aisle was reconstructed. The Primate of Ireland granted a 40-day indulgence to those who visited the altar or contributed to its beautification. 'Item', reads a later inventory, 'a blew cloth to oure Ladye in tyme of Lenton', when the statue would be covered. Richard Warner gave 36 pence from the rental of a tenement 'in the street in which pigs are sold' (Swine Street), '12d for the celebration of our Lady the Blessed Virgin, 12d to keep a waxlight before her altar and 12d for a lamp'.

By the mid-13th century, the Guild of the Holy Cross was a powerful religious community under a lay warden, Robert Hatton. The charter granted in 1269 by Godfrey Giffard, Bishop of Worcester, is worth quoting extensively for its charm and insights into the character of the Guild.

> Whenever a pious request is earnestly made it is meet that a gracious assent should be granted. It is therefore that our beloved children in Christ, Master Robert de Stratford [and] the brothers and sisters of the Holy Cross have humbly besought us that they might build a certain hospice, in the village of Stratford-upon-Avon, in honour of our Lord Jesus Christ and the Holy Cross, and also to erect an oratory and chapel there with bells, in order that divine service may be celebrated for the souls of their ancestors and all the faithful departed, and for the maintenance of those serving in the same chapel, and of the needy brothers and sisters of the same fraternity, and of the poor of the same town and also of needy priests who have been promoted without certain title by the Bishop of Worcester for the present.

The Guild was to pay the Bishop a token rent of a gallon of ale from every brewing, three cakes from every baking and 'certain rents in the same village, under the sign of the Holy Cross'. The hospice was to be 'immediately, in full right, subject to us and our successors'.

On the houses of the hospice and its tenants, a cross was to be erected and bells hung. Within the hospice a monastic community lived under the Augustinian rule. Such luxuries as linen garments were forbidden 'except for drawers, or for the sick and the infirm' and then only at the master's discretion. Their tunics were of russet 'as it comes from the fleece', with over-tunics furred in black and white sheepskin. Over this the brothers wore a cloak embroidered with a black cross surmounted by a white mitre. When riding out they wore a russet cape bearing the same emblems. The Order's nine laybrothers dressed in the same way, except for a scapular with the emblem in the centre, instead of on the cloak. No-one was allowed to eat, drink or go out of the hospice unless wearing his habit. The members of the Order ate together in the refectory and slept in a communal dormitory. It was forbidden for the brethren to eat or drink in Stratford without the Master's permission. The sick and the infirm were tended in the infirmary.

Novitiates took vows of chastity and obedience. At his investiture the ordinand lay on his face before the altar in the chapel while the majestic hymn *Veni Creator Spiritus* was sung, followed by the verse *Confirma hoc Deus quod operatus in nobis* and the response *A templo sancto tuo quod est in Jerusalem*. The Master's address took as its text *Omnipotens sempiterne Deus qui facis*. Each member of the Guild paid fourpence yearly. If a poor townsman died, or a passing stranger without means, the Guild provided the dignity of a requiem, with four candles, a winding sheet and hearse cloth. When a member died, a third of the fraternity were summoned to watch and pray by the body. To ensure the emergence of its members amongst the Church Triumphant, the Guild employed two chantry priests in its chapel.

The Guild acquired considerable property in Stratford. In 1353-4 it leased tenements with a total rental of £20 3s 5d. Times were hard that year, possibly through a slump in the wool trade. An unpleasantly long list of persons owed rent. A note of incentive appears in a bonus of twopence given to a roofmaker 'to get him to work better'.

It was probably after the promulgation of the Statute of Winchester in 1285 that the first structures of local government were formulated in Stratford. The Bishop's steward presided over a Leet Court of 12 citizens of substance which advised him on the annual election of a Bailiff, constables and other officials. A schoolmaster is first mentioned in 1295 when amongst those ordained deacon by Bishop Giffard were William Grenefield, rector of the church at Stratford and Richard, rector of the school. Grenefield was an eminent lawyer who later became Archbishop of York. The growing importance of Stratford in the early 14th century is demonstrated by the fact that he was one of three former rectors to become Lord Chancellor of England: the others were the brothers, John and Robert Hatton, who were probably sons of that Robert Hatton who was warden of the Guild of the Holy Cross. Like him they bore the suffix 'de Stratford'. Their seal punned on the family name, showing a figure with his *hat on*.

The Brothers Hatton de Stratford

John de Stratford was the first recorded Stratfordian to attend university, graduating from Merton College, Oxford, as a doctor of canon and civil law before 1311. Around this time he became rector of Stratford, but did not devote his entire energies to its spiritual welfare, holding plural benefices and regularly giving legal advice in Parliament. In 1319 he became archdeacon of Lincoln and his brother Robert, also an eminent lawyer, was installed as rector of Stratford. John de Stratford was a diplomat at the papal curia before becoming Bishop of Winchester. His role was as much political as spiritual. He played a crucial part in the abdication of Edward II in 1326. Edward III made him Chancellor in 1330 and he was principal advisor to the King for the next ten years, playing an ambiguous but moderating role in the French wars as virtual ruler of England during the King's campaigns. In 1333 he rose to England's highest spiritual dignity as Archbishop of Canterbury. His brother's star also rose: in 1331 he became Chancellor of the Exchequer and, later, Chancellor of Oxford University; in 1337 he became Chancellor of England and he was consecrated as Bishop of Chichester by his brother. A third member of the family, Ralph Hatton de Stratford, perhaps a nephew, became Bishop of London in 1340.

John de Stratford's primacy, like that of Thomas à Becket, brought him into conflict with the King, who was attempting to increase his power. When de Stratford was threatened with the same fate as his illustrious predecessor, he defended Magna Carta from the sanctuary of a Kentish monastery. After a jury of his peers acquitted him of all charges against him, he returned to the royal favour before his death in 1348. He was buried in his own cathedral, next to the shrine of St Thomas, where his tall, bearded effigy remains.

The de Stratfords were great benefactors to their native place. Robert's contribution was soundly practical. In 1332 he raised a toll on agricultural commodities to pave Henley Street, Greenhill Street and Old Town. John de Stratford's works were devoted to Holy Trinity. He erected a wooden bell tower, widened the north aisle and built the south aisle. There he established a chantry, endowed by the nearby manor of Ingon and dedicated to his special saint, Thomas à Becket, 'for the praise of God and for the soul's health of myself, Robert my brother and for the souls of Robert and Elizabeth, my father and mother, and for the good health of my lord, King Edward and that of my successors'.

In 1337 John de Stratford sought to appropriate the patronage of Holy Trinity from Simon de Montacute, Bishop of Worcester. A

1. South-west view of church, 1762, showing John de Stratford's wooden spire.

local layman, John Lacey, wrote a deposition in his support which revealed that the rector, like most of his predecessors, was mainly non-resident and that only two chaplains served the church. If it were appropriated the number of resident ministers would be increased to eight.

John de Stratford gave the endowment of the church to the chantry which he had founded. The office of warden, or *custos*, was a powerful one and he and the sub-warden were appointed for life, but the other priests were elected or dismissed at his discretion. The appropriation exempted the parish of Holy Trinity from much of the normal jurisdiction of the Bishop and gave it tenuous spiritual jurisdiction over the Guild of the Holy Cross. Two years out of three the Warden could exercise many of the prerogatives of the Bishop, including the prosecution of offenders against canon law in his own court. In 1353 Ralph de Stratford built a college for the chantry clergy near the church. The creation of the peculiar brought anomalies and friction between ecclesiastic and corporate jurisdictions which would endure for centuries.

2. Engraving of the College by R. B. Wheler, c.1800. It was built by Bishop Ralph de Stratford in 1353 and demolished in 1799.

Until the mid-18th century the seal of the Stratford peculiar bore the effigy and arms of John de Stratford. The archbishop is represented as standing in an attitude of benediction beneath a canopied tabernacle with this legend in a reeded border: S'PECULIAR JURISDIC-COIS DE STRATFORD SUP.ABANA.

Guild and Church

The growing power of the Guild is demonstrated in a complaint registered in 1377 by Thomas, Earl of Warwick, that 46 named Stratfordians and others, leading a considerable body of archers, had invaded the earl's manor at Fulready, breaking down fences and pillaging houses. They assaulted 'his men, servants, bondmen and tenants, whose lives they so threatened that they could not attend to his business . . . not daring to remain there any longer'. The cause of this aggravation is unknown, but it must have been serious for the list includes some of the most prominent brethren of Stratford.

By 1397 the Mary Guild had been absorbed into its richer neighbour, the Guild of the Holy Cross. Its guildhouse became a schoolroom and the schoolmaster lived there rent-free. In 1403 the combined Guild was refounded and incorporated as the 'fraternity and Gild of the Holy Cross of Stratforde-on-Avone and St John Baptist'. The officials consisted of a Master, eight aldermen and two proctors, elected annually by the fraternity. Sexual equality prevailed with the sisters voting together with the brothers. The proctors recorded fines for admission and the frequent legacies. They saw that repairs to Guild property were carried out and arranged the great feast. Their accounts illuminate contemporary manners and customs. Benefactors and their gifts are noted year by year with the communal principle prevailing of each contributing according to his ability. In 1408-9 Simon Groves, a carpenter, was admitted and excused 53s 4d he owed the Guild in return for building two bays at the eastern end of the kitchen. Other benefactions show the range of guild membership and the diversity of the gifts. Henry and Margaret Lyttleton of Handy gave two quarters of lime; Lady Joanna Clopton a canopy; in 1440, John Wydbury, Rector of Stretton, six quarters of barley, valued at 16 shillings; John Bultys, a pair of vestments; William Pyers, a hogshead of red wine. In 1454 Henry Newport of Daventry was admitted with his wife Joanna. He was a fishmonger who gave a 'lavetre [lavebo] with four cocks, for the use of the chaplains to wash at'.

Perhaps the most useful addition to the fraternity was John Prynce, admitted with his wife in 1416. Prynce was the Earl of Warwick's master cook and paid no fees 'on condition that he shall be always assiduous at the annual Communions of the Guild, to give council and assistance, if so previously required, annually during his life'.

Prynce lived at a time when there was little distinction between the secular and ecclesiastical meanings of the word 'feast'. On principal feastdays the Guild chaplains met the master and aldermen at the great white cross which stood in front of the Chapel and then they solemnly processed to Holy Trinity, splendid in their copes and liveries, bearing the Guild crosses and banners and feasting on their return. At Easter the great Guild feast was conducted so that 'brotherly love shall be upheld among them and evil speaking driven out . . .'. Everyone brought a leather drinking vessel, but before they drank, ale was given to the poor. Before the brothers and sisters ate the feast they prayed that 'God, the Blessed Virgin and the much-to-be venerated Cross, in whose honour we have come together, will keep us from all ills and sins'. They feasted at tables spread with 'napery' and groaning under the weight of a huge repast. In 1416 payments were made for wheat, malt, beer for the cook, seven calves, 16 pigs, boars' heads, four lambs, seven sheep, lard, 209 pullets, two geese, 12 capons, butter, milk, cream, vinegar, honey, salt, 1,900 eggs, three gallons of wine, fuel, pepper, saffron, ginger and mace. These Breughelian feasts were accompanied by music and dancing on the rush-strewn floor. After 1421-2 the Guild year dated from the feast of St Thomas the Martyr and the feast was held on that day: another mark of special devotion to the saint of Canterbury.

The coveted status of 'collegiate' was confirmed to Holy Trinity Church by Henry V in the Agincourt year of 1415. The church incorporated a college of priests which educated scholars to a high level of learning. After 1423, the warden assumed the title of 'dean'. Wills, testaments and accounts give us more information about the appearance of the church. A crucifix surmounted the rood beam. Three aumbury lights using seven gallons of oil each year burnt before the reserved sacrament. In 1465 William Bulle bequeathed two candelabra to 'serve' at the altar of St Thomas – one before the statue of St Dominic, the other before the *Pieta*.

In the 1420s, the reformed Guild began to build a grander chapel, paying an eminent lawyer, Sir Thomas Burdet, for services *pro ratificatione*. Early in 1427 John Harris, one of the chaplains, and William Bedley, a prominent Guild member, rode to Wedyngton to speak to the Bishop, presumably about the consecration. A schoolhouse was provided in the reconstruction – thus the origins of Stratford's ancient grammar school may be dated – and this John Harris was to be its first schoolmaster. 'On this side St Hilary', the Bishop was in Stratford, perhaps to view the new buildings. Later that year the chapel was elaborately and splendidly consecrated by the suffragan. Three ells of linen were used in the ceremonial cleansing of the altars prior to benediction. Scores of candles were lit and the air was thick and sweet with incense as the Bishop anointed 24 points around the building, marked by red and white crosses.

The growing autonomy of the Guild was causing concern at Holy Trinity. In 1428 a citation was served on behalf of the primate on the four chaplains (including John Harris) and three lay members of the Guild to answer complaints from Richard Praty, the warden of the church. A three-man episcopal commission investigated the matter. The Guild judiciously gave a dinner in their honour and sent Master John Foton to Rome with their charter. The church

authorities were active too, for the Bishop's judgement reaffirmed that 'the rule of St Augustine and the ordinances laid down by Godfrey, formerly Bishop of Worcester shall be observed by all concerned . . . under a penalty of 20s from the master . . . half of which shall be spent on alms, half on the cathedral church of Worcester'.

Other letters patent indicate the matters in dispute. Hay from the hospice grounds was eligible for tithes. The priests of the Guild were forbidden to conduct burial services or administer the sacrament, 'except the blessed bread and water to the sick in the said house'. All members of the Guild were to attend mass and vespers at Holy Trinity on the four principal feast days, when the Guild chaplains, 'wearing their correct surplices' (clearly another point of contention) would sing in the choir. To underline 'the superiority of the said Church', the hospice was to pay it an annual tribute of four shillings. The Guild appealed to the Pope and Master Thomas Hanwell was delegated to seek an audience. A Bull, now lost, which presumably confirmed the previous decision, was issued in 1432.

3. The Guild Chapel: an early 19th-century engraving.

This division of function ensured that the Guild no longer developed as a semi-monastic foundation, but as a lay body which impressively expressed the medieval ideal of community. The transformation was reflected in the changing functions of the buildings. The *frater* became a hall; the *dorter,* an upper hall and the livery, a costume for formal occasions. By 1480 the Guild's fellowship included merchants and bankers from a wide area and some of the greatest in the land were associated with it. The list reads like the *dramatis personae* of *Richard III:* the King's eldest son (the future prince in the Tower); Rivers, the Queen's brother, and the King's brother, the ill-starred and turbulent Duke of Clarence.

Stratford's development under the benign patronage of the Bishops of Worcester cocooned it from many of the troubles of the age – although they encroached to the very boundaries of the parish. In Henry IV's reign a Royal Commission investigated reports that 'certain evildoers, scheming to hinder the King's lieges, merchants and others, going by roads and highways between the town of Bermyngham and Stratford and the town of Alcestre, to the markets of Coleshull, Bermyngham, Walshule and Dudley . . . assembled in divers convecticles and veiling their faces with masks, with garments turned in the manner of torturers and carrying machines called "gladmeres" and other instruments, lay in ambush and assaulted the King's lieges going to and from the markets and put them and their horses to flight, so that the women and children riding on the horses with sacks filled with corn, fell off and some died and some were injured and cut the sacks and scattered corn along the roads'.

Yet so far as the little town was concerned the French wars might never have been and the inhabitants were shielded from the Wars of the Roses, although complete isolation could not be afforded from events so close, particularly when one of the main protagonists was Richard Neville, the 'Kingmaker' Earl of Warwick. In 1450-51 the Guild served wine in the house of Agnes Chacomb for Anne, Countess of Warwick and two years later spent 3s 8d on wine when 'the Earl rode by this way towards Wales'. Later the Kingmaker sent two deer 'to gladden the brethren and sisters . . . on the Feast of the Dedication of the Church'. After the Earl's defeat and death in 1471, King Edward IV and his army passed through Stratford: the first recorded visit to the town by a reigning English monarch. The brethren judiciously elected Neville's effective successor at Warwick, his son-in-law the Duke of Clarence, as a member of the Guild.

Stratford's fortune in being aloof from the lawlessness of the time is demonstrated by the sad affair of Ankarette Twynho. This friend of the Queen was seized by Clarence's soldiers in Somerset and brought to Warwick. Clarence was seeking revenge for the Queen's opposition to his projected marriage into the Burgundian ducal family. Ankarette's family and their servants were lodged in Stratford. She was executed on a charge of poisoning Clarence's wife, Isabella. The justices who had condemned her asked her forgiveness 'in consideration of the imagination of the said Duke and his might'. In the following year 'false, fleeting, perjured Clarence' was executed on a charge of treason a few weeks after Thomas Burdet from Arrow had been executed for being his necromancer.

Contemporary troubles did not divert the Guild's growth to prosperity. Most of its buildings were reconstructed between 1468 and 1480. A notable endowment came from a wealthy priest of the Guild, Thomas Jolyffe, who in 1482 gave the Guild his property in Stratford and Dodwell to provide an annual salary of ten pounds for a priest 'to teach grammar freely to all the scholars coming to the school, taking nothing of the scholars for their teaching'.

Stratford's prime benefactor in this era was Sir Hugh Clopton, who made a great fortune as a London mercer and became Lord Mayor in 1492. In Stratford he built the great house known as New Place, probably the town's first brick building, marking the start of a long transformation from wattle and daub. He bequeathed five marks each as dowries for 20 poor maidens 'of good name and fame dwelling in Stratford'; £100 to the town's poor householders and £50 to rebuild the cross aisle at Holy Trinity, as well as endowments to the hospitals of London and six exhibitions for poor scholars at Oxford and Cambridge.

Sir Hugh's greatest gift to Stratford was the 'great and sumptuous bridge upon the Avon', a wonder of 14 arches. It was over 400 yards long with its causeway. Leland, the antiquary, noted its benefits. 'Afore the time of Hugh Clopton there was but a poor bridge of timber and no causeway to come to it, whereby many poor folks either refused to come to Stratford when the river was up, or coming thither stood in jeopardy of life'. At the far end of this bridge was the Chapel of 'the Blessed Marie Magdalen'.

Sir Hugh started to rebuild the Guild Chapel and left instructions for its completion. 'Whereas of late I have bargayned with oon Dowland and diverse other masons . . . I will that the saide Masons sufficiently and ably doo and fynysshe the same with good and true Workmanshipp . . ., making the said werkis as wele of length and brede and hight such as by the advise of mine executors and other diverse of the substantialist and honest men of the same parish shall or canne be thought moost convenient and necessary . . . and in like wyse the covereing the rofyng of the same chapell with glaising, and all other fornysshments thereunto necessary to it, to be paide by my said executors as the werkis aforesaid goeth fourth.' The 'other fornysshments' included wall paintings. On the ceiling were scenes from the History of the Holy Cross; on the walls, pictures of Thomas à Becket and St George and the dragon. Above the chancel was a great painting of the Last Judgement. Its graphic gaping devils dragging lost souls to perdition contrasted with the blessed ascending to glory must have brought fascinated terror to children and served as an unneeded *memento mori* to the sick and infirm who chiefly used the chapel.

Substantial improvements were taking place at Holy Trinity too, wrought by two notable deans. Thomas Balsall rebuilt the choir as the exquisite structure which still survives. The work reveals two mastercraftsmen of very different character. Neither was familiar with contemporary trends in his craft. One created a delicate tracery throughout the choir, but in the Early English style of two centuries before, which he might have seen in the great cathedrals. The earthy creations of the other demonstrate the continuity of a peasant culture within the medieval *ecclesia*. He carved the fantastical and bizarre misericords on the choirstalls. The 26 carvings contain such folk memories of the Crusades as a saracen's head and a sphinx with a rider. An ostrich swallows a horseshoe, a mermaid combs her hair at a handmirror and the explicit sexual image of *Luxuria* or lechery as a naked woman rides a stag. Domestic discord is provided by a wife who seizes her husband's beard while pummelling him with a frying pan. Oddest of all is the depiction of two heraldic rampant bears, flanked by a chained ape which provides a urine sample for another ape to examine – perhaps a satire of a local dignitary? On the roof of the stalls the master paid due heed to the sacred but retained his basic flavour, creating 'uncouth images of angels and cherubs in profusion'.[2]

It was the collegiate Dean Ralph Collingwood who assigned lands in Stratford, Drayton and Binton for the maintenance of four choristers and left strict ordinances for their conduct. They were to attend daily matins and vespers which were sung according to the *Ordinale Sarum*. On entering the church they were to kneel and say a *Pater Noster* and an *Ave*. They were to sit quietly and say their offices distinctly. They were forbidden to go into the town or to fetch beer from the buttery. At dinner and supper they waited at table and read the Bible 'or some other authentic book'. Afterwards one of the clerics gave them singing lessons at the organ. Their bedroom (later the charnel house) adjoined the *sanctum* of the church and the boys shared two beds to which they retired at eight in winter and nine in summer. Before undressing they were instructed to say a *De Profundis* loudly, with the prayers and orizons of the faithful, before exclaiming: 'God, have mercy on the soul of Ralph Collingwood, our founder, and Master Thomas Balsall, a special benefactor to the same'.

Catholicism flourished in Stratford until the Reformation. Human failings were placed within a perspective in which worship was cared for and the sacraments made a living reality. Education was encouraged and charity extended far beyond the town. Yet, for most, faith brought demands rather than material rewards and it was the influence of the age which kept the fear of God before their eyes.

FOOTNOTES
[1]   Bede: 'A History of the English Church and People'; trans. Leo Sherley-Price. Penguin (1955).
[2]   This was demolished in 1790, but some of the bosses remain. I am indebted for some of the thoughts in this chapter to Mary Frances White in her 'Fifteenth Century Misericords in the Church of Holy Trinity . . .'; Stratford-upon-Avon (1974).

CHAPTER 2

'. . . A Body Corporate and Politic'

'The inhabitants of the borough of Stratford . . . have humbly prayed us that we would accord them our favour and abundant grace for the amelioration of the said borough and the government thereof . . . and that we would deign to make, reduce and incorporate them into a body corporate and politic.'

Charter of King Edward VI: 1553.

The Reformation at Stratford

The forces which produced the Reformation sent their ripples towards Stratford. The growth of national consciousness and the secular power of princes was breaking down Catholic universalism. Sheep farming was encroaching onto the Midland plains, destroying labour intensive farming systems and causing a drift from the land. 'In this shire . . . sheep turn cannibals', lamented a visitor to Warwickshire, 'eating up men, houses and towns; their pastures make such depopulation.' But there was another viewpoint: '. . . it is pleaded for these enclosers that they make the houses the fewer in the country and the more in the kingdom. How come building in great towns every day to increase . . . , but that the poor are generally maintained by clothing, the staple trade of the nations?' This economic revolution strongly influenced life in Stratford, where the wool trade was of increasing importance.

It would be incautious to interpret too much from occurrences in Stratford before the Reformation, which in a different chronology would not achieve such significance. Yet they are made significant by their proximity to momentous change. They had no doctrinal causation, but reveal a growth of individualism and the questioning of authority. Certainly they demonstrate an unwholesome increase in factionalism, alien to the spirit of brotherly love intended to pervade the Guild.

John Eylis, a former Master of the Guild, was appointed as the Bishop's deputy steward in 1509. His conduct aroused the opposition of three men of substance in the town: Richard Bentley, a smith by trade, who had been admitted with his wife Margery as long before as 1471, and two former Proctors, Thomas Thomasyn and John Staffordshire. Their behaviour led to a complaint to the King from Silvester, Bishop of Worcester.

At a . . . court holden for your supplyant at Stratford uppon Avene . . . elleccon [election] was made by xii men sworn . . . of too Constables for the for the conservation of your peas [peace] within the precyncte of the same town and of a Baily [Bailiff] . . . for the yere following as all weys hath be used there tyme out of mynde, one Thomas Thomasyn . . ., yoman, which have of his own presumptious mynde wold have be baily there for this yere, not pleased with the said ellecon assemble[d] with one Richard Bentley and John Staffordshire . . ., yoman and other persons to the number of xij, with bills, clubbys, stavys and swordes came riotously to the hous wher the . . . court was holden and then ther wold have slayne one John Elys deputie Styward sitting and kepying the said Court and there with exclamacon said that . . . William Cottoun which was ellecte baily . . . should not be bailly who so everwold sey naye, and with assautes & exclamacons riotously kept the said deputie styward & xij men tille hit was passed x of the clocke in the nyght, to the grete disturbans of your peas and in contmpt of your highnes & of your lawes to the perillous example of mysdoers enless they may have due punysion [punishment] therefore. In consideracon where of, that it will pleas your hignes to directe youre honorable letters of pryve seale to the said Thomas Thomasyn, Richard Bentley & John Staffordshire to appere before your highnes and your most honourable Counsaill at your palous at Westminster . . . there to annswere to thes premisses and to be punyshed for their said riotte and contemptes.

William Cottoun, whose election had caused such displeasure, was also a prominent member of the Guild. Admitted in 1492, he was a Proctor in 1499 and an alderman between 1502 and 1508.

The defendants replied that from 'tyme out of mynde' the Bailiff had been chosen by 12 of 'the most substanciall and honest persones', but Eylis had selected the jury from 'the senglest [silliest] and symplest persons . . . and some of them were but mennys servantes and left the substanciall men out of the same jurie. And after the said jurie was sworn they kuld not agree uppon oon of the Bayliffes and they so beying not agreed the John Eylis proclaymed Bayliffes and Constables at large in the sayd Town such as hym pleased'. It would appear that the King and his councillors found for the gerrymanders rather than the riotous legalists, for John Eylis continued as an alderman until 1520, but none of the defendants seems to have held office again.

Although the Reformation swept much away, its effects were less profound in South Warwickshire than elsewhere. There is little evidence of local zeal for change, although Hugh Latimer, soon to become the Protestant Bishop of Worcester, was arrested at Hampton Lucy while the King was still the Pope's *Fidelis Defensor*. This learned and austere man preached at Holy Trinity in 1537 and referred subsequently to the area around Stratford as the 'blind end' of his diocese.

If judgement were to be made on the scant evidence available from this one small town, the conclusion that avarice rather than doctrine was the prime motive for the Reformation would be irresistible. In 1535, following the King's defection from Rome, his commissioners seized plate from Holy Trinity. Before the end of the reign 260 ounces of silver and gold had been appropriated. In 1542 the lordship of Stratford passed from its creator, the Bishopric of Worcester when a new bishop, Nicholas Heath, described merely as the King's 'delegate', was obliged to surrender his manor of Stratford to John Dudley, Earl of Warwick, in exchange for lands in Worcestershire.

The Guilds and the College survived the reign of Henry VIII. In 1535 the College had an annual income of £128 9s 11d and was occupied by the Warden, five priests and four choristers. A glimpse of this little community emerges in a presentation of 20 June 1544 by Anthony Barker, Provost of the College, asking leave to appoint a *subcustos*. A number of people testified for the candidate, Master Giles Coventrie. On 27 December 1546, another *subcustos*, Edward Alcock, was appointed after Coventrie resigned. This was the last free recorded act of a College warden. In the following year, the first of the reign of Edward VI, all colleges and chantries were suppressed. Alcock did well financially from his brief tenure, gaining a gratuity of £6 13s 4d. All images in the churches of the diocese were ordered destroyed. Thus perished the remaining treasures of Holy Trinity: the gifts of the centuries, of the pious and of the placeseeker, together with the communal vision that produced them.

There were those in the town who understood the movement of the times. Thomas Bentley, physician to 'the late Kynge of famous memory Henry the viii' leased New Place in 1545. His will made in 1548 demonstrates the new formulae of secular and ecclesiastical power: 'Edward the syxte by the grace of God of England, France and Irelande Kynge, defender of the faith and in earth of the Church of England and also of Irelande supreme hedd'.

The changes made less impact on the Stratfordians than might be supposed. For the next two centuries changes in the state religion were frequent. Most citizens learned to accommodate change: the exceptions were considered fanatics or saints according to one's point of view.

Within a few years Catholicism was briefly restored and Roger Dyos, who had been a priest of the College, was restored as vicar. The Stratfordians disported themselves again in the great pageant of St George which had been abandoned as profane in the previous reign. The 'saint' rode through the town on horseback clad in armour, leading a dragon which belched flames and smoke from its nostrils. This was followed by a traditional Vice or buffoon in costume and warriors armed with pikes.

The Renewal of Local Government in Stratford

Although the Guilds did not fall in the reign of Henry VIII but in that which followed, their suppression was intended. In 1545-6 Royal Commissioners visited Stratford and reported that the Guild rents totalled over £50 and its outgoings were slightly more. The population consisted of some 1,500 'houselyng people together with seven lyttle hamlets thereto belong-ing'. £28 6s 8d went to maintain the four chaplains, the clerk received four shillings and 13s 4d went to Oliver Baker, the clockmender. The Commissioners noted the free school above the Guildhall, where William Dalem's annual salary was still the ten pounds bequeathed by Thomas Jollyffe. The Guild possessed almshouses and every year gave ten shillings worth of coal and 3s 4d in ready money to 23 poor brethren. There were moves to demolish the chapel which the commissioners resisted: 'Yet it is also a thinge very mete and necessary that the Gild Chapel of Stratford stand undefaced for that it was always a chapell of ease for the seperacion of sick persons from the tyme of plague and standith in the face of the towne.'

    The Guild was finally suppressed in 1547. Its properties were dispersed, chiefly to the Lord of the Manor, John Dudley. The town was left without local government or administration and for six years its life dissolves into a historical void. In 1553 a plea from the inhabitants, which stressed the continuity of local government in Stratford, gained a positive response on behalf of the dying boy King on 7 June. The royal charter ensured that most of the old Guild property returned to the corporate hands of the townspeople. The officers and functions of the new Corporation were much the same. The Master of the Guild became the Bailiff and the Proctors, the Chamberlains. This oligarchical government was to be conducted in a spirit of benevolent paternalism. The leading men of the town found themselves, by right and duty, members of the Corporation: an elaborate system of fines made it difficult to refuse service. In 1555 the school was reconstituted after the Corporation resolved to appoint 'a lawful and honest man lerned in gramr and in the lawe of god'. William Smart was paid £20 annually to 'gently dyly to employ himself, with such godly wysdom and lernynge as God hathe and shale endue hym with, to lerne and teche in the saide gramer scole such scholars and chylder as shall . . . cum together to lerne godly lernynge and wysdom, beying fet for the gramer scole'. Provision was made to maintain 24 of the aged poor in the almshouses and an overseer was appointed. A Court of Record was established which met fortnightly to consider small claims. The fortuitous fall of John Dudley early in the next reign and the reversion of his properties to the crown ensured that the income which had belonged to the College was given to the Corporation. In return £30 was to be paid towards the stipends of the vicar, his assistant and the schoolmaster and accommodation provided for them.

The rise of John Shakespeare

Around 1540 a youth left his father's farm in the village of Snitterfield and travelled the three miles to Stratford to take up an apprenticeship, perhaps with Alderman Thomas Dickson of the *Swan Inn*, whose wife came from that village. John Shakespeare served his master for seven years before paying 6s 8d to join the 'Mystery, craft or occupation of the Glovers, Whittawers and Collarmakers', one of the town's trade guilds.[1] By the early 1550s he was established in Henley Street.

The rise of John Shakespeare was rapid. He made an excellent marriage with Mary Arden, who brought her husband considerable wealth which his business skill expanded. This acumen had been observed by her father, Robert Arden of Wilmcote, who, having no sons, made John Shakespeare his effective chief heir. His will bequeathed his soul to 'Almighty God and to our Blessed Lady Saint Mary and to all the Company of Heaven'. His property was divided among his eight daughters, but the most considerable portion went to 'my youngste daughter Marye' who inherited his property at Wilmcote called 'Asbyes', with ten marks in money and a sixth of her father's goods which were valued at £77 11 0d and included painted wall hangings, oxen, bullocks, kine, 'wayning calves', sheep, bees and poultry.

For those who prefer the national poet to have appropriate genealogy, no better forebears could be found than the Ardens, whose very name recalls the ancient Warwickshire forest and whose Saxon ancestry may be traced beyond the Conquest. The family was connected with the Ardens of Park Hall, near Castle Bromwich, who were numbered with the county gentry. Robert Arden's extensive lands included part of the holdings at Snitterfield farmed by John Shakespeare's father, Richard.

Stratford's position ensured a prosperous flow of goods and traffic. Thirty ale houses slaked the thirst of inhabitants and travellers, over 50 malthouses supplied a wide area. Frequent fairs attracted the 'great concourse of people' observed by Leland in 1530. On market days John Shakespeare and his fellow glovers occupied a prime site by the High Cross. 'Brasyares' and ironmongers had their stands down Bridge Street; butchers sold flesh, hides and tallow in the High Street; pewterers paid fourpence a yard for their pitches in Wood Street; a 'sugarer' dispensed his commodity in Chapel Street. The butter sellers by the chapel were forbidden to light fires to soften their products; next to them were stalls for cheese, whitemeats, wickyarn and fruit. At the cross in the Rother Market raw hides were laid out. The saltwainers stood nearby.

This considerable trade was regulated by the Leet Court at twice-yearly sessions. The magistrates heard complaints and imposed penalties. The Leet's ale tasters – John Shakespeare was appointed as one in 1556 – guarded the people's brew against the introduction of hops and 'other subtle things'. The Leet fixed the weight of bread, checked its standard and ordained its price of a penny a loaf. In times of shortage it was assiduous in preventing the hoarding of grain. An order of 1554 reprimanded 'persons now having barley in their houses' and ordered them to release it or face a fine of 40 shillings.

Tudor Stratford was an Augean stable, with the stench of animal excreta mingling with the refuse of trade and markets, exacerbated by badly-paved streets and open ditches. The division between town and countryside was narrow. Stratford was beautified by 1,000 elms within its boundaries and its inhabitants kept pigs and other livestock in their yards. The officers of the Leet struggled to control abuses, but the persistence of their efforts implies their lack of efficacy. Butchers were the worst offenders and were frequently ordered to 'carry further of the borough at seasonal time the riddings of their beasts' bellies, garbages and beasts' pates on pain of a fine of 40/8d'. Fines were imposed on those who allowed their animals to stray on the streets, with errant ducks collecting a fine of fourpence and stray dogs, twopence. Housewives did their washing at the public pump and hung it to dry on the High Cross. The town's rubbish was gathered at six huge muckhills at its approaches. During wet and warm summers these tips became vermin-infested, stinking heaps. When the eye of heaven grew too hot, summer's lease brought plagues to ravage the town.

The street around the High Cross and the Guildhall was long swept by the Widow Baker, who was provided with a shovel, broomstick and branches for her task. She was paid 6s 8d a year and had the occasional duty of helping a man named Raven sweep the bridge. Other streets were supposedly cleaned by the householders. Fines were levelled to encourage compliance and it was for keeping an unauthorised muckheap outside his house that John

Shakespeare first appeared in the Stratford records in April 1552, when he and his neighbours, Adrian Quiney and Henry Reynolds, were fined 12 pence at the Leet Court. Three years later he was fined for not keeping the gutter clean. Amongst his co-defendants was the Bailiff, who was chairman of the Court, so Leet justice was clearly impartial.

The fines imposed by the Leet were no stigma. Every citizen occasionally violated its regulations. For John Shakespeare they were pinpricks in a steady advance to commercial prosperity and civic dignity. In 1556 he bought his Henley Street property from his landlord. Later the western side of the Birthplace was acquired and the two knocked into one. Property was also acquired in Greenhill Street and by 1572 he could lay out the considerable credit of £50 to a fellow glover from Banbury. The Henley Street property fronted a busy thoroughfare and its extensive premises housed domestic and trade employees. The long backyard was essential for white tanning, preliminary to the manufacture of soft leather gloves. The weathering of hides was prohibited near the town centre: the smell was too much even for the inhabitants of that town of many aromas. At the end of the yard, overlooking the Guild Pits where the townsfolk obtained their gravel, a large barn was built.

Like most Elizabethan tradesmen, John Shakespeare speculated in commodities. In 1557 he brought an action against Henry Field, a tanner of Bridge Street, for the cost of eighteen quarters of barley, probably the product of the family holdings at Wilmcote. Malting was a major trade in Stratford, so probably the crop was destined for the mash-tun. John Shakespeare was also a considerable dealer in wool. In 1559 he sued John Walford, a clothier who was twice Mayor of Marlborough, for a debt of £21 outstanding on a wool contract for 30 years. When the parlour floor of the Birthplace was relaid in the Regency era, woollen remnants were found embedded in the foundations.

Henley Street was a thoroughfare of many trades. Other glovers and 'whittawers' resided there and must have used the water from the adulterated stream which ran across the street and into Merepool Lane for dampening skins. The Shakespeares' immediate neighbour was William Wedgwood, a tailor of dubious reputation who was expelled from his native Warwick after behaviour so scandalous that it even attracted the attention of the mighty Earl in his castle. The *Black Book of Warwick* records that 'leaving his wief he went to Stretford and divers other places and there married another wief, his first wief yet living; besides that he is a man very contentious, prowde and slanderous, oft busieing himself with naughty matters and quarrelling with his honest neighbours, which condicions forcing him to leave the place of good government first went from hence and afterward was compellid to goo from Stratford'. In 1573 John Shakespeare witnessed a land sale between Wedgwood and his other neighbour, Richard Hornby, a blacksmith whose shop was also an alehouse. William Shakespeare sued Hornby's son for a debt in 1609. In *King John* there is an apparent memory of these childhood neighbours:

> I saw a smith stand with his hammer, thus, the while his iron did on anvil cool, With open mouth swallowing a tailor's news, Who with his shears and measure in his hand, Standing on slippers, which his nimble haste, Had falsely thrust on contrary feet.

Others in the street included Roger Green, a miller and alehouse keeper of doubtful credentials, who was fined for selling underweight candles and brewing 'unwholsum aell'. Alderman George Whateley, Bailiff in 1564, kept a woollen-draper's shop. From his profits he endowed a school at his native Henley-in-Arden. As a Catholic sympathiser, he did much to support his brother, Sir Robert Whateley, described in a recusancy survey of 1592 as 'an old massinge' [priest] whose wiles puzzled the authorities, 'resorting often thither, but hardley to be founde'. Whateley kept bees and had 'wax, honey and other things in the apple chamber'.

Infant mortality took a predictable toll of the growing Shakespeare family. The first child, a daughter named Joan, did not survive, for another child was christened with the same name in 1569. A second daughter was christened Margaret in 1562. In the following year John and Mary Shakespeare saw her little form lowered into the earth at Holy Trinity. The first son,

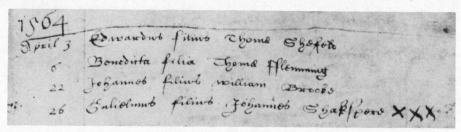

4. Baptismal entry for William Shakespeare, 26 April 1564.

William, was brought to church for baptism on 26 April 1564; another son, Gilbert, was born in 1566 and a daughter, Anne, in 1571. She died at the age of seven and 'Mr. Shaxper' paid eightpence for the funereal pall and bell. Richard was born in 1574 and there were perhaps miscarriages and still-births before Mary Shakespeare bore her last child, Edmund, in 1580. Five of her children survived to adulthood, not a low proportion for the age. In the year Edmund was born the Chapel bell tolled its funeral knoll 12 times for Stratford children.[2]

England's greatest genius narrowly escaped a little winding sheet in the first weeks of his life. On 11 July 1564, Oliver Gunn, an apprentice weaver, died at premises (now the *Garrick Inn*) in the High Street. In the burial entry the vicar, John Bretchgirdle, wrote the ominous words *'Hic incepit pestis'*. The plague was carried into Warwickshire by soldiers returning from the Earl of Leicester's expedition against Le Havre. Before the year was out 238 of the town's inhabitants had died: around one in eight of the population. It was by far the worst epidemic in Stratford's history. Mary Shakespeare may have fled back to Wilmcote with her baby. Her husband remained to attend the Corporation meeting on 30 August, held in the Guild garden rather than the stuffy atmosphere of the Hall.

In 1558 John Shakespeare was appointed one of the four borough constables and thus encountered many of the social problems which bedevilled Tudor England. The Elizabethan era has passed into national consciousness as the most triumphant in English history. The traumas of the age are often overlooked. Recessions were frequent, part-engendered by seemingly interminable wars. Stratford's poor were always with their Corporation and frequent levies were imposed on the capital burgesses for their relief. Rural depopulation caused a drift into the town, which was overburdened by the influx. The Corporation made regular appeals that outlying parishes should contribute towards the poor rates. 'No inhabitant', it was ordered in 1558, 'to harbour strange beggars who if refractory are to be punished with the stocks'. In 1559 Richard Mekyns was employed at 20 shillings a year, 'so long as he shall do his duties in drivinge out of beggars and vacabondes out of the towne and also shall whyppe such persons as shall be comanded hym to whyp'.

There was little room at Stratford's metaphorical inn for abandoned pregnant women. Their offspring became a charge to the borough and the Leet developed a regular obsession that 'no inhabitant of Stratford hereafter receive any woman to be brought to bed of child in his or their houses' on pain of a fine. Edmund Barrett of the *Crown* in Fore Bridge Street was fined 20 shillings around 1558 'for evell revell keepynge in hys hous and mayntaynenge and recevenge of a strumpet woman'.

As a constable John Shakespeare shared Dogberry's duty to 'comprehend all vagram men'. To him would have fallen the arduous task of enforcing the resolution passed in 1557 after a riot at the September fair. 'No sengle man dwellynge in Stratford . . . do weyre about hym wtin the burrowe or lybertyez of Stratford eny byll, sword, wood knyf or dagger, or anie such lyke wepon under payn of forfeyture of the same and their bodies to prison, there to remain at the Bailey's pleasure.' In 1553 Thomas Holtam was arrested for 'drawing his dagger and making a fray' on Richard Harrington, one of the constables. In the next year Thomas Powell of Shottery was fined 3s 4d for 'revelynge as well agaynst othere the quenes magestyez'. To maintain order the constables carried bills and were supported by a robust team of Stratfordians who could be called upon to deal with troublemakers.

In a society with inadequate means of law enforcement, penalties for wrongdoing were sharp and exemplary. Imprisonment was rare. The town lock-up was used to hold prisoners until they could be brought before the magistrates. Inmates paid a gaol fee of fourpence. More affluent prisoners tried to buy special privileges, for it was decreed that the officers were not 'toe presume to extorte, exact or take anie more or greater fee of anie persoune or persons upon payne of imprisonment' and a fine of 6s 8d. The unpleasantness of the gaol is revealed by one of its inmates, Nicholas Rogers, an alleged housebreaker, who petitioned the Bailiff that he might stand trial at the Quarter Sessions, protesting his innocence and stating that he was 'all most fyned for want of food and no rement to hide [his] karkas', since he was 'laden with irones'.

An elaborate system of fines existed and cruder punishments were available for persistent wrongdoers. The pillory was repaired at a cost of 6s 8d in 1567. Where much depended on the 'bubble reputation', slanderous talk was seriously regarded. A ducking stool for scolds deterred malicious gossips. In the Southampton Leet Court in 1608 it was recorded that a woman charged with slander in Stratford had been ordered to leave town. On failing to do so she was 'set in a cadge', with a paper detailing her offence. Economic sanctions could be taken, as with a local publican. A Corporation minute of 1575 ordered 'upon grevous complaintes made to the Bayliffe and Burgesses . . . that no inhabitant . . . shall sell ale to George Turner or hys wyf or servauntes, or to any of hys inmates, except yt be for the provision of themselves onlie'. Many such cases went before the peculiar court, under vicarial jurisdiction. Its propensity to try sexual offences gave it the nickname of the 'bawdy' court.

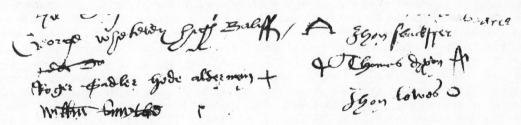

5. *John Shakespeare witnesses a corporation order, 27 September 1564.*

In 1559 and 1561 John Shakespeare assessed fines at the Leet Court, signifying assent with his mark of a glover's compass. This does not denote illiteracy. A fellow alderman, Adrian Quiney, also made a mark, although he could write a fine hand. Had John Shakespeare been illiterate the burgesses would not have made him Chamberlain in 1561 and in the two years following: the only person to be honoured with this consecutive burden. The two chamberlains had charge of the municipal property and presented the annual accounts. John Shakespeare had a gift with figures. The Corporation called on him in two subsequent years to rescue lesser men from the ignominy of failing to present a coherent account.

The spirit of the old Guild was reflected in the Corporation's orders. It was decreed that 'none of the aldermen nor none of the capital burgesses, neither in the council chamber nor elsewhere, do revile each other, but brotherlike live together'. The compilers were cautious enough to add a pecuniary inducement to fraternal accord – those disruptive of harmony were to pay 6s 8d for every default. One such contentious type was Alderman William Bott, a wealthy merchant of dubious character who lived at New Place. Bott's son-in-law said during a Star Chamber suit of 1564 that he had been 'openly detected of divers great and notorious crimes, as namely felony, adultery, whoredom, falsehood and forging'. 'Let every man beware of hyme', warned another witness, 'for he is counted the craftieste merchant in all our countery . . . and it is said that if Botte had made his righte he had been hanged long ago.' Bott, who had been accused of fraudulent conversion and forgery by William Clopton, was expelled from the Corporation in 1565 after speaking evil words about his colleagues. 'Ther was', he declared, 'never an honest man of the Councell or the body of the corporacyon of Stratford'. His place as an alderman was taken by John Shakespeare.

Bott's *confrère* in duplicity was Lodovick Greville of Milcote. Imperious, cruel and well-connected, he achieved the capital dispatch reckoned as Bott's desert. He was no respecter of persons, assaulting his cousin, Sir John Conway of Luddington, and threatening the great Earl of Leicester. When his son, Edward, shot an arrow in the air that killed his elder brother, his father jested about it, telling him 'it was the best shot he ever shot'. Lodovick coveted the land of one of his tenants, Thomas Webb, who was strangled by two servants during a visit to Mount Greville. One of them, Thomas Brock, was placed in bed, impersonating Webb, 'dolefully groaning' and making a will in Greville's favour before feigning death. The plot is worthy of the revenge tragedies of the age. The foul deed done, the horror escalated. Brock, 'in his cups at Stratford', let slip dark hints that it was in his power to hang his master, who had him killed by the other servant, Thomas Smith. When Smith was arrested he confessed all. Both were tried at Warwick. Greville refused to plead and stood mute. According to contemporary law it was impossible to convict, although a course of torture to any extremity was permitted and Greville was pressed to death on 14 November 1589. His estates, which would have passed to the Crown if he had confessed, were bequeathed intact to his villainous son, Edward: a courageous end to a dishonourable career which had terrorised the region.

Others found themselves in conflict with the Corporation. Robert Perrott, a cantankerous old Puritan who kept the *King's Hall Tavern*[3] in the Rother Market, was Bailiff in 1558, but subsequently refused to serve on the Corporation. The maintenance of the oligarchical system depended on the co-operation of all men of means. The quarrel was discussed by Sir Thomas Lucy, Clement Throckmorton and Sir Henry Goodere over wine and food at the *Bear*. The burgesses must have felt amply compensated for the bill of 37s 8d when the three gentlemen suggested that Perrott, of his 'free goodwill', pay £53 6s 8d he owed in back fines and that all should 'henceforth be Lovers and ffrendes'. Unfortunately, Perrott's goodwill did not extend to paying this enormous sum. The Corporation tried to force his hand by electing him Bailiff in 1567, but he declared he would never serve again. The choice fell on John Shakespeare, who had stood unsuccessfully the year before, perhaps indulging in the ploy of associating his name with the office. Alderman Perrott bore the council no lasting animosity. He endowed an annual sermon to be preached at Holy Trinity, with provision for the Corporation to 'make merye withall after the sermon is ended'.

The Election was on the Wednesday before the Feast of the Nativity of the Blessed Virgin (8 September). Afterwards the Corporation retired to the home of the new Bailiff to drink wine, so the household in Henley Street must have been the scene of bustling activity.[4]

The Friday week after, the Corporation held its annual 'Buck Feast' at the *Bear* at the bottom of Bridge Street, or at the *Swan* opposite. The *Bear* was a substantial hostelry employing 14 servants and was kept by the formidable Thomas Barber, who was three times Bailiff. The Feast was an elaborate affair when the Corporation and its wives entertained local dignitories like Sir Thomas Lucy and Sir Fulke Greville.

An account from nearby Banbury instructs that the Bailiff was to be 'a lanthorn in good usage and order as well to all the rest of his brethren as to the whole commonalty'. He was to 'wel and decently behave himself in all degrees and indifferently and rightly judge and deal with all men . . . according to the right of the cause and so likewise shall be comely attired in apparel and also at all such times as he shall be occasioned to go into the said town or the perambulation of the same whether on Fair days, market days or any other times and about the execution of his office, or together with his brethren touching any affairs or business of the said Borough, he shall have the Sergeant-at-Mace to be attendant upon him'. From 15 December until 20 days after Christmas he was obliged to hang a lantern outside his door 'to give light in the streets'.

The Corporation surveyed its property on the Friday in Easter week. At Rogationtide the Bailiff and burgesses perambulated their boundaries. The Bailiff and the Chief Alderman enjoyed the produce of the Corporation garden, except for the 'offal wood, trees branches and boughes dead, withered, fallen, cutt downe or playned', which was burned on the fire at Corporation meetings.

Companies of actors are first recorded in Stratford during John Shakespeare's bailiwick. In the summer of 1569 no less a troupe than the Queen's Players was paid nine shillings for playing in the Guild Hall. Later that year the Earl of Worcester's men gave less satisfaction and were paid a mere shilling. It is appropriate that John Shakespeare emerges as Stratford's first theatrical patron, although he could not have realised the destiny of his eldest son, then aged five. Many years later Robert Willis of Gloucester, born in the same year as William Shakespeare, wrote an account which reveals what must have happened at Stratford:

> When players of interludes come to town they first attend the Mayor to inform him what nobleman's servant's they are and so to get a license for their public playing and if the Mayor likes the actors or would show respect to their Lord and master, he appoints them to play their first play before himself and the Aldermen and common council and that is called 'The Mayor's Play' where everyone that will goes in without money, the Mayor giving the players a reward as he thinks fit to show respect unto them. At such a play my father took me with him and made me sit between his legs, as he sat on one of the benches, where we saw and heard very well. The play was called 'The Cradle of Security'. The sight of it made such an impression on me that when I came to man's estate it was as fresh in my memory as if I had seen it newly acted.

As a senior alderman, John Shakespeare enjoyed the trust of his colleagues. In 1571 the Corporation resolved that Adrian Quiney and he should 'at Hilary Term next deal in the affairs of the Borough according to their discretions' and six pounds was advanced to him for a visit to London. The business was probably connected with delicate negotiations about the rights of the town. A similar trip was made by Thomas Barber and the town clerk, John Jefferies, in 1590. Leaving Stratford on 15 May, they spent three shillings on that night's lodging which included supper and fodder for their horses. At High Wycombe the next night, the charge was 2s 1d, but at Uxbridge the following evening they were in the inflationary radius of the capital, paying 44 pence. A fee of 20 shillings was paid to a counsel, but either matters took a long time to resolve or the two men were enjoying the delights of the metropolis. On 27 May they hired a boat for eightpence and went down the Thames to Greenwich. Perhaps they were seeking the support of someone with influence at Court. If so they obtained it for they returned rapidly to Stratford, this time staying at Aylesbury and Banbury.

A meeting nearer home took place on 4 January 1574/5 when the civic fathers conferred with their fellows at Warwick about the terms of a legacy from Thomas Oken to the poor of Stratford. They were 'well recevid', but the Stratfordians were not happy about certain restrictive clauses. Adrian Quiney declared that the conditions could be considered a slight on their integrity. The men of Warwick were annoyed. It was the first they had heard of any criticism. In any case the conditions were not theirs, but the giver's. 'It was told to them

playnly that unles they did yeld both to the covenants & bond they should receive no mony.'
The Bailiff of Warwick chose his words judiciously:

'Though it be true that they be men knowen of good credit, honest behavior, upright
dealing & such as upon their credits might be trustid in as great a matter as this . . . they be
but men and therefore varyable and mortall & therefore must dye . . . It is not to be taken
amysse that some matter be devised in writing to tye their posterytie & successors for the
performance of the covennts being bothe resonable and easy to be performid by carefull and
good men whose travailes in that case being also but easy shall greatly benefyt their poore
neighbors whereunto we are all bound.' This eloquence appeased the Stratfordians. Agreement
was made 'and they of Stretforde sent mery homewards'.

Stratford was fortunate in Elizabeth's reign in having public servants of high calibre. The
pride in civic achievement and sound dealing is expressed in the charming epitaph of Alderman
Richard Hill, who died in 1590.

> Heare borne heare lived heare died and buried heare
> Lieth Richard Hill thrise Bailiff of the Burrow
> Too matrons of good fame he married in Godes feare
> And now release in ioi [joy] he reasts from worldlie sorrow
> A woolen draper beeing in his time
> Whose virtues live whose fame doth flourish still
> Though he disolved be to dust and lime
> A mirror he and paterne mai be made
> For such as shall succeed him in that Trade
> He did not use to sweare to glose gather faigne
> His brother to defraude in Bargaininge
> He would not strive to get excessive gaine
> In ani cloath or other kinde of tinge.
> His servant I this trueth doth testifie
> A witness that beheld it with mi eie.

FOOTNOTES

[1]   The company was apparently reformed in 1606, but had undoubtedly existed before then.
[2]   The infant death-rate at Stratford, 1570-99, was 190 per 1,000: see the unpublished doctoral thesis of
       J.M. Martin, deposited in the Warwick County Archive.
[3]   It was probably during Perrott's time that murals were painted depicting the story of Tobias and the
       Angel. They were discovered in what is now the lounge of the *White Swan Hotel* in 1927.
[4]   In 1574/5 Thomas Oken endowed an annual sermon in the Guild Chapel, to be preached after the
       election. Wine was provided afterwards.

1. John de Stratford, Archbishop of Canterbury.

2. Robert de Stratford, Bishop of Chichester.

3. Guild property, showing the Guild Hall, School Guild Chapel and Pedagogue's House.

4. The Guild Hospice, now almshouses, with the Guild Hall, School and Chapel beyond.

5. The sanctuary knocker at Holy Trinity church.

6. The Guild Chapel, rebuilt by Sir Hugh Clopton.

7. A water-colour reproduction, 1806, of a painting of the Last Judgement in the Guild Chapel, now much faded.

8. A water-colour reproduction, 1806, of a painting of St George and the Dragon in the Guild Chapel.

9. The old market house by James Saunders, prior to its demolition in 1826. John Shakespeare would have traded here with the other glovers.

10. The house of Thomas and Katherine Rogers, rebuilt after the fire of 1595. Their grandson was John Harvard, founder of the University, which now owns their house.

11. The much-restored *Garrick Inn* where the plague of 1564 broke out.

12. The Big School, Stratford Grammar School, where William Shakespeare was probably educated. The desks date from the 18th century.

13. Bust of William Shakespeare in Holy Trinity church.

14. Portrait of Michael Drayton, friend and alleged drinking companion of William Shakespeare and a patient of John Hall.

15. (*left*) Holy Trinity church, with the new spire built by Joseph Greene, 1762.

16. (*above*) 'Luxuria' or lechery: misericord at Holy Trinity church.

17. (*below left*) Portrait of Dr. Harvey, who treated a V.D. sufferer together with Hall.

18. (*below*) The Earl of Northampton, principal local Royalist protagonist at the start of the Civil War.

19. Portrait of John Trapp, Stratford schoolmaster.

20. Revd. Nicholas Brady, Vicar of Stratford (attributed to Hugh Holland).

21. Portrait of Revd. Joseph Greene.

22. 'The Revd. Destroyer', Francis Gastrell.

23. Portrait of David Garrick by Thomas Gainsborough, commissioned by Stratford
Corporation, 1769. Destroyed by fire in 1948.

24. At the Market Cross: the opening of the Jubilee.

25. Garrick reciting the Ode: note the statue of Shakespeare, the wrong way round.

26. Idyllic 18th-century panorama.

27. Band of the Warwickshire Militia by
James Saunders.

28. 'The Mayor and all his Brethren' by James Saunders.

29. The Revd. Stephen Nason, M.A., Vicar of Stratford 1763-87.

30. John Jordan, the wheelwright poet.

31. Believed to be a picture of Mrs. Mary Hornby, proprietress of The Birthplace.

32. Dr. John Conolly, founder of the Dispensary, later 'friend and guide to the crazy'.

33. Oil painting of the Corporation Beadle, John Hickman, by Edward Grubb, c. 1790.

34. Mrs. Elizabeth Hickman, the Corporation Cook, by Edward Grubb, c. 1790.

35. Shakespeare Jubilee celebrations, 1830, showing the procession outside the Birthplace. The figure on horseback is Charles Kemble.

36. Barn in Windsor Street used as a theatre, with the old workhouse on the left. The picture is by James Saunders.

37. Royal Shakespearean Theatre, Chapel Lane, before 1862 when the cottages on the left, once a barn built by John Hall, were demolished. On demolition of the Theatre, the portico was transferred to the *Shakespeare Hotel* and *The Red Horse* (now Marks & Spencer's).

38. *The Swan, c.*1845, showing the parish pump.

39. Engraving of Shakespeare's Birthplace, 1769, by Richard Greene, based on the earliest-known picture of the building, *c.*1762.

40. Earliest-known photograph of the Birthplace, *c.*1845. A constable of the Borough Force stands outside and it may be the amazing Mrs. Count looking through the servery window.

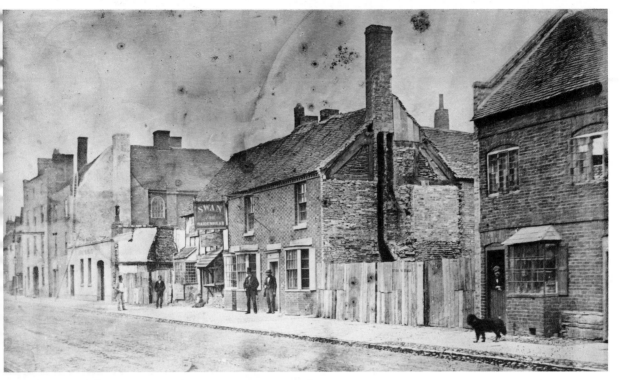

41. Birthplace, *c.*1850. The houses of Shakespeare's neighbours have been demolished. This gives a good view of the old drovers' public house, the *Swan and Maidenhead.*

42. 'A spick and span new villa': the Birthplace restored, *c.*1865.

43. Dr. Davenport, Vicar of Stratford, preaching his last sermon at the age of 92 in 1843.

44. Waggon from the old Tramway, now standing on Tramway Bridge.

45. Stratford Grammar School, c.1855. The Guild Hall had become the fire station. Note the gas lighting which contrasts with the bracket for the old obligatory 'lanthorn' outside the former house of Town Clerk, Thomas Hunt.

CHAPTER 3

'Thou Smilest and art Still'

'We ask and ask: thou smilest and art still, Out-topping knowledge.'
Matthew Arnold.

The frustration of delineating William Shakespeare's life is epitomised in Arnold's sonnet, yet we know more of him than of any Elizabethan dramatist. Many of his fellows are little more than names on a playbill. By contrast every major aspect of Shakespeare's life can be traced, but much of the information reads like programme notes, recording the author's dealings and endeavours, but telling little of his personality. Behind the stodgy, satisfied face of the bust in Holy Trinity, or the lugubrious eyes of the engraving in the First Folio, there existed the remarkable being who wrote the plays and poems. It is like finding the skeleton of a magnificent creature on a deserted beach. We can discern the bare bones, but the vital flesh which could tell us how it moved, breathed and had its being is missing. Apart from some contemporary and historical gossip, the main source of information about William Shakespeare is his works, but to construct the life and feelings of any author, particularly one of such complexity, from the internal evidence of his writings is hazardous. Yet Stratford-upon-Avon must have contributed greatly to the formative years of the child who was father to the man Shakespeare.

His father's civic status ensured him a place at the free school over the Guildhall which had a tendency to overflow into the chapel, necessitating occasional strictures from the Corporation to return whence it belonged. No records survive of Stratford School at this period, but the curriculum must have been as unvaried as that of other Elizabethan Grammar schools. Education began at five years. Learning was a mechanical pattern of repetition and the schoolroom echoed to chanting from the 'Absey' or A.B.C. book, whose loss, an early play informs us, could cause a schoolboy to sigh.

'They must reade English before they can learne Latin' was the stricture of one school benefactor and the young William's earliest literary efforts would have consisted of letters copied into a horn book. These first essays in learning would have taken place under the instruction of an under-master or his wife. The vicar, John Bretchgirdle, bequeathed in 1564 'to the common use of the scholars of the free scole', a copy of Thomas Ellyot's Latin dictionary. If the book survived the ravages of schoolboy usage, it would have been used by the young Shakespeare. Rhetorical methods were used, hopefully not as incompetently as by Sir Hugh Evans: 'What is he, William, that doth lend articles?' *William:* 'articles are borrowed of the pronoun and be thus declined: *singulariter, nominativo, hic, haec, hoc'*.

Stratford School was an academy of distinction whose masters were men of standing. William Shakespeare was too young to benefit from the learning of John Brownsword, a prominent poet in the 'Latin Empire', who left Stratford in 1567. He must have been taught by Thomas Jenkins, who arrived in 1575 and whom some have identified as the model for the Welsh schoolmaster, Sir Hugh Evans. The common Welshness does not extend beyond their surnames: Jenkins was a Londoner, educated at St John's College, Oxford. When he left Stratford in

21

6. Map of Shakespeare's Stratford.

TO HENLEY

TO CLOPTON

N

TO WORCESTER

TO WARWICK

GUILD PITS

WINDSOR

HENLEY STREET

GREENHILL STREET

ROTHER MARKET

WOOD STREET

BRIDGE STREET

BACK LANE

ROTHER STREET

ELY STREET

HIGH STREET

SHEEP STREET

BUTT CLOSE

CLOPTON BRIDGE

TINKERS LANE

CHAPEL STREET

NEW PLACE

CROFT

BANK

RIVER

AVON

TO BANBURY

WALKERS STREET

CHURCH STREET

SALMON TAIL

BULL LANE

OLD TOWN

SALMON JOLE

TO EVESHAM

THE COLLEGE

..... Borough Boundary.

HOLY TRINITY CHURCH

KEY

1. John Shakespeare.
2. Henry Field.
3. George Whateley.
4. Richard Hornby.
5. William Wedgewood.
6. George Badger.
7. John Wheeler.
8. Perrott's Tavern.
9. Richard Tyler.
10. Richard Hill, Abraham Sturley.
11. Adrian and Richard Quiney.
12. William Chandler.
13. Thomas Rogers.
14. July Shaw.
15. Thomas Nash.
16. Thomas Reynolds.
17. Matthew Morris.
18. George Badger.
19. Hamnet Sadler.
20. Daniel Baker.
21. The Cage, Thomas Quiney.
22. The Market Cross.
23. Henry Walker.
24. The Guild Chapel.
25. Guildhall and schoolroom.
26. Almshouses.
27. John Hall.
28. Thomas Greene.
29. John Combe.
30. The Bear Inn, Thomas Barber.
31. The Swan Inn, Thomas Waterman.

1579, he found his own replacement in an Oxford colleague, John Cottam, who paid six pounds commission to the canny Jenkins.

The most interesting of Shakespeare's likely schoolmasters is Simon Hunt, who came to the little academy in 1571. It was probably this Hunt who joined the Jesuits at Douai in 1575, although a namesake died at Stratford before 1598. In 1584 a request to send him into the dangerous rigours of the English mission was refused because 'Father Simon lacks sufficient learning'. Is this the source of the 'smalle Latin and less Greek' which Ben Jonson ascribed to his friend? The standard of comparison was high. Ben was tutored at Westminster by the great schoolmaster, Camden, while Hunt was being assessed as a Jesuit. Aubrey was probably nearer the mark when he said that Shakespeare 'understood Latine pretty well'. The works demonstrate classical knowledge; two-thirds of Shakespeare's classical allusions are from his favourite book, Ovid's *Metamorphoses*. 'As the soul of Euphorbies', eulogised Francis Meres in 1598, 'was thought to live in Pythagoras, so the sweet witty soul of Ovid lives in the melifluous and honey-tongued Shakespeare.' The fluent Latin of Stratford schoolboys is demonstrated in a letter from Richard Quiney, aged 11, to his father and namesake, the Bailiff, who was about the borough business in London. 'I give you thanks that from the tenderest age . . . you have instructed me in studies of sacred doctrine, nothing could be further from my mind than mere adulation, for not one of my friends is dearer and more loving towards me than you are and I pray sincerely that my special love may remain as it is.'

Whatever debts William Shakespeare owed to the memory of his early years, he recalled his schooldays with the lack of enthusiasm of his 'whining schoolboy, with his satchel / And shining morning face, creeping like snail / unwillingly to school'. 'Love goes towards love', Romeo tells Juliet, 'as schoolboys from their books, But love from love, towards school, with heavy looks.' Shakespeare's schoolboy eagerly awaits the moment when school breaks up and 'each hurries to his home and sporting place', or his mind wanders beyond the schooldoor to playing with tops, push pin, 'hide fox and all after', pursuing summer butterflies, birds' nesting, or wantonly killing flies for sport.

The Shakespeares may have travelled to see the festivities at Kenilworth in 1575 when Robert Dudley entertained the Queen to a 14-day extravaganza. Some of the cost of this progress fell on the Stratford Chamberlains, who contributed 16 shillings to the 'Quenes Carryage'. Elizabeth had been closer to Stratford in 1572, when she stayed with Sir Thomas Lucy at Charlecote.

Hard Times

John Shakespeare ran into financial difficulties soon after purchasing property in Stratford in 1575. Previously a regular attender at Corporation meetings, his presence is recorded only once after 1576. In 1578 he raised a loan from his brother-in-law, Edmund Lambert, offering part of his wife's inheritance, a house and 56 acres of land, as surety. On the same day, Alderman Roger Sadler, a High Street baker, made his will and recorded debts owed to him by John Shakespeare and Richard Hathaway, father of William's future bride. More of Mary Shakespeare's dowry was lost in 1579 when her share in two houses and 100 acres at Snitterfield was sold to her nephew for ten pounds. Impecuniosity was the likely cause of a petition by John Shakespeare to the Court of Queen's Bench in 1582, for sureties of the peace against Ralph Caudrey, Thomas Logginge and Robert Young, 'for fear of death and mutilation of his limbs'. The exaggerated phrase suggests that Alderman Caudrey, a volatile and violent man, was not a sympathetic creditor. The matter was resolved by 5 November when both men attended the election of a new Bailiff.

These difficulties confirm Nicholas Rowe's assertion in 1709 that John Shakespeare's need for William's assistance at home forced his withdrawal from school. Doubtless he accompanied his father on wool-purchasing journeys through the 'high wild hills and rough uneven ways' of the Cotswolds. Two plays, *The Taming of the Shrew* and *Henry IV, Part One*, show an intimate knowledge of the region.

John Shakespeare's precarious financial position was understood by the Commissioners for Recusancy in Warwickshire, who investigated those recalcitrant in church attendance. His name appears in March 1592 amongst a group of nine considered to 'absent themselves for feare of processes'. Church services provided an opportunity to serve writs and William Burbage was trying to recover seven pounds owed from a decade before, obtaining an order for payment in the following month.

The suggestion which has been made that the list of debtors was part of an elaborate plot to protect John Shakespeare from the rigour of the laws against recusants is unlikely. The nine were all in bad financial shape. The intriguingly named William Fluellen and George Bardell (or Bardolf) left widows to the care of the parish. William Baynton fled to Ireland to escape his creditors. John Wheeler had his goods distrained and his son's barn was 'readi to fall for rottenness' in 1599. These were hard times in Stratford. Some 700 people, about a third of the population, were on the poor roll. The wool trade had been decimated by the Spanish sacking of Antwerp in 1576, the year in which John Shakespeare's difficulties were first manifest. His troubles look less severe in this context. Although property was mortgaged, the house in Henley Street remained. Even in his pressing moments, he could stand credit for others, although his judgement was not always good. In 1586 he stood bail at Coventry for Michael Pryce, a local tinker charged with a felony. The money was forfeited when the defendant failed to appear. A month earlier he had guaranteed the debts of his unreliable farmer brother. When Henry Shakespeare defaulted John escaped jail only through the intervention of the good alderman, Richard Hill.

Where there were militant recusants locally, the Commissioners named them, including the influential William Clopton; Mrs. Frances Jeffreys, wife of the Town Clerk; Joan, wife of Alderman George Caudrey and their son George, suspected to be 'a semynerie preeste or Jesuite'; Edward Bromley, the town carrier and William Underhill of New Place.

Several of the Catholics, regarding a peaceful existence worth a litany, paid lip service to conformity and attended services. In September the Commissioners produced a second report naming those who had conformed and listing 'sutch dangerous and seditious Papistes and Recusantes as have bene presented to us or found out by our endeavoire to (have) bene att any tyme heretofore of or in this countye . . . and (are) now either beyonde the seas or vagrante within this Realme'. Amongst them was George Caudrey.

One name on the roll was that of Richard Dibdale of Shottery, 'who hath not bene at church this yere'. His brother Robert trained for the Catholic priesthood at the Douai seminary and sent a letter from there to his family. The bearer was Thomas Cottam, a priest from Lancashire, whose brother John was appointed Stratford schoolmaster in 1579. In the letter Dibdale told his 'right wellbeloved parents' that the 'cause of my wryting unto you ys to lett you understand that I am in healthe, commending unto you my especiall ffriend Mr. Cottame, who hath beene unto me the t[w]o halfe of my life'. Neither the letter nor some small gifts were delivered. Cottam was arrested at Dover in June 1580 and was ferociously tortured before being hanged, drawn and quartered at Tyburn, shouting 'God bless you all' to the onlookers.

Undaunted by his friend's arrest, Robert Dibdale followed him into the hazards of the English province. He was arrested and imprisoned, but did not suffer the torture faced with such valour by many of his fellows. On 3 November 1580, William Greenway, the carrier from Bridge Street, brought a letter, a loaf, two cheeses and five shillings from Dibdale's father to Newgate Prison. The prisoner was released on 30 September 1582 and fled to France, but soon returned, establishing a reputation as an exorcist, casting out devils from a servant-girl in Hertfordshire shortly before his recapture. This time he did not escape the fate of his friend and 'with constancy suffered martyrdom' at Tyburn on 8 October 1586.

The systematic harassment of his co-religionists produced an intense depression in a local Catholic, John Somerville of Edstone Hall, son-in-law of Edward Arden of Park Hall. On 25 October 1583, despair triumphed over reason and he set off for London, announcing 'I will go up to the Court and shoot the Queen with a pistol'. He was arrested near Banbury. His crazed imagination provided an opportunity to settle old scores. Sir Thomas Lucy of Charlecote, whose sympathy was with the new age, arrested Edward Arden and his wife on the order of the Privy Council. Margaret Arden was spared, but her husband, a former High Sheriff of Warwickshire, was hanged, drawn and quartered. As was customary, his head was placed on a spike on London Bridge and perhaps gave ghoulish greeting to his young kinsman, William Shakespeare, on his arrival in London. John Somerville, who precipitated the tragedy, was found strangled in his cell. Perhaps the authorities felt that the public execution of this demented youth would reveal the thinness of the case against Arden.

Sir Thomas Lucy prosecuted his campaign with vigour and enthusiasm. With the assiduous assistance of Thomas Wilkes, Clerk to the Privy Council, he searched a number of houses in the district with little success. Since no plot existed there was little to find. Wilkes wrote to London in evident frustration: 'Unless you can make Somerville, Arden, Hall the priest, Somerville's wife and his sister speak directly to these things which you have discovered, it will not be possible for us here to find out more than is to be found out already, for the papists in this country greatly do work upon the advantage of clearing their houses of all shows of suspicion.'

One who apparently so acted was John Shakespeare. In 1757 an extraordinary testament – six leaves of aged parchment stitched together – was discovered in the eaves of the Birthplace by workmen employed by Thomas Hart, his sixth-generation descendant. It passed to John Payton, owner of the nearby *White Lion Inn*. When the scholar Edmund Malone heard of it in 1785 he borrowed it. By then the first sheet was lost, but John Jordan, a local wheelwright, obligingly forged a replacement. Malone fortunately made a copy of the manuscript, for it was subsequently lost, probably by the great critic himself. He later expressed doubts about its authenticity, but in 1966 it was exonerated when one almost identical in format was discovered.

The document is an English translation of a triumphant affirmation of the Catholic faith written by St Carlo Borromeo. 'I John Shakespeare do protest that I will pass out of this life armed with the last sacrament of Extreme Unction, the which, if through any let or hindrance I should not be able to have, I do also for that time demand and crave the same, beseeching his Divine Majesty that He will be pleased to anoint my senses both internal and external with the sacred oil of his infinite mercy . . .'. The 'glorious and ever Virgin Mary' and John Shakespeare's 'patroness', St Winifred (perhaps he was born on 3 November, her feast day) are invoked to intercede for him.

The testaments were brought into England with the illicit Jesuit mission of 1580 led by Edmund Campion and Robert Persons. In the following year, William Allen, head of the English College in Rheims, told Rome that 'Father Robert wants three or four thousand more of the testaments'. This shortage necessitated the painstaking business for those in England of copying the limited supply, with the supplicant entering his name on a standardised text. Both Campion and Persons were in the Midlands during 1580. 'I ride about some piece of country every day', wrote Campion. 'On horseback I meditate my sermon, when I come to the house, I polish it. Then I talk with such as come to speak with me, or hear their confessions. In the morning after Mass, I preach. They hear with exceeding greediness and very often receive the sacrament.' In 1581 Sir William Catesby, a former High Sheriff, was imprisoned for refusing to say whether Campion had stayed with him at Bushwood House, in the Stratford parish, although 12 miles away at Lapworth. Perhaps John Shakespeare encountered the doomed priest, whom Lord Chancellor Burghley had described in happier times as 'one of the diamonds of England'.

It could have been sympathy for the old faith which caused John Shakespeare to be bound over to keep the peace by the Court of the Queen's Bench in June 1580. He was fined £20 for failing to appear and £20 for not bringing John Audley, a Nottingham hatmaker, into court. On the same day Audley was fined £70 which included £70 for not bringing John Shakespeare. Thomas Codey of Stoke-on-Trent, yeoman, was fined £30, £10 as surety for John Shakespeare, while two Worcestershire farmers were each fined £10 as sureties for Audley and Codey. One hundred and forty people from all over England were dealt with in a similar way. Perhaps the authorities were reacting to the known presence of the Jesuit mission. Certainly this would explain the link between such geographically disparate persons.

The Shakespeares may well have been 'Church Papists': conforming outwardly and nursing their sympathies until the spirit of the age might change. The authorities could be surprisingly tolerant. 'It was even lately proposed to certain noblemen to come', wrote Father Persons, 'if it were only once a year, to church, making if they pleased a previous protestation that they come not to approve of their religion or doctrine, but only to show an outward obedience to the Queen . . .'. At Warwick it was noted that there were those 'who come to church, but not to communion at all'. Doubtless the same applied in Stratford. Like most Englishmen in his position, John Shakespeare sought to minimise trouble. A like attitude was taken by his fellow councillors. The Corporation was an exemplary meeting-place of differing shades of religious adherence. Friction came through personality rather than doctrine – as with Nicholas Barnhurst of Sheep Street. In 1596 he was warned for calling George Badger a 'knave and rascal' and in 1599 he was expelled for 'his great abuse offered to the whole company'.

That his fellow councillors maintained John Shakespeare's name on their roll through his years of trouble indicates their esteem and belief in his recovery. Had they vindictively desired to persecute him they could have done so, for fines for non-attendance were high. Instead they lightened his burden by lowering his tax assessments: a considerable gesture in an oligarchical structure where much of the financial burden fell on themselves. Finally in 1586 the councillors replaced John Shakespeare and another impecunious alderman, adding the sad note that 'Mr. Wheeler dothe desyre to be put out of the Companye and Mr. Shakespeare dothe not come to the halles when they be warned nor hathe done of longe tyme'. If they had decided, after the longest period of non-attendance ever permitted, that the Shakespeare fortunes were irretrievable, they were wrong. The lost wealth was amply restored by William Shakespeare in the next decade, but it is not the function of a town council to assess the potential of literary genius.

To Have and to Hold

27 November 1582 is the first date after William Shakespeare's baptism which can be recorded with certainty. On that day the diocesan clerk in Worcester noted an application for a marriage licence *'inter Willelmum Shaxpere et Annam Whateley de Temple Grafton'* to secure the right to marry during the prohibited period between 2 December and 13 January. The complexity increased next day. William was joined by two men of Shottery, Fulke Sandells and John Richardson, who guaranteed a bond of £40 for the marriage of 'William Shagspere and Anne Hathaway of Stratford'.

Did William leave Anne Whateley standing at the altar? Some have thought so. The double marriage entry, William's youth – he was 18 – and the size of the bond imply strange goings-on. Frank Harris suggested that Shakespeare was enamoured of the Temple Grafton lass and intended to do the right thing by her. Meanwhile he dabbled with Anne Hathaway and the bun was in the proverbial oven. In a bold move he fled to Worcester to make Mistress Whateley his own, only to be thwarted by the burly husbandmen from Shottery, friends of the wronged woman's deceased father, who pledged the Bard to the shrewish and aging Anne, seven years his senior. He endured her until he could stand it no longer and fled to London. Thus Anne Whateley's loss is our gain. Had he settled in solid, rural, connubial bliss, this literary genius would have flowered unseen in a Warwickshire village.

However, Whateleys are not uncommon in South Warwickshire, but none of that name was recorded in Temple Grafton, a village five miles west of Stratford. William's other Anne probably never existed. Bishop Whitgift's strict ecclesiastical regime at Worcester would not have connived in youthful philandering and duplicity. The clerk must have made an error in his first entry, as he did in the same year when he wrote the same person down as 'Bradley' in one entry, 'Darby' in another. William Whateley, Vicar of Crowle, had been in the consistory court that day in a wrangle over tithes. Perhaps he distracted the clerk while he was dealing with the young man from Stratford.

Still, there was plenty on William's mind as he rode out that day. Anne Hathaway was three months pregnant – a fact open to many interpretations but only one cause. Had the young man seduced the older woman during the Warwickshire summer? Opportunity for such consummation was not lacking among the woods and fields of Arden:

> Between the acres of the rye. . .
> With a hey and a ho and a hey nonino,
> These pretty country folk would lie. . .

Spinster Anne, eldest sister amongst a large family from her father's two marriages, might have been carried away by the young man whom John Aubrey heard was 'handsome' and 'well shap'd'. 'I would that there was no age twixt ten and twenty or that youth would sleep out the rest', observed the shepherd in *A Winter's Tale* '. . . there is nothing in between but getting wenches with child, wronging the ancientry, stealing and fighting.'

Marriage and courtship customs vary according to society and age. In rural communities couples have jumped the broomstick, considering the approbation of God and their neighbours to be sufficient. Shakespeare's aunt, Agnes Arden, was recorded as the wife of Thomas Stringer several months before their marriage. There is a record of a couple from a nearby village exchanging vows before witnesses. 'I do confess that I am your wife and have forsaken all my friends for your sake and I hope you will use me well.' Some went too far. The rascally carpenter, William Slatter, confessed that he 'married himself in his chamber, nobody else being by and hopeth that marriage be lawful'. He hoped vainly. His homespun liturgy was declared invalid and he underwent a church ceremony.

Common Law marriage possessed some legal standing, but children from such liaisons were barred from inheritance. Extra-ordinary relations were not smiled upon in the Stratford peculiar. In 1584, two men were presented for not living with their wives and William Shepherd for cohabiting with Elinor Phillips while reported to have another wife. An undated entry upbrades 'Mr. Holder, curate at Bishopstone, for marrying wandering persons without license or banes asking'. If William and Anne were regarded as sexual transgressors, they would have had to do likewise, but the relevant records are lost.

The absence of John Shakespeare's name from the marriage bond does not indicate disapproval. The document would not have been issued without a declaration of parental consent. The marriage could have been a means to alleviate the monetary difficulties of the Shakespeares, with the legal prose of the licence masking a financial arrangement. Contracted marriages were the norm. They abound in Shakespeare's plays and the poet helped organise a match between the daughter and the apprentice of his landlord in Cripplegate in 1604. The Stratford records contain a number of similar suits. In 1593, Henry Wagstaffe was sued by

Charles Wheeler for breaching an undertaking to give him on his marriage with Rose Caudrey, daughter of Joan Caudrey, widow, ten bushels of rye and ten bushels of barley, 'which defendant had promised the said Rose, being his kinswoman'. William Slatter claimed that George Croftes had promised him money 'whenever he should celebrate a marriage with his daughter Anne . . .'. The marriage of an eligible daughter against her father's wishes could cause fury. In Armada year, Shakespeare's friend Richard Tyler married Susanna, eldest daughter of Richard Woodward of Shottery Manor. The bride's cantankerous old grandfather, Robert Perrott, cut her out of his will and added stern warnings to her sisters against her example.

7. An early 19th-century engraving of Ann Hathaway's Cottage which shows the building when it was still a working farm.

The Hathaways were a family of local standing. Their prosperity may still be seen in their farmhouse. John Hathaway, archer, probably Anne's grandfather, appeared on the muster of 1536 and later became a town constable. Anne's brother, Bartholomew, was twice churchwarden and his son, Richard, became Bailiff in 1626. Anne's father left holdings of over 120 acres in 1581. To his daughter 'Agnes' – the name was interchangeable with Anne, the 'g' being silent in the French fashion – he left ten marks for a dowry and expressed the hope that his chief heir Bartholomew would be 'a comforte unto his Bretherene and Sisters to his powers'. Fraternal largesse was expected. With the death of her father and the growth to maturity of his many children, Anne's domestic services were less essential. It was important to find her a husband.

The links between the families endured as long as William's descent. His grand-daughter left bequests to the five daughters of 'my kinsman Thomas Hathaway late of Stratford', four of whom bore the Shakespearean family names of Judith, Joan, Elizabeth and Susanna.

Anne was probably not residing at home when she married. Temple Grafton is the parish mentioned in the clerk's first marriage entry and it is there that she may have been living. The vicar was Sir John Frith, an old Romish priest, who received poor assessment in a furious Puritan survey of 1586 which described him with inadvertent charm as 'unsound in religion, he can neither preach nor read well; his chiefest trade is to cure hawks that are hurt or diseased for which purpose many do usually repair to him'.

The couple need not have married in church at all. The special licence enabled a valid ceremony to be conducted anywhere. Thomas Gardner was married in the alehouse at Haselor by 'Sir Roger of Preston' [-on-Stour]. Some Catholics obtained the licence to give a private ceremony secular standing and William could likewise have been married by the old rite. The unusually large surety is explicable if it were the rite which worried the authorities.

The awaited child was christened Susanna on 26 May 1583. Twins followed: Hamnet and Judith were baptised on 2 February 1584/5. The godparents were evidently the Sadlers, a couple who gave the twins their christian names. They kept a baker's shop on the corner of the High Street and named a son William in 1597. Hamnet Sadler travelled frequently on business as far as East Anglia. He was a loved and potent husband: his neighbour Abraham Sturley noted that 'Judith Sadler waxeth very heavy for the burden of her childing and the want of her husband'.

There were no more children for Anne. This could imply estrangement, but the women of Anne's line were not distinguished by fecundity. Perhaps there were complications undefined by Elizabethan medicine.

Whither William?

The lack of information about the nine years after William's marriage has enabled his biographers to wander freely. Some have noted his extensive use of legal terminology and articled him to a lawyer. The Elizabethans were keen litigants, although the Shakespeares indulged less than most. William Shakespeare, like a number of notable writers, does not appear to hold lawyers in great esteem. If he were so engaged, he did not find the experience edifying. Further speculation has put William in the military. Many Elizabethans had such experience, if only through the type of muster organised by Falstaff. 'Care I for the limb, the hewes, the stature, bulk and big assemblance of a man? Give me the spirit Master Shallow.' However, William Shakespeare's name is not amongst those summoned for duty during the Armada year of 1588. On 4 August the gentlemen of Warwickshire sent their levies to the great army assembled at Tilbury. At Stratford the town armoury was replenished and a little band of eight recruits was sent to war. They marched off, spent some time at Warwick, reached Banbury and then returned, presumably having heard of the Spanish fleet's dispersion and without, apparently, having reached Tilbury. The Chamberlains' Accounts reveal the costs of this heroic action:

pd. for the soldiers coates	£8
pd. for their conduct money [travelling expenses]	4s
pd. for the entrance of ther names in the captaynes rowle [the Queen's sixpence]	4s
Ther charges att Warwick	18. 8d
fridaie saturdaie and sondaie morninge – ther charges	24. 6d
pd. Wyll Baynton & Ryc. Tyler for ther swordes & daggers	15. 6d
pd. for girdles	4. 4d
pd. for mendinge iii flaskes	6d
pd. for mendinge Robert Smythes peece [musket]	6d
for xvijli of matche [matchlock muskets]	14s

for vjli of gonpoder	9s
for carryadge of the armor to Warw	2s 4d
pd. for fetchinge home a post horse from banburye	3s 6d
pd. to dawkes hys sonne for being guyde to the poste [-horse]	12d
pd. to mr. alderman for a Jacke [coat of mail, with overlapping plates], a byll (a sort of pike) & a scull [metal skull cap] to go with the cart	10s
Ther rest unpaid of the ceasures [levies] made in the wardes as per the bill brought in	10s 4d
pd for flaske lethers	4s
£24 gathered & to be gathered	

For William Baynton, Stratford was not a town fit for heroes to live in. By 1592 he had run into such debts that his name figures, with John Shakespeare, amongst those who did not attend church for fear of process.

The storms which swept aside the Armada had their effect on the Avon. The floods were so high that when three men going over Stratford Bridge reached the middle, 'they could not go forward and then returning presently, could not get back, for the water was so risen; it rose a yard every hour from eight to four . . .'.

The most likely occupation of Shakespeare's youth is revealed by John Aubrey's assertion that he was 'in his younger yeares a schoolmaster in the country'.[2] Perhaps like Simon Forman, the astrologer, he was undermaster in a grammar school, or, like John Donne, a tutor in a noble family which provided 'a kind of liberal profession for men of parts and gentle, but not distinguished birth'.

Most of the leading actors' companies passed through Stratford during Shakespeare's youth. The golden year was 1587 when five companies played including the celebrated Queen's Players who received the highest fee ever paid. Such was the crush to see these famous actors that a bench was broken. The Stratfordians were not always spectators. In 1583, 13s 4d was paid to 'Davi Jones and companye for his pastyme at Whitsontyde'. David Jones was a sadler whose second wife was a cousin of Anne Hathaway. Did William Shakespeare, then aged 19, take part in this performance at the Corporation's annual feast? That his daughter Susanna was born in the same month makes it likely that he was in Stratford

> . . . at Pentecost,
> When all our pageants of delight were played,
> Our youth got me to play the woman's part,
> And I was trimm'd in Madam Julia's gown;
> Which served me as fit, by all men's judgements,
> . . . I did play a lamentable part.
> Madam, 'twas Ariadne passioning
> For Theseus perjury and unjust flight;
> Which I so acted with my tears,
> That my poor mistress, moved there withal
> Wept bitterly.

Aubrey gives a further hint of the poet's youthful dramatic activity. After the dubious information that young William was apprenticed to a butcher, he adds that when he killed a calf, 'he would doe it in high style and make a speech'. This curious story gains credence with the knowledge that 'killing the calfe' was a popular charade played behind a door or curtain, in which the performer acted both the butcher and the animal.

Was William so overwhelmed by the romance of the players that he threw in his lot with one of the visiting companies? The Queen's Men were two actors short when they arrived at Stratford in 1587, for William Knell was killed by John Towne during a brawl in Thame.

Since Towne had struck in self-defence he was later pardoned, but, in the meantime, had his place been taken by a young man of theatrical enthusiasm from Stratford?

Whatever else William Shakespeare was doing during these lost years, he was maturing his poetic skills. The fortuitous combination of environment, epoch and genius would ensure an early blossoming of talent. In 1587 Anthony Underhill was buried in Ettington Church. His family knew Shakespeare and his valedictory verses have been preserved:

> As dreams do slide and bubbles rise and fall
> As flowers do fade and flourish in an hower,
> As smoke doth rise and vapours rain shall pour
> Beyond the witt or reach of human power,
> As somers heat doth perish in the grass
> Such is our stay, so lyfe of man doth pass.

If poetry of such quality was not written by the young Shakespeare, it is clear that Warwickshire was fertile in the potential to produce a great poet.

London Road

The London road was familiar to young Stratfordians. A number became apprentices in the great city. In 1577 Roger Lock, another glover's son, began a ten-year apprenticeship to Richard Pickering, a stationer. In 1579, Richard Field, son of Henry Field, the tanner in Back Bridge Street, entered the service of Thomas Vautrollier, a Huguenot printer. After his master died the young Stratfordian married either his daughter or his widow: it is not clear which. He did not forget the needs of his family in Stratford, taking on his brother Jasper as an apprentice after his father's death in 1592. Field printed many notable works, including Shakespeare's *Venus and Adonis*, the best-seller of the age, in 1593, and his *Rape of Lucrece* in the following year.

Stratford girls entered service in the City. In 1594, Elizabeth Trowte, sister of a local butcher, sued Elizabeth Hancocks for alleging that after the death of her mistress in London, she stole all her clothes 'and came down into the countrye and hyd her head for the space of halfe a yeare and afterwards flourished abroad in the said clothes lyke a gentlewoman, but after that she was taken and carryed to London where the same clothes were received agayne by her master without anye punishment'. Her airs and graces caught her Henry Prettie, another butcher, to whom she bore five children before she and her husband perished in the plague year of 1606. More respectable advancement was secured by Katherine Rogers, daughter of a High Street butcher and alderman. Her considerable fortune from outliving three wealthy husbands enabled her son John Harvard to endow the American university which bears his name.

A popular means of travel was to accompany the carriers who made regular journeys between Stratford and London. 'If ther be any cloth for mee to bee sent downe, send it by Edward Bromley', wrote Daniel Baker to Richard Quiney who was in London during 1598. Around 1605 John Sadler, son of the tenant of Stratford Mill, fled from an arranged marriage. 'He joined himself to the carrier and came to London, where he had never been before and sold his horse in Smithfield and having no acquaintance . . . to recommend or assist him, he went from street to street and house to house, asking if they wanted an apprentice and though he met with many discouraging scorns and a thousand denials, he went on till he light upon Mr. Brooksbank, a grocer in Bucklersbury.' This enterprising young man prospered, participating in the early colonisation of Virginia.[4] His partner and brother-in-law was Richard Quiney, brother of Shakespeare's son-in-law. The two grocers did not forget Stratford. In 1632 they presented the Corporation with a mace 'to be borne before the Bailiffe and Chief Alderman . . . for this time being for ever', which is still in use.

All these Stratfordians are eclipsed in memory by their fellow. The stage presented by David Jones and his Whitsuntide players had become too small for William Shakespeare. On an unrecorded date in the 1580s he crossed Hugh Clopton's great bridge to start his momentous journey. Stratford was the source of his genius, but only in London could he fulfill his destiny.

FOOTNOTES

[1]   The average age at first marriage in the Stratford registers, 1580-1624, was 25.3, see J.M. Martin's thesis in Warwick County Library.

[2]   Aubrey's source was the actor, Christopher Beeston, whose father was in Shakespeare's company.

[3]   If the most colourful legend of Shakespeare's youth is credited, his departure from Stratford was precipitate. At the end of the 17th century, a story emerged that he fled to London after a poaching incident to escape the wrath of Sir Thomas Lucy, whom he satirised subsequently as Justice Shallow. The fact that the story was not picked up by earlier chroniclers and the un-Shallow like character of the stern Sir Thomas argue against its validity. Perhaps the story reflects a half-forgotten memory of a clash between the Shakespeares and the Lucys at the time of the Somerville incident.

[4]   The story was told by his daughter in 'The Holy Life of Mrs. Elizabeth Walker, late wife of A[ntony] W[alker] D.D.' (1690).

A typical thatched mud wall, common in Shakespeare's Stratford.

CHAPTER 4

'Exits and Entrances'

'They have their exits and their entrances and one man in his time plays many parts.'
As You Like It 'Fame's Immortal Book'.

William Shakespeare is first recorded in London in a furious attack made on him by the playwright, Robert Greene, in 1592. By then he was an established dramatist. While his fame and fortune grew, he never lost contact with his home town. In 1587, when he was probably already in London, he participated in an unsuccessful action against his cousin, John Lambert, for the return of his mother's Wilmcote property. As with Dickens, the experience of family penury in youth had a deep effect. He developed an avid capacity for work, his output far exceeding any contemporary talent. The handsome earnings of this prolific genius were, apart from necessary professional investments, ploughed back into the Stratford area. The humiliations of the austere years had to be wiped out and the family prestige restored. Thus John Shakespeare resurrected a 20-year-old claim to a coat of arms, which was granted on 20 October 1596. The main device, a spear of steeled argent, was a clear pun on the family name. The motto 'non sanz droit' – 'not without right' – is defensive and was perhaps parodied by Ben Jonson as 'not without mustard'. The message is clear. This is not an award to an upstart, but to a man who had held high civic office, 'maryed a daughter and heyre of Arden' and

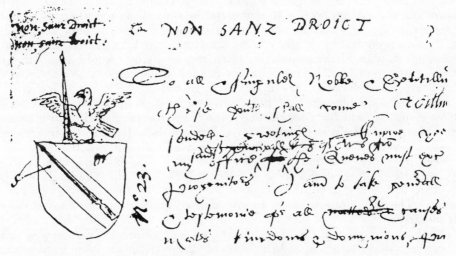

8. A sketch of the arms granted to John Shakespeare in 1596.

claimed an ancestor rewarded by Henry VII. In 1602 the Garter King of Arms, Sir William Dethick, was accused by the York Herald, Peter Brooke, of elevating base-born persons, including John Shakespeare. A successful defence was made of the Shakespeare claim both by Dethick and the Clarenceux King of Arms, William Camden, who knew both the London and Stratford ends of William Shakespeare's life.

Subsequently, John Shakespeare applied to pair his crest with that of his wife's family. The heralds sketched the arms of the Park Hall Ardens and later those of a junior branch of the family, but the application was never pursued. The enthusiasm of the Shakespeares was perhaps diminished by domestic sadness. Hamnet Shakespeare, aged 11, the only direct heir to the family name, was buried at Holy Trinity on 11 August 1596. Shakespeare's company was in Kent, but its chief playwright was probably in Stratford, working on his adaptation of *The Troublesome Reign of King John*. Thus he may have been in the sad group that carried the little body to the church. If any speech in his plays reflects his own feelings it is surely that in *King John*, when the stricken Constance mourns the loss of her son:

> Grief fills the room up of my absent child,
> Lies in his bed, walks up and down with me,
> Puts on his pretty looks, repeats his words,
> Remembers me of all his gracious parts,
> Stuffs out his vacant garments with his form.
> Then I have reason to be fond of grief.

Hamnet had probably followed his father to the grammar school, where a new pedagogue had arrived in 1582 who stayed for 40 years. Alexander Aspinall, described by Shakespeare's cousin, John Greene, as 'great Philip Macedon', married in 1594 a widow, Anne Shaw. Years later, Sir Francis Fane noted in his commonplace book:

> The gift is small
> The will is all:
> Asheyander Asbenall.
> Shaxpaire upon a peire of gloves that mas[t]er sent to his mistress.

One of Shakespeare's favourite *double entendres* is understood by adding 'y' to the 'will'. Gloves would have been a curious present, for the Widow Shaw's son was a glover.

It is easy to forget that Shakespeare was only 32 at Hamnet's death. In London he was a noted figure and the tributes flowing to him mark the start of the enduring cult of Bardolatry. To one contemporary he was 'honey-tongued Shakespeare', while another wrote of his name being in 'Fame's immortal book'. Even more adulatory was Francis Meres' declaration that 'the Muses speak with Shakespeare's fine-filed phrase if they would speak English'. His character was apparent from his earliest days in the City. Chettle, who published Greene's attack, apologised and declared that Shakespeare possessed 'demeanor no less civil, than he was excellent in the quality which he possesses; besides divers of worship have reported his uprightness in dealing, which argues his honesty and approves his art'. His conversation excited comment. 'Many were the wit-combats betwixt him and Ben. Jonson', wrote Thomas Fuller, 'which two I beheld like a Spanish great Galleon and an English man of war. Master Jonson (like the former) was built far higher in learning, solid but slow in his performance. Shakespeare, with the English man of war, lesser in bulk, but light in sailing, could turn with all tides, tack about and take advantage of the winds, by the quickness of his wit and intervention.' This Ben. Jonson, never to give praise lightly, declared 'I loved the man . . . this side idolatry'.

Like Joseph at the court of Pharaoh, William's success brought his brethren to his side. Gilbert became a haberdasher in St Bride's Ward, although he was often in Stratford, acting for his brother in land deals. Edmund, the youngest, became an actor of little distinction and fathered a 'base-born' son buried at St Giles, Cripplegate, in August 1607. Four months later,

Edmund Shakespeare, 'a player', was buried in the Bankside church of St Mary Ovarie with a forenoon toll of the great bell.

Of the other siblings, Shakespeare's sister Joan married William Hart, a Stratford hatter. Little is known of his brother Richard whose sole impact on the Stratford records, apart from baptism and burial, occurred when he appeared with three other men before the consistory court in 1608, on an unspecified charge. The four pleaded guilty and were fined 12d 'to the use of the poore of Stratford'. It is unlikely that Richard should be so little mentioned were he engaged in any trade or profession. Perhaps he was backward, living first with his parents and then his sister, helping with the simple business and household chores.

'A Praty House of Brick and Tymbre'

In 1597, Shakespeare bought New Place, 'a praty house of brick and tymbre', whose elegance had been noted by Leland. He secured this fine property cheaply[1] from William Underhill, a Catholic recusant, because it was in a state of 'great ruyne and decay and unrepayred'. Extensive works were necessary and 'Mr. Shaxpere' sold the Corporation 'a lod of ston' in 1598. His concerns creep into his current play, *Henry IV, Part Two*.

9. *A drawing of New Place, where Shakespeare lived from 1610 to 1616, done from memory by George Vertue in 1737 after the house's demolition in 1702. This is the only known representation of the house.*

> When we mean to build
> We first survey the plot, then draw the model
> And when we see the figure of the house,
> Then we must rate the cost of the erection.

The great garden of New Place was brought into order. A vehement local tradition maintained that the poet planted the mulberry tree which was cut down in 1758. Probably like Angelo he had a 'garden circumnured with brick, whose Western side is with a vinyard back'd', for in 1631 Sir Thomas Temple of Wolverton instructed a servant to ride to Stratford and 'desire Mr. Hall Phiscon[2] . . . to suffer Harry Rose or any better in skill to gather . . . 2 or 3 of the fairest of those budes or some shutes of last yeares vines'.

Anne Shakespeare ran her own household for the first time at New Place. This anonymous woman emerges fleetingly in the will of Thomas Whittington, the Hathaway shepherd at Shottery, who, in 1601, left 'unto the poore people of Stratford xls that is in the hand of Anne Shaxpere Wyf unto Mr. William Shaxpere and is due debt unto me'. Was the poet's spouse a scrounger from her brother's servants? More likely she was a trusted holder of savings.

Domestic chores would increase, although the retinue of servants living around the courtyard would diminish the burdens. Anne would be skilled in weaving and brewing. Inventories John Shakespeare made of the goods of two deceased neighbours show that equipment for these tasks was standard in Stratford households. Ralph Shaw's home contained barrels, a sieve, a spinning wheel, four pairs of wool cards, 20 quarters of malt, pails and looms. Henry Field possessed six beer barrels, five looms, four pails, two skips, one outing vat and three malt shovels. 'The chief trade here', observed Daniel Defoe, a century later, 'is in corn and malt of which last it makes great abundance.'

Troubled Times

Stratford's economic situation deteriorated in the 1590s: a misfortune compounded by two devastating fires which wiped out much of the town. 'Those that delighted themselves in downe bedds and silken curteynes are now glad of the shelter of a hedge', wrote an Oxford citizen in similar circumstances. Elizabethan Stratford was an elaborate incendiary device of wattle and daub, open hearths, thatch and timber. Every burgess was obliged to keep a leather fire bucket and the Corporation provided five great hooks to pull down stricken buildings. An order of 1583 compelled householders to erect chimneys, but this did not prevent the great fires of 1594 and 1595, which caused an estimated £20,000-worth of damage. Puritan preachers made much of the fact that both broke out on Sundays. 'That which is most strange within these late years', wrote Thomas Beard in *The Theatre of God's Judgements,* 'a whole town hath bene twice burnt for the breach of the sabbath by the inhabitants.'

The Corporation was more concerned with temporal practicalities. In September 1594, eight emissaries were appointed to travel and raise money for relief and rebuilding. Alderman Thomas Barber raised £21 0s 9d in Worcestershire; Mr. Parsons collected £10 11s 2d in Gloucestershire and Mr. Sturley, £4 3s 8d in 'Darby' and 55s 8d in 'Abrington'. Most successful was Richard Quiney, who raised £22 5s 3d in Northamptonshire and, with Shakespeare's friend Hamnet Sadler, the huge sum of £75 6s 0d in Suffolk and Norfolk.

Falling economic standards and high inflation[3] produced a rising crime-rate and the declining respect for authority epitomised by Elizabeth Wheeler *alias* Rundles, who was before the Bawdy Court in 1595 'for continually brawling and not attending church'. Her response was graphic. 'Goodes woundes', she told the Court, 'a plague a God on you all. A fart of ons ars for you.' A terse note adds 'excommunicated'.

The disastrous situation was compounded by the incessant war with Spain and a succession of bad harvests, which produced grave shortages. On 3 October 1595, the Corporation forbade innkeepers from home-brewing and baking and ordered them to use the public brewers and bakers. Milk was imported from 'the villadges about us . . . to the relievinge of our children and others'. In 1597 a survey of barley held by citizens was ordered as a measure against hoarding. At New Place the Shakespeares[4] held 18 quarters, a standard household quantity. Alderman Abraham Sturley[5] noted 'growing malcontent' against hoarders. 'God send my Earl of Essex down to see them hanged at their own doors', he wrote vehemently: Elizabeth's ill-starred favourite was a popular figure. A petition to the Queen stressed the hardship caused by the prohibition on household malting, 'in that oure towne hath no other especiall trade havinge thereby onlye tyme beyonde mans memorye lyved by exersysing the same, our houses fitted to no other uses, manye servantes amonge us hyered only to that purpose'. Such was the depth of the depression that the Corporation placed its treasures in pawn with John Combe, a local merchant and money-lender. 'Your cousin Sir Combe holds the silver and gold plate', wrote Sturley to Richard Quiney in 1598, 'on the advice of Daniel Baker, with whom indeed, he was very angry on thine account . . .'. We will hear more of this Baker, who was beginning to make a speciality of unilateral decisions.

Abraham Sturley had tried to enlist the aid of the lord of the manor, that fratricidal heir, Sir Edward Greville. On 24 January 1596/7, he wrote to Richard Quiney: 'Theare might bi Sir Ed. some meanes made to the knightes of the Parliament for an ease and discharge of such taxes and subsedes wherewith our town is like to be charged and I assure u I am in great feare and doubte bi no means able to paie'.

Relations between the Corporation and Sir Edward were good at this time, exemplified in a dinner given for him at Richard Quiney's house in 1596/7. Lady Greville was entertained in 1597 and amity appeared compounded at a meeting on 3 November when Sir Edward agreed to support an application for a new charter. Sturley wrote to Quiney that Sir Edward 'saith we shall not be at any fault for money for procuring the cause, for himself will procure it and lay it down for the time'. Yet Sturley had his misgivings. In considering the financial gains to be expected from the new charter, he suggested that half should be offered to Sir Edward, 'lest he shall thinke it to good for us and procure it for himselfe, as he served us last time'.

The 'last time' had followed the death of the Earl of Warwick in 1590. The Corporation petitioned for its right to appoint to appoint the schoolmaster and the vicar, but Greville moved faster and secured the lordship of the manor for himself. A strong antagonism between Quiney and Greville perhaps dated from this incident. In 1592 Greville exercised his right of veto over the appointment of Quiney as Bailiff. The Corporation lobbied Sir Fulke Greville at Warwick. On 5 October he wrote: 'Cosen Greville . . . If the cause of your refusall be for any wante of partes beseeking that place in the man himself, he is desirous to satisfie you in all objections'. Sir Fulke knew the volatility of his relative, for he added: 'In the meane tyme yor yeelding at this present to my request can no waie prejudice yor right and I hope yew shall have no cause to seek it violentlie of them'.

Greville conceded and relations improved, but Sir Fulke's suspicion was justified. After 1598 things worsened as Greville asserted his supposed privileges with violence. He claimed the right to enclose the riverside common known as the Bancroft and sent his men there to dig ditches and build fences in January 1600/01. Quiney organised the Stratfordians to destroy the works. A legal action by Greville, in which the great jurist Sir Edward Coke represented the Corporation, got nowhere. Quiney was defiantly re-elected as Bailiff in September. He worked assiduously against Greville's interest, visiting the Bishop of Worcester with Shakespeare's cousin, Thomas Greene,[6] to enlist his aid in withstanding unjust inroads into the town's liberties. Greville, believing 'we shuld wynne it by the sworde' sent his rowdy followers to make trouble in Stratford taverns. 'Ther came some of them whoe beinge drunke fell to brawelinge in ther hosts howse . . . and drew ther daggers uppon the hosts: at a faier tyme the Baileefs being late abroad to see the towne in order and comminge by in yt Hurley Burley came into the howse and commanded the peace to be kept butt colde nott prevayle and in hys endevor to stifle the brawle had hys heade grevously broken by one of hys [Greville's] men whom neither hym self [Greville] punished nor wolde suffer to be punished but with a shewe to turn them awaye and enterteyned agayne.' Quiney did not live out the month. On 31 May 1602, the 'Baily of Stretforde' was buried, the only one to die in office. Greville lost his estates through speculations during the next reign and died in poverty.

During Quiney's ill-fated bailiwick he compiled a list of senior and respected citizens who could vouch for the borough's historic rights, which included the name of John Shakespeare, who, according to an anecdote of his old age, was still to be found in his glover's shop, where Thomas Plume, writing half a century later, claimed Sir John Mennis saw him – 'a merry-cheeked old man – that said – Will was a good honest fellow, but that he durst have cracked a jest with him at any time'. Sir John was only two when John Shakespeare died. Perhaps the anecdote refers to an elder brother or perhaps he heard it from someone.

If Richard Quiney intended to use John Shakespeare's knowledge he was disappointed. On 8 September 1601, the old man was buried at Holy Trinity. His widow survived him by seven years.

'Loving Good Friend and Countryman'

In his letter telling Richard Quiney of the town's disasters, Sturley remarked that 'our countriman Mr. Shakspear is willing to disburse some moneys upon some od yardelande or other att Shotterie or neare about us; he thinketh it a very fitt patterne to move him to deale in the matter of our Tithes. By the instructions u can give him thereof we think it a faire marke for him to shoot att'. Shakespeare was not moved to fire an arrow on this occasion, but later he bought land and tithes in Stratford. Quiney took advantage of this growing wealth when he ran short of money during his visit to London. There was one man in the City to whom an impecunious Stratfordian could turn. Quiney wrote 'ffrom the Bell in Carter Lane the 25 October 1598' requesting a £30 loan from 'my Loveinge good ffrend & contryman Mr. Wm. Shackespere . . . you shall ffrende me much in helping me out of all the debettes I owe in

London I thanke god & muche quiet my mynde . . . I committ thys your care & hope of your helpe. I fear I shall nott be backe thys night ffrom the Courts. Haste. The Lord be with you and with us all amen.'[7]

Shakespeare's reputation as a man of wealth is revealed in a note written by the Reverend John Ward, the Vicar of Stratford after the Restoration. 'Hee spent att ye Rate of 1,000£ a year as I have heard.' Ward's informant was probably Shakespeare's daughter Judith. The sum seems absurdly high, but if it is reckoned as referring to the man's enterprises rather than his personal spending it falls into perspective. Shakespeare was a major shareholder in his theatrical company. The remark is one which an old lady might recall who had once asked her father for a new gown when he was overwhelmed by bills for costumes, salaries, touring expenses and other costly items.

It is inconceivable that a man of such self-made fortune, an acquaintance and entertainer of the greatest in the land, should not be a figure of note in his own town. The Stratfordians must have been aware of the source of the Shakespeares' regenerative wealth and taken a vicarious pride in their notable townsman. 'He was wont', says John Aubrey, 'to go into his native country once a year', when he would visit his family, deal with his affairs and, perhaps, work on his dramatic output. Yet, despite his attachment to Stratford, he never became involved in its civic affairs. This was right and proper for a man whose working life was spent elsewhere. The great writer would not retire to the country to become embroiled in the petty politics of a small town.

The confident face of Puritanism was encroaching on Stratford as surely as it was advancing elsewhere. While Abraham Sturley was Bailiff in 1596, he paid four companies of players and a show of the City of Norwich but in 1603 the Corporation, oblivious to Hamlet's warning against the players' ill-report, banned plays and interludes from its property, 'upon payne that whatsoever of the Baylief, Alderman and Burgisses of this boroughe shall gyve on license thereunto shall forfeyte for everie offense 10s'.

The leading Puritan and architect of this ban was Daniel Baker, a High Street mercer who dominated the town's councils for the next 40 years. He fulfilled the *cliche* of his kind, combining a strict public morality with an irrepressible sensuality. A widower, he was presented before the consistory court in 1606 on a charge of sexual incontinence. He failed to appear, but Anne Ward admitted that 'Mr. Daniel Baker is the true and undoubted father of the child with which she has been pregnant', saying that he had promised to marry her. She was ordered to make public penance in a white sheet. Baker was excommunicated for non-appearance. He appeared three weeks later and made his denials, but admitted there was public infamy about the matter. He was ordered to 'purge' himself,[8] with six others about whom similar rumours were circulating. When he failed to do this he was pronounced guilty, but may have escaped public humiliation by paying a fine. It was probably this incident which made him an intractable opponent of the vicar, John Rogers.

One who ignored the ban on actors was Henry Walker, who as Bailiff in 1608 revived the Guild Hall play. He was a friend of Shakespeare, who was the godfather of his son William. There were other breaches of the regulations and they were made more stringent in 1611. 'The inconvenience of plaies being verie seriouslie considered of with the unlawfulness . . . the sufferance of them is against the orders heretofore made and against the examples of other well governed cities and burrowes the Companie heare are contented . . . that the penaltie of 10s imposed for breakinge the order shall henceforth be £10 . . . this to bide untill the next common council and from thenceforth for ever, exepted that be their finally revoked and made void.' The Puritans had a point. The bloody skirmish which presaged the arrival of the Queen's Players in 1587, the Tyburn mark branded on Ben Jonson's thumb after he had killed a fellow actor in a duel and the violent death of Christopher Marlowe, all indicate that the epithet 'gentle' applied to Shakespeare was noteworthy because of its rarity amongst his fellows.

Adherence to the new regulations depended on the viewpoint of the Bailiff. When Thomas Greene's stepson William Chandler held office in 1618, 3s 4d was 'given to a company that came with a show to the town' and later five shillings *per* Master Bailiff's appointment to a company of Players'. As late as 1633-4, a strolling player arrested at Banbury had acted with his company at Stratford and Sir Thomas Lucy's house at Charlecote.

The poverty spiral was having its grinding effect in Stratford. In 1601, 700 people – a third of the population – were on the poor lists. Illegitimacy, drunkenness and violence increased and the Corporation castigated the alehouse keepers for contributing 'through their unreasonable strong drink, to the increase of quarrelling and other misdemeanors in their houses and the farther and greater impoverishment of many poor men haunting the said houses when their wives and children are in extremity of begging'. In 1601 Thomas Bailes was 'slaine at the Signe of the Swan upon the sabbath day at the tyme of the sermon being there drinking . . .'. In 1603 the Corporation prohibited inhabitants from 'tippling in alehouses unless they are labouring men partaking of drink in their dinner hour', which must have engendered initiative amongst those ingenious in evasion. The prohibition had little effect. 1609 was a notably violent year. William Robyns, a servant of Hornby the blacksmith, was killed in a quarrel over a jug of beer. Another murder took place in the low inner parlour of the *Swan* in Bridge Street. Lewis Gilbert, a veteran of Essex's disastrous Irish campaign, quarrelled with the host Richard Waterman, his wife and two daughters. When they attempted to eject him, he set his back against the door and resisted. 'He will spoil my father. He will murder my father', shrieked the daughters. Waterman's brother Thomas was sitting with Humphrey Acton by the fire in the hall. He forced open the parlour door and, seizing Gilbert by the collar, tried to eject him. Gilbert drew a long knife and stabbed him in 'the right side by the naval, from which he died'. Gilbert, of no fixed abode or means of support, fled. The Coroner's inquest, meeting over the body of Waterman, found him guilty of wilful murder.

The crime wave kept the courts busy. Richard Barrett of Henley-in-Arden and John Whittle of Bearley were summoned in 1610 to give evidence against James Lord 'in the felonious killing of William Langford'. A capital charge was faced by William Perry in the same year, 'a person suspected of having coined gold'. James Johnson and Nicholas Worrall were 'attached to answer Thomas Townesend for having conspired with one Hugh Browne . . . to defraud the plaintiff of divers sums of money at play in a game of cards called Newcutt'. Richard Smyth was 'attached to answer Henry Collins for scandalous words uttered, viz. "Thou art an arrant theife and wast whipped out of the countrie where thou didst dwelle for stealinge sheets of a hedge"'. In 1610 a revision of the charter extended the Borough's legal jurisdiction over the church, churchyard and Old Town, 'which last locality is much infested with beggars and vagabonds'.

For a while longer the 'spirit of brotherly love' intended to pervade the halls of the Corporation prevailed. In 1607 5s 2d was paid 'at Mrs. Queenes when Mr. Rodgers and Mr. Wright were made frendes'. Wright was the under-schoolmaster, just down from Oxford, whose precocious opinions must have upset the vicar. Around the same time the Corporation wrote to Henry Yelverton, the Attorney-General, on behalf of 'divers poore men . . . much grieved and oppressed by the hard and unconscionable course taken against them by William Slatter'. Slatter, the carpenter with marriage problems, was bringing actions in the Star Chamber against those too impecunious to defend and then extorting money from them in return for not proceeding. The Assize Justices ordered him to desist, but he ignored this injunction and was imprisoned. On his release he continued in his old ways, 'for he hath served poore women into the Starr Chamber for small or no causes and so terryfyed them therewith that some of them were constrayned to purloyne from their husbands to compounde with him . . .'. The Corporation's letter was scathing: 'The sayde Slatter ys very well knowne to us to be a fellow of verry lewde behavior, a stirrer up of suites, a contentious person, a contemner of authority . . . He standeth indicted . . . for a common Barrator and reformeth not himself, but groweth worst and worst . . .'. Yet it was difficult to take action against him because he had no fixed abode. 'Wherefore we desire that your worship will be pleased to have the compassion of the poore defendants and to take such a course that the countrye may be eased of so turbulent a fellowe.'

Gunpowder, Treason and Plot

Sectarianism invaded the Guild Hall in 1612, when old Thomas Barber of the *Bear*, who had been thrice Bailiff, was expelled from the aldermanic bench because his wife Joan was 'an obstinent recuscant'. Unless she changed her adherence he was not to be re-elected. There were other reasons for puritanical chagrin against Barber, who was likely to have defied the ban on players.

Catholic sympathisers were in a cleft stick. While their beliefs were ostensibly inviolate, the means of practising them were steadily denied and resources were drained by fines and forfeitures. Some Catholics resorted to desperate, hopeless plotting and those frail kicks against the pricks justified the authorities in further tightening their control. There is a tragic attraction about these Englishmen, struggling to keep alight the dwindling flame of faith amidst what they regarded as a new dark age. One such was Robert Catesby, whose father lived at Bushwood House, that enclave of Old Stratford near Lapworth. He was a familiar figure to Stratfordians. 'Yff you can learne where Mr. Robert Catesbie lyeth', wrote Daniel Baker to his 'Uncle Quyne' in London, 'I pray you goe to hym and dessier hym to have a care of mee for hys Father's debt according to hys promyse at Rolewright . . . Hee lyeth about the Strand in a back allie towards the Waterside.' Catesby was six feet tall, with a noble, expressive face and strong personal magnetism. He participated in the abortive Essex rebellion of 1601 and it was his fatal combination of charisma and naivete which led him into the Gunpowder Plot of 1605, a doomed escapade nurtured in the Stratford neighbourhood. Ambrose Rookwood rented Clopton House that autumn to be near his fellow conspirators who were mainly impoverished local Catholic gentry. They whiled away their time 'ryding of great horses and hunting'. On 4 and 5 November they attended local race meetings to be together when news came from London. On hearing the worst they fled across the county seizing horses from Fulke Greville's stables before making a last stand at Haddington in Worcestershire. Catesby was killed by a bullet in the head. The others were executed with that horror the age deemed necessary.

In Stratford the excitement was intense. This was as stirring as the Armada yet closer to home. The armour was again removed from its dusty repository and repaired and replenished. Musters were raised, gunpowder purchased and tactics discussed. Wild rumours circulated. On the night of 9 November the Corporation drank wine at Mrs. Quiney's tavern, 'when yt was said that Sir Fulke Greville's house was beseiged'. The horse-stealing had grown to a campaign in three days. An expedition was launched against Clopton House which the local militia was doubtless relieved to find unoccupied. Goods were seized, including chalices, crucifixes, surplices and other vestments. A further repercussion was a crack-down on those considered to be 'popishly affected', who fulfilled the obligation to attend church, but never received the sacrament. Amongst those so listed were the Sadlers and Susanna Shakespeare. Their names were later struck from the list, so it may be assumed that they complied.

Autumnal Years

This is the 'dark' period of Shakespeare's work, when a devastating vision of the universe produced dramas of superlative power. This vision is unlikely to have sprung from Stratford soil, except to the degree that great drama is rooted in universal experience. In his home town Shakespeare emerges as the man Abraham Sturley knew as interested in acquiring property.

Domestic concerns played their part in his sojourns. He must have been present on the summer day in 1607 when his daughter Susanna married John Hall. Susanna, 'witty above her sex' and heiress to a fortune, was doubtless pursued by numerous suitors, each carefully vetted by the Shakespeares. Hall was a Cambridge graduate born at Carlton, Bedfordshire in 1575, one of 11 children. He had become a doctor and taken up his practice in Stratford. Shakespeare got on well with him and, given contemporary inheritance laws, was content to regard him as his heir. Medical references are more closely observed in the plays after the marriage. That most fertile and creative of minds must have been fascinated by Hall's profession. 'Elizabeth, daughter of John Hall gentleman' was baptised on 21 February 1607/08.

Thomas Greene, Shakespeare's cousin, was living at New Place in 1609 with his wife, Lettice, and two children, aptly named William and Anne. Greene became Town Clerk in 1603 and may be the minor poet of that name who was criticised, with Shakespeare and Jonson, for failing to compose a funeral elegy to Queen Elizabeth. The accommodation provided by the Shakespeares was generously offered, for Greene wrote that he 'perceyved I might stay another year . . .' Much Corporation business must have been conducted from the parlour and it was presumably on Greene's behalf that a visiting preacher was entertained in 1611, who must have delivered one of the three annual endowed sermons at the Guild Chapel. The Corporation paid 20d for 'one quart of sack and one quart of clarett wine'. What Greene called his 'golden dayes and spirites' spent in Stratford's service is reflected in his surviving letters, including one to John Marston,[9] the dramatist, from his 'Lovinge ffrendes' in Stratford, but the subject is legal not literary. Another is written on behalf of the Corporation to Sir William Somerville, praying him to punish Michael Gybson of Knowle for the seduction of Dorothy Field; probably another example of public virtue coinciding with a strain on the rates!

In 1613, William Shakespeare contributed to a bill for the repair of the local highways. He had used them as much as most in Stratford, but in his autumnal years he was spending more time in the town, slowly disengaging himself from the metropolis. The hand which had written two plays a year was slowing down. *The Tempest,* written in 1611, was the last masterpiece. After that there was collaboration with the rising dramatist, John Fletcher. Probably Shakespeare worked from Stratford, sketching out plots, writing major speeches and setting scenes. Fletcher would complete the work. On 29 June 1613 the Globe Theatre burnt down during a performance of *King Henry VIII.* Within a year a new more splendid building had arisen, but William Shakespeare's name was not amongst the shareholders. England's greatest man of the theatre had made his exit.

'The latter part of his life was spent', reported Rowe, 'as all Men of good sense will wish theirs may be, in Ease, Retirement and the Conversation of his Friends. He had the good Fortune to gather an Estate equal to his Occasion, and, in that to his Wish and is said to have spent some Years before his Death at his native *Stratford.'* Yet the last years were not entirely tranquil. The Shakespeares were disturbed by a distasteful episode during the summer of 1613. On 15 July, Susanna Hall brought a suit for defamation in the Diocesan Court against John Lane the younger of Alveston who had 'about five weekes past' spread a story that she had 'the runinge of the raynes' (a graphic name for gonorrhea) and had 'bin naught [fornicated] with Rafe Smith at John Palmer'. Robert Whatcott, probably one of the New Place servants, appeared for Mrs. Hall. Lane failed to appear and was excommunicated for spreading false report. In 1619 he was presented for 'not receivinge holi communyon according to the canons' and, later in that year, for drunkenness.

The incident reveals the close-knit nature of Stratford society. Ralph Smith, one of the Armada volunteers, a hatter and haberdasher, was Hamnet Sadler's nephew. Lane's sister, Margaret, was married to Shakespeare's cousin, John Greene, the town clerk's brother. Lane's cousin, Thomas Nashe, married Elizabeth Hall in 1626.

'Overthrowne and Undone'

On 9 July 1614 Stratford was devastated by another fire, which was spread by the prevailing wind and destroyed 54 houses, 'many of them very fair' and much other property, to the value of over £8,000. The 'Brief for the Relief of Sufferers' written in the name of King James I makes pathetic reading. Not only were those who had lost their property in the three great fires 'utterly undone and like to perish', but the rest of the town was 'in great hazard to be overthrowne & undone'. The Stratfordians were 'no waies able to relieve their distressed neighbours in this their great want and misery. And whereas the said Towne hath been a great Market Towne whereunto great recourse of people was made . . . it is in great hazard to bee utterly overthrowne, if either the resort thither be neglected, or course of travellers diverted, which for want of speedy reparation may be occasioned. And foreasmuch as our distressed subjects the inhabitants of the sad Towne are very ready & willing to the uttermost of their powers to rectifie & new build the said Towne againe, yet finding the performance thereof far beyond their ability, they have made their humble suite unto us . . . and have humbly besought us to commend the same good & laudable deed and the charitable furtherance thereof, to the benevolence of all our loving subjects, not doubting but that all good and wel-disposed Christians will for common charity and love to their country and the rather for our Commendation hence of, be ready with all willingness to extend their charitable reliefe towards the comfort of so many distressed people . . .'.

The Corporation forbade thatching of houses and ordered existing thatch to be replaced by tiles and slates. The aldermen again embarked on their fund-raising tours for the stricken town, but in 1619 a petition described Stratford as 'the anciente (but now much decayed) Borough'. It was to be 200 years before this decline was reversed.

John a Combe

More stress and controversy blew up in 1614 with a plan by a cartel of landowners to enclose the common fields at Welcombe. To the peasant freeholders this meant destitution: to the Corporation, loss of historic rights and an increased burden of poor relief. The issue was explosive. In the spring of 1607, similar proposals had led to 'tumultuous assemblies' against 'depopulations'. Under Thomas Greene's guidance, resistance was planned. William Shakespeare was inadvertently involved as a titheholder.

The enclosers were men of the new age: Arthur Mainwaring, steward to the Lord Chancellor; William Combe, the High Sheriff, and his younger brother, Thomas, who had in 1598 denounced his cousins, the Sheldons, for harbouring a Catholic priest. The Combes represented new wealth. 'They say in Stratford that he cannot have less than 20,000li in his purse', wrote Leonard Digges of William Combe in 1632, 'increased by honest 8 and 10 in the hundred'.

This distate for usury also affected the posthumous reputation of the Combe brothers' Uncle John. The wealthiest man in Stratford, he lent money at interest and engaged in regular actions for its recovery. Within four years of his death in 1614, an epitaph was published 'upon John Combe of Stratford-upon-Avon, a notable Usurer, fastened upon a Tombe that he has caused to be built in his life time:

> Ten in the hundred must lie in his grave,
> But a hundred to ten whether God will him have?
> Who then must be interr'd in this Tombe?
> Oh (quoth the Divell) my John a Combe.'

Similar verses on an unnamed usurer had been printed previously and mock epitaphs were common. By 1634, it had been attributed to Shakespeare, Aubrey later adding the detail that it had been extemporised in a tavern. In fairness to Combe, he only charged the standard rate of interest. His will left £20 to the poor of Stratford and five pounds to William Shakespeare.

His monument was sculpted by Gerard Johnson, a young man of Flemish origin who worked near the Globe Theatre. Perhaps Shakespeare commended him to the Combes. Two years later he performed the same service for the poet.

FOOTNOTES
[1]   £60 is the figure in the fine but rarely does this represent the price paid.
[2]   John Hall, physician, Shakespeare's son-in-law.
[3]   Inflation ensured that the aldermen and burgesses had to subsidise Thomas Oken's bequest of wine after the election day sermon.
[4]   When things improved a member of the Shakespeare household sold 20 bushels of malt to Philip Rogers, an apothecary. Rogers failed to pay, so William Shakespeare undertook one of his rare lawsuits against him.
[5]   Legal agent to Sir Thomas Lucy. He married Anne, daughter of Alderman Richard Hill. Sturley lost his own house in the conflagrations.
[6]   This, the only extant letter sent to Shakespeare, was found amongst the Corporation papers and is presumably Quiney's copy.
[7]   The exact relationship is uncertain. 'Cousin' was an imprecise term. A Thomas Green was buried at Holy Trinity in 1589. His *alias* of Shakespeare demonstrates a link between the two names which could be the key to the exact relationship.
[8]   To make a formal confession before the minister.
[9]   Marston and his father had stood as sureties for the admission of Thomas Greene to the Middle Temple in 1595.

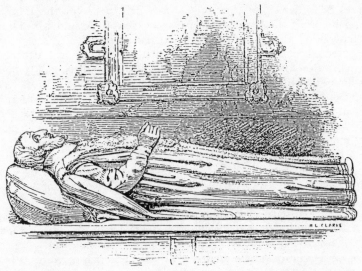

10. *An early 19th-century engraving of the tomb of John Combe in Holy Trinity church.*

CHAPTER 5

'No Peace where is no Unity'

'Hence I conclude what all the World can see
No Peace where is no Unity'.

Anonymous verse, 1619.

Both sides in the enclosure controversy wooed William Shakespeare. His tithe holdings were important, though not crucial to the project. Thomas Greene was in London on 16 November 1614. 'At my cosen Shakespeare commying yesterday to towne I went to see him howe he did: he told me that they assurd him they ment to inclose noe further than to gospell bushe & so upp straight (leavying out part of the dyngles to the ffield) to the gate in Clopton hedge & take in Salisburyes peece and that they meene in April to survey the Land & then to gyve satisfaccion & not before.'[1] Shakespeare's view was clear. 'He and Mr. Hall say they think ther will be nothing done at all': ultimately a correct opinion.

Shakespeare protected his position by agreeing with Mainwaring's attorney, William Replingham, on compensation for any losses through 'inclosure or decaye of tyllage' – a step taken also by other titheholders including Thomas Greene and Arthur Caudrey of the *Angel* who told William Combe that 'he would never consent without the Towne & that he hadd a house and other things more profitable to him than his Land was & that he rather loose his Land than loose their good willes'. The agreement was witnessed by the vicar, John Rogers, a vehement opponent of enclosure. That Shakespeare's behaviour was incontrovertible is demonstrated by the lack of any reproach from Greene, who was scathing about others, like the lawyer, Thomas Lucas, who lined his pockets from the dispute. Even Combe unctuously declared that this rascally advocate 'could not be an honest man for he had no religion in him'.

The Corporation attempted negotiation with William Combe, sending a delegation 'to present their loves and to desire that he would be pleased to forbeare to inclose & to desire his love as they wil be redy to deserve yt'. Combe preferred the profit of enclosure. With the end of the frost on 19 December his men started to dig a trench of 'at least fifty perches'. The Corporation wrote to Mr. Mainwaring and Mr. Shakespeare and sought the support of other landowners. 'I alsoe wrytte of myself', recorded Greene, now living at St Mary's House near Holy Trinity, 'to my cosen Shakespear the Coppyes of all oathes made then, alsoe a not[e] of the Inconvenyances wold grow by the Inclosure.'

Greene's stepson William Chandler and William Walford became tenants at Welcombe, thus increasing the number of claimants with whom the enclosers would have to deal. When they attempted to fill in the ditches Combe had them flung to the ground and sat 'laughingly on his horseback & sayd they wer good football playres' and 'puritan knaves and underlinges in their colour' – a reference to their acquisition of commoners' rights. Nor did he ignore bribery, offering Greene a mare worth ten pounds 'to propound a peace'.

Both sides rushed to law. On 26 January 1614-15, William Chandler wrote 'to my lovinge

44

father Thomas Greene Esquire at his chamber in the Mydle Temple' requesting him to *subpoena* William Combe and his associates in the Star Chamber. On 28 March the Corporation obtained a restraint order against enclosure at Warwick Assizes, unless it could be justified in open assize. Mainwaring gave up at this point, but for Combe the matter had become a vendetta. He beat and imprisoned poor tenants and depopulated the village of Welcombe. He told Arthur Caudrey that 'yf he sowed the said wheat land he would eate yt upp with his sheepe'. Those attempting to fill in the illegal ditches were assaulted and told that 'in the night their corn wilbe eaten and that they will not know against whom to find remedye and tellinge others . . . that their ould bones should be fetcht upp twice in a term or such like speeches'.

A sense of civic duty prevailed. When Combe asked Alderman William Parsons why he opposed enclosure, he replied: 'We are all sworn men for the good of the Borough and to preserve our inheritance. Therefore we would not have it said in the future that we were the men which gave way to the undoing and that all three fires were not so great a loss as the enclosures would be'. Parsons suffered for his probity. A week later he was beaten up by Combe's men.

On 19 April Lawrence Wheeler and Lewis Hiccox started to plough their land within the intended enclosure. Combe merely railed at them, which encouraged them to return next day with Mr. Anthony Nashe, who farmed Shakespeare's titheholding (which implies that his actions had the approval of the poet). In September Greene made an enigmatic entry in his diary: 'W. Shakespeare's tellying J. Greene that I was not able to beare the encloseinge of Welcombe'. Interpreted literally, this states the obvious. Perhaps Greene, without the advantage of inverted commas, was reporting the conversation verbatim.

The forces of legality were mustering. Sir Henry Rainsford of Clifford Chambers told Greene that the Combes would never succeed and that he intended to sue William Combe for trespass and riot and to seek sureties of £40 against Thomas Combe. Peter Roswell, gentleman, another freeholder, declared that he intended a similar course and that Sir Edward Greville 'would stick to him'.

On 1 March 1615-16 Combe had another try, his workmen digging out 27 ridges. Next day William Chandler sent his man Michael Ward to fill in the works. He was assaulted by Combe's men, one Stephen Sly shouting that 'if the best in Stratford were to go there to throw the ditch down he would bury his head at the bottom'. In a petition to the assizes, the Corporation demanded that Combe, 'being of such unbridled disposition . . . should be restrained'. Sir Edward Coke did not punish Combe because he was High Sheriff, but 'badd him sett his hart at rest he should never enclose nor lay downe his common arable land'. Despite this leniency, Combe considered himself ill-used and alleged that the Corporation had 'given money to work my Lord [Coke] and that was no good employment for the town's revenue'.

Combe made new proposals, but the Corporation told him that they desired his goodwill, but they would ever oppose enclosure. On 10 April 'Mr. High Sheriff' told John Greene that he 'was out of hope now ever to enclose'. This belated recognition did not soften his belligerency. Instead he launched a war of revenge against the Welcombe tenants. The Bailiff wrote to Combe in December that his conscience was 'blinded as yt seemeth with a desire to make your self Riche by other mens losse', so that he paid no heed to judges, 'nor the mynysters[2] Threatnyngs against Enclosures'. A petition to the Court of Common Pleas complained that Combe had not 'laid down meres according to my Lord Hobart's order . . . And that he hath decayed 117 ridges of tilling and neglecting the farming thereof contrary to his own word and promise made to the judge and justices at the time of their conferences'. Neglect had the same effect as enclosure. 'The grief for decaying is the destruction of our common and the decaying of the tilling is the loss of our tythes with which the poor are free.'

The Bailiff brought a contempt action against Combe in 1617. The warrant was delivered by Richard Hathaway, Anne Shakespeare's nephew. By this time Thomas Greene had moved to Bristol, selling St Mary's House for £640. Perhaps the departure of his old antagonist encouraged Combe, for his workmen began to dig a ditch to enclose Butt Close, next to Clopton Bridge, but the Corporation paid its own workmen 2s 4d to fill it in.

Combe's reputation was reaching the highest councils of the land. In 1619 he received a sharp letter from the Privy Council: he must restore the enclosures and abide by judicial rulings or face the consequences. At last he became alarmed and capitulated. He had lost in every court and a contempt action was pending. The Corporation judiciously decided to cut its losses. On payment of a four pound fine Combe was granted 'his pardon for enclosing'.

And Death Once Dead

On 20 February 1615/16, Judith Shakespeare, aged 31, and perhaps resigned to spinsterdom, married Thomas Quiney, four years her junior and son of that Richard who had been so assiduous in the public cause. The Quineys were vintners and perhaps the marriage had been long intended, for in 1611 Judith had placed her mark in witness to deeds for Elizabeth Quiney and her son Adrian. In the same year Thomas Quiney leased the tavern next door to his mother's in the High Street.

11. Thomas Quiney's signature, written in his capacity as Borough Chamberlain.

What looked a sound match, linking two leading local families, began disastrously. The bride and groom were excommunicated for marrying in the prohibited season, although this was lifted on payment of a fine. The offence was not serious and may be attributed to the greed and incompetence of the ecclesiastical authorities. Yet Quiney had a reason to marry in haste. He was seeking to exchange premises with William Chandler, his brother-in-law, who kept *The Cage* (formerly the town lock-up), opposite the Market Cross. Judith's marriage portion would help finance the move, which took place in July.

There was a more serious problem. On 26 March the Consistory Court heard Quiney's confession to carnal copulation with Margaret Wheeler, daughter of Randle Wheeler, a carrier occasionally employed by the Corporation.[3] This unfortunate young woman had died in childbirth. A sad entry in the parish register on 15 March 1615/16 records the burial of Margaret Wheeler and her child. The Court ordered Quiney to pay public penance on three consecutive Sundays, dressed in the customary white sheet: a penalty remitted on payment of what was, for this court, the considerable fine of five shillings and the performance of private penance. The incident does not seem to have affected Quiney's standing in the town, for he became a burgess in 1617 and was Chamberlain in 1621 and 1622. His first account was unsatisfactory, but was later ratified. His second account carries his elaborate signature and a misquoted couplet from the French poet, Saint-Gelais:

> Bien heureux est celui qui devenir sage
> Qui par le mal d'autrui fait son apprentissage.[4]

Quiney's transgressions led his father-in-law to revise his will, changing a draft which had been made in January. He must have been severely ill when he signed this document on the day before the Bawdy Court met at the Vicarage opposite New Place. The three signatures are written with difficulty. Perhaps the poet was lying in bed and struggled to rise before falling back on the pillow. He knew he was dying, for he bestowed the interest on £150 on

Judith if she were alive in three years, which assumed he would not be. Her husband could not touch the capital sum unless he settled lands on her to the same value.

Clustered around the bed were the witnesses. There was Juline Shaw, a wooldealer who lived two doors away. In 1613, the Corporation, 'much approving his well-deserving in this place, for his honesty, fidelity and good opinion of him', had elected him an alderman. There was Hamnet Sadler, a life-long friend, and two men who were probably Shakespeare's servants, Robert Whatcott and John Robinson. The will is a lawyer's draft by Shakespeare's attorney, Francis Collins. The opening statement that the signatory was 'in perfect health and memorie' is legal convention, as is the religious declaration which follows. There are no phrases of endearment. It is 'my wife' and 'my daughter', not 'beloved wife' and 'dear daughter'.

Despite the death of Hamnet, the desire to pass the estate to a male heir remained. If not of the name, he should be of the blood. Shakespeare's property was entailed through Susanna to her eldest son. Although she had no sons, at 33 there was still hope. Failing this, the estate was to pass through her daughter Elizabeth to her sons. If she had none, then through Judith to her sons. Only if all these contingencies failed was the estate to pass 'to the Right Heires of me the said William Shakespeare for ever'.

Judith was given an ample cash settlement: £100 for her marriage portion and £50 if she renounced her claim to a cottage in Chapel Street: perhaps it was

12. Various specimens of William Shakespeare's signature.

intended for her before her marriage to Quiney was arranged. As a keepsake she received her father's 'broad silver-gilt' bowl. Other bequests follow. Joan Hart, the poet's sister, received £20, his clothing and the life tenancy of the Henley Street house, half of which had been converted into a tavern, the *Swan and Maidenhead*. It is curious to think of Shakespeare as the owner of a public house. Joan's three sons were left £20 each, although no-one present could recall the name of the youngest. Elizabeth Hall received his plate. The poor of Stratford got £10: William Walker, Shakespeare's godson, £20 in gold: Thomas Combe was bequeathed Shakespeare's sword, but his aggressive brother, William, was ignored. Some old friends were left 28s 6d to buy memorial rings: William Reynolds; Anthony and John Nashe, the next-door neighbours and 'my ffellowes John Hemynges, Richard Burbage and Henry Cundell', the only members of the theatrical profession to receive bequests.

Another recipient of ring money was Hamnet Sadler, whose name replaces Richard Tyler's in the second draft. Tyler too had known Shakespeare all his life, but may have been deleted because of suspicions about his character. He was one of five Stratfordians authorised to collect abroad for the victims of the great fire of 1614. An audit in the month Shakespeare made his will found 'every one prefferinge his owne private benefittes before the generall good' and 'exhibitinge to us bills of charges excediing theare collectiones'.

The most famous bequest is to Anne Shakespeare. 'Item I gyve unto my wief my second best bed with the furniture'. This has frequently been interpreted as a posthumous slight: by implication, the best was reserved elsewhere. Yet the bed was probably the one shared by William and Anne, the best being reserved for guests. Others made peculiar provisions about beds. In 1609, Thomas Combe, in another will drawn up by Francis Collins, left his best bedstead to his son, William. Shakespeare's best bed would not pass to the Dark Lady or some other mysterious paramour, but to his heirs, the Halls.

The only recorded indication of the cause of Shakespeare's death is another curious note by the Reverend John Ward in 1662. 'Shakespeare, Drayton and Ben Jonson had a merry meeting and it seems drank too hard for Shakespeare died of a fever there contracted.' If such revelry occurred it could have been in London. Ben had cause to celebrate in early March when he received royal patronage, with an ample allowance of wine as part of his stipend. Perhaps Shakespeare's return was through the winds of March over roads which were a quagmire. But perhaps this is already too late. Shakespeare was presumably well when he spoke to Thomas Greene in September 1615. By January, when he made the first draft of his will he could, with the perspicacity of pre-industrial man displayed by many of his contemporaries, have been aware of his approaching death. The putative meeting could have been in Stratford. Ben was a great traveller, walking the length and breadth of Britain, while Drayton was regularly in Stratford, sojourning with his friends, the Rainsfords of Clifford Chambers.

Shakespeare's death may have been caused by his residence in an insanitary corner of a pestilent town. Along the length of Chapel Lane ran an open, festering ditch. Many were the complaints about it, the Corporation making futile efforts to clean it up over three centuries. The issue was compounded by the pigs which the inhabitants kept in the street. Chief offender was the vicar, John Rogers, who pleaded the necessity of poverty. In 1613 his neighbours petitioned the removal of these sanctified swine, but they crept back under his successor.

'He dyed a papist', wrote Archdeacon Richard Davies late in the 17th century, who, as a member of the Anglican hierarchy, was not a special pleader. Given the lack of decisive evidence it is best to be agnostic about Shakespeare's religion, but it should be noted that he allegedly *died* a Catholic rather than *lived* one. Such returns are not without parallel. Catholic priests were still to be found in Stratford. William Reynolds, Shakespeare's recusant friend, also lived in Chapel Street and it was to his door in 1603/04 that a 'supposed semynary escaped at Stratford' was seen running, wearing green breeches, high shoes and white stockings. In August 1615 at Clifford Chambers Reynolds married a Frenchwoman, Frances de Bois, 'of London in Philip Lane'. Perhaps the Shakespeares were present at the wedding.

On 17 April, 1616, the funeral *cortege* of Shakespeare's brother-in-law, William Hart, the hatter, wound past New Place. The poet must have heard the great bell of the Guild chapel tolling its melancholy tone. On 23 April, the day posterity deemed his birthday, he died. Two days later his funeral procession departed from the courtyard of New Place, crossed the stagnant ditch and passed the gate of the school where he studied as a boy and the Guildhall where he probably saw his first play. Holy Trinity would have been filled with the names which composed Shakespeare's Stratford: Quiney, Sadler, Greene, Hall, Reynolds, Nashe, Walker, Hathaway (Shakespeare's nephew, Richard Hathaway, had just been made a church-warden) and the rest. As the minister intoned the burial service, the body was lowered into its grave at the High Altar: the privilege of a titheholder rather than a mark of esteem. Thus the world saw the last of Shakespeare the man. The literary legend would not be confined in the Stratford earth.

'Together, by the Ears'

The Vicar did not receive a fee for burying the greatest figure of the age. It had been decided that such monies would go towards repairing the dilapidated chancel. Relations between the Corporation and its vicar were good at this time. That year wine was sent 'to Mr. Rogers when his brother preached'. In similar spirit a supporting testimonial was sent in June 1617 on behalf of the lawyer, Thomas Lucas, whose devious ways had got him into trouble at Gray's Inn. Relations with the two men deteriorated rapidly soon after. The probable reason is to be found in the will of Francis Collins, made the day before his death on 26 September. He recorded that he and Rogers were trustees of a charitable legacy consisting of two houses, but that Rogers and Lucas 'did combyne themselves togeather and keep it from the poore most uncontionably'. Lucas had responded by suing Collins and making false accusations against Thomas Greene, the Town Clerk. The Corporation banned dealings with him and he got a local dignatory, Sir Clement Throckmorton, to plead for him: 'that which is good in Mr. Lucas I wish much good to. I hope his ills the divine light will be in time making him see'. If Lucas dropped his suit against Collins and apologised to Greene, Sir Clement hoped that the Corporation would continue to employ him. This appeal had its effect, for the Corporation replied in a conciliatory tone. They also went out of their way to cajole Rogers into better behaviour. On 30 January 1618, they gave him 'a fitt gown of good broad cloth . . . in hope that hee will well deserve the same hereafter and amend his former faults and failings'.

Rogers failed to take this generous hint and gave his enemies the golden opportunity by obtaining a second benefice elsewhere. Lucas, who had made his peace with the Corporation, turned on his former *confrere* and advised how to dispose of him. His replacement, presented by Lord Chancellor Verùlam on 6 March 1619 and endorsed by the Corporation by 18 votes to seven, was a well-known Puritan divine, Thomas Wilson of Evesham. Rogers, who refused to leave the vicarage, had his friends. Perhaps his easy-going ways appealed to that considerable body of citizens whose religion did not exclude cakes and ale. When Wilson arrived to conduct his first evening service on 30 May, he was met by a wild crowd armed with swords, daggers, bills, pikes and stones, screaming 'Hang him, kill him, pull out his throat, cut off his pockie and burnt members. Let us hale him out the church'. A way was cleared through the mob and Wilson hurried inside, the great doors slamming behind him. Some of the crowd broke in. Others battered at the doors and threw stones through the windows. The most ferocious rioters were women. On 24 July, five of them and two men were presented before the curate, John Owen. One of the men was Thomas Lucas, who had engaged in a fracas with a minister, Master John Bursye (a friend of Rogers?), 'striking and using him unreverently, calling him scurvy rascal knave'.

In September the opposition found a cohesive cause for traditionalist and hooligan alike. Doubtless encouraged by the approbation given to dancing and 'such harmless recreations' by King James, the townspeople erected a maypole on the newly-repaired church path. It was

removed by order of the Bailiff, John Wilmore, but it was stressed that it was because it was
an obstruction, 'not for any dislike to the pole', which the townspeople could re-erect six yards
away. Re-erect they did, at least 40 of them, but in the same place to 'the great danger of
raising a mutiny'.

The Corporation responded by enacting a Bill in Chancery, drawn up by Lucas, against
those whom they considered the instigators of the disturbance, who included John Nashe
(uncle of Elizabeth Hall's future husband), William Reynolds (Shakespeare's friend and, like
Nashe, legatee), John Lane, gentleman (defamer of Susanna Hall), John Rogers (the quondam
vicar), John Pinke (a local satirical poet), William Nixon (the corrupt apparitor of the
consistory court), William Hathaway (half-brother of Anne Shakespeare), Thomas Courte,
blacksmith (son of John Shakespeare's neighbour), Raphe Smith, haberdasher (with whom
Susanna Hall was scurrilously said to have 'bin naught') and 'divers other persons for
malicious, libellous and riotous behaviour'. It is tempting to see the episode as a last flourish
of the personalities of Elizabethan Stratford.

The 'libellous' offences consisted of circulating scurrilous verses. The Star Chamber proceedings reveal the literary vigour of some of Shakespeare's neighbours. 'A Satyre to the Cheife
rulers in the synagogue of Stratford' identifies the leading Puritans in the town and protests
against their oligarchical control:

> Stratford's a town that doth make a great show
> And yet it is governed by a few.
> O Jesus Christ of Heaven,
> I think there are but seven,
> Puritants without doubt,
> For you may know them, they are so stout.
>
> ....
> A heavy curse (O Lord) upon them send
> Because they have bereft us of our best friende
> And in his stead here have they placed
> A fellow that hath neither shame nor grace.
> Yet these men are True Religious without quirks,
> For one of the chiefest hath read far in Perkins[5] Works.
> But soft my satire be not too free,
> For thou wilt make them spurn at thee,
> For rubbe a horse where scabbe be thick
> And thou wilt make him wince and kick.
> Be sure their lawyer is of God accurst,
> For he began this business first,
> And with his malice and his spite
> Was first that brought this 'lapse' to light.

The lawyer was, of course, Thomas Lucas.

Another onslaught took the form of a letter: 'Sirrah ho! The greatest news since Pentecost.
Where there is report that all the old biting and young suckling Puritants of Stratford are
joined with their two Justasses a piece maliciously to displace and utterly undo their Minister
and to bring in his place an arrant a K——————— as themselves, of purpose to assist them
in their hypocracy and now seeing they have set all the town together by the ears, which is
the true office of a Puritant and finding their plot hath not had the desired effect, it is thought
that divers of them will run horn-mad: therefore I would have thee make haste up hither.'

The writer 'skibs' at one Puritan as 'too busy', another 'shows like a monster with four
elbows . . . because he useth in his gait or going, as some observe, to shake his elbows'. Another
is 'a cobbler turned divine'. The conclusion is that 'some death-unconscionable knaves will

hearken to nothing but their greedy desires. Therefore, farewell from Romany, this merry month of May; thy honest friend (if thou do not turn Puritant). F.S.'.

'Divers of them will run horn-mad . . .' One of them, according to a a broadsheet by Joh[n] P[inke] had had carnal knowledge of Margery Gunne, wife of John Gunne in a barley-close called The Farm:

> The Puritants are now found out, their walking late and early,
> Beshrew their hearts, they spoil men's grass and do not spare the Barley.
> The ancient leading Hypocrite, that is of all that sort,
> (Some say), a sermon lately lost to wait afield for sport;
> But now 'tis meant in better sort (as some of them do say):
> The cause why he neglected church was but to save his hay.
> But take heed how you do him charge with doing any harm;
> He'll drive the countery of him that tells him of the Farm.

Perhaps the Puritan in question was Daniel Baker, around whom still clung the memory of the scandal of 1606.

Now it was Rogers' turn to lament, a burden assumed on his behalf by a sonneteer of some merit:

> Who will relieve my woe? My heart doth burn
> To see man's state wane as the wind doth turn.
> He wars and wins and winninge lost by strife.
> War is another death, a sure uncertain life.
> Try then and trust, give credit by delay.
> The feigned friends with feigned looks betraye.
> Baker had never lived to vanquish me,
> Had it not bene for Lucas treachery.
> Shall I of Chandler and busy William speak,
> That bade me make a tale and it to break?
> Hence I conclude, what all the world doth see -
> There is no peace where is no unity.
> Thou I on earth for thee receive disgrace,
> Live I in Heaven, see Jesus face to face.

The introspective effect is marred by a scurrilous chorus about Wilson:

> June, July, August and September,
> Although he comes he shall not mortify one member.
> A very rogue he is -
> He cannot draw his pintle for to piss.

The reference to Chandler and 'busy William' (probably Walford, his collaborator in resistence to the Combes) is unclear. Apparently they encouraged the vicar and then let him down.

Under a new Bailiff, William Wyatt, father of one of the accused rioters, some attempt at compromise was made. It was resolved to pay Rogers five pounds to end his squat in the vicarage. The outcome of the Star Chamber proceedings is unknown, although they do not seem to have affected the later careers of the defendants. William Reynolds resisted the charges strenuously, replying to the Attorney-General that he was 'persuaded his name is inserted uppon some causles mallice'. At a subsequent consistory court, the wife of Will Piggott, a maltster, was presented 'for revyling and miscalling Mr. Wilson our vicare, gyving him the tytle of a knave'.

Shakespeare's Monument

In 1634, an army officer, Lieutenant Hammond, visited Stratford. He recorded the story that Shakespeare had extemporised verses on the usurer, John Combe. At the church he admired the 'neat monument of that famous English poet, Mr. William Shakespeare, who was born here'. The monument had then been in place for at least 11 years, for Leonard Digges, a poet with local connections, had referred to it in a prefatory poem to the First Folio of 1623. There had been, according to a sonnet written by Willaim Basse, a proposal to reinter the poet's remains in Westminster Abbey, but the erection of the monument must have inhibited any such move.

The epitaph is more disinterested than one composed for the family, concentrating on Shakespeare as artist rather than father or husband. It demonstrates a lack of knowledge of Holy Trinity and that the poet was buried in a grave rather than a tomb. Presumably Shakespeare's London associates had overseen the creation of his monument. It would be difficult to hurry past the monument at the High Altar:

> Stay passenger, Why goest thou by so fast?
> Read if thou canst whom envious death hath plast
> Within this tomb. Shakespeare with whome
> Quick Nature dide, whose name doth decke this Tombe
> Far more than cost. Such all yet he hath writt,
> Leaves living art but page to serve his WITT.

Shakespeare, it seems from traces of the original paint, had hazel eyes and auburn hair. The kindest view of the stodgy face is that it is taken from a death mask. The sculptor would have required such an image and the face, with its tongue thrust between the teeth, is in the attitude of death.

The bust was clearly a sufficient likeness to satisfy Shakespeare's family and friends. Perhaps his old company came to see it in 1622, when they attempted to play in the Guild Hall. This caused some embarrassment for the Corporation. The regulations forbade plays and yet these actors were under the patronage of the King. The Chamberlain's accounts reveal a compromise: the King's Men were paid 6s 'for not playing in the Hall'. Doubtless they got a warmer welcome at New Place.

The inscription on Shakespeare's grave has caused much speculation:

> Good friend for Jesus sake forbeare
> To dig the dust enclosed heare
> Bleste be the man yt spares these stones
> And curst be he yt moves my bones.

The verse is not addressed to the passer-by; nor is it a prophetic vision of those who would seek to exhume the Bard in the hope of proving that the Works were the product of another's genius. The 'good friend' is the sexton, who disinterred bones to make way for newcomers; a custom evocative of Hamlet's distaste as he watched the gravediggers dig up the remains of Yorick. 'Did these bones cost no more in the breeding, but to play at loggats with 'em? Mine ache to think on't.' William Hall, who visited Stratford in 1694, declared that Shakespeare wrote the lines to frighten off ignorant clerks and sextons, adding that he 'descends to the meanest of their capacities and disrobes himself of that art which none of his contemporaries had in greater perfection'. Yet it is unlikely that Shakespeare wrote his own epitaph. Few do so for obvious reasons.

No matter who wrote it, the inscription has succeeded in its purpose. Near the bust is the outline of a door which once led into the charnel house where disinterred bones were stored. Such was the fate of the mortal remains of Shakespeare's family. Their bodies were disinterred, their graves occupied by others and their epitaphs wiped out.[6]

Minister Wilson

As expected Thomas Wilson proved a dedicated Puritan. Of all Stratford's vicars he was the one who most assiduously strove to uphold public morality. Presumably he enjoyed a brief honeymoon of favour amongst his adherents, but their factiousness and his stern moral code would lead inevitably to friction. Although Wilson was regarded as a fine preacher, no word of his has come down to us. What effect his preaching had on the morals of his congregation is impossible to say, but the fragmentary records of the Bawdy Court give a picture of those on its fringes who upset convention.

Holy Trinity was built to hold the whole of Stratford's population. Indeed, with the canons demanding compulsory attendance, it had to do so. The small group of recusants continued to pay fines rather than worship against their consciences. Others were too infirm to attend. 'Neither did old Sibel Davis communicate', reported the churchwardens in 1622, 'by reason of her extreme povertie and want of clothes'.

The spectacle of an entire town attending church was not always edifying. The consistory court regularly heard offences against ecclesiastical propriety. On 28 May 1622 Richard Baker, a shoemaker, was presented for 'stryking in the church in time of sermon . . . the son of John Rogers of Shatterlie'. He claimed that the boy was playing and 'keeping a noyse' and he could not hear the preacher. He admonished the boy to desist but he would not, so he gave him 'a little tappe uppon the head'. The Vicar dismissed him with the caution that 'from henceforth he stryke no more but yf such offence be in church he shall complayne to the magistrate that such boys may be whipped'. It must have been a dull service that day, for Edward Rogers was also presented 'for stryking the servant of William Castle, glover, in sermon tyme'. He admitted that he 'did swing the boy by the eare because the said boy did fight and jostle with another boy and did disturbe the congregacon'.

As may be expected with increasing Puritan domination the most frequent charge was Sabbath-breaking. In March 1621, Thomas Couper was presented for 'playing at cards and soffring other in prayer tyme on ye Sabothday' and in July Arthur Brogden and David Ainge for opening 'their shoppes and sellinge ffleshe on Sabaoth dayes'. The court was usually lenient with such offenders, who were generally let off with a warning on promising to reform, but in 1624 John Mase was presented for 'suffering drunkenes and fightinge with much disorder in his house on the Sabaoth day in tyme of praires'. He was obliged to confess before the magistrate, churchwardens and minister and to pay a shilling for the poor. When he failed to pay in full, he was presented for not attending catechism and for 'a common drunkard'. He must have reformed, for in the following May the court licensed him to practise something related to medicine, perhaps as an apothecary.

A matter which occupied the court during the period 1619-22 was the affair of William Bromley and Elinor Varney. William, born in 1580/81, was the son of Edward Bromley, the carrier. Elinor was born in 1585 and her father was registered as a pauper in 1596. In 1609, the year of his death, he sued 'Peter Ruswell and others', including Gilbert Shakespeare. When Elinor served Ruswell with the writ, he 'did vyolently snatch it . . . and refused to redeliver it unto her and delivered his staffe he then had in his hand to a stander by who therewith did assault and beate this deponent out of the house'.

Elinor was servant to William's widowed mother, Joan Bromley. She must have been related to the Bromleys, or perhaps she assumed the status of a foster-daughter, for the relationship she developed with William was deemed incestuous. On 3 February 1618/19, an 'infant of Elnor Varines de Shotery, uncrisoned, a b. . .' was buried. William Bromley was later presented for begetting a bastard. The verdict of the court is lost, but it did not inhibit the relationship. In July 1621, during the triennial period when the functions of the court passed to the diocesan authorities, William was presented for sexual 'incontinence'. In August the couple were presented by the churchwardens to the Bishop of Worcester 'for Incestuousness together'. The lack of his court increased the bureaucratic duties of the vicar. During this period, he was in correspondence with John Trewman of Feckenham about Will Ball, a servant, who promised to marry Anne Deloes of that parish and then moved to Stratford, where he pledged himself to Mary Watson 'contrarie to all truth'.

With the reversion of the powers of the court, an Elinor Bromley was presented for fornication, so she may have assumed her lover's name. Bromley was excommunicate by the following May when Thomas Woodward, who 'hath ben heretofore admonished to desist from the same', was presented for keeping company with him. Woodward appeared and failed to appear several times in the next few months for the same offence and for 'being in alhouses uppon the Sabaothe day in tyme of divine service and not coming to the church'. Presumably William and Elinor had left town together by then. Neither appears in the burial register. Woodward's continued association with them must reflect a sympathy, or an indifference to moral sanctions.

Blasphemy was another serious offence. In May 1624, Eleonor, wife of Thomas Silvester, was presented for 'saing that God did doate and that God knew not what he did, with manie other blashemous speeches and cursed oathes'. This precurser of Nietsche admitted that she 'did speak such wordes'. She was ordered to attend the parish church on the following Sunday week 'and then to performe her pennance'. This had little effect; in July she was presented again 'for blaspheaming of Godes most holy name'. She did not appear and was referred to the magistrates. Her fate is unrecorded, but the secular arm of the law was more severe and we think of the ducking-stool by the Avon. On the same day as her first appearance, Stephen Lea was presented for 'singing prophane and filthie songs, scoffing and deriding on ministers and the profession of religion'. On promising to reform, he was dismissed with a warning.

Under this Puritan regime the ancient Mayday revels were anathema. In 1621 Thomas Clarke was presented for 'playing with his tabor and pype upon the First Daie of mai in evening prayer tyme at Bishopton'. In 1622 a number of Mayday revellers appeared before the court. George Quiney the curate presented 'Mr. Birch's man for dauncing the morris in eveninge prayer tyme'. John Allen, William Plymmer and Humphrey Brown were presented for the same reason 'on the feast day of Phillip and Jacob', which was Mayday. They were ordered to perform public penance. John Rickitts of Shottery, who had made up the foursome, was excommunicated for non-appearance. Further insight into the Mayday festival is given by the presentation of Francis Palmer, also of 'Shatterlie ... for being the Maid Marrion' – presumably in a pageant of Robin Hood. It was probably because of his youth that he was pardoned.

Allen was in more trouble at the next session. He had failed to perform his penance and 'committed the lyke offence againe'. He was 'enjoined that the next Sabaoth day presently after the reading of the gospell he confes his falt in the midle ile that the congregacon may take notice of it'.

In these censorious attacks a 'Merry England' emerges that the Puritan ascendancy was seeking to extinguish. Yet its diminution would not bring renewed unity to society, for that Puritanism would prove divisive of itself.

FOOTNOTES
[1]   Greene's fragmentary diary is reproduced in Ingleby's book on the enclosure controversy: see bibliography.
[2]   Thomas Rogers, the Vicar.
[3]   The details remained hidden until 1964 when the records of the Stratford consistory court were discovered in the Kent County archives.
[4]   'Happy is he who to become wise, By the difficulties of others serves his apprenticeship'.
[5]   William Perkins was a moderate, Puritan divine of the Elizabethan era.
[6]   The epitaphs, which were recorded by William Dugdale in the 1650s, were recut in 1844.

CHAPTER 6

'From the very Jaws of Death'

'. . . restoring me as it were from the very Jaws of Death'
Quotation from the casebooks of John Hall.

Sometime after the Battle of Edgehill, Dr. James Cooke, a surgeon from Warwick, joined the Parliamentary garrison at Stratford. The town had at least one compensation. John Hall, one of the great doctors of the previous generation, had lived there and Cooke was delighted when an army colleague, a relative of Hall's, invited him to New Place, where Susanna Hall showed him some books 'left by one that professed Physick with her husband, for some money'. He noticed that two of the documents were written by Hall, 'I being acquainted with Mr. Hall's hand'. Susanna disagreed. 'She denyed, I affirmed till I perceived that she began to be offended'. He agreed to reimburse what she thought had been paid. The mistake does not indicate that Shakespeare's daughter could not read; rather that 60-year-old ladies can be weak of sight. An illiterate would not dispute handwriting with a learned doctor.

Although Hall had prepared his casebooks for publication, it was 15 years before Cooke got them into print. There were the difficulties of deciphering a doctor's idiosyncratic handwriting, but such was Hall's reputation that the task of translation from the Latin was considered worthwhile by all whom he consulted. One of the volumes (the other was lost at some point) was published under the curious title, *Select Observations on English Bodies*.[1] Cooke added a preface, a few cases from other practitioners to bring the total to 200 and a postscript explaining 'I had almost forgot to tel ye that these Observations were chosen by Hall from all the rest of his own, which I conjectured could be no lesse than a thousand, as fittest for public view'.

A second preface eulogising Hall's contribution to contemporary practice was written by John Bird, Professor of Medicine at Cambridge, who added that Hall intended the posthumous publication of his casebooks 'when men more willingly part with what they have'. The book was successful. Three editions were published in the next 20 years. Some of Hall's patients were still alive and did not welcome the intimate revelations of the casebooks. 'Fluxes of the courses', 'worms', 'whites' and 'stools' – such terms must have brought a blush to many a faded cheek. In his preface to the third edition, Cooke apologised for naming names – although he had had the discretion to render anonymity to a case of gonorrhoea.

The casebook tells us much of Hall the doctor and something of Hall the man. Frustratingly, the prefaces give little biographical information. It is known that his father William Hall, an astrologer and alchemist, was keen that his brightest son should follow him in these arts, which held an esteemed place in Elizabethan society, although some had their doubts. The father left his books on astrology and alchemy to his servant Matthew Morris, since John would have 'nothing to do with these things'.

Matthew Morris followed John Hall to Stratford. He married there in 1613 and named two of his children Susanna and John. Perhaps he fulfilled any demand for astrology and alchemy amongst Hall's patients. Hall's trust in his assistant was shared by his father-in-law. In

1617/18, his house in Blackfriars was conveyed to John Greene of Clement's Inn and 'Mathew Morrys' of Stratford 'in performance of the confidence and trust in them reposed by William Shakespeare deceased'.

13. One of the earliest known pictures of Hall's Croft, supposed home of John Hall.

Around 1810, Robert Bell Wheler saw in some old papers 'that Dr. Hall resided in that part of Old Town, which is in the parish of Old Stratford'.[2] The large Tudor house now known as Hall's Croft is one of a handful of properties which fulfil this criterion. If the Halls lived there, they moved after Shakespeare's death, for in 1617 Thomas Greene paid a debt 'to Mr. Hall at Newplace'.

Some have observed Hall in the character of Cerimon, the aristocratic doctor of *Pericles:*

> Tis known I ever
> Have studied physic, through which secret art,
> By turning o'er authorities, I have,
> Together with my practice, made familiar
> To me and to my aid the blest infusions
> That dwell in vegetives, in metals, stones;
> And I can speak of the disturbances
> That nature works and of her cures . . .

Hall certainly overturned authorities. 'It seems', says Cooke, that he 'had the happiness to lead the way to that practice almost generally used by the most knowing of mixing scorbutics in most remedies: it was then, and I know for some time after, thought so strange, that it was cast as a reproach on him by those most famous in the profession.' Long before such terms were categorised, Hall realised that scurvy was a deficiency disease. His cure, a mixture of scurvy-grass, watercress, brooklime, juniper berries and wormwood, rich in vitamins, cured many sufferers. The eldest son of Mr. Underhill of Loxley, aged 12, bore the excruciating agonies of this harrowing disease. 'I found him grievously afflicted with the scurvey; on the right side he had a tumour without discolouration, so that I judged there was a Tumour of the Liver. He was grown as lean as a Skeleton, was Melancholy, with black and crusty ulcers appearing in the legs. He had a loathing of Meat, a disposition to Vomit and an Erratic Feaver; his Urine was red, as in a burning Feaver, yet without thirst or desire to drink.' That this variety of abominations was cured demonstrates Hall's medical brilliance.

The earliest dated observation is in 1617 (the year after Shakespeare's last illness, but Hall mainly recorded his successes), when Hall treated Baron Compton for toothache. When Compton became Lord President of the Council of Wales, Hall was summoned to Ludlow Castle – a considerable journey – to treat his family.

The *Observations* contain names familiar in Shakespearean biography. The poet would have known the brilliant George Quiney, younger brother of Thomas, who became curate and assistant schoolmaster after graduating from Balliol College, Oxford. In 1622 the Corporation – or Daniel Baker – attempted to replace him with its own nominee, John Trapp. Sir Edward Greville, the Lord of the Manor, appealed to the Lord Treasurer, but the action was abandoned 'uppon advice taken and the truth appearinge . . . and the towne sithence hath quietlie enjoyed the same'. Quiney died of tuberculosis at the age of twenty-four. 'Many things having been tried to no purpose', wrote Hall, 'peacefully he fell asleep in the Lord'.

The most interesting cases are those of Hall's wife and daughter. When Susanna suffered from colic he tried a complicated herbal cure which brought no relief, so he resorted to a traditional remedy. 'I appointed to inject a Pint of Sack made hot. This presently brought forth a great deal of Wind and freed her from all Pain.' Elizabeth Hall, 'my only daughter', was cured of *'Tortura Oris'* (toothache?) and general constitutional disturbance with a fomentation of *acqua vitae* and spices. A curious manuscript note adds that 'she eats nutmegs often'. Perhaps she was addicted to this mild narcotic.

Much of Hall's ministration was to the effects of excess. The contemporary diet of huge meals and a virtual lack of fresh vegetables was formidable, but it would be a mistake to judge the general health of the population from a doctor's notebooks. Obesity had its sad side-effects. 'Mrs. Sheldon being corpulent . . . was wont to miscarry often, the second month after conception.' Hall put her on a diet and she achieved her desire. 'She . . . brought forth a lusty son and after that more.'

Excess of a different kind troubled a gentleman of Northampton who suffered from gonorrhoea. Hall and Sir William Harvey, discoverer of the circulation of the blood, tried various cures, but they were only partially successful, for the disease kept recurring. Hall's unsuccessful formula consisted of a powder made from sarsparilla, bark of guaicum, cinnamon, senna, dodder, hellebore root and fine sugar.

Hall's care was not restricted to the wealthy and influential. The record of one Hudson, a poor man suffering from vertigo, indicates labour amongst the needy. In 1632 the Corporation paid 4s 7d 'for a portell of sack and a portell of claret given to Sir Thomas Lucie and Sir Robert Lee . . . at the Swan, when they came to confer with Mr. Hall about the poor men which were arrested'.

Hall favoured the use of purgatives. There is a note of satisfaction when a treatment is successful: 'Mr. Fortescue (Catholick) of Cook-hil, aged 38 (a great Drinker, of very good habit of Body, sanguine, very fat, fell into a scorbutic Dropsy by a Surfeit, with difficulty of breathing, hard tumor of the Belly, Cods and Feet, Wind in the Sides, the yellow Jaundice spread over the whole Body and tumor of the Sides and Belly, and by all these was much troubled.' Hall purged him every three days, took him off the beer and substituted a cold herbal drink. 'After to sweat was this prepared: Guiacum shaved . . . Water nine pints, boil it to the half, towards the end cast in Soldanella dried . . ., the inner Bark of Cinnamon . . .

Raisons unstoned . . . after they are boyled enough, pour them into a Glass Vessel in which there are three pints of White wine. Of which take . . . in the morning . . . and evening, covering him well . . .'. The purgative of jalap, cream of tartar and an electary of tamarinds gave six stools. 'By these means in six weeks he was perfectly cured. Glory and honour to God.'

The case of Mrs. Wilson, the Vicar's wife, provides an example of taking the waters. 'As she thought she was tormented with the Stone', she went to Bristol and 'drank of St Vincent's Well too greedily, to the quantity of eighteen pints a day . . ., so that thereby cooling her Body too much, she fell into a Palsy. She presently got herself conveyed to the Bath . . . where she was restored'. Returning home in tempestuous weather, 'that night she was assaulted with the Mother, with a fainting and a light Palsy on the left side.' Hall prescribed 'a powder worth Gold, which I always carry about with me.' This 'delivered her both from her fainting and trembling of her Heart, with which she had usually been troubled'.

Much of Hall's success was due to psychological insight. Dr. Thornborough, the 86-year-old Bishop of Worcester, 'had very unquiet Nights from salt and sharp humours, and Vapors ascending to his Head; and if he did sleep, it was with terror, which happened from the sudden slaughter in one of his Family, which did much To terrify and perplex his Spirits and afflicted him grievously with Melancholy'. Editha Staughton, aged 17, suffered from intense hysteria and depression, 'her Courses as not yet having broken forth . . . she was very easily angry with her nearest friends, so that she continually cried out that her Parents would kill her.' The good doctor advised that 'there should be few to trouble her'.

The casebooks give glimpses of the reaction of patients to illness. Simon Underhill, aged about 40, 'troubled with extream Vomiting, wind of the Stomach, difficulty of breathing, constipation of the Belly and Scurvy . . . said I should either cure him perfectly, or kill him'. Hall achieved the former. Mrs. Woodward of Avon Dasset, 'a Maid very witty and well-bred, aged 28', suffered from chronic scurvy and believed that death was imminent. 'Towards evening she expected her unwelcom Enemy with grief of Mind.' Mrs. Mary Talbot, sister-in-law of the Countess of Shrewsbury, 'a Catholick, fair, was troubled with the Scurvy, with swelling of the Spleen, erosion of the Gums, livid spots of the Thighs, Pain of the Loins and Head, with convulsion and Palsy of the Tongue; her Pulse was small and unequal, her Urine was troubled and thick. The Countess asked me whether there was any hope of Life? I answered, Yes, if she would be patient and obedient'. He forbade all drinks except his scurvy cure. '. . . afterward she began to walk, and at last was very well'.

Over the years, Hall treated the Rainsford family of Clifford Chambers. He described Sir Henry Rainsford's widow as 'dedicated to sacred literature and conversant in the French language'. The poet, Michael Drayton, had been a page in her father's household and dedicated much of his voluminous output to her. If Thomas Fuller's description is credited, Sir Henry was unlikely to have regarded the poet as a threat to his marriage bed: 'Very temperate in life, slow in speech and inoffensive in company'. Indeed Drayton felt that Sir Henry shared Lady Rainsford's affection for him:

> He would have sworn that to no other end
> He had been born, but only for my friend.

'I am stopping at a knight's house in Gloucestershire', Drayton wrote in 1631, 'to which place I yearly used to come in the summer time to recreate myself and spend two or three months in the country.' During one of these visits John Hall treated 'Mr. Drayton, an excellent Poet, labouring of a Tertian'. He prescribed syrup of violets with his Emetick infusion. 'This given wrought very well both upwards and downwards.'

Hall clearly impressed Drayton. In *Poly-Olbion*, his monumental description of the counties of England, the book on Warwickshire opens with a lengthy description of a pious and learned doctor, skilled in herbal remedies, who is disillusioned with the ways of man:

His happy time he spends the works of God to see,
In those so sundry herbs which there in plenty growe.

The picture neatly fits Hall. His practice covered a wide area. He was probably called in as a specialist when all else had failed and frantic messengers must have hammered on the door of New Place to summon him to distant bedsides. His dedication is demonstrated during an illness of his own. 'About the 57th year of my age, August 27, 1632 to September 29 I was much debilitated with an immoderate Flux of the Hemorrhoids; yet daily was I constrained to go to several places to Patients. By riding, a hardness being contracted, the Flux was stayed for fourteen days. After I fell into a most cruel torture of my Teeth, and then into a deadly, burning Fever, which then raged very much, killing almost all that it did infect.'

This devotion was returned by Hall's patients. 'Noble lady', wrote Lady Eliza Tyrell to her friend Lady Temple, 'I have lately heard of your worthy knight's mischance for which I am heartily sorry. And both Mr. Tyrell and myself have purposely sent to inquire of his recovery. Madam, I am very glad to hear that Mr. Hall is the man of whom Sir Thomas Temple hath made choice of. In regard, I know by experience that he is most excellent in that art.'

A Broken Pledge

By 1625 Thomas Wilson, the vicar, was in conflict with Daniel Baker. Perhaps his efforts to impose a sterner moral code had conflicted with the alderman's selectivity, for Baker's past peccadilloes would not have been forgotten. It is a measure of the dislike which Wilson engendered amongst his former friends that they attacked him for his failure to observe canon laws which they would equally oppose. An opportunity was given when the churchwardens reported to the Diocesan Court that 'our . . . minister is desirous to make known . . . [that he] doth not constantly weare his surplice and hood according to the injunction of 58 canon'. Wilson trod a doctrinal tight-rope, or at least theologically bewildered his flock, for the note adds enigmatically 'but it is not for that he refuseth to conforme unto that ceremony'. On 8 March 1625/6 the Corporation gave Wilson its 'Certificate under the Seale', but warned him to conform 'to the Church Cerimonyes as kneeling at the Sacrament, enjoyning others thereunto, wearing the surplice, baptising with the Crosse, marryinge with the ring and all other orders of the Church'. Later that year he was cited before the diocesan court and the Court of High Commission 'because he laboured to shake the jurisdiction of the Bishop . . . and govern the people of Stratford according to his own will, as if he had been another Calvin or Bera in Geneva'. Baker's brand of Puritanism was hostile to a theocracy of divines. Yet when the Bishop excommunicated Wilson, the Corporation sent a delegation to plead for him. Perhaps it was a triumph of Christian forgiveness, or they preferred the vicar to the Bishop, but it is a mistake to see too many doctrinal innuendoes in local disputes.

Before the dispute, John Hall sold some of Shakespeare's old tithe holdings to the Corporation for less than their value to enable them to increase the stipends of the vicar and the schoolmaster. This they had failed to do, apparently at the instigation of Daniel Baker. Hall was furious at what he regarded as a broken pledge and sought to prove that Baker and two others were personally responsible for the debt of £400 due to him. He was out-manoeuvred, for an Indemnification of 26 March 1626 assumed collective responsibility. Once good relations with Wilson were restored, the Corporation fulfilled its obligations, voting the vicar an additional £20 annually for his 'learned sermons'. Later that year an old dispute resurfaced when Wilson was accused of exceeding his rights to churchyard timber. On 14 December the annuity was withdrawn and Hall must again have been furious. A sniping battle continued until 1631, when the Corporation requested Sir Thomas Lucy and Sir Greville Verney 'to hear and to judge wherein the Bailife and Burgesses have wronged or abused Mr. Wilson oure

Vicare'. Perhaps it was they who advised the co-option of John Hall to the Corporation in the hope that the doctrine of collective responsibility might silence a persistent critic. If so they were mistaken, for he proved 'acrimonious and quarrelsome', making 'abusive speeches against the Bailiff'.

In June 1633, Hall retaliated against the civic fathers with a grand gesture. Since the time of Thomas Greene the wives of the Corporation's senior officers had used the box-pew in Holy Trinity belonging to the owner of New Place. Now Hall caused the erection of a new pew there for his own use. By relegating the municipal dowagers from their exalted station, he released an intense feeling of *lese-majeste*. If Thomas Wilson directed his eloquence to the Gospel injunction to seek the lowest place, it can only have been with a sense of irony. In the furore which followed Hall was on strong ground, securing the support of his aged patient, the Bishop. The Corporation appealed to Canterbury, but Hall's claim was upheld by Sir Nathaniel Brent, the Vicar-General.

There was an echo of Hall's dispute in the Church Court in December. William Smythe was charged with disturbing the congregation during divine service. He replied that his behaviour was 'occasioned by the intrusion of Mr. Richard Castle . . . who went about by violence to thrust . . . [him] out of his usual sitting place'. He boasted to the Court that he was 'ancient to . . . Richard Castle as well as in bearing the offices of churchwarden and alderman . . . and hath alwayes held his place among the aldermen in the said parish church . . . and . . . is above the said Castle in all taxations and payments and hath always had precendcy'. On 15 January 1635, John Eston 'was wished to forbeare sitting in the Burgissers seate by John Smithe' and replied: 'Who will keep me forth?' Sir Nathaniel's report included the weary phrase, 'here are many contentious about seats in churches'.

Perhaps Hall's profession gives a further hint of the reasons for his civic disenchantment. A man used to examining the stools of the influential is unlikely to be impressed by the verbal diarrhoea of the petty bourgeoisie. That he never permitted his municipal duties to interfere with his medical practice is revealed by a pleading note from Sidney Davenport of Bushwood House on 5 July 1633.

> Good Mr. Hall – I sent my boy to you this morning to carrie my water & acquainte you with what danger & extremities I am faullen into in respect of my shortness of breath & obstructions of my liver that I cannot sleep nor take anie rest . . . I will not eat or drink untill I see you . . . I received a note from you howe that you cannot be here at Bushwood with me to morrow in respect of some private meeting at yor hall concerning the affairs of yr Towne. You saie you are warned to be there and if you are absent you are threatened to be fined. I did not expect to have received such a kind of excuse from you, considering the daungerous estate I am in, as maie appear by my water . . . therefore I think it is not anie Towne business that can hinder you but rather that you have promised some other patient and would put me off with this excuse . . . Therefore I councell you as a friend never be bounde: as long as you may be free you shall but derogate from yor . . . studie wch deserveth the whole imployment of anie man had he 100 years to live longer. . . .

A postscript adds: 'My brother Colmore's Phisick is ended & all is taken. He staieth at home purposely to speak with you tomorrow morning for further directions'.

The hypochondriac brothers had their way. Hall sent the letter to the Corporation as an explanation and apology, but the burgesses were in no mood to be understanding towards the troublesome doctor and he was fined for non-attendance.

The factiousness of the Corporation led to a resolution against canvassing being passed in 1633. '. . . the greater number of the Company have declared themselves that the course of goinge from house to house to gett the voyces or the hands of the Bailiff, Alderman and burgesses is altogether unfitting and not hereafter in any sort to be practised'.

Hall also had family matters to trouble him. His brother-in-law, Thomas Quiney, had not achieved much success. In 1633 his business was handed over in trust for his wife and sons to his kinsmen John Hall, Thomas Nashe and Richard Watts. Sadly none of his sons survived to his majority. Shakespeare Quiney died in infancy; Richard and Thomas within weeks of each other in 1639 probably in an epidemic.

14. *The joint signatures of John Hall and his son-in-law, Thomas Nashe, from the vestry minute book.*

More from the Bawdy Court

Whatever the ecclesiastical regime, the Bawdy Court continued its efforts to control the town's morals. The case of Margery Warner, wife of John Warner, heard in 1624, was highly unusual, in that she confessed her offence unilaterally: the vengeful gesture, perhaps, of a spurned lover. She 'accused herselfe of adulterie with Robert Wilson of the Crowne . . . and now she appereth personalie, and in publick courte she confesseth herselfe guiltie . . . and upon her oathe shee declareth that she did 2 severall tymes committ adulterie with the said Robert Wilson . . .'. She was ordered to perform public penance both in church and at the Market Cross on the next market day. Wilson had fled the town.

A Rabelaisian note is struck in the next year. Rumours were circulating that John Hemings, the aged Beadle, had taken advantage of his access to the Guild Hall. The story reached the ears of the Consistory Court and thus the pen of its clerk. 'Wee present that there is publicke fame that John Hemings alias Ames and Elizabeth Court weare in a very unseemly and filthy manner conversant alone (according to the said John Hemings his confession) in ye chamber of the towne of Stratford the dore being fast locked . . . when the said Elizabeth Court did provoke him the said John to Incontinency and did kisse and stroke him and use other meanes and that hee had her upon the fforme in the chamber and took up her coates and was very unmannerly with her but had not carnall knowledge of her body, in regard he could not by reason of his age or inability althoughe shee consented thereunto and that he did handle her privities by her willing consent . . .'. The passage dealing with Heming's alleged impotency is struck out. Perhaps it was not a defence which impressed the court, any more than would at least one of his six 'honest neighbours' whom he had chosen as 'compurgers',[3] who was Thomas Woodward, that regular visitor to the Court. The Beadle was ordered to appear at Morning Service 'with a white sheet hanging down from his shoulders to his feete, holding a white rod in his hand and penitently to acknowledge his fault'. There can have been few malingerers from church that day. His cohort of the chamber, Elizabeth Court, failed to appear and was excommunicated.

The ire of the Court could extend to outsiders. On 3 December 1625 Richard Hill 'Citizen and haberdasher of London' (perhaps a grandson of his namesake, the alderman), wrote to the churchwardens freely acknowledging his 'ffalts comitted at Stratford uppon Avon in unlawfull frequenting and haunting of Alehouses and playeinge at unlawful games . . . and in giving evell words to the offices and Constables there: for all of which I am heartily sorry and promise Amendment for the tyme being to come'. Since repentance was a prime object of the Court, it may be presumed that the apology was accepted.

The court records reveal Stratford's 'problem' individuals and families. Often these were ordered to attend weekly catechism classes, presumably in the remote hope that greater knowledge of religious discipline might activate reforming instincts. The Bartlett family represented a continuing headache. On 22 May 1624, Richard and William Bartlett were presented for refusing 'to come to be cattechised'. Neither had appeared by the time the Court sat, so they were excommunicated and it was ordered that they 'hereafter . . . doe come diligentlie to be cattechised everie Sabaoth day untill [they] can answer the minister in the principles of the christian religion'. At this point William appeared. The apparitor 'delivered that the said William Bartlet did when he was cited speak reproachfull and revilinge words of this court, viz. "Shyte uppon the court"'. He was ordered to make a public confession in his own clothes.

The Bartletts were not strong on catechetics. On 16 July William was cited for failing to answer the questions in the catechism and Richard and Stephen were excommunicated for failing to attend. Bigger trouble was on the way for William. Five cases of slanderous abuse followed: the churchwardens had occasional crackdowns on particular offences. Richard Wheeler was cited for calling Richard Brookes' wife 'whore and sowlike whore with divers other filthy speeches'. In his defence he declared that the woman 'calling him a rogue, he replyed that if he were a rogue she were a whore'. Anne Lane was presented for calling 'Katherine Trowt whore'. She admitted the offence and 'sayth moreover that William Bartlett hath publicely confessed before witnesses that Katherine Trowt did come to bed to him'. The churchwardens were ordered to denounce and cite him. On 3 September he denied the charge and was ordered to 'purge'[4] himself at the next Court in the presence of of Katherine Trowt. This appears to have been delayed until 8 June. The outcome is unclear, but the Bartletts must have continued to provide the Court with regular business. Their last recorded case was in 1627, when Richard was presented for 'revelling in the night and carrying himself disorderlie towards his neighbours servants calling them up at midnight to dance with him and to revell.' Little of the Puritan spirit infected the Bartletts.

The Court records for 1628 reveal another hidden current beneath the surface of Stratford society. Elizabeth or 'Goody' Bromley was presented for abusing the wife of Adrian Holder in terms redolent of the black arts. She threatened to 'overlook her and hern' (to put the evil eye on them) and Mistress Holder exclaimed, in Shakespearean language, 'Aroint thee witch!'[5] She told her 'to get her home', or, echoing the King James' version, 'a would brush the motes forth of her dirty gown'. Such invective gives another insight into the verbal vigour of the age.

Hall was churchwarden in 1628 and gave a carved pulpit[6] to the Church. He held the position again in 1633, presenting one man 'for loitering forth of church in sermontime', another for sleeping in the belfry, with his hat on, upon the Sabbath; another for 'keeping drinking in his house after evening prayer' and a fourth for being a 'common romler'.[7] He may have cracked down on extreme Puritans, for four men were presented for the iconoclastic gesture of 'wearing a hat in church'. Another Shakespearean echo is heard in a presentation for 'putting hands in plackets' (the opening in the front of a woman's dress), one of the peccadilloes against which Lear's Fool admonishes.

'Medicus Peritissimus'

In the mid-1630s two mighty projects were undertaken to revive Stratford's economic fortunes: the Market Hall was rebuilt in 1634 with the intention of increasing vital trade. At the same time an engineer, William Sandys, was working on the ambitious enterprise to make 'the River of Avon passible for bringinge of wares from sondrye places to this borough of Stratford'. Even the Corporation forgot its strife and expressed its 'approbacion, commendacion and alowance'.

Meanwhile, the conflict with the vicar continued. The keys of the Guild Chapel were taken away from him, probably because of dissatisfaction with the way he kept the building. Hall, still seething from the swindle of the tithes, launched himself against the burgesses again. On 20 July 1634, the clerk recorded that 'Mr. Hall charged some of the company to be forsworne villains'.

The acrimony extended through the vicar's household. When Wilson was asked 'to permitt his maide Elizabeth Edwards to come and speak with Mr. Baliffe', he replied that she would not come without a warrant. When the Bailiff sent his warrant by Tymbrill, a constable, Wilson took it away and would not return it though the constable pleaded for it. Eventually the maid was prevailed upon to appear. 'Then Mr. Wilson did affirme (coming with her) . . . in the Hall that she was sent for as a felon and bade his mayde not to reveale who tolde hir certayne speeches which she spake tending to the disgrace of the companye.'

Hall and Wilson made common cause against the Corporation in a Chancery suit in 1635, which mainly concerned Hall's lost tithe revenues. The Corporation retaliated by expelling Hall from its number. Since he was a reluctant burgess, it is unlikely that this sanction cut him to the quick. The Corporation now petitioned for the removal of Wilson whom they accused of such bizarre behaviour as wandering around the Church during prayers. 'In his sermons and lectures [he] doth particularize somme of his parishioners' – it is not difficult to guess who they might have been – and 'he hath prophaned the chapple by sufferinge his children to playe at bale and other sports therein and his servants to hange clothes to drye in it and his pigges and poultrie to lye and feed in it and alsoe his dog to lie in it and the pictures [presumably the wall-paintings] . . . to be defaced and the windows broken.' Even stranger was the vicar's behaviour during a funeral. He was not asked to give the address, so he sat on the pulpit steps to prevent the curate from doing so.

The subtle difference between the Congregational viewpoint dominant on the Corporation and Wilson's theocratic authoritarianism might explain some of the mutual hostility. If such considerations were voiced, however, they were obscured by clashes of personality. John Hall was not alone in his criticism of his fellows. Alderman Thomas Smith pointedly gave five pounds for a weekly lecture 'as long as Thomas Wilson shall continue as vicar'. In 1635, William Smith was expelled from the Corporation after alleging that 'noe honest man could have favour in this place' and that 'the Bailiff and Burgesses weare not so good as chaffe'.

Hall appears to have shared something of the intense disillusion of Shakespeare's dark period. His fight against corruption included vigorous opposition to those who purloined money intended for the poor. He paid a ten pound fine in the reign of Charles I, rather than accept a knighthood at a time when the sale of honours was a national scandal. It is apposite to recall Cerimon, whose medical practice gave

> More content in cause of true delight.
> Than to be thirsty after tottering honour,
> Or tie my treasure up in silken bags,
> To please the fool and death.

Hall's distrust of institutionalised man stemmed from his faith. 'Thou, O Lord', he prayed on recovery from illness, 'which hast the power of Life and Death . . . and drawest from the Gates of Death . . . without Art or Counsel of Man, but only from thy Goodness and Clemency, thou hast saved me from the bitter and deadly Symptoms of a deadly Fever, beyond the expectation of all about me, restoring me as it were from the very jaws of Death to former health.' We think again of Drayton's Warwickshire doctor:

> . . . who of this world the vileness having seen,
> Retyres from it quite and with a constant mind
> Man's beastliness so loathes, that flying humane kind . . .
> Indifferent are to him, his hopes on God that staies . . .

Hall was no bigot. He describes Lady Rainsford as 'modest, pious and kindly' and adds 'praised be God' after curing a Catholic priest, Father Browne. His greatest admiration is for the Reverend John Trapp, the schoolmaster, whose 'piety and learning' he considered 'second to none'. Hall treated him for a hypochondriac melancholy: the result of overstudiousness.

The Church register records the death of 'John Hall, gent., *medicus peritissimus*' ('most learned physician') on 25 November 1635. There had been fever in Stratford and it is likely that he had laboured too hard and too often. His verbal will, made the day before his death, left the bulk of his property to his wife and daughter. A Bill in Chancery filed by his widow reveals his wealth. His goods and chattels alone were worth £1,000. He was buried close to William Shakespeare. Part of his Latin epitaph translates:

> Hall lies here who was renowned in the healing art
> Awaiting the delightful joys of heaven.

Had he chosen his own memorial, Hall might have selected the Latin inscription he wrote in his manuscript: 'He who practices medicine without a cause is as one who navigates without a rudder and oars'.

Ship Money

With Hall's death, Minister Wilson lost his strongest ally. He conceded the charges against him and was suspended by the diocesan authorities for three months. When the portly Mrs. Wilson was asked about the arrangements for her husband's absence she said he had spoken to Mr. Simon Trappe, the curate. 'If he did not, she would provide none', but Trappe grumbled that he had 'had nothing for his paynes and therefore he forebears to preach'.

The curtailment of Wilson's activities enabled Bishop Thornborough to report to Archbishop Laud in 1637 that he was 'less troubled with non-conformists since Mr. Whateley of Banbury gave over his lecture at Stratford': which was presumably the one endowed by Alderman Smith. Wilson retained his living until his death in 1638, after which the Corporation sought control, withholding its share of the stipend while attempting, unsuccessfully, to buy the right to present the vicar and schoolmaster.

Times were changing fast. In 1635 the introduction of the 'ship money' tax by Charles I set in train the events which led to civil war. On 14 June 1637 the Corporation resolved to petition the Lords 'for to lessen our ship-money'. On 1 January 1638/9, it was decided that 'Mr. Duppa is to goe to London to petican the Lords in behalf of the Boroughe to same of ship money'. Poverty was a legitimate plea. The sum required (£30) contrasts with the assessments of £160 at Birmingham and £500 at Coventry. The deterioration of the times – a further fire devastated the town in 1640 – and the brooding air of expectation is reflected in the minutes of 26 June 1640: 'Att this hall yt is ordered that everye Ald and Burgesse shall have 2 pownde of gunpowder and 2 pownde of droppe shot of that wch belongs to Corpacon and shall pay for the same'.

Daniel Baker, that vehement old Puritan who reflected personally the growing factiousness of 40 years, did not live to see the triumph of his party. He was buried at Holy Trinity on 30 July 1641, bequeathing to the church 'there to remain for ever my book of Mr. Greenham's[8] works for the use and benefit of such as shall be well disposed to read the same'. The book was to be fastened with a chain 'for the more better and safe keeping thereof'. On 24 November, the Corporation underlined its Puritan disposition by removing decorative effects from the Guild Chapel. 'The perticion between the Chauncell and boady of the Chappell' was taken down and the walls washed with white lime.[9] The pulpit was moved and 'conveniently placed', centre aisle, to stress the supremacy of the word. In 1642 Henry Twitchett, styled as 'vicar', was replaced by 'minister' Will Hawling. In August, the King set his seal on the nation's divisions by raising his standard at Nottingham. The minds of the burgesses, so long obsessed with nuances of civic dignity, would soon be concentrated on wider issues by rival armies in Stratford's streets.

FOOTNOTES
[1]	There is a facsimile of the second edition in Harriet Joseph's *Shakespeare's Son-in-Law, Man and Physician*: see Bibliography.
[2]	James Halliwell also saw this document some time before 1864, but it now appears to be lost.
[3]	Guarantors of the integrity of the confession.
[4]	Swear an oath of denial before witnesses.
[5]	cf. *Macbeth* I.iii.6 and *Lear* III.iv.129.
[6]	It was removed around 1792.
[7]	A word defined in the *Warwickshire Dialect Dictionary* of 1886 as meaning 'coarse' and 'crude'.
[8]	A Puritan divine of the previous century.
[9]	This is when the murals were painted over. Not, as some have asserted, when John Shakespeare was Chamberlain.

CHAPTER 7

'The Times hath bin Troublesome'

'For watch and ward the Times hath bin Troublesome'
Jury presentment, 1646/7

The principal local antagonists at the start of the Civil War were both former patients of John Hall: Lord Brooke and Spencer Compton, Earl of Northampton. Brooke was in Stratford in July 1642, raising over 600 men from the district, two-thirds of them armed, the remainder a militia for which William Combe was obliged to pay as lord of the manor. The Stratfordians panicked at the sight of the armed battalions. It was rumoured that the Bailiff and the vicar had offered them billets, but they were exonerated at the Hall of 3 August. 'Whereas yt. Mr. Bayliffe & Mr. Twitchett were accused for using theis words . . . that they had betrayed the Towne and that they had sett their hands to a note for builletinge soldiers here, the Companie doe free and acquite them'.

The Corporation was wary enough of Compton's proximity to raise a subscription for the King, donating £50. Other contributions included five pounds from the vicar and two from Shakespeare's godson, William Walker. The highest donation of £100 came from Thomas Nashe. This was impressive in view of the property worth £255 he had lost in the fire of 1640. Despite these deprivations, the Stratfordians looked generously on the plight of others. They were aware that others had contributed in their extremities and would do so again. In September, £85 19s 0d was collected for the 'reliefe of his maiesties distressed subjects of the Kingdom of Ireland'. Spencer Compton read the Royal Proclamation in Stratford that month, the Corporation paying 11s 2d to trumpeters 'when the Lord of Northampton lay in the Towne'. The Royalists plundered the College, home of the politically suspect William Combe. That autumn the bloody and futile battle at Edgehill ensured the district's hour at the centre of the national stage. The noise of battle resounded through Stratford. As far away as Alcester, the Puritan divine, Richard Baxter, preaching on the text, 'The Kingdom of Heaven suffereth violence' found his sermon punctuated by the noise of cannon.

After the battle the retreating Parliamentary army clogged Stratford's streets. Waggons clattering northwards, the array of weaponry and uniforms reflecting haphazard recruitment; cannons heaved by straining horses and sweating men; the Puritan chaplains admired by John Trapp, the schoolmaster as 'Those gallant spirits at Edgehill battle, with their reboated "Now for the fruit of prayer" and of many psalms sung by that religious armies . . . whereof I have been an eyewitness . . . down go the anti-christians immediately by the power and prowess of the Christian armies, thus edged and encouraged by their preachers'.

The Chamberlains' accounts recorded 'monyes disbursed and given unto the Parliament soldiers which weare wounded and died in the Towne after Kinton Batell', including some who had served under 'Captain Crumell'.

The Battle of Stratford-upon-Avon

Early in 1643 a troop of Royalist horse commanded by Colonel Wagstaff occupied Stratford and recruited a number of locals. On 25 February Lord Brooke, advancing from Warwick, resolved on an early morning surprise attack. 'Yet a countryman and friend of theirs', records the Parliamentary chronicler, 'espying us two miles on this side, crossed the fields and gave the enemy advertisement: upon which they drew themselves out under a hill, where they could view us in our march. We drew the greatest part of our Artillery to the Vanne, they having the greatest part of our Horse and we expediting the first charge there, but withall suspecting their weaving about, we drew up our reere, so that we stood triangle upon three hils in full

15.   *The old Town Hall, Stratford, as it was rebuilt after the Civil War, from a drawing by James Saunders.*

view of each other. From the reer division we let flie a drake, which ran through the midst of them and forced them to wheele off towards the Town and we hasted after them so fast as our Carriages and the Plowd Lands so well softened with the raine would permit us'. Faced by superior fire-power, Wagstaffe retreated, leaving two dead behind. His local recruits had fled at the first sign of danger.

The Parliamentarians had not heard the last of Wagstaffe. Learning that a military council was to be held in the Town Hall, which sheltered an ammunition dump, he crept into town and laid a 'traine of powder to a piece of match left at such a length as should . . . just meet the powder at the time of their sitting'. The building went up, but prematurely. 'When they thought all had been quiet and well and the Lord Brooke and the Colonels and Captains were going to the Council, they heard a noise as if some houses had fallen down and saw the Town Hall in pieces in such a manner that it is utterly ruined, one of the townsmen slaine and four more burnt and bruised, who are very ill and this all the hurt it did. O the great cause we have to praise God for such deliverances as these!' The destruction of its 'very faire Hall', which had been built less than a decade, was a desperate blow to the Corporation. Other property was pillaged, including part of Shakespeare's Birthplace. At the *Swan and Maidenhead* the 'orphan children of Jane Hiccox (Thomas and Anne) lost silver when Lord Brooke's forces came'.

Next month the antagonistic Warwickshire noblemen were drawn northwards with fatal consequence. Compton fell at Hopton Heath. A month later John Trapp mourned 'that thrice noble Lord Brooke who lost his precious life at Lichfield'.

'The Queen Majestye'

In July, Stratford's bells rang as Queen Henrietta Maria arrived at the head of 2,000 foot and a thousand horse, with artillery. She was met by Prince Rupert with another force. The Queen lodged at New Place with Mrs. Hall. 'She preferred it to the *College,* which was in the possession of the Combe family, who did not so strongly favour the King's party.'[1] Combe professed to be a Royalist, but it was complained that he 'sat at home'.[2]

More expense fell on the impecunious burgesses: £18 6s 0d was paid 'when the Queen Majestye laye in the towne', including six pounds for six footmen and the 'cochman and porters'. No chance was taken with the royal person: three pounds was paid to 'Mr Bayliffe of Warwick for their fortifications', probably barriers to exclude the curious or malignant.

It was probably during the Queen's visit that Susanna Hall presented Colonel Richard Greene, Chamberlain to the young Duke of York, with a copy of Henri Estienne's *Mervaylous Discourse upon the lyfe of Katherine de Medicis*, printed at Heidelberg in 1575. An inscription records the gift: *Liber R: Gracei ex dono amicae D. Susanne Hall.*

When the Royalists left Stratford, they carried off the little schoolmaster, John Trapp, who had subscribed two months' salary – five pounds – to the opposing cause. He became 'one of God's poor prisoners' at Oxford, 'from which death God graciously delivered him' through a prisoner exchange. Trapp, regarded by fellow-Puritans as 'a man of singular Prudence and Piety, of an acute wit, of a sound judgement and of an indefatigable spirit' became minister at Welford. 'That's the best sermon', he once homilised, 'that's dig'd out of a man's own breast', but his new parishioners heard little of his eloquence, for he spent 'his daily labours amongst the soldiers and in the midst of the noises of guns and drums'.

An admirer, Thomas Dugard, Rector of Barford, dedicated a poem to him:

> One of this Age's Greatest Little Men,
> Great in Good Works, witnesse his golden pen.
> His pen hath drawn his learned hand in part,
> His Holy Life proclaimes a Gracious Heart,
> Should any mee consult how hee might rise
> Unto compleatnesse, I would say,
> Trappize.

Others were probably less adulatory. Trapp inveighed energetically against theatre, masquerades and dancing.

Stratford's position ensured continued involvement on the fringe of the war. Early in 1645 500 Royalists rode into the town and demanded £500 to refrain from plunder. There were skilled diplomatists around, for they rode off after settling for ten pounds. After this Parliament ordered an arch of the bridge to be demolished, 'for securing the county and preventing the incursions of the enemyes'. In such precarious circumstance, the Stratfordians refrained from open partisanship, each side accusing them of favouring the other.

A Journal of the Plague Year

The battalion of troubles was compounded that year by devastating plague. The community's response to this disaster is uniquely recorded in 'A Note what hath beene paid to the Infected wth the Plague and kept up for feare of further spreading'. It represents a tale of suffering, but also a community at its best, organising with compassion for the general good.

On 24 May 16 people were registered as infected. The first payments are two shillings to William Adams 'for drawing a Corps to grave' and 2s 6d to 'Granams for buryinge a corps'. This is John Granams, who is listed as 'infected' – presumably a term denoting contact with infection – who was paid fivepence a day. A little village of 'pest houses' was built outside the town in a place called 'the Hill', which was probably at Welcombe. The sufferers were paid their subsistence from a monthly levy of ten pounds on the borough and district.

Granam's wife, Mary, was in charge of the isolation colony with Richard Rogers and they were paid eightpence a day. In May tenpence was spent on 'a Coast [side] of Veale' for them and twopence 'for tobacco and candles for Richard Rogers'. The graveyard was established and the sufferers' livestock kept in a nearby field. Sixpence was paid to George Bridges 'for coving of graves & for worke in the Ffield' and fourpence to William Hornby 'for work in the Ffield about Pesthouses'.

As the numbers of sick increased the accommodation was expanded. Five men were paid eightpence each for 'helping to sett up the Pesthouses' and £1 18s 5d for materials.

During the first week in June the Austin family was decimated:

Ffor making a grave for Austin's boy....	4d
Ffof prunes jd & raisins, jd for Austin & Granams....	2d
Ffor more prunes, sugar, cloves & cinnamon for them....	4d
Ffor suger, candles & making a grave for Austin's wench...	6d
Ffor a sheete to wrappe Austin's wife in	1.0d
Ffor half a strike of brans to burie the Corps	4d
To Alexander Hornbe wch he paid Mary Granams to bury one of Austins children	2.6d.

Considerable organisation was needed to maintain the colony. As the infection spread more help was required. On 11 June payment was made to 'Goodwife Hopkins for her husband & her own wages for this weeke watching, warding & tending the people at the Hill'. William Burforde was paid 4s 2d for 'watching & warding . . . for a weeke'. Better facilities were needed and John Hobbins was paid for 'fetching stuffe from Luddington to make a cabbin for the Warders at hill'.

The plague brought one blessing. On 12 June Fairfax's great army arrived at Stratford. Normally hundreds of soldiers would have been billetted with the townsfolk, but, fearing the infection, they camped at Cross o' the Hill above the town. Next day the bridge echoed to the sound of an army on the march as it passed to decisive victory at Naseby.

At 'the Hill' there can have been little concern for this momentous movement of national events. The death rate was increasing with the summer heat. Coffins were ordered in bulk. George Cole was paid 9s 4d for 'boards, pitche, nailes, coard & making coffins for the infected yt died' and 'more which he laid out for Mountford's wife and sonne'. George Bridges was paid for 'drawing ye Corps & making a grave for goodwife Mountford's' and 'for making Mountford's sonnes grave'. On 15 June George Badger was paid fourpence for making 'a grave for Francis Cowper's motherlawe' and tenpence for 'Cook's wives grave' and for 'helping to drawe the Corps'. Twopence was paid for 'sugar candie for Cook's wench' and twopence for 'a peck of brans for their swine'. Eightpence was paid 'ffor a strike of Charcoale for them at Hill' and 3s 7d to 'Goodwife Hopkins for sope for them; jd for bread, meate & drinke for them wch. they had for Satirday, Sunday and Monday'.

After 9 July, when George Bridges was paid a shilling for 'making the graves & haling the coffin for Clark's wife and child', the plague could no longer be isolated, but was rife in the alleys of the town. On 2 August, 2s 6d was paid 'to the infected in the sheepstreet maze'. To coax people into isolation they were paid in advance. 2s 8d was given on 9 August 'to Tasker a weeks paie beforehand to remoove unto the hill'.

By autumn the disease was on the decline. Sixty-one people had died, of whom 41 lived in the Borough. The Corporation became preoccupied with the collection of the district levies, which were predictably slow in appearing. On 24 September, 6s 4d was received from William Matthews, Constable 'of Hampton Episc. [or Lucy], a fortnights paie[ment]', but other places were not as forthcoming. In October George Cowper was paid a a shilling for going 'to Claverdon & other townes about money for the infected'. There must have been muted joy when on 21 January 1645/6 two shillings was paid to Robert Taylor for 'pulling downe the pest houses'.

'The Times hath bin Troublesome'

'For wach and ward the times hath bin troublesome', declared a jury presentment, with considerable understatement in January 1646/7. Law and order had broken down in the countryside with a resultant effect on trade. Gangs of marauding horsemen terrorised travellers. The number of tenants in arrears had doubled to a fifth of the total. Local parishes defaulted on the Poor Rate, so increased burdens fell on the burgesses. 'Parishes and schools are polled and robbed of their maintenance as if they meant to starve us all', preached John Trapp and came to a pedagogue's conclusion: 'Man that was once Captain of God's school, is now, for his truantliness, turned into the lowest form, as it were, to learn his ABC again'.

A kind of anarchy had been unleashed. On 20 March 1645/6, Edward Welles swore before John Smith, the Bailiff and Thomas Horne, the Chief Alderman that two years before at his house in Stratford, John Powse of 'Noball' (Newbold-on-Stour) had said 'yt our Saviour CHRIST was a bastard, & our Virgin Mary a whore, & yt hee desired a bible to shewe a proofe of it, & yt our Sovaigne Lord the Kinge is both a knave & a foole, & had not soe much wit as hee had'. When Welles was asked why he had not reported this before, he said 'yt hee did reveale it to some particular men, but durst not speake it openly in regard of the times'. His testimony was supported by three others, including Eleanor Welles, who had reported the matter. When Powse was examined he said he was at Welles' house frequently during the 'period alledged but denies any recollection of the imputed to him'. The verdict of the Court is lost, but it is noteworthy that the magistrates investigated heresy and at least nominally defended the integrity of the monarch. In the same year the compiler of the vestry minutes at Holy Trinity ceased to describe the local highways as 'the King's'.

A survey of 1646 analysed the losses caused in the town by the war. The 119 claims against the Parliamentary forces totalled £2,542 – mainly for quartering soldiers. The cost of plunder by Lord Brooke's forces was recorded as £135, but some claims were spurious: 'It is true that the Mayor of Eson's Coronet[4] took an old gown to watch in, but it was redelivered.' Claims against the Royalists were smaller – and even less likely to be paid – £1,412, mainly in taxes, loans and contributions. In 1649, a token £41 was laid out by the Corporation.

The coming of peace meant an upsurge in trade. With the roads relatively free of outlaws, the horse-fair of 1646 did record business, dealers coming from six counties. In more relaxed mood, the Corporation bought a china fairing for the curate's wife.

Peace brought an opportunity to clear the backlog of civil cases. At the Quarter Sessions, Abraham Tibbits was indicted for watering his hides in William Combe's fishing ground, an offence committed five years before, and William Ingrams and 11 others were fined for carrying away four cartloads of Combe's soil. On 30 April 1647, a case was heard concerning the taking of two deer from Sir Greville Verney. A man named Taylor was alleged to have had one and 'a souldier quartering with Mrs. Nash', the other. Chapel Street, four years after its welcome to the Queen, had become a base for poaching soldiers.

Mrs. Nash was newly-widowed at this time. Her husband, Thomas, died on 14 April. His will shows the continuing adhesion of the Shakespeare circle, with cash bequests 'to his mother Mistress Hall' and to his wife's cousins, Thomas, Elizabeth and Judith Hathaway. 'To his uncle and Aunt Nash', to Richard Quiney and his wife and to 'his cousin Thomas Quiney and his wife', he left 20 shillings each 'to buy them rings'.

'Our Light shall Come'

From 1646, the minister at Holy Trinity was Alexander Beane, 'a studious man . . ., who at home and abroad was highly esteemed for his solid useful sermons'. Richard Quiney bequeathed in 1656 to 'Master Beane, minister of God's word at Stratford-upon-Avon, forty shillings for his pains taken in preaching my funeral sermon'. Beane was a signatory of the *Warwickshire Ministers Testimony to the Truth of Jesus Christ* and *The Solemn League and Covenant* of 1647: 'That although at present the sunne be covered and air darkened with mists risen out of the bottomlesse pit, yet ere long our light shall come and the glory of the Lord shall rise upon us'. This fervour was observed by the Quaker, George Fox, who in 1648 met 'a great company of professors in Warwickshire, who were praying and expounding the scriptures in the fields'.

At the school a delicate situation existed. In January 1649/50, the schoolmaster, John Trapp, wrote to the Corporation:

> Gentlemen all and my very good friends, your ancient curtesy to me (though now for some years discontinued) as it calleth for my renewed thanks, so it give me boldnesse to remind you, that for these five years past I have received but one yeares pay of that five pounds that you were pleased, fifteene yeares since to add to my stipende . . .

Trapp had abandoned teaching to minister to the Parliamentary armies, but his party's ascendency meant that he had to be handled carefully, so the Corporation paid him ten pounds. In 1650 he was appointed to assist the Commission which ejected those who refused to subscribe to the Covenant and substituted his son-in-law, Robert Dale, as schoolmaster with the consent of the Corporation.

Thomas Combe became Recorder of Stratford, an office he held until he died in 1657. Brother William, the former tyrant of the fields, did not fare so well. His fire was spent, wasted by advancing age and the deprivations of war. 'My uncle Combe is far in debt', wrote George Willis in 1650, 'and the land that he hath about Stratford is sould or now upon sale.' The sad epitaph in Holy Trinity of his daughter Judith shows that the family had a human face. She was to have married her cousin, Richard Combe of Hemel Hempstead, 'had not death prevented it by depriving her of her life, to the extream grief and sorrow of both their friends, but more especially of the said Richard Combe, who in testimony of his unfeigned love hath erected this monument for perpetuating her pious memory. She took her last leave of this life the 17th day of August 1649. In the armes of him who most intirely loved and was beloved of her even to the very death.'

In 1651 Stratford was near the front-line again. On 27 August, the New Model Army marched through the town to rout Charles II's Scottish army at Worcester. Oliver Cromwell wrote from Stratford to the 'dubitating' Lord Wharton. 'The Lord's work needs *you* not, save as he needed the asses beast to show his humility, but you need *it,* to declare your submission and own yourself the Lord's and His people's.' After the battle, the young fugitive King skirted Stratford to avoid the heavily-guarded bridge, probably fording the river below the town. Again the ratepayers bore the cost. On 2 September a general levy was announced 'for the collecting of soo much as is charged upon this Towne by vertue of an order for provisions for

Major-General Lambert's Regiment'. On 13 September the Corporation paid 15 shillings for wine and tobacco 'wn. my Lord Protector was proclaimed'.

The rule of the Saints did not curtail all conviviality. 'Att this Hall', read the minutes in 1652, 'Mr. John Wolmore senior is fined xxs for breaking the ancient and laudable custom of nott invitinge our wives to the feast'. In the following year the Corporation received 'Richard Castell's bill for sacke sent to the Cheezcake feast, white wine sent to Mr. Batliffe's feast, &c'.

War damage was repaired. The bridge was renovated at a cost of £20 by Thomas Sargerson of Coventry in 1652. A year later a fund was opened to rebuild the Town Hall. Meanwhile the Corporation met in the old Guild Hall. On 9 December 1653, it was agreed to alter the maces 'according to the injunction of a Act of Parliament' and Commonwealth crowns were substituted for royal ones. Another symbol of the disappearance of monarchical power was the change of name of Stratford's leading inn. The *Crown* became the *Woolsack*.

There were other urgent matters to hand. Another fire had devastated the town, caused by inadequately supervised malting kilns and lack of fire-fighting equipment. Collections were again made throughout England towards the 'great losses'. The Corporation petitioned the Lord Chief Justice to 'restrayne all thatched houses in our towne'. It was requested that the number of statutory fire-buckets should be increased to two dozen and that the Chamberlain should provide 'spoutes . . . and to make som fire-houkes more and mak some ladders more'. No fire was to be kept under any kiln, or any straw left in the kiln-house after eight o'clock at night – 'nor any children under twelve years of age or any blinde body imployed about the keeping of fire under any kilne upon the penalty of twenty shillings'. Each alderman and burgess was to provide, at his own expense, two leather buckets 'to keep in his house betwene this and ester next upon payne of forfeitinge twenty shillings'.

Once again, in the midst of their troubles, the Stratfordians remembered others. Within a year the Bailiff paid £20 3s 9d collected in the town to the Lord Mayor of London's fund 'for the distressed Protestants of the Duke of Savoy countrie': Milton's 'slaughtered saints' massacred in Piedmont.

Religious controversy continued, although it is not possible to be specific. On 12 January 1653/4, the Corporation agreed that Mr. Wade, 'who lately preached in the High Church, shall be admitted to preach again in the same place upon the next Lord's day but one, or in case he shall meet with any disturbance that he cannot preach there, hee shall bee permitted the use of the Chappell for that day'.

The Corporation's regular obsessions also continued. A meeting of 1653/4 fined Richard Castell five pounds for disclosing 'the speeches of some members of the Company at a common Councell'.

'Witty above her Sexe'

In 1649 the widow Nash was wed privately at Billesley Manor to John Barnard of Abington, near Northampton. At the Restoration he was knighted for services to the Crown during the Commonwealth period. Susanna Hall died two months after her daughter's remarriage. A charming epitaph adorns her tomb in Holy Trinity:

> Witty above her sexe, but that's not all,
> Wise to salvation was good Mistress Hall;
> Something of Shakespeare was in that, but this
> Wholly of Him with whom she's now in blisse.
> Then passenger, hast ne're a teare,
> To weape with her that wept with all?
> That wept, yet set herselfe to chere
> Them up with comforts cordiall . . .

A document of 1685 describes Thomas Quiney as having been 'a citizen and brewer of London'. Whether he abandoned his wife cannot be said; more likely he went to work with his successful elder brother Richard, who in 1652 had assummed the sole trusteeship of his business. He was presumably still alive on 9 February 1662, when 'Judith uxor [rather than *vidua]* Thomas Quiney, Gent' was buried at Holy Trinity. Thirty years later a visitor was told that Shakespeare's wife and daughters 'Did earnestly Desire to be Layd in the same Grave with him', but that the verse with the curse had exercised its spell. With the death of Elizabeth, Lady Barnard in 1670, Shakespeare's direct line came to an end and the property he had so assiduously acquired for his dynasty was dispersed.

Restoration

A sense of unrestrained joy was apparent amongst Stratfordians at the return of Charles II: a rare occasion when a change of government was not accepted passively, but greeted with widespread enthusiasm. The royal arms were restored to the bailiff's mace (the Sadler mace still carries its Commonwealth crown). Richard Phillips was paid 'for drawinge the Kinges Armes in the Chamber in the Hall' and 'for Gildinge the Crown at the Church'. The town was indulged in the Latin manner 'for wyne . . . was put in the crose pump at the proclaiminge of the Kinge'. In 1661 a receipt was issued 'for the Voluntary Contribution of Henley St Ward to King' – perhaps in preparation for Coronation celebrations.

The Restoration Parliament suppressed dissent. In 1662, the County Commissioners removed three aldermen and three burgesses from the Corporation, although in 1665 when Richard Smart refused the Oath of Loyalty, he was duly elected.

The vestry minutes refer briefly to the Reverend Alexander Beane as 'Vicar' before his Puritan conscience overpowered him. On St Bartholomew's Day in 1662, he was ejected for failing to pledge 'unfeigned assent and consent' to the Book of Common Prayer. 'His labours in this place had been so great and successful that he could ill be spared', lamented a fellow-Puritan. 'Soon after his ejectment he preached privately and was disturbed. When endeavouring to secure himself by flight, he took a surfeit and quickly died.' His resistance was courageous, for he had a wife and six children to share his penury. To its credit, the Corporation granted him a gratuity of £6 13s 4d. Surprisingly the militant Puritan John Trapp conformed and retained his living at Weston. Perhaps the years had mellowed him. A curious entry in the Chamberlains' accounts in 1662 noted the payment of £1 to 'Mr. and Mrs Trappe and his son for preaching'.

Local nonconformity had lost its potency. A survey conducted by Lord Compton showed that only 1.6 per cent of the townspeople were dissenters. A major objection to this small band was financial. In 1682 Richard Bromley, Richard Hull and John Copeland were presented for 'not coming to church to heare divine service & for refusing to pay the rates levied for repaire of the church'.

At Holy Trinity the sacraments were restored and '2 gilte chalices with covers and a damaske tablecloth . . ., a pulpit cloth and cushion, a carpit for the Comunin Table and a hearsecloth and a great cloth and a Flagon' were acquired. John Ward, a bachelor who had studied medicine at Barber Surgeons' Hall, was appointed vicar. In 1663 he was paid three pounds 'for his extraordinary paines as Vicar, there being no assistant Minister yet provided', although financial circumstance had forced a reduction of the stipend.

Ward's attitude to medicine was similar to John Hall's. He rejected bizarre cures compounded of 'the foot of a tortoise, the liver of a mole and the dung of an elephant' as 'strange and monstrous trash', favouring an analytical approach. He examined breast-feeding, dissected cancerous tissue and denounced the bleeding of patients. When the plague wrought its devastation he noted that the only cure was to sweat twice a day 'and when the malignity is collected into one bubo . . . to poltice and ripen it, that it may break and so dissolve it'. He noticed the effects of the climate on the health of Stratfordians. 'After a cold winter, a cool Spring and a very hot Summer, children had the meazles extremely and men about July had agues and feavours in abundance'. A sad case gives a glimpse of the high infant mortality. 'A fellow that lives in Kineton had 27 children, most of them born alive, yet not one lived above a month: this man I spoke with myself.' He realised the unhealthiness of the stifling atmosphere of the contemporary bedchamber: 'Have a care in curing children, that they be not kept too hot by people lying with them; to give them breath is very good'.

A further reminder of the pestilence occurs in 1665. 'In respect of the plague being soe hott in London and spreadinge into many parts of the cuntry', the Corporation cancelled the September fair and ordered John Woolmer, junior to send to London by the next post 'to have it put into the news booke that thereby the cuntry may the better take notice of our resolutions'.

Ward's sermons struck a sure note. The confidence and calm of the phrases he jotted in his commonplace book imply that, while past storms are not over, more tranquil times lie ahead. 'Those mercies that we obtain by prayer, we must keep by praise', he exulted in a phrase reminiscent of George Herbert. The shallowness of man's affections was noted. 'Favourites are like dials, no longer looked upon than while the sun shines upon them.' He expressed distaste for slanderous gossip. 'The good name of a man is like a Venice glass which one drop of ink will defile.' Yet the message was one of atonement. 'He that does wrong never forgives, but he that suffers wrong may.'

Ward exhibited great progressiveness. In 1671 Mrs. Isobel Bates was elected as the only woman churchwarden in the history of Holy Trinity. Yet this radicalism did not inhibit general esteem. At the episcopal visitation of 1674, the churchwardens noted with satisfaction: 'Our church and churchyarde . . . are . . . in good order and repair. Our minister is episcopally ordained, leagally instituted & inducted, & performeth his ministeriall office with much care & diligence, & is a person of good sober life and sivell conversation'.

Educational provision was extended by John Smarte of Romford, Essex, who endowed free places for 20 poor men's children to be taught by 'some auntient woman of your Towne'. The children were to take their Bibles to Church and read them at home to their parents; 'for Parents are oftymes taken more with their childrens reading than with that they heare at Church'. Smarte also provided a loaf of bread each Sunday for 20 poor men and women selected by the Corporation 'if they come to Church, or bee not hindred by Sicknes or age. And that it may bee the better Bread for them I desire that when Wheat is best cheap there may bee soe much bought as may serve them for the whole yeare'.

The reason for Smarte's philanthropy towards Stratford is unclear. Because he lived 'out of London & know not where to send the carriers' he requested that the Corporation 'appoint some boy in London to call for the Books and mony at my sonn's shop at the Black boy in Lombard Street at Ste Clements Lane end a woolen Draper his name Mr. Joseph Smart'.

'Obedient and Loyal Subjects'

Stratford's body politic was in a state of confusion born of the financial crisis of the times and accentuated by the steady decline in the town's economic status. Measures were taken to reduce expenditure in 1663, 'in respect of the poverty of the Chamber & the improbability of being out of Debt'. The town clerk's annuity was reduced to a mere pound and the 20 marks payable to the Bailiff at Oken's Feast was discontinued. Even so, the Mayor (the title was first used in 1665) and town clerk had to wait two years for their money. A major problem was the compulsory renewal of the borough charter, which the impecunious government decreed in 1664. Despite considerable effort and expenditure, this matter never quite came right. The town's poverty earned it a general jury exemption in 1671.

The old problem of encroachment continued. The new lord of the manor, the Earl of Dorset, claimed rights over the Bancroft and accused the poor inhabitants of carrying off his timber. The Mayor and justices were summoned to London to answer charges of aiding and abetting this. A long wrangle ensued during which they were accused of illegal coining. This was true. Illicit invention had relieved the town's impecunity. The Exchequer did not mint lower denomination coins because of the cost and communities and traders issued their own. Less than a quarter of the small change in circulation was genuine. Six pounds of halfpennies were coined in Stratford in 1669, a practice on which the authorities were obliged, officially, to frown. In 1672 Parliament forbade further manufacture, but Stratford was still minting in 1676.

The first recorded use of the word 'Mop' to describe one of the fairs occurs in the Chamberlain's Accounts for 1675, when the Beadle, John Mumford, was paid fourpence 'for cryinge the moopp' and given sixpence for two ounces of tobacco and two dozen pipes on the same occasion. A contemporary reference[3] shows that 'mop' was a regional word used to describe a fair at which young people gathered to be hired as servants; the origin of the word is obscure, but has been suggested that it derives from the symbols of trade worn by those seeking work.[4] The Chamberlain's Accounts give no indication of when this Mop took place, so it cannot necessarily be identified with the October fair which still bears the name.[5]

The Corporation participated energetically in the furore over the 'Popish Plot', even if its efforts again recall Dogberry: 'All persons shall watch in their own persons and that there bee apoynted 6 persons every night to watch till they see cause to the contrary'.

The townspeople regarded their patriotism, if not their efficiency, as second to none, sending a declaration of loyalty to their sovereign in 1681:

> Dread Soveraigne.
> Wee yo: Maties
> most obedient and Loyall subjects looking back upon the dismall designs and bloody practizes of the late rebellious tymes which yet wee cannot with-out horrour and amasement reflect upon. . . although others have appeaared before us in their Addresses of this Nature, yett wee declare none shall goe before us in reality and zeale to your Majesteyes service . . .

In 1682, the Corporation sent an address to the King 'to shew our dislike to that Association drawn upp by sume of the protestinge Lords'. Yet some burgesses supported this attempt to exclude the King's Catholic brother from the succession. In the following August it was resolved to exclude three burgesses from the aldermanic bench until 'they doe acknowledge and subscribe their abhorrence to the Association formed in the Earl of Shaftesbury'. After the Rye House conspiracy the King was congratulated on 'his happy deliverance from that horod plot designed for the murdringe of his sacred majesty and his deere brother the Duke of Yorke'. The Corporation could not resist adding a line to this loyal address about its difficulties over its charter.

Lack of financial probity is revealed by an inquiry into the misuse of charitable funds instigated in 1682 by the County Commissioners. The Corporation was instructed to 'produce all evidences, together with accompt of the Anne Loyes money, Mr. Okens money,[6] etc.'. The outcome is unknown, but the investigation underlines a decline in civic standards.

A Grand Design

In 1667, an engineer, Andrew Yarranton, began repairing locks on the Avon which had fallen into disrepair during the Civil Wars. He developed a scheme which demonstrated the energy and invention characteristic of the pioneers of the industrial revolution. Although it was well before its time its scale might have ensured a return of manufacturing prosperity to the depressed region.

Yarranton proposed the building of twin cities outside Stratford: one at Milcote, named New Harlem, where 10,000 inhabitants were to be employed in growing flax and manufacturing thread. The other was to be over the river at Bridgetown and called New Brunswick because a German beer called Mum was to be brewed there.

The engineer may be pictured, tramping the water meadows, measuring and calculating his grandiose plan, which he called 'the brat of my brain when I conceived it'. He envisaged that it would make Stratford 'to the West of England, Wales, Shropshire and Cheshire as Danzig is to Poland'. By 1674 construction had begun, but the project was wrecked by the volatile peasantry. The Privy Council received a complaint that mobs of 'the poorer sort of people' had stopped up the locks and sluices, broken into the mills and seized the corn.

Yarranton's description of the proposed spinning school is worthy of Thomas Gradgrind. Two hundred children would sit spinning on benches around a large room. In the middle

16. A sailing barge on the navigable Avon, by R. B. Wheler, c.1800.

would be a box 'like a pulpit' where the grand mistress would sit with a white wand in her hand. 'If she observes any of them idle, she rings a bell, by which a little cord is fixed to a box and out comes a woman. She then points to the offender and she is taken away to another room and chastised and all this is done without one word speaking. And I believe this way of ordering the *young women* in Germany is one great cause that German women have so little of the *twit twat*.'[7]

Although his grand design was never completed, Yarranton restored the navigation, giving Stratford the appearance of a small seaport. Daniel Defoe, on a visit in 1712, noted the 'exceeding advantage' of the waterway. 'For by this river they drive a very great trade in sugar, oil, wine, tobacco, iron, lead, and ... all heavy goods ... and, in return, the corn, and especially the cheese – for Gloucester cheese is excellent in its kind, and this county drives an excellent trade in it.'

The Start of Legend

In 1680 died the last person who certainly knew William Shakespeare, his godson, William Walker. Legend could now take the poet where it willed and that it began to do. The first Stratfordian to embroider legends to suit local topography was probably the aged sexton, William Castle, who, on the strength of his birth in Stratford two years before Shakespeare died, established himself as a resident expert on the Bard, telling visitors that Shakespeare wrote the ghost scene in *Hamlet* in the charnel house at Holy Trinity at night in order to gather atmosphere and that he was 'bound apprentice to a butcher, but that he run from his master to London'. The sexton's insolence, negligence and avarice caused problems to his 'masters and superiors', the vestry admonishing him for taking excessive fees. He had even hired out the hearse cloth.

FOOTNOTES

[1]   Theobold: Preface to *Works of Shakespeare* (1733).
[2]   Symond's *Diary* (Camden Society, p. 191f).
[3]   Plot. *Oxfordshire,* 1677; quoted as the first-known use of the word by the *Oxford English Dictionary*.
[4]   A suggestion which the O.E.D. records as first having been written from hearsay in 1830.
[5]   See below p. 112.
[6]   The unease expressed by the Warwick burgesses a century before had been realised. See above p. 19.
[7]   *England's Improvement* by Andrew Yarranton; 1667.

CHAPTER 8

'In Statu Quo'

'Everything is *in statu quo* at our Town.'

Revd. Joseph Greene, 1735.

The Corporation sent loyal greetings on the accession of King James II. During Monmouth's rebellion, Sir John Clopton raised horsemen with 'powder and bullett for four days' and a month's pay 'if there be occasion'. Three years later the deposition of the King passed unremarked in the Stratford minute-book.

The bells of Holy Trinity clamoured national pride at the victory on the Boyne in 1690 and the Corporation paid £2 15s for 'Cyder and Wine on the Kings return from Ireland'. In 1692 the Vestry Minute Book recorded the payment of 14s 'for ringing the Victory at sea [La Hogue] and November 5th'. More local sensations continued to impinge. In 1694 £12 was sent after a dreadful fire engulfed Warwick.

Not that it required a national triumph for the Corporation to celebrate. When the schoolmaster left in 1691, it was decided to turn his 'old cole-house' into 'a bruehouse between this and Mayday next, for . . . the Company doth resolve to make use of it themselves'. In 1698 the Corporation petitioned unsuccessfully for the right to send two members to Parliament.

In 1687, Joseph Smith, an ironmonger, was fined a shilling for selling dissenting literature: two years later he was charged with permitting his premises to be used as a meeting-house. Things improved for dissenters with William III's Toleration Act of 1689, which granted a certain freedom of worship and proved to be a small first step towards pluralism. At subsequent Quarter Sessions the houses of Joseph Smith, William Hunt, woollendraper, and Richard Bromley were licensed as dissenting meeting-places.

A mandate from Sir Timothy Baldwin, diocesan Vicar-General, in 1694, reveals the severity of excommunication: 'Elizabeth Hiccocks, Widdow . . . wilfully lacking of all obedience to the King and Queen's Majesty's Laws . . . doth stand lawfully excommunicated and so hath obstinately continued for a a long time . . . disobediently refusing to submitt to the Government of the Church of England as by Law it is now established and to the Magistrates and Ministers thèreof. Tnerefore you are hereby admonished and required to eschew and avoid her . . . as a rotten member cutt off from the Church and that no person or persons within this parish or elsewhere doo give unto her entertainment in their houses, nor eat, drink, buy, sell or otherwise communicate with in publick or private but do turn her out of their houses, society and company . . . untill her submission and conformity to the Law'. The churchwardens were required to make 'diligent Enquiry' into offenders against the order 'that proceedings against them may bee made'.

Mrs. Hiccocks was, perhaps, a non-juror – one who refused to accept the validity of William III's accession on religious grounds. If so, it was particularly painful for her in the next year when the Chamberlains paid 1s 4d for 'cleaning the Bridge when King William and Queen

Mary were coming' and the Stratfordians turned out to cheer their progress, surrounded by a great concourse of nobles.

The vicar from 1702-05 was Nicholas Brady, a chaplain to the King. It demonstrates the narrow perspectives of the time that it was said that this Irishman would undoubtedly have gained high preferment had 'the singular humanity and benevolence of his disposition . . . suffered him to have run in with the violence of either prevailing party, or had he not settled in a country where he was regarded as a foreigner'. Not too much can have been seen of this amiable cleric in Stratford, for he also held the plural livings of Richmond and Clapham and much of the care of the parish would have fallen on the assisting minister; yet Brady must have been regarded as an ornament to the town as co-author with Nahum Tate of the *New Metrical Version of the Psalms*, which includes such familiar hymns as 'Through all the changing scenes of life' and 'As pants the hart for cooling streams'.

The next incumbent, Richard Synge, was presented by the churchwardens in 1707 for 'neglecting to doe divine service' on the previous Sunday morning and for 'providing no parson in his absence'. On the same day, a letter to the Bishop signed with the mark of Thomas George, chapelwarden at Bishopton, accused the vicar of 'notorious and scandalous neglect' in not officiating since 15 July. He was prosecuted 'with great severity' and forced to quit the living.

A sequel to the affair emerges in a letter from the Reverend John Jeffcott, Vicar of Evesham, to the Bishop, pleading for the borough chamberlain, Joseph Smith. Mr. Synge had promised 'to preach no more in ye church or chapel of Stratford, and therefore went on a Lord's Day in ye afternoone to Bishopton to preach there, whither abundance of people went to hear him'. It was a very hot day, the little church was packed and some of the women fainted. Smith was approached about whether glass could be removed from the chancel window 'that those within might be relieved and those without heare'. He replied that it was not his responsibility, but 'desired them if they tooke any downe to take care it might not be broken, but kept safe to put up againe . . ., which he says was onely an act of mercy and charity. If this be true, as I hope it is, I am ready to thinke it rather deserves praise than censure and therefore, most humbly pray by your favour on his behalf yt he may not be forced to any public penance, nor troubled with further attendance. I assure you I know him on a long and good experience to be a very pious, sober, prudent and good man, which encourages me to expect that you'l grant this request of your humble servant'. The outcome is unknown.

'The Dreadful Consequences of a Licentious Passion'

In 1714, the Corporation spent £6 10s to celebrate the proclamation of George I and sent an extravagant address to the new sovereign, expressing the hope that God would 'blast the attempts of any pretender that shall rise up against you'. Yet some of the local gentry were Jacobites: Sir William Keyte, recorder of Stratford and owner of the College, proclaimed the Pretender at Shipston and was removed as a Commissioner of the Peace. The oaths of Allegiance, Supremacy and Abjuration were administered at Stratford in 1723. Some 100 people signed a declaration against Popish doctrines, acknowledging 'before God and the World that our Sovereigne Lord King George is lawful rightfull King of this realm . . . And I doe sulumnly and sincerely declare that I doe Believe in my conscience, that the person pretended to be Prince of Wales, during the life of the late King James, and since his decease, pretending to be, and taking upon himself the style & Tytle of King of England by the name of James the Third . . .' was not what he claimed.

Amongst the signatories was Ann, wife of Sir William Keyte, who thus doubtless greatly offended her husband. Despite their numerous children, the Keytes were incompatible; a situation compounded when the lascivious eye of Sir William alighted on Mary Johnson, one of his wife's maidservants. His suspicious wife bribed the butler to reveal all and her unrepentant husband fled with his mistress and elder children to a house at Aston Subedge. After several years of increasing penury and irascibility, Sir William quarrelled with his mistress and children and threw them out. His fancies turned to a dairy maid, 'with no other beauty than what arrives from the bloom of youth'. Belated recognition of the harm he had done turned his mind. On a spring day in 1741 his remaining servants were alarmed to see smoke pouring from his bedroom. William Whiston, a Stratford tailor, who was delivering liveries, tried to pull him out and struggled with him, but the flames forced him to retire. All that remained of Sir William were the hip-bone, the vertebrae, some keys, a gold watch – and, of course, the huge debts, which obliged Lady Keyte to write a pleading letter to Mrs. Welchman of the *White Lion*. 'I shall deem it a great kindness if you will take all opportunities to assure those I owe money to in Stratford . . . that I will honourably pay what is due to them from me & pray don't let that bad woman Mrs. Ward come and kant at yr. house, for she has used me very ill.' Lady Keyte would have concurred with a contemporary judgement that the tragedy was 'the dreadful consequence of a licentious passion, not checked in its infancy'.

The End of the Bawdy Court

Those of less exalted rank continued to have assistance in checking their licentious passions. During the first decades of the 18th century, a trickle of penitents continued to appear at public confession. Some cases evoked public sympathy. A petition to the diocesan court in 1703 from neighbours prayed for a money commutation of a public penance imposed on William Smith and Susannah Hurdis, *alias* Smith, 'their marriage having been disolved as incestuous on the ground that she was sister to Jane his first wife'.

The case of Thomas Hudson, a weaver, provides the words used by penitents. He stood through Divine Service clad in the white sheet on 30 March 1716 and after the Nicene creed repeated after the Minister in 'a distinct and audible voice': 'I Thomas Hudson do here in the presence of God and this Congregation humbly confess and acknowledge that not having the word of God before mine eyes, but being seduced by the Devil and my own sinful lusts I have committed the foul sin of Adultery and have two bastard children unlawfully begotten . . . Whereby I have greatly offended Almighty God, endangered my own soul and gave an evil example and scandal to all good Christians, for which offence I am heartily sorry and do humbly beg pardon of God and this congregation for the same hereby promising (God assisting me with his Grace) never to offend in the like again, but to live more chastely hereafter, asking this congregation to pray for me and with me to say, "Our Father . . ."'.

A few weeks later Sarah Adams made an identical confession, the minister substituting her name and offence of 'ffornication' for Hudson's on the sheet, adding that she had borne a child 'begotten on her body by William Edes the younger', a butcher who had fled before the charges were brought. Eleonor, wife of Thomas Marshall, cordwainer, performed semi-public penance for ante-nuptial fornication and confessed 'most devoutly and solemnly'. Either the same Eleonor, or a namesake of Shottery, 'singlewoman', confessed fornication with Thomas Horsly 'and by him had a bastard child, though I wrongfully charged it upon one Thomas Green, who never had knowledge of my body'.

This ceremony of humiliation and redemption was accepted by saints and sinners alike as an act of penance in which offender and congregation participated. The last extant case was that of Ann Edwards who confessed fornication in 1733. Within two decades Stratford's first newspaper arrived on the scene. *Keating's Stratford, Shipston and Alcester Journal*, 'a good family paper', pursued the course later sanctified by overwhelming usage, providing succulent information about rapes, murders, executions and the peccadilloes of the famous: all lasciviously presented in a tone of unctuous condemnation. Public penance and pillory was delegated to the Fourth Estate.

Town Life

In 1724 occurred the last meeting of that useful body, the Court of Record, which, despite collapsing through lack of organisation, continued to provide a succession of Stewards. After an Act of Parliament granted overseers the authority to build workhouses and refuse relief to those unwilling to enter, a House of Correction for 'punishing & Employing the poor or other Disorderly persons belonging to this Burrough' was established in 1725 in Henley Street. In the same year Mrs. Sarah Woolmer, an Alderman's wife, donated £100 to instruct six poor boys and six poor girls 'born of honest parents' to 'reade a Chapter in the Bible, distinctly say the Creed, Lord's Prayer and Ten Commandments in the vulgar tongue and be fully instructed in the Church catechisme'. They were to be known as 'Mrs. Woolmer's Charity Children'.

In 1726 it was decided to give the Mayor-elect 'for the time being to come a present of halfe hogshead red wyne' in lieu of his entitlement of three dozen bottles. He was to select his vintage and the Chamberlains would pay. The coronation of George III was celebrated in due style in 1727 and five shillings was paid to 'ye Morris dancers' on the Queen's birthday in 1732. That year Sir Hugh Clopton gave an annual rent of £16 from Ingon Farm to provide a blue coat biennially for the 24 almsmen and women and to endow an Oak Apple Day sermon by the vicar in the Guild Chapel, for which he would receive one pound, the parish clerk five shillings, and each almsperson a shilling. The rest of the annuity was to buy straw hats and aprons for the almswomen, or was to be spent in any fit manner. At its next Hall, the Corporation 'fit and properly ordered that a bole of punch be prepared this evening to drinke to the good health of Sir Hugh Clopton, Knight'. In 1733, despite the Chamberlain being obliged to meet current deficits from his own pocket, five shillings was spent, with Shakespearean phraseology, on 'Cakes and Ale'. Yet financial stringency led to the abandonment, in 1736, of the custom of escorting the retiring Mayor home. Instead it was resolved that 'the late Mayor doe make a present to the new Mayor of a dozen of wine'.

There was antagonism to the Whig administration. The Corporation encouraged the County members to vote against Walpole's excise scheme in 1733. In the next year the burgesses declined to present a loyal address on the marriage of the Princess Royal to the Prince of Orange.

A familiar dispute with the Vicar re-emerged in 1735 concerning the appointment of a curate. Two senior lawyers, Sergeant Willes and Councillor Makepeace, awarded all costs against the Corporation and judged its claims 'illegal, Nay, Oppressive'.

'Ye Gentle Joseph'

A putative factor in Stratford's illegitimacy rate was two troops of dragoons, stationed in the town, at least from 1713 when £1 1s 6d was paid by the Chamberlains for 'Ale the Troopers drank'. Some at least appreciated their presence. 'All things are *in statu quo* at our Town', wrote the Reverend Joseph Greene to his brother in 1735, 'excepting that the Landlord and his lady at ye Crown in ye Highstreet, have battled it out to some purpose very lately. I can't imagine what's the matter with the man, but to be sure he damn'd her grievously t'other day, only because he catch'd her in bed with a Trooper: one wou'd think he might put up with such trifles as those, but he swears he won't bear it, neither will he.' Another letter declares that 'we encounter as many Fools and Knaves as ever; but run some risque of having more Whores and Bastards before ye Feast of St Michael next; especially if our Pacifick forces alias Review-Warriors continue to quarter upon us.'

Joseph Greene was another civilised and humane clergyman who flourished at Stratford.

Born at Shipston in 1712, he became curate at Preston-on-Stour in 1734, which he combined with the post of master of Stratford School. In 1736 he fell in love with Cecilia ('Tilly'), daughter of Richard Bartlett, an apothecary who was twice Mayor. The courtship was opposed by Bartlett's third wife, Martha, desirous of cementing her alliance by providing Tilly for her own son. 'I wonder Miss', she would say to her step-daughter, 'you'll be so much with Jo. Greene' and she persuaded Bartlett to forbid the relationship. Greene passed his time composing scurrilous verses about the Bartletts and plotting his revenge, which occurred on 17 July 1737. 'I took Miss Tilly privately to my Church at Preston & there I married her; the consequence you may easily guess at; Stratford bells ringing, and all ye old women in ye town hobbling up and down the streets to spread the News. Our friends laughing and rejoicing without ceasing; The father of the Bride sometimes meloncholy & then raving and weeping by turns; the old Mother-in-law whisking about as if stung by a Gad-bee, with her face as red as a newbrick, & fuming like an old smoakers tobacco pipe; We in ye interim wisely took occasion to keep out of these fits of various madness, & bedded together at Parson Holyoakes at Wolverton where we were to blame if we did not make one another hearty amends for being kept so long at so great a distance.'

Throughout this letter to his brother Greene calls his bride 'the good ship Cecilia' and himself 'a mid siz'd privateer called ye Gentle Joseph'.

'The Strolers'

A letter of Greene's in 1734 mentions the arrival of a company of actors in Stratford. He does not record who they were, or what or where they performed, but he does not regard the event as remarkable, so such visits were not infrequent. A local poet, William Somerville, wrote a *Prologue for the Strolers at Stratford-upon-Avon:*

> We to this place where Shakespeare dwelt of old,
> On foot, on horseback, or in carts have strol'd.
> Be kind this night, each honest score we'l quitt
> And give for sterling money, sterling wit.

Perhaps this was written for Roger Kemble's Company. In 1740 they presented a 'Speaking Musical Pantomime', entitled *Harlequin's Invasion or Shakespeare Triumphant,* which it was reckoned would 'certainly give real pleasure to the inhabitants of this polite circle where the immortal bard first drew breath'. The dialogue was 'universally allowed to be the masterpiece of the celebrated David Garrick', then 23 and in the first flush of fame. This high priest of the growing cult of Bardolatry visited Stratford in the summer of 1744, with his fellow actors Denis Delane and Charles Macklin. They paid the obligatory visit to the famous mulberry tree at New Place, 'planted by Shakespeare's own hand', which Sir Hugh Clopton loved to show visitors. Neither Stratford nor Garrick could know how their futures were intertwined.

The first recorded performance of the poet's work in Stratford occurred through a curious process. By 1746 natural decay and the depredations of souvenir hunters had reduced Shakespeare's bust in Holy Trinity to a lamentable state. Joseph Greene resolved to restore it and enlisted the aid of John Ward, whose company of actors had recently played at the Town Hall. Ward 'very genteely' offered to perform a play by Shakespeare and donate the profits towards the appeal. The play that evening was *Othello,* with Ward in the title role and 'several Entertainments of SINGING, between the ACTS'. Greene wrote a prologue '& received greater marks of respect ... than I could have presum'd to expect'. It was spoken by 'ye ingenious Mr. Ward, who entered fully into my sentiments & expressed every sentence as I could wish, with ye justest Emphasis & most exact propriety, notwithstanding he had the composition but a very short time in his possession'. He considered the company 'much ye best set I have seen out of London, & in which opinion I am far from being singular. Ye characters . . . (except that of Brabantio) were well presented, & the whole conducted with much decorum, & in consequence, applause'.

The performance raised seventeen pounds. A limner, John Hall, was engaged to repair and 'beautify' the monument. Greene had not anticipated the foibles of the woodenheaded churchwarden, John Spur, a blacksmith, who refused to sign the contract with Hall, 'ridiculously vaunting it that his word would go for 100 pounds'. He was finally prevailed upon to. declare that when the monument was completed, he would pay the money without delay. The restoration was meticulous. 'Care was taken', recorded Greene, '. . . not to add or to diminish what ye work consisted of, & appeared to be, when first erected.' The restored colouring offended the taste of the age. 'Lady Caroline Petersham is not more vermillion', complained Horace Walpole on a visit in 1757.

Greene's talent for historical research enabled him to find a copy of Shakespeare's will in the diocesan records in 1747. He was depressed by his discovery, regarding the document as 'so dull and irregular, so absolutely void of ye least particle of that spirit which Animated our great Poet, that it must lessen his Character as a writer, to imagine ye least sentence of it his production'. Contemporary sensibility demanded that even the poet's last testament should be in blank verse.

Extant play-bills show that other companies of actors played at Stratford. Charles Booth, the founder of a famous theatrical dynasty, played Hamlet there in 1758. The Kembles returned in 1763. No record remains of their performance, but on 12 February 'Mary, daughter of Roger Kemble, Comedian', was baptised at Holy Trinity. They returned five years later to perform Tate's dissected version of *King Lear* with its happy ending at 'The Histrionic Academy' in the Rother Market. Mrs. Kemble played Cordelia and Mr. Siddons, Albany, while Miss Sarah Kemble, aged 13, sang. A fortnight later, the season closed with a benefit performance of *As You Like It*. Mr. Siddons played Orlando; Mrs. Kemble, Celia and Miss Kemble, Phoebe. This prodigy is better known as the subsequent wife of Mr. Siddons.

'The Devil, doubtless'

On 13 January 1743 Stratford became part of John Wesley's world parish. 'I had scarce sat down', he recorded in his *Journal*, 'before I was informed that Mrs. K., a middle-aged woman of Shottery . . . had been many weeks past in a way which nobody could understand; that she had sent to a minister, but almost as soon as he came began roaring in so strange a manner (her tongue at the same time hanging out of her mouth, and her face distorted into the most terrible form) that he cried out, "It is the devil, doubtless! It is the devil," and immediately went away . . . I asked "what good do you think I can do?" "One cannot tell but Mrs. K. earnestly desired you might come, if you was anywhere near, saying she had seen you in a dream, and should know you immediately:" but the devil had said . . . "I will tear thy throat out before he comes." But afterwards she said his words were, "If he does come, I will let thee be quiet, and thou shalt be as if nothing ails thee till he is gone away."

'A very odd kind of madness this! I walked over about noon, but when I came to the house, desired all those with me to stay below . . . I went straight to her room. As soon as I came to the bed-side she fixed her eyes and said, "You are Mr. Wesley. I am very well now, I thank God; nothing ails me; only I am weak." I called them up and we began to sing . . . After singing a verse or two we kneeled down in prayer. I had but just begun (my eyes being shut) when I felt as if I had been plunged into cold water, immediately there was such a roar that my voice was quite drowned, though I spoke as loud as I usually do to three or four thousand people. However I prayed on. She was then reared up in the bed, her whole body moving at once, without bending one joint or limb just as if it were one piece of stone. Immediately after it was writhed into all kinds of postures, the same horrid yell continuing still. But we left her not until all the symptoms ceased, and she was (for the present at least) rejoicing and praising God.'

Later Wesley preached at the Market Cross. 'Most of the hearers stood like posts, but some mocked, others blasphemed and a few believed.' Despite Wesley's visit and exorcism, Joseph Greene could tell his bishop in 1764 that 'about 30 years past there was a monthly meeting of the People called Quakers in the Town, but they too have wholly now quitted it, and no Dissenters of any sort remain, unless a few illiterate mechanic Methodists deserve that Appelation, who venture not however to enlist their nonsense except in some private families.'

Energy and Inertia

That Georgian necessity, a spa, known as 'Perry's Mineral Spring', was modestly established in 1744, 'at the end of a cornland' in Shottery Fields. Edward Wyles, a dragoon stationed at Stratford in Major-General St George's Regiment, had his right leg 'full of sores and breakings out for two years' which had baffled all treatments, so he tried the mineral water. Each morning he drank up to six pints and bathed his leg in it. In a few weeks he was cured. A devotee of the waters saw 'the vestiges or cicatrices of the many sores' on his leg. The waters cured another dragoon of violent diarrhoea. Leonard Sherrington, Warden of the Tower of London, hearing of the water's 'great character', tried it and his 'persistent gout was cured'.

Between 1726 and 1769 the local main roads were turnpiked. The improvement was relative. 'The roads are not only very slippery, but in some places deep,' wrote the Nonconformist divine, Dr. Doddridge from Stratford in 1743, 'and we had thirty-three gates between this and the last market town, most of them very heavy, and made fast with latches.'

However, improved transport spelt disaster for the town's staple industry of malting. 'Since the Roads have been made so good that Business is Cheifly Transferred to Birmingham. There was upwards of 60 Officers Formerly Employed in Town for that purpose, but now there is no more than 20.' The resultant slump led the Corporation to seek advice about establishing a permanent debt in 1744, although this was not undertaken for another 30 years.

Economic decline was paralleled in civic life. Despite fines and exhortations, many Corporation meetings were abandoned as inquorate. Even the constables were fined in 1745 for 'not attending to proclaim the Fair'. When burgesses moved away, they could not be released from office lest failure to replace them led to the collapse of the flimsy structure of local government. Yet Stratford was fortunate in its town clerk, Thomas Hunt, who, from his appointment in 1750, initiated virtually every positive policy pursued by the Corporation. Corruption played its part in the system. In 1753, Mr. Pixell of Worcester, a young gentleman of 'taste and good family' who was seeking a situation in the town, sought the advice of Mr. John Reynolds of Wooten Wawen. He said that the only way he knew, was for Mr. Pixell's father to get nine or ten aldermen drunk and 'consequently they would be friends to the son'. Stratford was not unique, for he added that 'This kind of proceeding prevails in England sooner than merit.'

The decay was reflected in the appearance of the town. Visitors commented on its dilapidated state. Horace Walpole, who should have appreciated a Gothick ruin, found Stratford, 'the wretchedest old town that I ever saw, which I intended to find snug and pretty, and *antique*, not old'. Insanitary conditions prevailed. The ditch along Chapel Lane was the receptacle for 'all manner of Filth that any person chose to put there and was very obnoxious at Times'. The inevitable *sequila* was disease. The plague had exhausted its virulence, but a new scourge had emerged from the East. 'The small-pox is ruining my school as fast as it can', wrote Joseph Greene in 1747 with heart-felt understatement. A survey in 1765 showed that 1,260 of the Borough's 2,287 inhabitants had suffered the disease.

Yet some saw rural virtues and were oblivious to the poverty. 'Stratford', enthused one writer, 'is most pleasantly and happily situated upon the fine navigable Avon. It is a country of beauty, plenty and cheapness and the town is very neat and is capable of accomodating a considerable number of strangers'. Alveston Field, which was some five miles in circumference, had been 'with great justice' styled 'The Montpelier of England' because of its fine hard gravel soil. 'But if it is condusive to health on the one hand, it is no less adapted to those rural recreations which almost all gentlemen delight in on the other; such as hunting, shooting and riding as an exercise.'

Little John Jordan

Basic education was still available to the humblest. As soon as John Jordan, the wheelwright's son, could walk he went to school to 'a poor old woman' in Tiddington. He learned to write in a horn book. Soon after 'one Kemsley came and taught . . ., a man whom Nature had left unfinished for he came into the world with only one hand . . . Being thus incapacitated from labours he was bred to letters and . . . being of an unfettled and whimsical Eccentric turn of mind he was weak enough to put some confidence in judicial Astrology and Occult Philosophy: in which sciences he vainly thought himself so great a proficient that he could as Shakespear says "Conjure spirits from the vasty deep" and which experiment he had the vanity to try, but failing in the enterprise it affected his mind to such a degree that he became Meloncholy, which affliction he attempted to avert with the charms of the bottle. . . in a short time his faculties were damaged and he grew distracted and was obliged to give up his school . . . Among all his fits of Paroxism he. . . beat many of the scholars most unmercifully', but he treated little John with the 'most tender respect'. Not surprisingly, he was soon the only pupil left. One day Kemsley declared in a flood of tears that he could teach no more, but he was sorry they must be parted. He was sent to an asylum where he was 'perfectly cured . . . and was many years after a teacher at Aulcester'. Perhaps poor Kemsley exercised a formative influence over Jordan's later career as an inventor of legends. In 1756, when he was ten, John left school. There were five younger children at home, and to help support them, he worked with his father as a wheelwright. Even after he was 18 he was obliged to work without wages to keep his siblings, 'who have since treated me with the most excessive ingratitude especially after the decease of my Father and Mother'.

'The Reverend Destroyer'

Sir Hugh Clopton had maintained the aristocratic tradition of freely opening mansions to the curious. His successor was in a different mould. The Reverend Francis Gastrell, a Canon Residentiary of Lichfield Cathedral, acquired New Place in 1753, but felt 'no sort of pride or pleasure in this charming retirement, no consciousness of being possessed of the sacred ground which the Muses had consecrated to the memory of their favourite poet'. It is a measure of this wealthy cleric's obnoxiousness that he even stirred the Corporation from its lethargy by evicting tenants and indulging in long wrangles over his poor rates. Matters were exacerbated by the steady tramp of the visitors whom Sir Hugh had welcomed so freely, but whose demanding presence tried the limited patience of this irascible parson. As his temper grew he rationalised his disagreeable humour so that the celebrated mulberry tree became the focus of his disaffection. He considered it overshadowed his windows and made the house damp. In 1756 he screwed his courage to the chopping place. One John Ange did the dastardly deed by night. Next morning all that remained of the living link with Stratford's most cherished son was a pile of logs in the yard.

'The people of Stratford were seized with grief and astonishment when they were informed of this sacrilegious act and nothing less than the destruction of the offender in the first transport of their rage would satisfy them. The miserable culprit was forced to skulk up and down to save himself from the Stratfordians, who as a first instalment of their terrible revenge, alleviated their fury by breaking the reverend destroyer's windows.' Amidst this vehement chaos, one man realised his hour had come. Thomas Sharpe, clockwinder and repairer to the Corporation, purchased the remains of the tree and transferred them to his premises over the way. He realised that cults require relics. The mulberry-wood would satisfy an insatiable demand. He was to create sufficient objects from the 'original' wood to consume groves of mulberry trees. In 1768 one Judith Brawne denied rumours that he had bought more mulberrywood from her family. After he acquired a walnut tree growing in front of the Birthplace, a verse on the master and his craftsman circulated in the town:

> Gastrell the Mulberry Tree cut down
> Tom Sharp he cut it up;
> But Gwinnett turns a Walnut Tree
> Into a Mulberry Cup.

Sharp's sales technique was cunningly simple. He nailed a piece of the real tree to his workbench and placed one hand on it while disposing of the spurious article with the other, declaring to his credulous customer: 'I do solemnly swear that I hold in my hand a portion of the tree Shakespeare himself planted'.

All was not over between Parson Gastrell and Stratford. In 1758 he petitioned to demolish three barns, but was told that he must pay full land tax. The Corporation should have known that the iconoclast was liable to act erratically when upset. When an effort was made to extract the full poor rate for New Place, despite Gastrell's frequent absence, he angrily declared *'that* house should never be assessed again'. In 1759 he razed it to the ground and left Stratford 'amidst the rage and curses of the inhabitants'. According to one report, the populace solemnly vowed never to allow anyone of the same name reside in Stratford again. It was fortunate that the perpetrator of the outrages was not a Smith or Jones!

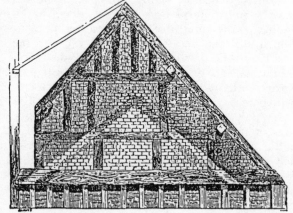

17. *A drawing by J. T. Blight, c.1860, showing the building line of Shakespeare's New Place on adjoining property.*

In fact little remained of Shakespeare's New Place, for in 1700 Sir Hugh Clopton had completely rebuilt the property. The surly Gastrell lost a considerable investment by his eccentric action and his rage turned to self-pity. 'I shall hardly ever entertain any thought of returning', he wrote to Hunt, 'to a place where I have been so maltreated.' He gained a pyrrhic revenge on the Corporation by being in continuous debt with his poor rates. 'This is not payd' was still being recorded against his assessment 20 years later.

Despite the loss of this attraction, the number of visitors viewing such aspects of the town as might be evocative of the 'Immortal Shakespeare' continued to increase. Stratford's most celebrated inn was the *White Lion* in Henley Street, which boasted a 'bill of fare equal to that of the Piazza Coffee House, Covent Garden'. The proprietor was the ebullient John Payton, who 'by a secret peculiar to publicans of making general favours appear particular ones . . . brought the house into great vogue'. He did much to stimulate the nascent tourist trade, even providing that trippers' essential, an excursion. In 1762, a correspondent of the *British Magazine* stayed there. The 'cheerful landlord' showed him the Birthplace and was 'so complaisant' as to accompany him to visit two young women, 'lineal descendents of the great poet', who kept a little alehouse near Bidford. On the way, he showed him a crab tree, called 'Shakespear's Canopy' where the young poet was said to have spent the night after a drinking contest with

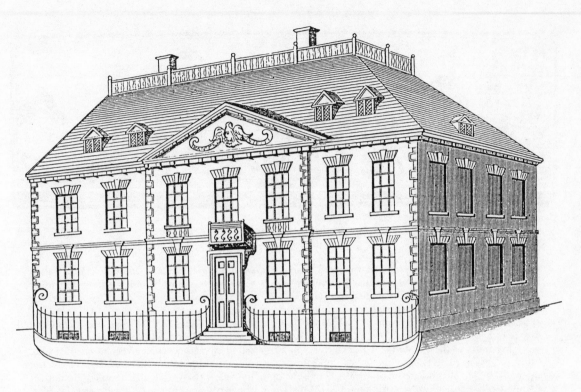

18. Drawing of New Place before demolition, ascribed by J. Halliwell to Winter and dating from 1759.

the local topers. When Joseph Greene heard this story of Shakespeare's imbibing, he considered it 'no more than the Fiction of some wag'.

A Sporting Centre

Stratford was becoming a noted racing centre, with a course in Shottery Fields. A ballad recorded its hazards:

> Many a good 'un was down on his luck
> When he first clapped his ogles on Shottery brook.

The annual meeting at the end of August was a 'great source of amusement to the neighbourhood and sporting world', which chose as its meeting-place the *King's Head* in the Rother Market.

More reprehensible sports occurred. Joseph Greene wrote a furious letter to the *Oxford Journal* in 1767 which must be quoted in full for its vigour and sincerity:

The Deities of Stupidity, Avarice and Cruelty, conscious of the Influence they have over that numerous and sagacious corps of this Kingdom called the Mob and how many virtues they can enumerate in the Town of Stratford in particular, have given notice that they intend to hold their solemn Festival in the said Town, on ye approaching 3d day of March, commonly called Shrove Tuesday, when it is expected that there will be a temporary infraction of every social law: to make amends for which, the following Irregulations will be observed.

First, in imitation of the Ancient Heathens (an excellent pattern undoubtedly for Christians), a spacious Altar of turf will be erected within the Licensed precincts of a Mansion dedicated to Bacchus or some other inferior though equally reeling Deity; some laudable deviations will be however made

19. Stratford Races, by James Saunders.

from the early items of simplicity; for instead of killing noxious animals, certain Domestick Birds called Cocks will be despoiled of the beautiful plumage which nature gave them, be obliged to mount upon the Turf almost naked (like half their spectators) and be encouraged by way of sacricice to tear one another to pieces, to the excessive sport of the pious Devotees that surround them.

Secondly, none will be initiated or admitted to a participation of these sacred mysteries below the degree of a scoundral, whether with or without a shirt, from the small striped ostler's waistcoat to the glittering tunic of the steady-fac'd Buck; unless he promises to swear and curse every moment, to lie, bully and over-reach as often as he has opportunity, like the rst of the infernal Associates; and in the intervals of the Solemn Rites of Sharping, Gambling and Hooking with avaricious triumph, gulph down plentiful Libations of intoxicating liquors, 'till the woul'd be gentleman & ye chimney sweep lovingly unite in the same edifying conversation.

Greene's letter had its effect. The Mayor issued a proclamation prohibiting cock-fighting which the town-crier shouted through the streets on Shrove Tuesday morning. 'Which notice,' wrote Greene, 'however mortifying, was duly complied with; and thus for once I procur'd the poor innocent cocks a reprieve.'

'Small Beginnings'

Old controversies were stirring. In 1766, the Corporation resolved unanimously to oppose 'by all lawful means' any petition presented to Parliament for enclosing Stratford or Bishopton fields. Support was enlisted and plans for resistance prepared.

Early in 1769 Stratford's innkeepers petitioned the Secretary for War that 'the great unusual No. of Dragoons in this small borough is a most heavy oppression upon the Inhabitants – and must infallibly reduce many of the lower victuallers to Distress and Ruin and bring their families upon the Parish, which must eventually greatly injure and oppress those who are now scarcely able to bear the present heavy Load of Taxes'. The soldiers had brought smallpox, which was 'raging throughout the Town' for the first time in many years. The reason for Stratford's poverty was clear. 'There is no manufacture in this place.' The petition brought temporary relief when the dragoons were transferred to Warwick.[1]

Despite the vilification Gastrell received for knocking down a building, it was clear that, unless urgent steps were taken, the town's chief edifices would collapse of their own volition. The wooden bell tower at Holy Trinity was removed in 1762. The indefatigable Joseph Greene raised £250 to build the stone spire which still reigns over the church. In April 1767, the Corporation agreed to rebuild the Town Hall, which was in 'a dangerous and Ruinous State', but restricted its own contribution to £200. Since the lowest estimate was £678, William Hunt compiled a list of potential donors. A number of local worthies subscribed, but a substantial shortfall remained. A single gift of an appropriate object for the new building might stimulate largesse. In common realisation, two men decided independently that David Garrick, then at the height of his fame, would be the ideal benefactor. 'The Common Observation', it was said later, 'that great events have small beginnings was *never* more verified than in the progress of Shakespeare's Jubilee!' This beginning was no more than an empty niche above the entrance of the new Town Hall.

FOOTNOTE
[1]   The transfer was fortuitous in view of the great Jubilee in the following September.

CHAPTER 9

'The Lad of all Lads'

'For the lad of all lads was a Warwickshire lad.'

Jubilee song, 1769.

'A Proper Letter'

On a trip to London in 1767, Francis Wheler, Steward of the defunct Court of Record, learned of David Garrick's adoration of anything Shakespearean and his susceptibility to grand flattery. He thought that it would be 'an ornament' to the Town Hall if Garrick could be persuaded to donate a 'Handsom present'. A means towards this might be to make the actor an honorary burgess. The Corporation agreed, so he wrote 'a proper letter', which was delivered by George Yeate, a minor poet and acquaintance of the actor. A judicious balance of boldness and deference was observed.

> It would be a Reflection on the Town of Stratford to have any publick Building erected here without some Ornamental Memorial of their immortal Townsman, And the Corporation would be happy in receiving from your hands some statue Bust or Picture of him to be placed within this Building, they would be equally pleased to have some Picture of Yourself that the Memory of both may be perpetuated together in that town wch gave him birth & where he still lives in the mind of every inhabitant – The Corporation of Stratford ever desirous of expressing their Gratitude to all who do Honor & Justice to the Memory of Shakespeare, & highly sensible that no person in any Age hath Excelled you therein would think themselves much honoured if you would become one of their Body; Tho' this Borough doth not now send members to Parliament, perhaps the Inhabitants may not be the less Virtuous and to render the Freedom of such a place the more acceptable to you the Corporation propose to send it in a Box made of that very Mulberry Tree planted by Shakespeare's own hand . . .

Doubtless Yeate provided an amusing account of Stratford's war with Parson Gastrell. The actor was delighted to accept this extraordinary honour. Wheler's letter was the spark that set Stratford alight. Garrick wrote on its back that it 'produc'd ye Jubilee'.

Meanwhile, John Payton of the *White Lion* was entertaining his friend George Alexander Stevens, the celebrated comedian. Hearing of local regrets that there was no statue of Shakespeare in the niche outside the new Town Hall, Stevens offered to approach Garrick, warning that the actor was fond of both praise and profit. While he would be flattered by the approach, he would seek to turn it to his financial advantage. Returning to London, he visited Garrick and sent Payton a vigorous letter:

> He informed me your Recorder had been with Him & told him about the bust of Shakespeare to be in the Town Hall – Out Sir was my answer. Mr. Recorder & the Corporation of Stratford want Shakespeare to be out – out I mean to Everybodys view . . .

Stevens thought that Garrick would produce the required gift and suggested the lines on which Payton should write: 'Set forth his great merits, & that there is not a man of greater propriety for a Bust or Statue, say Shakespear the father of the English stage, Garrick the Restorer of Shakespear – & some other such phrases for all great men love to be praised'.

90

The Jubilee was afoot. If Wheler was the first to approach Garrick it was Stevens who proposed the statue in the niche and a celebration to launch it, offering to compose an oration set to music. Given Garrick's showmanship, the extravaganza which followed was inevitable from the first.

'Warmth and Rapture'

The first priority was the preparation and exchange of the precious gifts so lavishly promised. The elaborate flattery of Garrick produced the desired effect. He determined to present a statue *and* a portrait of Shakespeare, commissioning John Cheere to cast a fine lead effigy. He dabbled with Thomas Gainsborough, but was shocked by the portraitist's lack of reverence towards the Bard, so commissioned instead a lesser but more complaisant artist, Benjamin Wilson.

The warning that Garrick would turn any situation to advantage was soon realised. In a neat reversal of position, he revived Wheler's proposal for a portrait of himself. It would appear vanity if he commissioned it, so the Corporation picked up bills from the reinstated Gainsborough and from the frame-maker, Thomas Davies of Edgbaston, who also carved the box. The Borough got infinite value for money, for Gainsborough created a happy portrait of an elegant Garrick embracing an amiable bust of Shakespeare.[1]

The cost of relations with Garrick was soaring, but there was no going back. On 11 October 1768 '. . . the greatest theatrical genius of the Age . . . who has done the highest Honor to the memory of the Immortal Shakespeare' was unanimously elected an honorary burgess. Garrick would have been gratified to know that he occasioned the first mention of Shakespeare in the minute book.

The presentation occurred next May in London. The Freedom was accepted 'with warmth' and the box 'with rapture'. At the close of the London season, Garrick invited his audience to join him in Stratford later that year. In June he visited the town and was received 'with public honours, bells ringing'. At a dinner at the *White Lion,* he outlined his plans with 'much perspecuity and to . . . perfect approval'. The scale of his proposal was staggering – to bring his personnel, properties and adherents to an obscure little town with no theatre and scant accommodation – and all this to be achieved in ten weeks.

The first question was vital. Who was to pick up the bills? The Corporation, although spellbound by Garrick, knew that the enterprise was beyond its resources. Thus Garrick agreed to bear the cost, aided by local supporters. Payton would take his own gamble by organising the accommodation and catering. The centrepiece would be a great rotunda on the Bancroft, where Garrick would deliver his 'Ode Upon dedicating a Building and erecting a Statue to Shakespeare'. The leading native composer, Dr. Arne, would compose some of the settings and an oratorio. A more reluctant composer was the talented Charles Dibdin, whose spendthrift ways had resulted in undue dependence on Garrick. This caused friction and, after a series of quarrels, he walked out.

Despite such setbacks, the number of events was escalating. Plans included civic banquets, a masked ball, a Shakespearean procession, a firework display and a horse-race: the latter the inspiration of a group of local gentlemen who gained Garrick's approval for this 'well-imagin'd thought'. The provisions to supply the anticipated 'Jubelites' would have sustained an army. Payton ordered a huge turtle and hired Gill the celebrated chef, brother of a noted Stratford drunk, to cook it. Three hundred waiters were engaged – they alone would place a severe strain on accommodation – empty houses were leased and 1,500 beds sent up from London. Despite this, due to accommodation difficulties, some Jubelites would be pitching tents in the common fields. Extra hands were employed to complete a new turnpike between Dudley and Stratford. Hunt had promised that Stratford would be beautified and set a splendid example by erecting an elegant pagoda in his riverside garden. Many Stratfordians – to the regret of the antiquarians – whitewashed their houses.

At the College, Garrick's brother George was in charge of technical preparations. The celebrated John French from Drury Lane was painting transparencies to adorn prominent buildings, but to work he needed an ample supply of drink and George's stimulating conversation. To clear the site for the Rotunda, riverside willows were felled, revealing a charming view of the bridge. The timber was bought by Thomas Sharpe 'of mulberry-wood notoriety', who found ample use for it during the ensuing celebrations.

The papers were full of the forthcoming Jubilee. 'To such a pitch of excitation was almost every individual throughout the country raised that a literary man . . . observed that the people of England were always falling out of one fit of madness into another and that the passion for Mr. Wilkes' politics had totally given place to Shakespeare-mania.' Not all the publicity was sympathetic. A man of Garrick's position and personality was bound to draw detractors and there were those who sensed the difficulty of the situation. It was equally inevitable that Stratford should not escape the attention of the sharp-witted. The confrontation of corrupt sophistication and rural naivete is traditionally comic and this would be a classic encounter. The papers were full of hilarious stories allegedly emanating from Stratford and many a legend was founded before the Jubilee began. To fulfil obligatory criteria, rural officialdom must be grasping and pompous. Whatever the Corporation's claims to the latter quality, it was surely abrogated from the former by its generous support for the Jubilee. Yet in a satirical piece in the *London Chronicle,* James Solas Dodd claimed that while staying at Stratford's principal inn he had overheard a meeting of the Corporation; '. . . several songs were sung, one of which for very obvious reasons was ordered never to be performed before any company but themselves'. The alleged 'anthem' was a parody of one of Garrick's songs for *A Winter's Tale:*

> Come brothers of Stratford, these flocks let us shear,
> Which bright as if washed-in our Avon appear.
> The coolest are they who from fleeces are free;
> And who are such trimmers, such trimmers are we?
> Sing Tantarara, Shear all, &c., &c..

It was announced that, to boost the local economy, Shakespeare's statue would wear a woollen nightcap and that 'the fat landlady at a noted inn fell out of a hayloft into the manger while she was practising the chamber scene in *Romeo and Juliet* with one of the candle snuffers'. A leading Stratfordian allegedly named his daughter 'Doll Tearsheet' in honour of the Bard, while the Mayor was supposedly taking lessons in deportment from Mr. Baddeley, 'who played the Lord Mayor of London in Richard III'. Many Stratfordians must have pondered the efficacy of this way of opening a Town Hall.

After feverish work the preparations were completed, although hammering was heard from the Rotunda to the last. A building had been created 'to make a lover of art sigh to think how soon it would be demolished'. French's elegant transparencies were hoisted into position: at the Birthplace a huge sun rose from the clouds over the inscription, 'Here dying clouds contend with growing light'. At the Town Hall Shakespeare rode a pegasus, flanked by his characters and lit by scores of back-lamps. Admiring crowds gathered, although those Stratfordians whose fundamentalism was compensation for their ignorance expressed apprehension at such idolatry, which they regarded as 'peculiarly entitled to the Vengeance of Providence'. The correspondent of the *St James Chronicle* was particularly scathing: 'The low people of Stratford-upon-Avon are without a doubt as ignorant as any in the whole island . . . I talked with many, particularly the old people, and not one of them but was frightened at the Preparations . . . Many of them thought that Mr. G--- would raise Devils, and fly in a Chariot about the Town'. The writer's comment on the discrepancy between the inhabitants and Stratford's greatest son was to be much repeated. 'Providence seems by producing Shakespeare and the rest of his Townsmen, to shew the two Extremes of Human Nature.' The man from the *Gentleman's*

20. The Jubilee Booth 'or Amphitheatre'; from the Gentleman's Magazine, *1769.*

Magazine found the inhabitants 'pursuing their occupations in the old dog-trot way, or staring with wonderful vacancy of Phiz at the preparations, the purpose of which they had very few ideas about'. The reports alarmed Garrick, who was not sure whether they were part of the hilarity, but wrote to Hunt of his concern in hearing that 'the Country People did not seem to relish our Jubilee . . . I suppose this may be a joke, but after all my trouble, pains, labor & Expense for their service & the honor of ye County, I shall think it very hard, if I am not to be receiv'd kindly by them.' Yet there was one area where the most ignorant Stratfordian exercised tolerance. 'They found our money worthy of acceptance', observed one correspondent.

By contrast, the correspondent of the *Public Ledger* was rarely enlightened in relating Stratford's problems to its poverty. The town was 'much worse than the ruins of St Giles, with a sort of people equally needy and equally desirable of removing their necessities by honourable means'.

Stratford filled up two weeks before the Jubilee. Cooks were working day and night in every available kitchen. Sedan chairs were trundled from London and Bath. 'If a person has but money', eulogised one reporter, 'he cannot stand in need of any article his desires may demand.' The bustle was not to everyone's taste. 'The company', reported the *Public Ledger's* fastidious correspondent, 'consisted not of persons whose rank in life was likely to do honour to the Festival; on the contrary, they consisted chiefly of itinerant hairdressers and figure dancers from the Theatres'. The priggish scribe was not long disappointed at the lack of names to drop. On 1 September, David and Eva-Maria Garrick set out, followed two days later by a great convoy of actors and musicians. The roads were congested with Jubilee traffic. 'All the inns and roads from London are filled', declared a traveller, 'as if an army was on the march.' Some avoided the congestion by taking to the water and a little fleet floated on an Avon swollen by summer rains.

Jubilee fervour touched James Boswell, newly returned from a Corsica in revolt against

Genoese tyranny. He had contracted venereal disease and his forthcoming marriage increased the necessity for a cure. To his delight, the pox-doctor agreed that a trip would be an admirable precursor to treatment and the young writer prepared an inevitable Corsican costume for the Masquerade Ball.

Garrick's apprehension about his reception was unjustified. He was greeted by 'joyful demonstrations', the Corporation delivering a formal welcome at his lodgings in Hunt's house. Those with foresight had booked accommodation and some odd households emerged. Many 'highly respectable' people lodged in the almshouses. The Duke of Dorset was with the Widow Hatton at Nash's House; the Whitmore's of Swine Street hosted a national hero in Admiral Rodney, while the Earl and Countess of Pembroke and the future Parliamentary star, Charles James Fox, boarded with Tom Sharpe. The number of mulberrywood souvenirs they obtained is unrecorded.

Joseph Craddock, a friend of Garrick's, lodged at 'a clean baker's'. His family were to dine at the *White Lion*, but there were so many loose horses around that the ladies could not safely alight. Fortunately the unflappable Payton appeared and led the coach round by another route. The inn was jammed with people, but he sat them in Mrs. Payton's bedroom until supper was served at a table on the landing.

At the *Bear*, a little band settled whose hope was to see the Jubilee founder. Most dangerous was Samuel Foote, the noted actor and satirist. The hilarity began when Charles Macklin discovered that they were lodged above the store of the pyrotechnicist, Dominic Angelo. In mock apprehension, Foote declared that 'a new Gunpowder Plot was being hatched against them. Should they be blown up, it would give the laugh so strong on Garrick's side . . . that were he to hear of it in the other world, he should be eternally unhappy.'

At the Birthplace Mrs. Hart was showing visitors 'the chair in which he used to sit when he wrote'. She soon tired of explaining her husband's descent from the poet's sister and temporarily assumed the name of Shakespeare. Her daughter of 14, in whom the imaginative discerned a likeness to Shakespeare, was a great attraction. In a moment of euphoria, Garrick's partner, James Lacy, announced that he would train her for the London stage. Fortunately there is no evidence that he did so.

The little town was beginning to creak under the seemingly endless arrivals. Visitors were diverted to outlying villages, but soon these were overflowing. 'Every Inn, House or Hovel now swarms with company; and the very stables are no longer confined to the reception of Horses, or even Grooms or Postilions, the Haylofts over them being cleared for the Reception of Families of the first Credit'. Hunt had recommended a charge of a guinea a night for lodgings, but the norm soon became the minimum. One arrival reflected poetically:

> To bed I must go – for which like a ninny
> I paid like my betters, no less than one guinea,
> For rolling – not sleeping – in linen so damp
> As struck my big toe ever since with the cramp.

It was too much for one Jubelite. On 21 September, the *London Post* attributed the death of John Henry Castle, 'at his lodgings in Clopton . . . to his having laid in damp sheets at Stratford-upon-Avon, where he went to amuse himself at the so much talked of Jubilee'.

During Jubilee week, crowds surged through the river meadows, where Angelo, 'looking another Marlborough', strode around selling fireworks. The noise of their explosion was exacerbated by the regular thumping of 30 small cannons. Showmen were exhorting the curious to inspect such sights as 'the surprising Porcupine boy with the man Tiger'. At the Masquerade warehouse in Chapel Street, ballgoers were sorting through costumes. A discreet silence was maintained about the ladies of the pavement who had followed their patrons to Stratford, although one correspondent sighed over the 'wenches . . . there was never any Paradise so plentifully or beautifully inhabited'.

'Let Beauty with the Sun Arise'

Early on Jubilee morning, the Garricks awoke to a serenade led by a recalcitrant Charles Dibdin, whose defiance had evaporated in a London denuded of fashion. The harmonies of his fantastically dressed singers vied with the dawn chorus under Garrick's window.

> Let Beauty with the Sun arise,
> To Shakespeare tribute pay,
> With heavenly smiles and sparkling Eyes,
> Give Grace and Lustre to the Day.
> Each smile she gives protects his Name
> What face shall dare to frown?
> Not Envy's self can blast the Fame,
> Which Beauty deigns to crown.

Garrick was enchanted by this compliment to Eva-Maria and apologised to Dibdin for his churlishness, although the musician declared that he 'knew what credit to give to his protestations'.

The singers moved round the town, serenading society beauties at their lodgings. Stratford was waking up and the thudding cannon on the Bancroft added to the swelling noise. Tiring of their original ditty, the singers broke into songs intended for performance later in the day. The theme was taken up by the resplendent band of the Warwickshire Militia. The testy correspondent of *Lloyd's Evening Post,* who had considered returning to London, was overwhelmed by 'this tumult of perfect satisfaction', although his euphoria was soon tempered by an encounter with an avaricious sedan chairman.

At eight o' clock, the Corporation, fully robed, assembled at the Guildhall to elect a new Mayor and then process to the Town Hall. It is not to be doubted that the fashionable wags greeted the little column with every weary Stratford joke uttered in the preceding weeks.

At the Town Hall, William Hunt presented Garrick with his insigniae as Steward of the Jubilee: a medal and a wand of the inevitable mulberrywood. Garrick, splendid in a gold and brown suit, made a short, graceful speech before the company donned its Jubilee ribbons and devoured breakfast. The movement was then to Holy Trinity where Dr. Arne was conducting his Oratorio, *Judith.* Leading singers performed the airs 'in the best style', but the choruses were sung by enthusiasts amongst the Jubelites and were thin. The Oratorio over, crowds inspected Shakespeare's monument, so decked with bay leaves that it 'resembled the God Pan in an old picture'.

Garrick's conversation with a group of admirers was interrupted by the arrival of a weird and filthy young man, with long dank hair and wearing a scruffy grey coat. To everyone's surprise Garrick warmly greeted this strange creature. The newcomer was James Boswell who had arrived at noon, having ridden postilion in a coat borrowed from a small groom. On crossing the Avon he was overwhelmed by 'those feelings which men of enthusiasm have on seeing remarkable places'. He went to the *White Lion* in the forlorn hope of finding accommodation, but that fortune which pursues the young and charming was with him. A maid directed him to Mrs. Harris, an old woman who lived opposite the Birthplace, who, for a guinea a night, let him 'a tolerable old-fashioned room with a neat, clean bed'.

Boswell was elated by the gathering in the church. 'My bosom glowed with joy when I beheld a numerous and brilliant company of nobility and gentry, the rich, the brave, the witty and the fair, assembled to pay their tribute to Shakespeare.' Although he missed the Oratorio, he reviewed it euphorically for the *Scots Magazine*, adding the pious wish that there had been prayers and a short sermon. 'It would have consecrated our jubilee to begin it with an act of devotion.' On greeting Garrick, Boswell slipped him a note, 'to let him know I was incognito, as I wished to appear in the Corsican dress for the first time they should know me'. Many of the onlookers asked who the curious stranger was. 'A clergyman in disguise', Garrick replied.

Outside, a procession formed behind the singers and musicians. Niceties of rank were forgotten in the good-humoured crowd. At the Birthplace a new chorus burst forth:

> Here Nature nurs'd her darling Boy,
> From whom all care and sorrow fly,
> Whose Harp the Muses strung:
> From Heart to Heart let Joy rebound,
> Now, now we tread the enchanted Ground,
> Here Shakespeare walk'd and sung.

At four, the movement was to the Rotunda for dinner. Such was the crush that the less honest diners escaped without paying and the less honest waiters pocketed cash, leaving Payton out of pocket. Ribaldry about Stratford continued, scurrilous verses circulating about its chief magistrate:

> The Mayor scarse able to keep ope his Eyes
> Peeped at the food . . .
> & licked his lips (to stir in vain he tryes)
> At length as sweet in soft arms he stretches
> The snoring magistrate be sh't his Breeches.

As the meal closed, Garrick's health was proposed. He replied with 'the truest liveliness and hilarity'. The reporter from the *Gentleman's Magazine*, who had enjoyed the wine, led three cheers for Garrick as the orchestra and singers appeared to perform *Shakespeare's Garland*. Soloists were the tenor Joseph Vernon and Mrs. Sophia Baddeley, a soprano of great beauty of voice and form, whose profligacy always guaranteed interest. Scores were available, so the Jubelites thundered the choruses. After the already-obligatory *Warwickshire Lads*, Mrs. Baddeley sang the Jubilee's most popular and silly lyric:

> The pride of Nature was sweet Willy O,
> The first of all the swains,
> He gladden'd the plains,
> None ever was like to Sweet Willy O.

After the concert a group of young enthusiasts seized a mulberry cup which Vernon had used in a song. 'Nothing would satisfy them till it was filled with the best of wines that they might have the pleasure to drink to the memory of the Immortal Bard.' There followed the Jubilee's most charming scene. *En route* for his lodgings, the cup bearer met some friends who requested the pleasure of drinking what they called 'Shakespeare's ale' from the cup. It was filled in a nearby alehouse and passed round 'every lad and lass, as well as every Darby and Joan'. A Jubelite with a good voice sang Jubilee songs and all joined in jolly dancing. A spirit of goodwill prevailed. As the Jubelites emerged for the Ball, they found that the Stratfordians had 'testified their Joy' by illuminating their windows, which 'made the Night as cheerful as the Day'.

The Rotunda was transformed into a fairy palace, lit by a thousand lamps. The floor was soon crowded with dancers. James Boswell appeared to inspect the company 'and to be able to say I had been there.' He was so tired that he could hardly stand, so he went home to bed. 'My landlady got me warm negus and seemed to be a good motherly woman. I told her that perhaps I might retire from the world and just come to live in Stratford.'

Samuel Foote went to bed with less satisfaction. Things had gone too well, but the winds blowing up the Avon even as the dancers danced would bring the disruption he desired. The Corporation took no chances with the London wags. Two men were hired to guard the statue of Shakespeare in the Rotunda. They would have heard the first patter on the roof. When Stratford woke, sheets of rain poured down, filling the gutters and the sodden meadows while the Avon rose relentlessly.

A Wet Ode

A depressed David Garrick surveyed the dreary scene from Hunt's window. On the crucial morning the one chance item, the weather, had failed him. To make matters worse, his barber, perhaps suffering a hangover, cut his chin while shaving him. Pulling himself together, he went to the College, where 145 actors from Drury Lane mingled in confusion with the locals selected to process with them. James Lacy greeted his partner with unanswerable invective. 'Who the devil, Davy, would venture forth upon the procession under such a lowering aspect? Sir, all the ostrich feathers will be spoiled and the property will be damnified five thousand pounds!'

But if the procession were abandoned, what of the Ode, which depended on the carnival atmosphere it would engender? And what of the assembled enthusiasts and carping critics, now breakfasting in the Town Hall? Garrick took the bold and only decision. The orchestra and singers were dispatched to the Rotunda; 500 leaflets were run off, announcing that the pageant was postponed, but that the Ode would be performed.

At noon a damp audience packed the Rotunda. Garrick was aware that a pack of literary wolves was waiting to pounce and looked nervous as he took the rostrum to waves of applause. He paused for Arne's overture, raised his voice and spoke:

> To what blest genius of the isle
> Shall Gratitude her tribute pay . . .?

His ascendency was total. 'He never showed more powers', wrote James Solas Dodd. The highly critical correspondent of the *London Chronicle* acknowledged that 'after all the expense, fatigue and disappointment . . . we were overpaid by a single recitation of the Ode . . . [which] . . . gave so perfect a satisfaction that I should not hesitate at another Stratford expedition to hear it'. With his gift for combining artistry and novelty, Garrick had devised a new dramatic form: a recitative monologue to music. His three lady singers were closed in so that 'their musical punctuation to Garrick's mellifluous voice came like a crash of thunder'. Frequent applause interrupted the performance. Such was its power that many considered they had heard a masterpiece, rather than the mundane composition objective examination showed the Ode to be.

There was even solidarity in the fight against Enclosure:

> And may no sacrilegious hand,
> Near Avon's banks be found,
> To dare to parcel out the land,
> And limit Shakespeare's hallow'd ground.

As Mrs. Baddeley sang the closing lines

> Thou soft-flowing Avon by the silvery stream
> Of things more than mortal, sweet Shakespeare would dream
> The fairies by midnight dance round his green bed,
> for hallow'd the turf which pillow'd his head.

the huge doors of the Rotunda opened to reveal the Avon, anything but soft-flowing, the sort of touch for which Garrick's instinct was unerring. The audience burst into wild applause and the benches gave way in a domino effect, culminating in a door crashing down, injuring several spectators.

When the debris and wounded were removed, Garrick recited Milton's sonnet on Shakespeare and boldly asked if anyone wished to make a contribution. The comedian Tom King emerged and launched into an extravagant parody of the critics of the Jubilee. Not surprisingly, this met a mixed response. Garrick made a mild defence, embroidered around an appeal to the ladies to protect the reputation of the Bard, and the audience spilled into the rain.

Despite Garrick's brilliance, the spirit of the Jubilee was lost. As the Avon rose, so did the exasperation of the Jubelites, slowly realising that they were marooned in a ramshackle little town. Amidst this gloom, one man's hour had come. From Samuel Foote flowed joke after joke about Garrick, the Jubilee and Stratford. This masterly humorist made an elaborate jest of the entire town, not inventing stories, but exaggerating outrageously. He claimed he was charged nine guineas for six hours sleep[2] and two shillings when a local told him the time. The theme was taken up by his circle and the tall-story became the Stratford joke. It was claimed that 'an eminent actor was charged a shilling every time he repaired to the *Temple of the Graces* at a particular Inn and that those rated at eighteenpence . . . who did not lodge in the house' and that the chickens were only half plucked because the cook felt that, since the visitors were so overcharged, 'they should have their property entire'.

It was not the visiting gentry who claimed discomfort, but the fastidious press corps. At the next event, the dinner where Gill's huge turtle was eaten and claret drunk, one correspondent declared that 'we might as well have been regaled on neck of Beef and Southampton port'.

Garrick's distress about the weather was shared by Dominic Angelo. The Stratfordians had shown lively interest in his huge firework display and huge crowds gathered, but the event was a damp squib. A few pieces fizzed into the night before a regretful announcement postponed the show until the following evening.

Masquerade

The Ode inspired James Boswell to write verses on the inevitable subject of Corsica. Delighted with his effort, he rushed round to one Fulke Weale, who 'advertised printing at an hour's notice, I suppose taking for granted that Stratford would produce a general poetic inspiration which would exert itself every hour . . . But Mr. Angelo's fireworks turned his head and made him idle. He preferred them to all poetical fire.' So Boswell went round to the bookseller and printer, Mr. Keating, who had a lad called Shank. 'I found him a clever, active fellow and set him to work directly.'

As the waters rose, exotically-clad masqueraders struggled over the soggy Bancroft to the Rotunda. The confusion afforded fine entertainment for the locals. 'A young gentleman of London, very eminent in the musical way', fell into a ditch. He grabbed a stump and clung to it while shouting for help. A gallant masquerader who went to his aid also slipped in. Fortunately the Stratfordians suspended their hilarity long enough to rescue them.

The interior of the Rotunda was now surmounted by the Imperial Crown made from multi-coloured lights. The arduous passage to reach this wonder had taken its toll. 'So completely was *the wet blanket* spread over the Masqueraders, that each, taking off the mask, appeared in true English character, verily grumblers.' Garrick's friends worked hard to relieve the misery. The orchestra struck up a minuet and an Aesopian ass took the floor, 'in droll contrast' to his partner, a sultana. Many costumes from the postponed procession now appeared. Notable were three hideous witches, who, after much cackling and squealing, were revealed as the society beauties, Lady Pembroke, Mrs. Bouverie and Lady Crewe. All remarked on the 'astonishing contrast between the deformity of the feigned and the beauty of the real appearance'. A highly offensive devil encountered Mr. Cook, a young clergyman disguised as a sweep, who flicked his brush at him, saying that he should be used to soot. The response was a hefty thump.

A mere flood could not hinder James Boswell, who delayed his entrance to give his costume maximum effect and then underlined his arrival by conversing with Mrs. Garrick. His bizarre dress aroused as much comment as it would have in Ajaccio and he received enough attention to declare himself 'as much a favourite as I deserved'. The only disappointment was that Shank had not printed his verses in time for distribution.

Outside an expatriate Stratfordian argued with the doorman. 'Do you know who I am?'

'Yes, I know you well enough. I knew you when your father was refused the place of Beadle
. . . and although you have now got some money, you must not think to domineer here.'

The man from the *Gentleman's Magazine* was unique amongst the press corps in continuing
to enjoy himself, although he conceded that 'a masquerade taxes the abilities in general too
high', for few of the participants sustained their roles. There were few witticisms worth
recording. Best charade was the dinner, which was 'inambigu, not one thing . . . as it really
was'. Payton's fare worked wonders for morale. The stately minuet was abandoned for the
wilder pleasures of the country dance. Yet the jollity was still forced. 'All zealous friends',
said the loyal Craddock, 'endeavoured to keep up the spirit of it as long as they could.'

As dawn broke over the lake which the Avon had become, the problem of evacuation arose.
A lengthy queue waited tentatively to cross planks laid across the flood to carriages standing
in two feet of water. Braver spirits hitched up their costumes and waded grimly. The surly
devil attempted to exonerate his obnoxiousness by heaving a large female to shore. When a
gust of wind revealed breeches under her outer garments, he disgustedly dropped his burden
in the flood.

A promised repetition of the Ode was out of the question and was quietly abandoned. As
the Jubelites returned to their damp lodgings, most shared Boswell's reflection that he was in
'a little village in wet weather, and knew not how to get away, for all the Post Chaises were
bespoke'. Arrivals were spread over several days. Now all sought to leave within hours. 'We
were like a crowd in a Theatre. It was impossible we could all go at a time.' Payton, at least,
was happy with this captive custom.

Aftermath

For the locals – and those Jubelites remaining after the first rush – one highlight remained.
A huge crowd watched five horses wade relentlessly round a Shottery meadow knee-deep in
water. The winner was Mr. Pratt, a groom whose horse swam home by seven lengths. The
Jubilee whimpered towards its close. Angelo exploded his last fireworks before a thin crowd.
At the Town Hall a sparse ball was only remarkable for Eva-Maria's vivacious dancing. Next
day the Garricks left Stratford – the receptacle of their shattered dreams – for ever.

Generously, Garrick bore the full Jubilee costs, although he was under no legal obligation
to do so. Faced with the depressing combination of debt and ribaldry, he defeated his creditors
and critics with a masterstroke. A Jubilee play and pageant was a wild success, achieving a
record run and amply replenishing Garrick's accounts. In *The Jubilee*, he turned on his 'fellow-
burghers' and lampooned them unmercifully, as a sample of dialogue reveals: *'Mary:* "But
Ralph, have you been down to the College, where they keep all their conjurations, Hobgoblins
and gunpowder plots?" *Ralph:* "Oh, I saw how it would be when they wouldn't let his Image
alone in the Church but the show folks from Lunnonshire would paint it all over like a Popish
Saint – Oh I see how it be . . . as sure as sartain tis a plot among the Jews and Papishes."'
Other scenes featured a fight between rival mulberrywood sellers and the injunction of
Stratfordians to their women: '"Don't stir out for fear the Pagans should . . . ravish you."'

Garrick's contempt for the little town he had so happily adopted even extended to contriving
a quarrel over money with the splendid Hunt. His letter brought an eloquent and dignified reply
listing the execrations Hunt had suffered, including, 'The Abuse of my neighbours of the lower
sort for endeavouring to prevent their Exortation – the sneers of the Witty – & the Pity of the
Grave & Solemn – Thanks from no Person living that I know of – This I could have laughed at,
all this I cou'd have despised, & have sat down happy with a Balance so amply in my favor; for
the Greatest Genius of the Age, condescended to call me his Friend – I now, alas, find Felicity
vanished also & my Credit side become a total Blank – Experience . . . remains . . . sagely to
advise me . . . never to meddle with what I do not understand – nor aim at Friendship beyond the

reach of my Abilities to preserve.' Hunt's difficulties increased with the return of Mr. J. Fullerton of the College, who demanded compensation for damage to his property. 'What right', he fumed, 'Mr. Garrick ever had to the Keys I am quite a stranger to.'

Most Stratfordians, blissfully unaware of the derision crackling around them, returned sophisticated scorn with a goodwill which would have been saintly if not born of ignorance. Even those who had regarded Garrick as a dangerous magician now viewed him as a universal provider. The Corporation formally thanked him for 'the great Honor he hath done . . . in the Execution of the Office of Steward of the late Jubilee & for the great Expense and trouble he was at'. Delight was expressed with his solidarity. 'Our Hearts overflowing with Gratitude, can never forget that Attention, and Regard, you have shown to our Prosperity, in so elegantly expressing your Abhorrence in your most incomparable Ode, of that cruel Design, to destroy the Beauty of this situation by inclosing our open Fields.' Thus encouraged, the Corporation held a meeting at the *White Lion* to oppose enclosures. The choice of venue was ironic, since John Payton was promoting a scheme with Thomas Mason, a local lawyer and titheholder.

On 6 September 1770, the anniversary of the Jubilee was celebrated at Stratford 'with uncommon festivity' – an annual commemoration abandoned after six years because of further decline in the wool-trade. When Hunt proposed a yearly Jubilee to Garrick he received a caustic reply. The actor advised his 'friends' that the celebration should be on Shakespeare's birthday, but avoided the possibility of his own presence. 'The Manner how', he declared, should be for the Stratfordians, characteristically going on to advise what to do. 'The Bells should ring & Bonfires should blaze, ye Ladies should dance and the Gentlemen be Merry & Wise . . . There should always be proper Songs introduced . . . and joined with the Hearts and Voices of all the Company . . .' Their priority should be to decorate the town, '(ye *happiest* and why not ye *handsomest* in England) let your streets be well pav'd, & kept clean, do Something with ye delightful Meadow, allure Everybody to visit ye *holy Land;* Let it be well lighted, & clean under foot, and let it not be said. . . that the Town which gave Birth to the first Genius since ye Creation, is the dirty, unseemly, ill-paved, wretched-looking Town in all Britain.'

Yet nothing could temper Stratford's veneration for Garrick. The *Greyhound Inn* was renamed in his honour. His artistry had had its impact on the Corporation. After the Mayor-making it became the custom for a number of years after the Jubilee 'to proclaim theatrically His Worship' at the Market Cross. The burgesses processed in full regalia, preceded by a band, which struck up 'Warwickshire Lads' on its return to the Town Hall. Mulberrywood objects pursued Garrick for the rest of his life as the townsfolk dreamed of the return of their Prince Charming. A typical appeal arrived in 1771 from Henry Cooper of Swine Street: 'I am a Painter, Carver and Engraver, and in short Jack of all Trades, . . . and I should take it as a great favour if your Honour would be so good as to give me an Order.'

The extraordinary achievement of the Jubilee was not at once apparent. In the Middle Ages pilgrims travelled to religious shrines. Now Garrick had given the Age of Reason its first secular saint, indubitably laying the foundations of Stratford's tourist industry; a point realised by the poet Cowper:

> For Garrick was a worshipper himself,
> He drew the liturgy and fram'd the rites
> And solemn ceremonial of the day,
> And call'd the world to worship on the banks
> Of Avon, fam'd in song.'

FOOTNOTES
[1]   Sadly, it was destroyed by fire in 1947.
[2]   Mr. Franks, who shared Foote's Jubilee lodgings, declared that this was untrue.

CHAPTER 10

'For Want of a Quorum'

'No Business can be done for want of a Quorum'.

Corporation Minute Book, 1784.

Like the Combes before them, the enclosers realised an interest might make the burgesses more amenable. After hard bargaining the Corporation secured a good concession. It promoted legislation and borrowed £400 to enclose, thereby instituting the first permanent debt. In 1779 a further £200 was borrowed for enclosure at Drayton and Shottery.

The peasantry reacted in the spirited manner of its forebears. Game was destroyed 'by Poachers and unqualified Persons'. It was announced that anyone caught poaching, or pulling down enclosure works would be prosecuted 'with the utmost vigour of the Law'. Direct action was a forlorn gesture, but as late as 1792 Ralph Greenaway of Shottery was reported for stealing fences and doubtless the dispossessed expressed forcible views in the expanding workhouse.

The break-up of the ring of common land enabled the first growth in Stratford's street-pattern since the Middle Ages. The thoroughfares of a small estate off the Guild Pits were named John Street and Payton Street after their creator.

The Corporation – or Hunt – was aware of the necessity to participate in the communications revolution. In 1775, Parliamentary petitions for a cut to the projected Stourbridge canal came to nothing. In 1777 the Grammar School contained one pupil and Hunt could not remember more than five there in the previous 20 years. One in ten houses was empty. On Sundays, bread was distributed at church, but the charitable funds provided only a shilling a week. The only tenuous link with prosperity was the well-supplied and crowded weekly market. To encourage this trade the Corporation declared the town toll-free in 1787. At the Ram and Cheese Fair on Michaelmas Day, the youths wore red waistcoats and gay bandannas and the countryfolk, elaborately embroidered smocks. Rother Street swarmed with tumblers, fire-eaters, poker-swallowers and boxers. There was a considerable hop exchange and cheese was sold in such quantities that 'upward of 200 Waggon Loads have been here at one time'.

Around this time a new hiring fair bearing an older name, the Mop,[1] held during the first two weeks of October,[2] seems to have emerged in response to the pool of dispossession following enclosure. The labourers and servants seeking work stood 'like cattle waiting to be hired by the first comer'. The indenture between employer and employee was binding for a year. The 'Runaway' Mop, a smaller fair on the following Friday week, gave a second chance to the dissatisfied.

Economic decline was paralleled by political disintegration. Around a third of Corporation meetings was abandoned as inquorate. Burgesses paid fines rather than attend. In 1772 a dissenter, William Bache, was illegally co-opted, but he indignantly rejected this chance to advance his sect. Involuntary election ceased in 1793 when John Cox, a mercer, refused co-option and won a High Court action after his goods were distrained. In 1788 fines for non-attendance were increased. The first 'neglect' cost five shillings, the second ten, and the third, a guinea. Burgesses had been registering their names and leaving, for it was prescribed that those departing early were liable to all the penalties. A copy of the minute was sent to the Mayor of Jubilee year, Nathaniel Cookes, who had long been absent.

The Corporation still possessed the volition to continue its ancient jurisdictional tiffs with the vicar. In 1775, the Reverend Stephen Nason gave notice to his assisting minister, the Reverend James Davenport, citing 'the Many Complaints made to me against you by my Parishioners'. The burgesses were not amongst the complainants, for they requested the withdrawal of the notice. Davenport had secured the plural living of Weston-on-Avon, so Nason disposed of him by bringing forward the sermon-time at Holy Trinity. Davenport, stranded at Weston, was unable to preach and was obliged to resign. Nevertheless the Corporation continued to pay him its share of the stipend as minister of the Guild Chapel and master of the moribund school. On Nason's death in 1787, the Corporation used its influence to secure the living for Davenport, whose brother-in-law, Thomas Ashford, was a former Mayor.

Such was the ascendancy of Thomas Hunt's legal practice over the town's affairs that on his death in 1783 a dynasty of Hunts had to be created. An acting Town Clerk was appointed until Charles Henry Hunt reached his majority. When C.H. Hunt resigned in 1792, he was succeeded by his brother Thomas.

In one matter at least the Corporation showed a progressive spirit, petitioning Parliament in 1788 for the abolition of the slave-trade.

The Constables' Supper

One of the highlights of Stratford's official calendar was the Constables' Supper, held at the *Falcon* on 5 November, when punitive powers were conferred on the minor officials. It was an incentive that money raised in fines was spent on the feast. The first Supper was held in 1784, when the company comprised 'merely the inferior officers of the Borough, such as petty-constables, aletasters, bread and butter weighers, gutter groupers, &c . . ., but the feast was noted for its conviviality and soon the higher functionaries dignified it with their presences'. Soon it was considered that, although the Mayor was officially elected at a Hall of the Corporation, the real selection occurred at the Supper.

Before the constables were invested with the power to arrest rogues and vagabonds, definition was called for. The answer was that these terms applied to any wandering beggar over seven, or those wandering abroad without a lawful 'pastport', giving no good account of themselves. There were superior varieties, like 'scholars and seafaring men that beg, wandering persons using unlawful games, subtle crafts, or *plays*, or pretending . . . to have skill in telling fortunes; all counterfeit Egyptians (or gipsies, not being felons), all jugglers (or sleight of hand artists, pretending to do wonders, by vertue of Hocus Pocus, the powder of Pimper le Pimp, or the like), tinkers, peddlers, petty chapmen, glassmen, &c.'. The Constables were required to 'look after' orchard-robbers, 'hedgbreachers' and wood stealers; repress profane swearing and search for the horses of Popish recusants 'above the value of £5 a piece and to seize the same for His Majesty's use'. The archaic tone of the address with its quaint definitions and virulent religious sentiments perhaps dates it to the Restoration era.

On the evening of the Supper the town was 'pretty well in the hands of the mob – the authorities to show their antipathy to Popery, tacitly allowing all sorts of riotous behaviour'. Bonfires were lit in the streets and guns fired. 'Violent hands were laid on anything combustible.' Once a four-wheel waggon was dragged to a bonfire in the Guild Pits, while 'those of a better class' ran away to avoid being implicated if any offenders were brought to justice.

The injunction against travelling entertainers was long obsolete. At the *Wheatsheaf* in 1770, Mr. Hickman allowed anyone to load a pistol and fire it at any part of his body between his thigh and his chin. The Kembles returned in 1774 to present *The Beggars' Opera* at the *Woolpack*, but

By Mr. Kemble's Company.

At the THEATRE in *Stratford-upon-Avon*,
On *This Evening* 1774,

WILL BE PRESENTED

The Beggars Opera.

Captain *Macheath*, by Mr. CHAMBERS,
Lockit, by Mr. SIDNEY,
Peachum, by Mr. JOHNSON,
Ben Budge, by Mr. MORRIS,
Jemmy Twitcher, by Mr. DONNELL,
Wat Dreary, by Mr. WHARTON,
Filch, by Mr. HINDE,
Crook-Finger'd Jack, by Mr. LEDWITH,
Drawer, by Mr. SMITH,
And *Mat o' the Mint*, by Mr. BROWN.

Polly Peachum, by Mrs. SIDNEY,
Mrs. Peachum, by Mr. KEMBLE,
Jenny Diver, by Mrs. OSBORNE,
Sukey Tawdry, by Mrs. ADAMS,
Mrs. Slammerkin, by Miss WILLIAMSON,
Mrs. Coaxer, by Mrs. SYDDALS,
Moll Brazen, by Mr. DONNELL,
And *Lucy Lockit*, by Mrs. DONNELL.

To which will be added a FARCE, call'd THE

Spirit of Contradiction.

Mr. Partlet, by Mr. SIDNEY,
Captain *Lovewell*, by Mr. HINDE,
Bat Steer, by Mr. BROWN,
Ruin, by Mr. LEDWITH,
And *Randell* (the Gardener) by Mr. DONNELL.

Mrs. Partlet, by Mrs. DONNELL,
Miss Harriet, by Mrs. SIDNEY,
And *Betty*, by Mrs. OSBORNE.

PIT 2s. GAL. 1s. *To begin exactly at Half after Six o'Clock.*

21. *Playbill for 'The Beggar's Opera', performed in Stratford in 1774 by Kemble's Company.*

without Mrs. Siddons who had joined Garrick at Drury Lane. In the same year the Masterman Company played its version of *King Lear and his Three Daughters*. A contemporary note was struck by a 'Petit Piece (in two Acts) called AMERICAN CRUELTY or THE FATE of MAJOR ANDRE (Humbly Attempted by Mr. Masterman)'. This closed with a Dead March, but to ensure the audience departed in cheerful mood, the evening finished with a musical farce, *The Quaker*.

'Lord of the Company'

The Warwickshire Militia often held its annual manoeuvres at Stratford, once to the advantage of the actor, Joseph Munden, who found 'the temptation of visiting the birthplace of the matchless Shakespeare . . . too strong for his romantic mind to withstand'. He fell in with a volunteer and learned that with great numbers assembled it would be difficult to find accommodation. His new friend suggested that he obtain a billet by presenting himself as a recruit. His companions, numbering between thirty and forty and bearing 'an uncanny resemblance to Falstaff's ragged regiment', assembled in a rickety old tenement. 'After the cravings of nature were satisfied . . . our young actor drew forth a fund of entertainment which encircled the evening and rendered him *King of the Company* . . . heroes fresh from the barn door . . . listened with pleased attention and congratulated each other on the acquisition they had gained, in a genius, who would convert three months of duty into so many months of pleasantry.'

When bedtime was called, 'the mirthful crew' retired to a large gothic apartment, where spiders' webs obliterated the light. Straw was spread on the floor and each man given a mattress and quilt. 'Full many a snore, which to nicer ears, would have murdered sleep interrupted the stillness'. Munden woke to find the sergeant smothering each man's hair with soap suds to make his helmet fit, 'enabling each simple rustic to pass in review before his Colonel; the scarlet popinjay of a month's buffoonery'. After breakfast the drums beat to arms and the regiment mustered. Munden, realising his tricky position, left rapidly, 'choosing to enlist under the banners of Melpomene rather than those of Mars'.

An Age of Credulity

The trickle of pilgrims filtering through the humble door of the Birthplace was boosted by the Jubilee. That once-fine house had descended to a 'mean-looking edifice of wood and plaster', where the Harts had assembled 'some antiquated lumber . . . imposed upon the world as its original furniture in the period of Shakespeare'. They were quick to follow the precedent of Thomas Sharp. Old Mr. Hart sold a 'Shakespearean' manuscript for 30 guineas, his credulous benefactor keeping 'the poor, old man from want for the rest of his life'. The Harts should not be judged too harshly for taking advantage of their hereditary good fortune. Like many Stratfordians they were heavily in debt and the buyers refused to be deterred. The premises were inspected in 1781 by the Hon. John Byng:

> 'How do you do, Mrs. Hart? Let me see the wonders of your house.'
> 'Why, there, sir, is Shakespeare's old chair and I have been often bid a good sum of money for it. It has been carefully handed down by our family, but people never thought so much of it till after the Jubilee, and now see what pieces they have cut from it, as well as from the old flooring in the bedroom!'
> 'I bought a slice of the chair equal to the size of a tobacco stopper and I eagerly eyed the lower cross bar of the chair, curiously wrought, which Mrs. Hart would not be tempted to part with.'

At the Church, Byng 'pilfer'd (in common with other collectors)', a tesselated tile from the top of Shakespeare's gravestone.[3] Returning to the *White Lion* for dinner, he met Mrs. Hart again and had 'another chaffer' for the cross bar in vain, but as he passed on his evening walk she accepted his offer and he proudly obtained this 'ceremonial memorial of theatrical antiquity'.

Whatever was left of the chair was sold to a Polish aristocrat, the Princess Czartoryska for twenty guineas in 1790. Byng noted its absence with displeasure on a return visit. 'The evening was cold and gloomy. I walked about the town in a Shakespearean reverie. At the house of his birth they would have tempted me in, but I said: "Where is his old chair that you have sold? I now enter not." My words seemed to shock them; and they have discovered that they have sold the goose which laid the golden eggs.' He reflected that had the Harts been 'makers of Italian policy, they had always kept an old chair ready to succeed the one sold, or rather kept the old one and parted with the substitute'.[4]

The Hathaways at Shottery were equally enterprising, selling in 1793 the chair on which 'Shakespeare had sat with Anne on his knee'. In 1830 a local directory revealed that the cottage had been provided, some years before, with several pieces of furniture, 'affirmed to have belonged to the poet', including his 'courting chair'.

The Jubilee had awakened Stratfordians to their heritage. 'The people seem all alive to the honour of their town having produced Shakespeare', commented a traveller. 'The tailor will descend from his shopboard, or the cobbler shut up his stall and volunteer to guide you to the points connected with the history of the great poet.' The local guide *par excellence* was John Jordan, who nurtured the Shakespeare legends, producing a polished and persisting version of the Bidford drinking tale. Equally enduring was his designation of a fine old farmhouse in Wilmcote as the girlhood home of the poet's mother. He was dangerous to cross. When the Harts upset him, he denigrated their famous abode and mercenary behaviour. 'Even the house that for upwards of half a century has been shown for and venerated as the place of his birth is a most flagrant and gross imposition, invented purposely with a design to extort pecuniary gratitudes from the credulous and unwary.' He selected Brook House on Waterside as a rival temple of nativity, but even his powerful invention could not deflate the mystique of the Birthplace.

Jordan possessed poetic pretentions. He wrote a turgid narrative called *Welcombe Hills* with the assistance of the Reverend Joseph Greene (who found his style 'low and prosaic') and undertook research on the scholar Malone's behalf. He possessed the peasant instinct to provide what was required, 'discovering' poems from Shakespeare's youth in secret drawers. Malone was aware of the shortcomings of his assistant and expressed occasional exasperation. He too was sufficiently a child of his time to indulge in predatory vandalism, hacking John Hall's signature from the parish records and losing John Shakespeare's Testament. At Holy Trinity the poet's multi-coloured monument offended his neo-classical sensibilities. He was delighted to find that the Reverend Davenport shared his view and the bust was repainted in a dreary off-white, to suit 'the taste of the present age.'[5] 'By – ', said Charles Lamb, 'if I had been a justice of the peace for Warwickshire, I would have clapped both commentator and sexton in the stocks, for a pair of meddling, sacrilegious varlets.' A wit was moved to verse in the Visitors' Book:

> Stranger to whom this monument is shown,
> Invoke the poet's curse upon Malone;
> Whose meddling zeal his barbarous taste betrays,
> And daubs his tombstone as he mars his plays.

In 1793, the Harts leased their half of the Birthplace to Thomas Hornby, a butcher. His wife, Mary, soon claimed lineal descent from the Bard and assembled an impressive collection of relics, including two chairs 'said to be given' Shakespeare by the Earl of Southampton, with the Earl's coronets and supporters; the painting of Shakespeare as Petruchio, 'said to be done' by his nephew, William Shakespeare Hart; an old basket-hilted sword 'which looked as though it had laid buried for a century or two on the field of Edge-Hill or Worcester, but which was in fact no such thing, but the veritable sword with which Shakespeare performed in Hamlet . . . and *pièce de résistance*, the very matchlock with which he shot the deer in Charlecote Park.'

Yet the highlight of a visit to the Birthplace was the 'Birthroom', where the surface of the walls and ceiling was covered with the names of visitors. Those who did not sign their own names chose that of a celebrity. Mrs. Hornby who 'endeavoured to impose on all was in this respect imposed on by others'; yet if 'this very decent nurse-like woman' minded, she never showed it, incorporating true and false signatures in her itinerary.

The Age of Reason was an age of credulity: the Harts and Hornbys merely mute, inglorious Chattertons. The Shakespeare craze led to the demand for documents connected with the Bard. Records were plundered and archives ransacked, but the results of the great quest were thin. The search was occasionally hampered by the local peasantry. In 1793 Samuel Ireland, a naive London bardolator, explored Stratford's outlying farms in the hope of uncovering relics. At Clopton he encountered Mr. Williams, a yeoman, who must have been alerted to droll possibilities by previous pilgrims. In response to Ireland's probing, he exclaimed dramatically: 'My God, I wish you had arrived a little sooner! Why it isn't a fortnight since I destroyed several basketfuls of letters and papers . . . and as for Shakespeare, why, there were many bundles with his name upon them. Why it was in this very fireplace I made a roaring bonfire of them.' Ireland was horrified. 'My God! Sir you are not aware of the loss which the whole world has sustained. Would to heaven I had arrived sooner!'

In compensation the farmer solemnly presented an illuminated picture of Elizabeth of York, keeping a straight face while explaining that being on vellum, 'it would not do to light the fire'. The joke exploded on Williams, who 'excused himself of the indiscretion' after Malone wrote a stern letter to his landlord.

Such episodes were not lost on Ireland's son, William, who produced a series of forgeries beyond the dream of any Stratfordian. A play which he wrote on Shakespeare's behalf was performed at Drury Lane. Malone exposed its flaws and the young man confessed. The scandal had a ripple in Stratford. A letter in Mrs. Hornby's collection, 'addressed by Shakespeare from the playhouse in London to his wife', was judiciously mislaid.

Depression, Discontent and Duty

In 1791 the line of a canal to Birmingham was surveyed. Two years later a company was floated and the enabling legislation obtained. Such was the speculative boom that £120,000 was subscribed, of which a quarter came from Stratford. The project was beset with difficulty and in 1795 ambitions were reduced when Josiah Cloves was engaged as engineer of a branch to the Grand Union Canal at Lapworth.

The foundation of a Sunday School in 1791 represents a realisation that religious instruction could teach 'the habits of cleanliness, subordination and order'. Basic literacy was a side-product of the curriculum. By 1797 this attempt at mass education had expanded to seven schools, including two at Shottery.

In reaction against events in France a local 'Church and King' mob hanged in effigy two leading radicals, Joseph Priestley and Tom Paine, in 1793. Next year a scheme by Malone to celebrate the silver jubilee of the Jubilee was abandoned 'in consequence of the national gloom arising from the horrors of the revolutionary war'.

One carried away by patriotic enthusiasm was Thomas Sharp's son, John, an excellent workman in his father's trade, although regarded as very wild. Four decades after his purchase Sharp was still purveying his mulberrywood articles. At least he had convinced himself. On his deathbed in 1799 he testified 'before the four Evangelists, in the presence of Almighty God' that he had only used wood from the miraculous tree. By then much of his wealth had been drained away by his son, who enlisted on 32 occasions, but was each time bought out by his doting father. Even Sharp's death did not curtail the flow of souvenirs. As late as 1812, Thomas Gibbs, the clockmaker, bought 'the remaining part of that celebrated tree' from his widow.

In 1794 a Warwickshire Regiment of Fencible Yeomanry Cavalry was raised, composed of 'respectable men of the district, whose *Amor Patriae* is above the fear of being exposed to the necessary toils of a military education'. The local troop was commanded and equipped by

Captain James Shirley of Ettington Park. Its main function was to aid the civil authorities in quelling unrest. It was so engaged in 1795 when a riot of Irish dragoons shattered the peace.

The Fifth Regiment of Dragoons was billeted in Stratford and aroused considerable hostility which erupted with seasonal impropriety on Christmas Day. It appears that troopers were refused service in certain alehouses and a footpatrol was attacked. Either on genuine suspicion or to settle old grievances, Corporal William Ridley decided to arrest Thomas Baker, landlord of the *Malt Shovel* (now the *Old Thatch Tavern*) in the Rother Market. Troopers broke into his premises, smashed crockery and beat him severely. Passions were running high. 'By our Dear Jesus and the Holy Ghost, we will massacre the first man we lay hold of', yelled the soldiers in their Irish brogues. The terrified landlady alerted the constable, William Bullard, who enlisted the aid of some townsmen. Arming themselves with staves from a woodpile, they ran into a group of dragoons in the Rother Market. Bullard shouted 'Peace', but the soldiers struck at him with their swords. At the corner of Hell Lane (now Windsor Street), he stood against the wall and defended himself against three soldiers. A townsman, Joseph Pinfield, was struck severely and cried 'O Lord!' repeatedly as he staggered home to Mere Pool Lane. The soldiers' blood was up. A local drinker, Hiron the carrier, was told that his entrails would be cut if he came near. They smashed windows and broke into houses, seized implements as weapons and chased Pinfield home. His wife bolted the gate and begged for mercy. 'By the dear Jesus and the Holy Ghost, we will massacre him', screamed the dragoons. Forcing entry, they chased him up the yard and struck blows of such severity that Trooper James Kelley bent his sword. 'By the Holy Jesus', he exulted. 'Did you ever see my sword work so well about his head before?'

The soldiers possessed no monopoly of aggression. Trooper James Anderson staggered back to his billet at the *Red Lion* in the early hours, declaring erroneously that his life was ebbing away. The arrival of the dragoon officers at last brought calm. For the next two nights Captain Shirley's Yeomanry and 30 specially-enrolled constables patrolled the streets before the arrival of soldiers of the King's Own Troop. On 28 December an inquest was held at the Town Hall before John Payton, the Mayor, with Joseph Pinfield, 'then and there lying dead', as the mutest of witnesses. Corporal William Ridley and Troopers James Anderson, Patrick Welsh, William Howard, James Kelley and Samuel Irwin were committed to the next Assize and escorted to Warwick. Identification was made possible by Welsh and Irwin turning King's evidence. At the Lent Assize their testimony was supported by that of 30 Stratfordians. The four prisoners were convicted and were presumably executed.

As a response to this affair, the magistrates issued regulations to curb 'the various and increasing Evils arising from ill Regulated Public Houses, so hurtful to the morals of the lower order of society'. It was forbidden to serve drunks, known or reputed thieves, rogues, vagabonds and common prostitutes. Landlords failing to keep orderly houses would lose their licences.

Tally Ho

The patrician world surrounding Stratford was epitomised in this era by John Corbet, 'the Warwickshire Squire', Master of Fox Hounds from 1791, who rented Clopton House for his large establishment, increased in the season by the many gentlemen who partook of his hospitality. His hounds, in the charge of his famous huntsman, Will Barrow, were kennelled in Bull Lane. Hearing of a local gentleman who disposed of his foxhounds because of his wife's nagging disapproval, Corbet declared: 'If my wife had done so I would never have kissed her again till she took off her night-cap and cried "Tally-ho"'.

Once Corbet's hounds pursued a fox for 35 miles. Of over a hundred huntsmen, only Corbet and five others were in at the death. This famous old fox was enclosed in a glass case in the club-room at the *White Lion*, whose proprietor, Bill Barke, was 'a conspicuous figure with the hounds'. Members dined on alternate Thursdays during the season wearing their scarlet coats embroidered with the letters 'S.H.'. When Corbet left in 1809, Lord Middleton took over patronage of the Hunt.

'My Dear Betsy'

A glimpse of middle-class life is revealed by the journals of Elizabeth Davenport Ashford, which possess a Janeite mixture of domesticity and sensibility. She noted recipes – 'Peas Pudding is much better with butter boiled in it' – and recorded her reading, sharing the contemporary taste for Gothic novels. In 1797 this 19-year-old received 'amusement and instruction' from Mrs. Radcliffe's *Italian, or the Confessional of the Penitents* and she found *Women as They Are*, 'a novel by Mr. Parsons . . . very sentimental. Well worth reading'. Events in France were not ignored. She read *The History of a French Emigrant and his Family* and the *Anti-Jacobin Review*. There is a reminder of the Terror in the contribution she made to 'the Distressed Clergy' – Catholic refugees from revolutionary France.

This sheltered life was shattered by sadness. Her father, Thomas Ashford, had resigned from the Corporation because of bad health, but he continued to ail. On 4 February he suffered a paralytic stroke. Elizabeth sat with him all night. Next day, Mr. Bray, the doctor, laid 'blisters' (poultices) on his head and stomach. He lingered for another week and another blister was laid on his back. On 12 February her 'dear Father departed this life for a better'.

A period of family mourning followed, but this had finished by May when the Booth company returned to Stratford. Its repertory ranged over 36 pieces, from cameo sketches to full-length drama. Elizabeth, an avid theatre-goer, saw 20 of them,[6] although she gives no indication of where the theatre was. The most popular was Stratford's own play of *The Jubilee*, which was performed three times. Elizabeth's mother gave her a box ticket on 9 May, when it was a double bill with *The Crook'd Husband* and she saw it again on 29 May as a double bill with *The Way to get Married*. Her uncle, the vicar, paid three shillings for her ticket, so there was no clerical disapproval of the theatre. The following evening a series of benefit performances began. The season closed on 4 July with performances of *Which is my Man? or A Soldier for the Ladies* and *No Song, No Supper*. Mrs. Booth, accompanied by Elizabeth, made her eleventh theatre trip.

On 12 June, Elizabeth went to an auction at the College. Edward Battersbee, the owner, could not afford to maintain this ancient and beautiful building in these depressed times and demolished it while it was still 'handsome, capricious and strong'.

During 1798 Elizabeth fell in love with a young attorney, Robert Hobbes. Most middle-class marriages at Stratford occurred within the neighbourhood circle. Decorum reigned and a young lady could wait anxiously for a nervous lover to declare himself, so for several months Elizabeth had to be content with glimpses of Robert in church. Her main social indulgence was an occasional visit to the Card Assembly, where she usually lost her small stake. Her reading taste was becoming more catholic and serious. She was devoted to Cowper's poetry and she devoured Hannah More's *Treatise on Female Education* and Isaac d'Israeli's *Curiosities of Literature*.

In the spring Robert Hobbes began to pay tentative court, greeting her as she emerged from church. Two weeks later she missed him at morning service, but was rewarded in the afternoon, when he escorted her part of the way home. Two days after rejecting an offer from another suitor, 'D.D.', possibly her cousin, David Davenport, she 'receiv'd some nods from R.H. as he rode up the Lane with the Yeomanry'. On 21 July he stopped his horse under her window on his way to the theatre in Birmingham. Within four days she had obtained and read the play he saw, *Pizarro*. She was no longer to be resisted. On 13 August she joyfully recorded: 'Mr. Hobbes declared himself my lover this evening. I am the happiest of beings'. Three weeks later he obtained a partnership in his firm, so the way was clear to marry.

The couple could now walk out together. At the Ram and Cheese fair he bought her a canary for a fairing and at the Mop they went to see the bull-roast in the Guild Pits. His sister began to call and to accompany her to the Card Assembly. Bridecakes were ordered and the marriage settlement prepared. The ring, trousseau and household goods were bought. On New Year's Day the lovers had the obligatory tiff and reconciliation. Robert, whose journal for 1800 takes up the story, went to a Dancing Assembly at the *White Lion* on 13 January and lingered to 'nip' with friends until half-past three. This was something of a stag-night, for two mornings later he was up at seven and off to Holy Trinity to receive the hand of 'my dear Betsy', while outside another couple waited 'to be tacked together'. After a wedding breakfast at Mrs. Ashford's, they set off for Oxford, each in a sedan chair. They honeymooned in London before returning to their new house on Waterside at the end of the month. On Easter Sunday they received the Sacrament for the first time. Elizabeth was pregnant and suffering morning sickness. A few days later she was bled for the first time in her life.

'Great Discontent'

Economic depression increased as the war progressed. Investment in the vital navigation project was reduced. By 1798 it had crept southward to Hockley Heath and there it stopped. The touch-stone of the town's hopes, the canal shares, fell drastically. Robert Hobbes bought one for 40 guineas from Thomas Edkins of Welford, who had paid £100 for it five years before and forfeited £4 interest in his eagerness to shed his investment.

Stratfordians followed events with concern. Edmund Malone ended his Shakespearean enquiries to the vicar with summaries of the dispatches. Joseph Hill, the Sheep Street barber, gloomily discussed the latest French successes in his shop. In May 1800, a public meeting sent a loyal address after the King survived an assassination attempt.[7]

Pauper children were found places in trade and industry. Between 1794 and 1796, 30 were sent to the model cotton manufactory at Measham in Derbyshire. Some, at least, felt they were badly treated there or became homesick, for they returned to their parents in Stratford, presumably walking the hundred-odd miles. After Thomas Smith, a 'poor unfortunate boy' had returned to Stratford, his father, another Thomas Smith, a brickmaker, lost his temper while taking him out on a job and 'in the heat of his Anger, bruised his Arm in a dangerous Degree; which was afterwards increased by a violent Blow he unfortunately received from a brickbat thrown by his Sister'. He was returned to Measham, where despite medical treatment, the arm continued to fester. When his father heard of his son's plight, he went to Measham and took him away again, announcing that he 'would himself endeavour to gain a Cure'. On his return to Stratford, the father declared that the injuries were due to 'the rigid treatment of his Masters at Measham'. At home the condition of the arm was exacerbated by 'a bad Scrophulous Habit of Body'. After six months, the boy was 'recommended to the General Hospital of Birmingham, where 'no Possibility could be taken, to preserve his Life, without submitting to the Amputation of his Arm'. Despite this disability, he returned to Measham soon after to renew his apprenticeship.

The case aroused strong feelings in Stratford and Mr. Bolton, a churchwarden and Mr. Dadley, one of the Overseers of the Poor, were sent to Measham to investigate conditions. When they arrived at the mill, all the Stratford children were assembled in a room and asked to make their complaints. Not surprisingly there were only a few trivial mutterings and the majority of the children expressed their great happiness. Mr. Wilks, the proprietor, said that strict attention was always paid to the childrens' 'Obedience in our excellent Religion' and that the Sunday School education was comparable to that in Stratford.

It is impossible to discern how perceptive the two Stratfordians were in their analysis of the childrens' conditions, but they reported that their diet was very good, their apparel clean, their faults were corrected 'with that Mildness which is becoming Those who have the Care of Children; and they are indulged with their youthful and customary Recreations' at Whitsuntide and Christmas. Small monetary incentives were given for the childrens' work, which they generally spent on 'some trifling Articles of Dress; somewhat inferior to the usual Apparal worn at the Manufactury'.

The Stratford gentlemen interviewed poor Thomas in private and he speedily revealed the source of his injuries and, falling on his knees, 'supplicated the Pardon of Mr. Wilks for raising so scandalous a Report . . ., saying the Reason he durst not declare the Truth in Stratford, was, lest his Father in the unrestrained Moments of his Anger should deprive him of Life'.[8]

The Corporation set an example of austerity by abolishing public feasting for the duration of the war. With the chilling precedent of the Terror to concentrate minds, offenders against the civil code were treated ferociously. On a hot summer day in 1799, a man named Cox from Hell Lane was whipped for stealing cabbages. In October, the Corporation lamented the high price of bread and voted the almspeople another sixpence a week. Both public and private violence increased through the winter: a soldier billeted in the town received 300 lashes for stealing a leg of mutton. On Boxing Day a 'Church and King' mob stormed the little dissenting chapel at Shottery.

By spring the situation was desperate. The Corporation allocated five guineas towards a soup kitchen. The summer brought day after day of rain and the harvest was a disaster. The price of bread soared and there were food riots in many parts of England. Robert Hobbes noted 'great discontent' amongst the poor of Stratford. On 12 September a mob rose and plundered a broad-wheeled waggon. That night the authorities were powerless. An uneasy peace prevailed next day, but in the evening the mob rose again in great numbers. The Yeomanry Cavalry cleared the streets and a day of calm followed. Four days later the frenzied and hungry mob smashed the windows of the Guild Hall, which was being used as a foodstore. On market-day the authorities tried to relieve tension by selling corn at reduced prices, but passions were too high. Blocks of butter and baskets of provisions were seized from helpless stallholders and flung into hungry hands. That night the remaining Guild Hall windows were smashed. Three of the mob who broke into the cheese store were captured and escorted by the Yeomanry Cavalry to Warwick. Rain did as much as authority to clear the streets. Next day all was quiet and yeomanry sergeant Robert Hobbes took Betsy for a drive in their new gig. Four days later he took her out to tea, but he was called away to a vestry meeting, which opened a subscription with a £50 grant from the Corporation.

The Corporation posted notices offering a reward to anyone providing evidence leading to the conviction of rioters. On 9 December 1801, 20 guineas was paid to Joseph Stiles after Samuel Sambridge, a dyer of Sheep Street, was bound over at the Quarter Sessions with eight others in the sum of £40 to keep the peace, particularly towards John Powys of Bethnal Green, who was perhaps a trader whose stall had been plundered.

Robert Hobbes was concerned about his poor neighbours and did much to help them, but the middle classes were cushioned from the worst effects of the depression. His social round was unaffected by the disturbances. On 2 October, he dined at the *Shakespeare* and drank lots of wine, coming home 'non se ipse'. Two weeks later he was 'very poorly and sick in the morning from eating Walnutts and high living'. At five the next morning Betsy's contractions began. He went for Mr. Gamble, the surgeon. At noon she was delivered of a 'fine, large bumping boy and had an excellent time of it'. She remained in bed for ten days. On 14 November she was churched and the baby was christened Robert.

The greatest flood recorded in Stratford occurred that month. The ground floors in Waterside were awash. On 18 November the local sensation was the discovery of a woman's body with its throat cut in the weir-break at Welford. She had been slain by her husband, William Palmer of Snitterfield, who had hoped that the flood would carry her away. Palmer fled but was arrested two days later, brought to Stratford and then taken to Warwick Gaol. Ten days later, his sister was charged as an accessory.

Six weeks after the birth of their son, the Hobbes went to 'a most furious Assembly' of 32 couples. Robert declared himself 'wholly tired of my legs', but for Betsy, there was 'not much dancing at present . . . poor Soul'. They got to bed at three. Robert was 'quite fagged' the next day and did not get up till 11. In the evening the baby was inoculated against smallpox. This was a bold step, only four years after Jenner's first experiments. Understandably Betsy was 'quite low', an apprehension which deepened two weeks later when the baby was 'exceedingly ill with the small pox which is come out very much'. Her morale rose next day when he was much better. That month, her uncle, who had preached in support of vaccination, supped with them on oysters.

Another innovation occurred in December when Robert paid an income tax demand for seven pounds. This tax had been introduced on incomes over £60 in the previous year.

Robert was active with the Bread Committee through the long winter, drawing up lists of those eligible for aid, organising distributions and raising donations. On Christmas Eve he gave his poorer neighbours sacks of potatoes. He was a rising man, doing legal work for the Corporation, having his portrait painted by local artist, Edward Grubb, and becoming a churchwarden. In January he was bottling and racking 'madewines' and spirits from 'Harvey'. If this was the Bristol shipper, the river must have consigned the order from door to door. Robert fasted and went to church on Ash Wednesday, but he broke his Lenten discipline by rolling back late from the hostelry. Expiation was sufficient, for he found Betsy 'as cross as two sticks'.

Palmer and his sister were hanged at Warwick on 1 April. The sister's body was sent for dissection by Robert Hobbes' friend, Gamble. Next day he saw it twice in the surgeon's garden. It is a measure of the brutality of the times that this humane man expressed no distaste at the sight of the executed woman. He was equally dispassionate two days later when he saw Palmer's corpse conveyed through Stratford on a sweltering Good Friday to be gibbetted at Cranhill Leas. At the same Assize a Stratfordian whom the local press did not even name was transported for stealing a pocket-book containing money bills.

Despite such sensations, life at Stratford was generally a steady plod of familiarity. 'The town holds but one market a week', commented a visitor. 'It renders the town extremely lively . . . when put in contrast with the apparent dullness observable on other days.'

Mock War and Peace

On 23 April 1801, Robert Hobbes bled his horse in preparation for the annual manoeuvres of the Yeomanry Cavalry. On 18 May, he was 'up at seven and busy soldiering'. The Troop met in Banbury Lane and exercised at Clopton. Robert was quartered at the *Shakespeare,* but he slipped home to Betsy and bed. For the next three days the Troop 'performed wonders'. On the second evening Robert escaped to the churchwarden's supper at the *White Lion* and was 'very jolly, like a true Churchwarden'. On the final day, General Greenfield reviewed the regiment and Robert acted as his Orderly ('no way out of that'). The day was a great success. That evening the sergeants dined at the expense of a delighted Lord Aylesford. Robert staggered home at two a.m., drunk almost to oblivion for what he claimed, with true drinkers' contrition, would be 'the only time'.

We follow the Hobbes through 1801. Betsy was 'as ill tempered as the Devil' when Robert came home late once and 'behaved cursedly ill' on another occasion, 'being in her tantrums'. This entry is smudged, perhaps by Betsy. On 22 July, Robert attended a meeting about the plight of the poor, perhaps making plans for the winter. In the afternoon he was 'snugly alone' with Betsy. Ten days later they were 'snug as two G.G.'s' after supper. She was four months pregnant again.

On 3 October news of an armistice brought scenes of heartfelt joy. At night a great illumination was made. That month, Thomas Sheldon, who had only been a burgess for two weeks, refused the Mayoralty and John Payton was elected in his place. Afterwards the 'Jury and Officers' dined at the *Windmill* at his expense. Robert Hobbes stayed till 12:30 and came home sober, as he did when his Yeomanry Captain, Evelyn Shirley, gave a dinner of 'famous venison' at the Town Hall to celebrate the peace. The party lasted till two, but Robert left early because Betsy was nearing her time. Three days later at two a.m., his wife produced 'a fine Girl'. A month later she was churched and this was the occasion for a small celebration. The couple drank a bottle of port and made merry. Robert had been excluded from Betsy's bed during her confinement, but that night he went 'to bed to wife. comfortable as usual'. She was a sturdy nursing mother; in February the couple danced every dance at the Assembly, returning home after four. Later that year Robert entered one of the town's inner circles when he was received into the third degree of freemasonry. Hopes of better times were compounded on 30 March 1802, with the news of the Peace Treaty of Amiens. Another great illumination was made and the streets were 'all bustle and joy'.

Peace brought renewed interest in the canal project. Shares rose to £105, but hopes proved illusory. Later that year, Robert Hobbes drafted a stern letter from the Corporation to the Company stressing the 'propriety and absolute necessity of continuing your canal'. The town was 'nearly ruined' by the completion of the Warwick Canal. Its market and trade would be 'utterly sacrificed' if the Stratford Canal was not completed.

On Christmas Day, Betsy Hobbes was delivered of her annual child, a boy, described by her husband as 'a fine Xmas box'. She was up and about three days later. The ferocious winter – one of a series in the 1800s – was again causing suffering amongst the poor. Things got so bad that the churchwardens decided to distribute the sacrament bread and Robert organised the hand-out outside the *Falcon*.

FOOTNOTES

[1]   See above p. 75. Joseph Hill, the barber, noted that 11 October 1800, 'gave the best Mop that as [sic] been *since it was established'* (my italics). Wheler noted seven fairs in 1806, of which several had begun recently. There are a number of 'Mops' in the South Midlands.

[2]   By 1806, Wheler reveals that the date had settled as the morrow after old Michaelmas day. From the 1850s it was held on 12 October.

[3]   Around this time, someone stole the feet from the effigy of John Combe. In 1894 the vicar received a letter from a gentleman who claimed to have the missing feet, which proved a perfect fit.

[4]   John Byng: *Torrington Diaries*, 1781.

[5]   The colours were restored in 1861.

[6]   Amongst those she missed were *Hamlet, Wild Oats* and *The Rivals*.

[7]   Another meeting was organised by Robert Hobbes in 1803 after another such attempt.

[8]   'A General Statement of the Accompts of the Overseers of the Poor . . . from Easter 1794 to Easter 1796': Birthplace Library.

CHAPTER 11

'Demand and Supply'

'The price of every commodity will be regulated by the demand and supply.'

Warwick Advertiser 1811.

With the renewal of hostilities with France, a Corps of Stratford-upon-Avon Volunteer Infantry was formed, commanded by Major the most Noble Marquis of Hertford, abruptly dismissed in the Corps records as 'non-effective'. Its strength numbered 12 officers, nine sergeants and 240 men. Their golden hour came in 1806, when the volunteers were drawn up before the *White Lion* and received the Prince of Wales with presented arms.

These would-be defenders were a mixed blessing to the townspeople. The effect of an annual break from families and vocations was predictable. 'The Yeomanry Cavalry came into town and behaved very ill', noted Hill in 1807. Not surprisingly, the regiment's official history tells a different story: 'The four Troops . . . were inspected by Col. Corbett, who expressed himself highly satisfied; and observed that he had never seen a Corps better disciplined or that made a more soldier-like appearance.' Next year, members of the Yeomanry pulled down the sign of the *Swan and Maidenhead*, declaring that 'as the only maidenhead left in Stratford was a wooden one, they would destroy it'.

An annual notice ordered all men who had not previously trained with the Militia to assemble in the Rother Market before being 'trained and exercised' for three weeks. Some passed to regular regiments and the recruiting officer made regular visits to assist in raising men for the Permanent Additional Force, thus saving the parish financial penalties. A Churchwarden and an Overseer of the Poor were required to attend: the paupers' rolls made good recruiting lists.

A more colourful approach was adopted by Captain James Saunders, the local adjutant. His extravagant poster offered the 'splendid chance . . . of assisting the renowned and victorious general, Lord Wellington, in exterminating the rapacious myrmidons of the French; or of serving in the Artillery of the Hon'ble East India Company and at the expiration of twelve years returning to their friends Loaded with the riches of the East. Gallant hearts, men and boys, actuated by such honourable motives will meet a kindly reception'. The number exterminated by Stratford lads is unrecorded and none appears to have returned laden with the riches of the East.

Some recruits were of low calibre. Mr. Duke of Tiddington hired John Hickman as his coachman at Warwick Mop, but he disobeyed orders and was frequently drunk on duty, purloining his master's horse to collect liquor. Robert Hobbes, the parish clerk, advised the despairing Duke that misconduct had to be proved by witnesses. At the next Assize, Hickman, who had enlisted in the 14th Light Dragoons, sued unsuccessfully for breach of contract.

Crime and Punishment

Grinding poverty produced a desperate crime wave which in turn motivated a brutal judiciary. In October 1805, Henry Blun received 232 lashes at the Market Cross for stealing hay from

William Bache. The odd number implies he collapsed and could take no more. Other traditional punishments were given. Two stall-women, a mother and daughter, were placed in the stocks for profane cursing and swearing and riotous behaviour in the market. The stocks were set on the ground floor of the Town Hall, where iron bars excluded mockers 'from the degraded and uncomfortable offenders within'. Drunks provided most of the custom.

In 1806, the Assize judge sentenced Sarah Hiron, aged 26, to seven years' transportation for stealing money and clothing at Stratford. Three local men faced capital charges during 1808 and 1809. There were humane attitudes outside the judiciary for, in two cases at least, those they had wronged pleaded for their lives. Job Edkins, aged 16, a postboy, embezzled money-bills from a Bromsgrove bank. The judge told him that he had not been capitally indicted because of the leniency of his prosecutors and, because of his youth, the punishment would be 'very slight indeed in proportion to his offence' – 16 months in the House of Correction. Thomas Quayle was sentenced to death for stealing, at Stratford, a silver watch from William Tompson, but was reprieved, possibly through Tompson's intervention. John Wesson stole a sheep in the parish of Old Stratford, but was reprieved through 'the humane interference of the prosecutor', Henry Robbins.

Market-day was a favoured time for muggers on the Warwick Road. In December 1811, two footpads rushed at James Waring of Warwick, knocked him down, beat him severely and robbed him of fourpence. Fortunately for him, they missed £100 concealed in his coat. Another victim was Mr. Green of Snitterfield. Two footpads cruelly beat him and robbed him of his loose cash, but missed £70 hidden in his pocket-book.

There was some recognition of the economic cause of this lawlessness, although it was frequently combined with a reluctance to interfere with the *status quo*. The main newspaper circulating in Stratford, the *Warwick Advertiser*, deplored the hardships endured by 'the labouring classes', but considered this 'trifling' compared with what they suffer if mob-rule prevailed. 'They would empty the granaries, break open the magazines – they would compel the farmer to bring his stock to market, and they would sell it at their price.' Famine would follow as stocks were exhausted. 'All the horrors which history records . . . would ensue; the rich would have no means of relieving the distress of the poor, for money could not procure what is not in existence.' Given contemporary economic and social thinking, the conclusion is unremarkable: 'the price of everything will be regulated by the demand and the supply'.

Slow Change

A symptom of the decline amongst Stratford's old families may be found amongst John Shakespeare's descendants. In 1804 Thomas Hart was forced to offer the Birthplace for sale, but found no takers. While there were eager bidders for every sham relic, no-one wanted to acquire the prime Shakespeare memorial. Perhaps its authenticity was off-putting! At an auction the following year there were no offers, but in 1806 Thomas Court, landlord of the *Garrick*, met a distracted Mr. Hart at four a.m. on Stratford Bridge. Perhaps he was contemplating ending his troubles but the outcome was happier. Court bought the building for £210. The Harts moved to Tewkesbury, but continued to visit Stratford, singing as they went the old Jubilee songs of 1769, the family's finest hour.

The Corporation was becoming more conscious of its heritage. In 1807, James Saunders and Robert Bell Wheler were appointed to transcribe and classify its archives. Saunders combined a well-developed sense of rank with military earthiness. He headed a notebook with the quip:

> Where fools have scribbled, fools will scribble more,
> As dogs will ---- where dogs have ---- before.

Robert Bell Wheler was the son of Garrick's friend. In 1806, at the age of 21, he published the first history of Stratford. This 'kind and amiable' lawyer filled notebooks with memorabilia in a minute and precise hand. Both Saunders and Wheler extensively sketched contemporary Stratford. Without them much material would have been lost.

In 1806 it proved so difficult to find a Mayor that Joseph Walker, who lived at Worcester, was elected. Meetings were arranged to suit his availability which was restricted by seasonal requirements on his farm. At Rogationtide he declined the obligation to perambulate the boundaries because of his 'Barkharvest'.

Nevertheless, the Corporation was beginning to take an active part in arresting Stratford's decline, rather than passively accepting stagnation. The Barkes at the *White Lion*, successors of the Paytons, had established a considerable coaching network, the continuation of which was inhibited by Stratford's ancient bridge, which was narrow, dilapidated and 'very incommodious for the Travelling and Posting Business'. In 1805 the Corporation petitioned Parliament for permission to demolish it and erect a new one. Richard Wyatt, a 'skilfull architect', reported that the old bridge could be widened, but financial considerations prompted a caution increased by the reluctance of any authority to accept responsibility. In 1811 the Crown won an action against the Corporation for the 'non-repair of a bridge'. A further petition for demolition was prepared, but the bridge passed precariously to the future. In 1814 it was widened and a tollhouse built.

The coaching heyday produced vigorous competition. In 1811, 329 Stratfordians, including the Mayor and the vicar, pledged themselves to patronise the Leicester and Bristol Telegraph Coach and to ignore the 'very unhandsome Opposition which has lately started'. The sound of the coach-horn and the clatter of horses' hooves on the cobbles drew Stratfordians to their doors to watch the arrival or departure of the stage coaches, but such events were too frequent to arouse more than brief interest. First in view at six a.m. was the *Regent* coach from London *en route* for Birmingham, Wolverhampton, Shrewsbury and Holyhead. In the three hours there followed the *Union, Old Post, Ancient Briton* and *Mail* coaches along the same route. Passengers for Warwick and Leamington changed for the *Vittoria* light coach leaving at nine thirty. In the evening the equivalent coaches returned towards London.

In 1808 the Corporation subscribed £2,000 to bring the canal another mile and a half to Wooten Wawen. An 'Assembly of the Proprietors' during 1809 resolved to raise £90,000 in £30 shares to complete the project.

In 1811, the Corporation increased endowments at its decaying Grammar School, in the hope that 'some of the more respectable inhabitants' would send their sons there. Twenty boys were given free instruction in English grammar and 'the learned languages'; other courses were paid for 'according to the usual terms'. A guinea was paid to the Master on admission, 2s 6d per year for fuel and pupils provided their own books. Applications were passed by the Corporation to the Master, who accepted those 'duly qualified (according to long established custom) by being at the age of seven years and able to read'. Admission was restricted to inhabitants of the borough, which meant the sons of the middle-class. Nine pupils in 1811 had fathers for whom the appellation 'gentleman' was sufficient. Others included two attorneys, a surgeon, a grocer, a hotelier and a banker. After an initial rush of entries, there was a shortfall in numbers for some time.

Austin Warrilow, writing master at the preparatory school attached to the Grammar School, ran an independent boarding establishment in his house next to the *Falcon*. An account survives for David Rice, son of the vicar of Alderminster. Half a year's board, including instruction in English and writing, cost eight guineas. Each language taken cost half a guinea and David learnt Latin, English, Greek and French. His generous personal allowance of 3s 6d a week was about half a farmworker's weekly wage, but there is no record of how it was spent. He was equipped with a Bible, an English reader, 'Jonson's Dictionary' and an 'Eton' Grammar. His seat in church cost a shilling; 'Fire and Candle', 2s 6d. Personal and stationery charges, including a 'Blacking Ball', a visit to the 'Haircutter' and servants' fees of two shillings, complete a bill for £11 15s 5d. The curriculum reflects the desire of the middle class for a utilitarian education – land surveying, geography, 'with the use of the Globes'; music, drawing and dancing.

The beginning of a universal education system is reflected in Stratford by the foundation of a National School in Bull Lane to educate children in the principles of the Church of England, some time between 1811, when the National Society was founded, and 1817, when two sermons were preached on behalf of the school at Holy Trinity and the children sang hymns.

Rising evangelical fervour led to the foundation of a Bible Association at Stratford in 1819, with the intention of making the scriptures available to all households. Out of 120 families visited, only six possessed a Bible. 'Too much praise cannot be given to those ladies who have given so much of their time and trouble to visit the poor in their respective neighbourhoods, but have enabled them to supply themselves by small weekly contributions, with copies of the Scriptures.' Within a year, most households in the district were subscribing.

Continuing religious factiousness emerged in 1817 when John Perry of Stratford, a printer, reported Benjamin Appleby of Stratford, also a printer, for disturbing a meeting of Protestant dissenters at Snitterfield. In 1819, Matthew Pearce opened his house in Wood Street for a Methodist Society of just six members. By 1822, the society was meeting in a barn in Meer Street.

Popular Entertainment

The deprivations of war did not curtail the range of popular entertainments. A woman was sent to the House of Correction in 1808 for 'pretending to tell fortunes'. Mr. Hathaway's Cabinet of Wax Figures was more favoured. 'The most interesting characters in the World' included the Royal Family, 'the unfortunate Royal Family of France', many other 'illustrious Personages, both living and dead' and a grand tableau of Lord Nelson's funeral.

Sometimes an entertainment accompanied a touring play. After a production of 'Tobin's admired comedy of *The Honeymoon*, Mr. V. G. Yngell displayed his peculiar and interesting Experiments . . . with the WONDERFUL LEARNED GOLDFINCHES, some new and popular Airs on the MUSICAL GLASSES, whose sounds are, of all others, the most celestial; concluding with OLYMPIC EXERCISES, consisting of balancing in a most astonishing manner'.

There were more brutal diversions. Cocks, a local maltmaker, fought an unnamed plumber for a purse of five pounds, knocking him down 118 times. Regular cockfights took place: Joseph Greene's 'reprieve for the poor birds' of 60 years before had proved only temporary. A less formal version of the 'sport' was available. Outside the *Red Horse* stood a muck-heap where game-cocks were penned. Boys could throw at them for a penny and all they killed, they took.

Peace at Last

The seemingly endless war ground on far away, having little immediate impact on Stratford-ians, but striking into everyone's lives. During 1812 a national 'Peace' petition was circulating locally which deplored the growing despondency and mourned the 'multitudes of valiant men' killed or incapacitated in the war.

> . . . while our Youth, at an Age, and in Numbers, hitherto unencamped, are ballotted for Military Service, and seduced or forced away, from the useful and meritorious Employments of Husbandry and Trade, your Petitioners . . . lament the past and approaching Ruin of our once opulent Manufacturers and the Melancholy condition of our Artisans, formerly . . . a contented, industrious and honest Race, but now disheartened by dreary Poverty, degraded by Galling dependence . . . by which they may be precipitated into such Acts of Violence, as would render the Forfeiture of their lives a necessary, but most deplorable measure of Public Justice . . .

46. Garrick Court in the 1890s, one of Stratford's old alleys later demolished to build the Picture House. Note the bird cages on the walls of the cottages.

47. Perambulators and other traffic in Henley Street in the 1890s.

48. Labourers plying for hire at the Mop, 1899, by Benjamin Stone, M.P. Stone was one of the first men to realise the importance of photography as a social record.

49. Women gossiping at Shottery, 'the once benighted hamlet'.

50. Ox-roasting at the Mop.

51. Women fetching water from Shottery Brook. Ann Hathaway's cottage is in the background.

52. Dr. John Day Collis, Vicar of Stratford 1870-9, educationalist and reformer.

53. The Revd. George Arbuthnot, Vicar of Stratford 1879-1907.

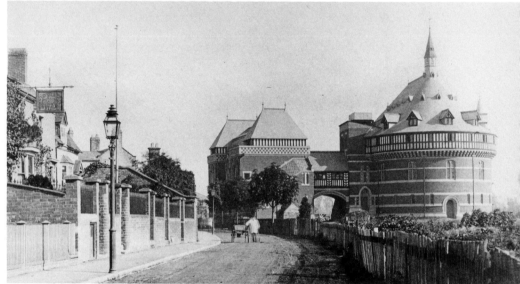

4. (*opposite top*) The Tercentenary Pavilion in Charles
Flower's garden off Southern Lane, 1864.

5. (*opposite centre*) The Shakespeare Memorial
Theatre, *c*.1878. The auditorium is complete, but the
water tower has not yet been built. Note the labourer
in a smock and the osiers for basket-making growing
in what became the Theatre Gardens.

6. (*opposite below*) The destruction of the Memorial
Theatre by fire, 6 March 1926.

7. (*above*) Charles Edward Flower, 'The Founder' of
the Shakespeare Memorial Theatre.

8. (*top right*) Edward Flower, founder of the brewery,
in mayoral regalia, 1864.

9. (*right*) 'Miss Marie Corelli presents a Cup to Stratford-
on-Avon Boat Club.' This is one of six scenes of Miss
Corelli in Stratford produced by a local stationer. Shortly
after they appeared, the entire stock was bought out,
presumably by Marie, who hated pictures of herself.

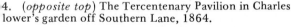

60.   Frank Benson as Shylock. This step outside the auditorium of the Theatre was much favoured for Bensonian photographs.

61. Mrs. Constance Benson as Rosalind.

62. The G. W. R. station decorated for the arrival of the Benson company, *c.*1910. The inscription from *Richard III* reads: 'To meet you on your way and welcome you'.

63. Mr. and Mrs. F. R. Benson outside Shakespeare's Birthplace with an admirer, photographed by Benjamin Stone, *c.*1908.

64. Sarah Bernhardt, who played Hamlet at Stratford in 1899. She described her visit at 'one of my heart's memories'.

65. The American actress, Mary Anderson, whose performance as Rosalind in 1882 was the Theatre's first great success.

66. Oscar Asche and Lily Brayton.

67. An autographed postcard of Ellen Terry. 'A star danced and under that was I born'.

'A star danced, + under that was I born' =

Ellen Terry

68. The Picture House, *c.*1912.

69. Women's suffrage meeting at the Fountain, 1913, which ended in a riot.

70. Birthday procession, 1900. Photograph by Benjamin Stone.

71. The May Day procession, 1911.

72. The Fairies' Dance from *A Midsummer Night's Dream*: girls rehearse in the Theatre Gardens. 'Hand in hand with Fairy Grace/ Will we sing and bless this place'. Photograph by Benjamin Stone, 1899.

73. F. R. Benson crowning the May Queen outside the Theatre.

74. Marching off to war, 1914-18.

75. The convalescent hospital at Clopton House, 1914-18.

The burden of taxes had led to exorbitant increases in the cost of food and substituted 'a factious, precarious, and fluctuating kind of property in paper' for the coin of the realm. The gazettes were filled with bankruptcies, the gaols with debtors and the workhouses with paupers.

The deprivation was selective of position and class. The *Warwick Advertiser* was not surprised that the 'fashionably attended' Christmas Assembly at the *White Lion* was regaining its former splendour, 'as the form is so well calculated to exhibit the graceful movements of female elegance'. A year later the local 'nobility, elegance and fashion' attended the Hunt Ball. One of the decorations depicted 'The flight of Bonaparte across the Rhine', a touch which indicated that the war was at last drawing to a close. In April 1814 Stratford was illuminated in celebration of Napoleon's departure to Elba. With the news in June of the Peace Treaty the Stratfordians spontaneously illuminated their houses. Four days later 100 gentlemen held a celebration dinner at the Town Hall and great numbers of women held tea-parties in the streets. At Alveston, a large ox given by John Higgins, Esq. was distributed to the parish poor: a gesture the *Warwick Advertiser* considered 'a far more acceptable method of testifying gratitude to the Great Controller of Events, than all the pomp and parade of show'. Yet the Alvestonians felt a more public occasion should seal their joy. A week later, at two o'clock, grace was said, a band played 'Oh, the roast beef of old England' and the parish poor, numbering nearly 400, sat down in a special booth with, according to the reporter, 'hearts and minds blessing their benefactors'. In the evening crowds flocked out from Stratford to join the festivities. In the 'most gratifying scene imaginable', the oldest inhabitant of the parish, aged 92, 'anxious to evince her joy, in unison with her neighbours, opened the rustic dance . . . upon the green in front of the booth, under which an immense concourse of persons of all ranks were . . . giving vent to their feelings by frequent and loyal songs and toasts accompanied by loud cheers'.

Stratford was not outdone by its smaller neighbour. A week of celebrations in July began with a grand illumination. The houses of Lord Middleton, Dr. Davenport, Mr. Hunt and Mr. Hobbes were lit with 'a degree of taste and splendour never before equalled in this Borough'. A 'very liberal' collection enabled plentiful supplies of beef and beer to be distributed to the poor, which were 'gratefully received and produced the utmost joy and satisfaction.' Those of more genteel pretentions attended a ball at the Town Hall. At six a.m. 'the company separated highly delighted with the order and conviviality which manifested the amusements of the evening'.

The peace was shortlived and the 100 days of war which followed even shorter. The great battle which closed the Napoleonic era was marked at Stratford by two sermons. Fifty-four pounds were collected at the church door for 'poor sufferers Friends at the Battle of Waterloo'. Two further sermons were preached on 20 August by the vicar and the Reverend J. T. Jones, the curate, for the 'relief and benefit of the widows and orphans of the brave men killed, and of the wounded sufferers in the signal victory'. From the proceeds the Waterloo Benefit Society was formed in 1821, Stratford's earliest such society, with the prime aim of helping those who had fought in the wars and their dependents, who numbered 'many a Veteran Waterloo hero'.

Less auspicious was the military career of William Price, a Stratfordian who at 18 enlisted in the 33rd Regiment of Foot in 1813. Three years later he deserted at Sunderland. His description, conveyed to his home town, shows that he was not really cut out for a soldier's life: he was short and stout with large feet. Perhaps the poor fellow was tired of his comrades chaffing him about his singular shape.

Crime upon Crime

The long looked-for peace did not bring prosperity. Poverty and deprivation continued unabated, generating in their turn a further crimewave. At the Lent Assize of 1818, 62 felons were condemned, of whom five forgers were hanged. One who escaped death was William

Salmon, indicted for possessing £64 in forged notes at Old Stratford. His sentence was commuted to 14 years' transportation.

In 1820, the magistrates ordered Samuel Edwards to pay William Evetts £1 for apples he had stolen. Through pride or poverty, he refused. The Beadle was then ordered to 'strip him from the middle upwards and whip him until his body be bloody'.[1]

An Association for the Prosecution of Felons was formed in 1818 and sought convictions through 'blood money'. In 1820, it offered the huge reward of £30 for the conviction of those who had broken into the offices of Mr. Wyatt, the solicitor, and stolen a few obsolete and valueless banknotes. Informers could suffer. Thomas Lench and Joseph Price were convicted of stealing apples on information provided by Joseph Calloway. On Mop night they encountered him in the *Windmill* and Calloway was struck, pursued into the street and beaten violently. Lench and Price were taken before the Mayor, who refused bail and remanded them to 'the hole' until they were sent to Warwick Gaol the next day.

Court proceedings offer another glimpse of those brutalised paupers who emerge rarely into the historical light and then only through transgression. In 1820, Richard Smith, a labourer, was bound over for threatening to drag Mary Adams out of bed by the heels and throw her in the Avon. Two years later, Smith committed an act of vagrancy by going away leaving his common-law wife and several children to the public charge.

The severity of the penal code was an oblique incitement to violence. If wrongdoers were punished with drastic brutality, they had little to lose by committing more heinous crimes. Such may have been the case on 4 November 1820, when Henry Adams (known locally as 'Black Harry'), Nathaniel Quiney and Samuel Sidney, of Waterloo Cottages on Banbury Lane, met with Thomas Heytrey of Pimlico Farm, Alveston, to plot a highway robbery. All four were known villains who had attacked travellers already that week. Necessity was a powerful motivator: Adams had to support a large family on 1s 9d a week. At Littleham Bridge near Alveston, they pulled William Hiron, a local landowner, from his horse and battered him mercilessly. He never spoke again and died soon after he was found.[2] John Ashfield's suspicions fell on the four, who were brought to Stratford and filled with drink to ease their confessions. Foolishly they had concealed banknotes stolen from the murdered man in their homes. At the Easter Assize, a chain of evidence was established, which left 'not a shadow of a doubt that the right men were doomed to suffer for the awful crime for which they were arraigned'. The ministrations of the prison chaplain brought them to 'a state of hope they never expected to experience'. On the morning of 21 April, they were taken to the prison chapel and received the sacrament. The 'deep tolling of St Mary's bell now summoned them to their ignominious end'. Adams wept bitterly. His wife had died in childbirth since his commital and the thought of leaving his six children as orphans was 'a weight too heavy for him to support'. Heytrey, whose sister had been hanged from the same scaffold the year before for the murder of her mistress, could hardly stand after he was pinioned. After a short time in prayer, the drop fell 'and in a few minutes there was an end to their earthly suffering'.

After this 'awful and melancholy event', Stratford Corporation employed an officer 'to keep strict look out after dubious characters'. The deterrent effect was not great. Soon after, the Overseers donated five shillings to Private William Hughes of the 3rd Light Infantry after he was attacked and robbed outside Stratford. Some months later, a groom was hailed by two women on the Warwick Road. They were immediately followed by two men, who knocked him off his horse with a bludgeon. They stripped him, robbed him of £12 and left him naked.

A lighter note occurred when two Herefordshire prostitutes, Mary Turner and Elizabeth Rose, were discovered *in flagrante delicto* with six local lads in a wood behind Banbury Lane. The women were sent to the House of Correction for a month for 'wandering about the boro' in a riotous and indecent way'. The boys had fled 'beyond our jurisdiction' and were discharged *in absentia* with a severe reprimand.

Mrs. Hornby's Waterloo

The constraints of war removed, the bi-centenary of Shakespeare's death was commemorated by a breakfast, a dinner and a Ball, but still no word of the poet's elevated or confused the occasion. At the Birthplace, the sitting tenant, Mary Hornby, was moved to add a distinctive note to the national triumph. So absorbed in newspaper accounts of Waterloo that sleep was impossible, she utilised her insomnia to compose a poetic tragedy on this mighty theme, proudly claiming the inheritance of some of Shakespeare's genius through a literary osmosis of habitation and descent. The work was described by a sympathetic critic as 'the queerest thing imaginable' and by an unsympathetic one as 'the most execrable verses that folly ever produced'. Such was her attraction that even the Prince Regent found her irresistible. He visited the Birthplace in 1815 and entered thoroughly into the spirit of the place, signing his name on the wall and offering to buy Shakespeare's 'old sword with which he had played Hamlet'.

Mary Hornby's social success led to her downfall. Her landlord, Thomas Court, died in 1817. His widow, noting the growing queue of pilgrims, doubled the annual rent to £20. The demands rose with the tide of pilgrims. Soon the rent was £40, beyond the wildest dream of touristic return. In October 1820, Mrs. Hornby moved to premises across the street, taking with her the celebrated Shakespearean relics. Determined that her rival should not seize gratuitously what she had painstakingly amassed, she took a pail of whitewash and washed over all the scores of names on the walls. 'At one fell swoop, out went the illustrious signatures of kings, queens, princes, princesses, ambassadors and ambassadresses, comedians, bishops, Lord Chancellors, lord chief justices, privy councillors, senators and famous orators; all the sweet tribe of duchesses, countesses, baronesses, honourables and dishonourables- out went they altogether with as little remorse as if death himself had been wielding the broom of destruction. Mary Hornby, having executed this sublime execution of so many dignities, marched out with a lofty sense of the vacuum she had left behind, carrying with her her Albums into the bargain. The new tenant on entering was struck with a speechless consternation! In the immortal bard's own words, all the precious relics had

> Vanished like the baseless fabric of a vision,
> And left not a wrack behind.'

Ada Court tried threats, bribes and litigation to secure the return of the vital relics, but to no avail. The only option seemed to begin again with clean books and clean walls. Yet 'as the disconsolate successor ruminated on the means – lo! a most happy and inspired idea occurred to her. Mary Hornby had been in a passion, and perhaps she had forgotten to put any size into her whitewash'. A brush was applied and the hope became a certainty. 'The millions of pencilled names once again appeared in all their original clearness! The relics were at once pronounced humbug; new albums were opened and the Shakespeare showroom was restored to its ancient value.'

The great entertainment in Henley Street doubled in value. The rival dowagers stood at their doors to abuse each other and their respective visitors, 'frequently with so much acerbity as to disgust and even deter the latter from entering either dwelling'. A traveller was moved to verse:

> What – Birthplace here – and relics there!
> Abuse from each! Ye brawling blowses! -
> Each picks my pocket – 'tis not fair -
> A stranger's curse on both your houses!

Mrs. Hornby's invective must have gained pungency when her rival's daughter was impregnated by George Skinner, the chaise driver at the *White Lion*. He absconded but, like a good

Stratfordian, was induced to return by the hope of living at the Birthplace after making a decent woman of Miss Court.

It was surely Mrs. Court who induced William Shakespeare Hart to place an advertisement in the *Warwick Advertiser* in 1822, declaring that his family had never owned the relics. Mary Hornby was undaunted by this reductionist ploy. She persuaded Jane Iliff, 'only surviving daughter of the late Thomas Hart . . . *(and Aunt of William Shakespeare Hart of Tewkesbury)*' to affix her mark to an advertisement in the following week's paper, declaring that, when Thomas Hornby rented the Birthplace in 1793, he purchased all the articles which had 'from time immemorial, been shown as Reliques of the Great poet'. William Shakespeare Hart, who was born at Tewkesbury, was then a little boy 'and never was in the house many times while my father was living . . . and that he cannot know anything, or but very little *"traditionally"*, and, of course, with *"no degree of certainty"*'. She had often heard her old grandfather and her father say that all the relics had been in the family since Shakespeare's death.

Such was the destructive rivalry between the two women that a mere street could not contain both. Mrs. Hornby removed herself to new premises near the Town Hall, where she exhibited her 'Collection of Reliques of William Shakespeare certified to be genuine by T. Kite and Jane Iliff, the nearest descendents of the immortal bard'. 'Do not omit to see this museum', urged a visitor. 'Every relic will make you laugh.'

Yet Mesdames Hornby and Court were making a more serious contribution than was generally realised. As the *Monthly Magazine* commented in 1818, Stratford had lost its woollen trade and 'having no manufactury would be one of the begging places of the Kingdom – but for the renown of Shakespeare, and the numerous visitors drawn to the place'.

The Canal Opened

In 1813, the Canal Company bought the Avon Navigation. This once-flourishing trade was boosted by an increase in West Indian produce shipped from Bristol. To complete the canal, the Company employed William James of Henley-in-Arden, an architect endowed with the creative energy of the new age. On 24 June 1816, it opened amidst great festivities.

The celebration was not misplaced. Soon 48,000 tons of coal were being shipped annually to Stratford, of which 18,000 tons was consumed there. The barges discharged their cargoes at two great basins on the Bancroft, where it was sold. The main return cargo was limestone, shipped from quarries near Wilmcote. Lime kilns were established by the canal at Stratford. In 1819 Thomas Lucy from Surrey, who it was rumoured had come into the district to lay claim to the family estate at Charlecote, bought and rebuilt the old flour mills by the church, reputedly using the proceeds of an out-of-court settlement, and shipped corn up the Avon, after 1830 in a steam vessel which puffed its way up and down the river. The new trade soon found its way into the records. In 1819 a bargee was arrested for assaulting a constable.

In 1820, six years before the opening of the Stockton-Darlington line, William James launched a grand new enterprise: a Central Junction Railway, to link Stratford's waterway system with London. Thomas Telford, the consultant engineer, costed the first stage to Moreton-in-Marsh (with a branch to Shipston) at £45,000. George Stephenson advised James to use steam power, but, despite James patenting the tubular locomotive boiler in 1821, this was unwisely rejected for the certainties of horse locomotion. The enabling legislation was secured and capital of £35,000 raised. The financial commitment was too much for James and he was imprisoned for debt, although later he surveyed the Liverpool and Manchester railway. 'His fluency of conversation I never heard equalled,' opined the great engineer, Robert Stephenson, 'but he was no thinker at all in the practical side of the work he had taken up.'

A Sad Ending

The story of that devoted couple, Robert and Elizabeth Hobbes, has a sad ending. In an era of enterprise and speculation, fortunes were easily made and lost. By 1812 Robert Hobbes was a moneyscrivener, 'receiving other men's money into his trust and custody and making merchandize thereof'. In 1816 he overreached himself in land speculation and became indebted for £669 10s 9d to the Stratford bankers Oldaker, Tomes and Chattaway. A commission of bankruptcy was issued against him and he was required to 'surrender himself' to the Commissioners on three successive days. His legal partnership was dissolved and assignees were appointed from amongst his creditors to dispose of his property. As well as the family home in Waterside, there were four cottages in Chapel Lane, a meadow on the Warwick Road and a new schoolhouse in Ely Street, where Betsy was going to open a school.

Robert's troubles came not as single spies. The Assignees had permitted him to dig up his potatoes. On his way to the plot he saw his friend Gamble the surgeon, who was involved in unrecorded trouble with the Corporation. Robert told him he disapproved of his conduct and added 'perhaps laughingly (certainly not exultingly) that the Corporation would play the devil with him, or some such expression'. This remark found its way back to 'those who have been indefatigable in their Exertions to defame me', who may have 'artfully' converted it into 'an expression of Triumph or Contempt to the Body Corporate'. He was in a tricky position. If his debts were called in he could be imprisoned, so his reputation was of vital importance. In a dignified affidavit to William Chattaway, one of his Assignees, he declared that Gamble would vouch for the truth of his statement, 'with his

22. The former home of the Hobbes family, where Mrs. Hobbes later opened her school. Drawn by J. T. Blight in 1840.

usual candour and kindness'. This sad episode of conflict with the Corporation he had served so well is the last we hear of Robert Hobbes. He was as yet only 43 and capable of strenuous work, yet on 2 January he died from unspecified causes. He was buried at Holy Trinity five days later.

Elizabeth Hobbes faced huge problems. At 39 she was the widow of a bankrupt, with 11 children to bring up. She possessed sympathetic friends. Her uncle the vicar was instrumental in the appointment of Elizabeth Ashford Hobbes, aged 15, as the organist at a salary of £40 a year. This must have been planned before Robert's death: the meeting confirming her appointment took place 18 days after his burial.

The Corporation shared something of Robert Hobbes' penury. The vicar despatched a furious letter on 8 October, declaring that he would no longer be 'deluded' with promises of an increase in his stipend. If this were 'to be delayed till you are out of debt, you all know that it may be Half a Century before it can possibly take place. I have only to add that from this day, as a Corporate Body I take my leave of you for ever'. When the Chamberlain called for an explanation, he was subjected to personal abuse and violent invective against the whole Corporation. In retaliation the vicar was ordered to quit the Mayor's garden, next to his own, which he had been permitted to use for 40 years. To underline this division between ecclesiastical and civil jurisdiction, a dividing wall was built.

Either through skilful handling of her affairs or through friendly largesse, Elizabeth Hobbes retained the family home. Yet income would have to be generated if the family were to remain solvent. The answer was that she should open her school at home instead of in Ely Street. Ten weeks after Robert's death she advertised in the *Warwick Advertiser* that she would open a

*Mathews as a River god
by Mr Edwin Landseer*

23. *Caricature of Charles Mathews as a River God,
by Landseer.*

school for young ladies in the summer and engage a teacher 'fully qualified ... both as to acquirements and morals and she hopes that her utmost exertions for the present improvement and future happiness of her Pupils, and the support of herself and her numerous family, will meet with every encouragement from a Benevolent Public'.

There were a number of small private schools in Stratford. A survey in 1818 recorded seventeen. Mrs. Hobbes' standard boarding charge of 25 guineas per annum included tuition in English grammar and needlework: 'Parlour Boarders', who lived with the family, paid 40 guineas: 'Day Boarders' (i.e. weekly) paid 14 guineas and 'Day Scholars', four guineas. It would be interesting to know who the pupils were and from whence they came, but financial considerations would ensure that they were from affluent backgrounds.

Elizabeth Hobbes fought with tenacity for her 11 children. In 1819 she measured their heights, which ranged from two feet 11 inches for four-year-old Harriet to just under five foot three for 18-year-old Robert. Elizabeth at 17, measured five feet and Mary, a year younger, an inch shorter. Their shortness surely reflects a pattern amongst the population as a whole.

Robert Hobbes, junior was found a position with a firm of lawyers in London. His brother William followed him into the profession. For the six Hobbes daughters, the feminine accomplishments of embroidery and music could be acquired, but the best long-term prospect was marriage. Not all Stratford's maidens achieved such conjunction. The assertion that the only maidenhead in town was on the pub sign of that name was contradicted by the battalions of spinsters conducting lives of private tuition and drapery. 'Miss Whitmore', wrote a Stratfordian in 1818, 'still holds out against the sieges of those horrid creatures, men, as do our neighbours opposite and all the spinsters of the town and neighbourhood.'

The marital prospects of 37 of the town's maidens prompted a wager over dinner at the *White Lion* in 1820. Joseph Cresswell bet William George Morris, with Robert Hobbes, junior as witness, that seven would be married within five years. The stake was a dinner for the winner and four of his friends. Cresswell probably won, since at least four of the maidens were married within a year, including Elizabeth Hobbes, who had improved his chances by marrying him.

'Aye, I had a hand in that'

The dramatic arts were chiefly represented in Stratford at this time by Mrs. Nunns of the Warwick Theatre, who frequently brought her company, once with sad effects when one of her actresses, Mrs. Frimbley, hanged herself while 'lunatic'. Despite such setbacks, the company always performed to the 'utmost applause'. So much did the 'genius of this unrivalled band grow in the minds of its votaries', that it was resolved to build a theatre, 'that the birthplace of the matchless poet may boast of a trophy dedicated to the memory of his immortal genius'. All that remains of Mrs. Nunns' reputation is a fleeting record of local approbation, but to her must be ascribed the first inspiration for a Shakespearean Theatre at Stratford.

The suggestion that Stratford should have a theatre dedicated to Shakespeare was picked up by the noted comic actor, Charles Mathews, when he performed at the Town Hall on 10 December 1820. His show was called *A Trip to Paris* and he played all the parts in monologue. No record survives of his performance, although the correspondent of the *Warwick Advertiser* anticipated a 'delectable treat'. Yet the visit was historic, for next evening he convened a meeting at the Town Hall, with Captain Saunders in the chair, to consider 'the best mode of erecting, in the form of a THEATRE, a NATIONAL MONUMENT to the IMMORTAL MEMORY of SHAKESPEARE'. Mathews made a memorable speech, observing that 'the Literary and Dramatic World' had long regretted that the birthplace of Shakespeare did not possess 'some token of NATIONAL respect and gratitude to such an immortal genius'. He appealed to his listeners 'to lend their mite were it only in the gift of 5/-, as it would be the proudest boast of any person's life to say in after times when passing by this Building, "Aye, I had a hand in that."' He sat down to loud cheers. A committee was formed, with Mathews as President. Next spring he selected a site in New Place garden and appointed Mr. Chantry of London as the architect. Fund-raising was boosted by the news of Sir Walter Scott's support. Not all showed such approbation. The *Warwick Advertiser* considered that 'more moral evil than good and less pecuniary advantages derived to the inhabitants by the erection of a Theatre than of a Mausoleum'.

FOOTNOTES
[1]   The punishment had a limited deterrent effect. In 1825, James Palmer, the Town Crier, flogged 'Young Wheeler and Saml. Edwards' for stealing pears.
[2]   The place where his head had rested became known as 'Hiron's hole'. For many years afterwards, men on the way to work scooped it out, 'so that this foul deed should never be forgotten'. *Looking back at 91.* Mrs. Elsie Powell, 1970.

CHAPTER 12

'Success unto Trade'

'A bumper I claim, and I am not afraid
But you'll join me in drinking – success unto Trade!'

Shakespeare Club drinking song.

'My dear Robert'

From her window on Waterside, Elizabeth Hobbes could see the transformation of the Bancroft. Two large basins, lined by warehouses, received canal traffic. Despite William James' bankruptcy, work on the railway continued. A graceful brick bridge was built to carry the wide-gauge tracks over the Avon in 1823. In that year Elizabeth found places for two of her sons: Thomas, aged 17 and 11-year-old John. She wrote to her son Robert in London from the *Mitre* at Oxford, to give him the good news of John's admission as a chorister of Magdalen College:

> I brought him here on Tuesday, his voice was tried yesterday and his name is to be entered in the books today. I am now going to seek out for Board and Lodg[ing] for him, to pay entrance to the different Masters, Fees to the Servants & purchase cap, Gown & Surplice, &c. We are much indebted to our friend the Proctor for without his weight and interest, He would not have succeeded; John's age being very much against him. I have heard of a suitable situation for Tom with the same Gentleman with whom D. Rice served his time but more of this hereafter. God bless you and believe me in great haste to remain always your affect. Mother, E.D. Hobbes. John desires his love and hopes you will call upon him when you pass through Oxford. How grateful I feel to Providence for his protection and Assistance.

Here influence is being used for a not unworthy purpose: the placing of the bright son of a genteel but impecunious widow, who was solicitous of her children's welfare.

A last glimpse of this admirable lady is afforded by a fragmentary journal she kept during 1824. The year opened on a poignant note: 'January 2nd. The anniversary of my dear Robert's death, never absent from my thoughts during the whole day'. Her life was dominated by large washdays and the routine of school-life. In the summer her married daughter resigned as organist and her mother used her influence again. Her uncle, the vicar, called 'to speak about organ, agreed to give notice in church to get Anne elected'. On 19 September the mother was at church twice to hear Anne play. Life was not all soap and salvation, for she fitted in an occasional game of backgammon with her daughter's mother-in-law, Mrs. Cresswell. On 14 October, the pupils were given a holiday for the Mayor's feast-day. Robert was now practising in Stratford and it must have seemed like old times when his mother recorded his return from the festivities at the Town Hall in the early hours.

At the Runaway Mop, Mrs. Hobbes hired Mary Ann Savage as a cook at eight pounds a year – and two other domestics who had worked for her before: Sophia Plumb as housemaid and Sally Hiron as washerwoman. The difficulties associated with Mop-hiring asserted themselves. On 3 November the cook and housemaid ran off early in the morning, leaving 'nobody but Sally Hiron' and Mrs. Hobbes registered a complaint for breach of contract.

On 16 November Miss Tomlinson, the teacher, took the children to a Diorama at the *White Lion*. Stratford was up with the times. It was only three years since Daguerre's first showing of his three-dimensional exhibit in Paris. Four days later, Mrs. Hobbes went to see the celebrated comic-actor, Mr. Sims, perform at the Town Hall. This was her last recorded excursion. Next day she concluded her journal with the laconic entry 'Not so well tonight'. She wrote no more. She must have been ill through the winter and died in the spring, aged only 46. Her passing was noteworthy in Stratford. On 18 April 1825 James Palmer, the town crier, recorded in his journal that Mrs. Hobbes was buried. The school was closed and the house let. Her six children still at home must have gone to live with their lawyer brother or married sister. Elizabeth Hobbes had worked hard to keep her family after the death of her beloved Robert. She would have been gratified to know that, in Stratford's terms, each achieved a fit marriage or profession.

A Great Reformer

There were those in Stratford who would ensure that the lethargy of the Georgian era would give way before Victorian energy. The town was fortunate in 1822, when Dr. John Conolly became Borough Surgeon at the age of twenty-seven. This great doctor, 'a reformer by nature and hearty liberal in politics, ardently devoted himself to the furtherance of every measure of progress'. His first great work was to establish a public dispensary for the sick poor, with a surgery and two small wards, at the Old Bank Building in Chapel Street. The scheme was intended to help those to whom sudden illness or injury would be a disaster. Subscribers had the right of nomination, deficits being made up by public appeals. The annual Dispensary Ball became a feature of the social calendar. In the first year 330 patients were treated.

In August 1824, after a severe case of smallpox was diagnosed, a vaccination was organised of those claiming parish relief and later of the other inhabitants. Conolly did not doubt that Stratfordians would comply 'with so respectable a recommendation', but warned that anyone wandering abroad who had been in contact with the contagion would be prosecuted. His zeal for public health led to his calling a meeting in September to discuss the hazards of lime kilns proposed on the canal-wharves and he sought advice from a specialist in Uttoxeter. That year he founded a local 'Society for Reading and Lectures' to expand educational opportunity for working people, which included a 'Tradesmen's Library' and a fund for visiting lecturers.

Soon after arriving in Stratford, John Conolly was elected to the Corporation, rapidly becoming alderman and Mayor, and a valued diplomatist in local disputes. His interest in the town continued after he was appointed the first Professor of Medical Practice at the new London University in 1828. He resigned in 1831 after administrative difficulties and went into private practice in Warwick. In 1839 he became resident physician to the Middlesex Asylum. Here this 'friend and guide to the crazy' abandoned the prevailing system of restraint, pioneering the recognition of the nature of mental illness. His work and energy effected a revolution in the treatment of the mentally sick.

Christian Fervour

In 1824 a branch of the Church Missionary Society was formed, 'with every good wish and sincere desire for the conversion of the poor benighted Heathen'. The Reverend Francis Fortescue Knottesford of Alveston Manor chaired the inaugural meeting, when it was resolved to petition Parliament for governmental protection for missionaries within the British Empire. In 1826 another petition, for the abolition of negro slavery, was presented.

Mr. Knottesford was also the local correspondent of the National Committee for Abolishing Climbing Boys; those poor mites who shared the fate of Kingsley's 'Water Babies'. It says little for the Stratfordians that his efforts were depressingly sterile. He arranged for a 'clever mason' to be trained to sweep mechanically in the hope of encouraging by example; a scheme which was reluctantly abandoned 'on finding that the *sine qua non* generally with the inhabitants for its admission into their houses, was whether their favourite sweeper should be employed or not. At first he willingly adopted it, and spoke highly of its convenience; but time has convinced us that he is playing the same trick that so many of his fraternity have played before . . . he serves his own purposes merely by obtaining the use of an additional boy that neither eats nor drinks, and yet such is the prejudice of the neighbourhood, that if we were to take it from him at present, he would retain all his customers.'

The Committee attempted to 'bind out his eldest boy, a poor deformed lad, as apprentice to a tailor or basket-maker', but this was frustrated by the Overseers for Old Stratford and the borough, 'who each deny that he belongs to them and will not admit him until that point be settled. There will then be two more boys to get rid of'. Like many frustrated reformers, Mr. Knottesford saw public legislation as the means towards private morality: 'Our greatest hope rests on the passing of the bill to be brought forward the next session'. This splendid clergyman concludes with the hope that Stratford's parsimony was untypical of the nation. 'I sincerely trust that this will be the most discouraging report you receive from your numerous correspondents.'

Such worthy activity received little support from the vicar and his colleagues. 'When I come to consider,' wrote Captain Jenkinson of Alveston, secretary of the Church Missionary Society branch, 'that the Clergyman of the Parish is not inclined to favour our proceedings and the prejudice that exists with some of the principal inhabitants, I cannot but be very thankful for the success it has pleased God to give us . . . I have applied to one of the principal Gentlemen of the Corporation, who seems to think that there can be no doubt of our obtaining the Town Hall for a meeting; to obtain the church for a sermon, would, I fear, be difficult.'

The increasingly irascible Dr. Davenport was in the fourth decade of his long incumbency and was sturdily maintaining his tradition of latitudinarian inactivity. His fondness for the bottle led to his nickname of 'dive-in-port', while his resultant tetchiness caused Captain Saunders to fix a Shakespearean quotation on him: 'If I can fasten but one cup upon him / With that which he hath drunk tonight already / He'll be as full of quarrel and offence / as my young mistress' dog'.

Dissatisfaction with the Established Church was revealed in a survey of church pews, conducted by John Conolly in 1828. Many parishioners were vociferous about being unable to obtain sittings – their children were sometimes turned away from church for this reason. Some had left the Established Church altogether. Dissent, for a century and a half a puny flower in Stratford's religious soil, began to take new roots, although old prejudices died hard.

Nonconformists were taking advantage of the Acts of Indemnity which ended their exclusion from public office and the Mayor in 1824, John Tasker, was a dissenter. At the Mayor's Feast, Mr. Jones the curate upbraided him for his beliefs, 'rather catechetically and without regard to time and place'. With dignity he replied that he considered the Established Church, 'thro' neglect and lukewarmness in prescribed duties, to be not only the greatest dissenters themselves from what they inculcate, but by preaching it to be Orthodoxy, the cause of it in the minds of others.'

The Independent meeting in Rother Street was reviving through the inspiration of a remarkable pastor, the Reverend Thomas Helmore, who was born an Anglican in 1783, but was ordained in the Independent ministry after hearing the noted preacher, Dr. Styles. He came to Stratford in 1820 and his indefatigable energy soon made its mark. In 1823, he founded a boys' school at the Rother Street Chapel, under the auspices of the British and Foreign Schools Society. In 1825, a girls' school was opened. Soon there were 300 pupils in the 'British Schools', compared with 40 at the National School.

Helmore taught in the British Schools until he trained a schoolmaster, William Pardoe, to take charge. 'He drilled the boys, taught them to sing, drew and coloured maps which he mounted on frames.' His youngest son, Frederick, aged seven, led a band of fifes. 'The indefatigable minister' was assisted by little Mrs. Corbett, the postman's wife. A future Mayor, William Pearce, recalled that she delivered letters in the morning and beat him in the afternoon. The pupils were taught to sing and act their school songs and to do 'useful exercises'.

The children's morning hymn was sung before fund-raising sermons preached by Helmore:

> Let grateful songs arise,
> Jehovah's name to praise;
> Who from the lofty skies
> Regards our infant lays:
> Let all rejoice to see the day,
> When children learn to read and pray.
> Our Sabbaths once we spent
> In folly and in sin;
> On play our minds were bent,
> And pleasure sought therein:
> But now we learn to read and sing and pray.
> To aid this good design,
> May all our friends unite;
> May those in glory shine,
> Who freely gave their mite,
> To teach our youthful feet the way
> That leads to realms of endless day.

When Helmore realised that his sons possessed musical talent, he taught himself music at the age of forty. Frederick remembered sitting with a large music book, playing an imaginary accompaniment to his father and brother's struggles on their flutes. The elder brother, another Tom Helmore, possessed exceptional ability. After his return from Mill Hill School, his father put him in charge of the chapel singers. Soon there was a fine choir and a great deal of singing was introduced into the service. At the age of ten Frederick played the second violin part in Corelli's trios, but on the flute, with old Edmund Payne the timber merchant on first violin and Tom on the cello – the only two stringed instruments in Stratford. 'One day to my great joy my dear father presented me with the skeleton of a violin he had purchased in a sale. I ran with it down Sheep Street and Edmund Payne (who seemed as delighted as myself) rigged out my instrument and lent me a bow. I took it to bed with me and next morning was up before 4 o'clock and in the loft set to work on my scales. As soon as I could play as far as 4 sharps and 4 flats in tune I got Challenor's tutor and played all through that'. Before he went to bed he could play a little gavotte. He had practised 14 hours. 'I practiced as hard as my blistered fingers would let me all through the Summer vacation.' He then had lessons, which he relayed to some of his schoolfriends. Tom taught William Pardoe the violincello and within a year they had a 'fair orchestra', which supported the choir. The brothers Helmore formed a unique quartet of three flutes and a bassoon, for which Tom arranged a number of pieces. Mr. Rainsford, the music publisher, declared it, years later, to be 'the sweetest and most perfectly executed chamber music he had ever heard'.

Frederick recalled the moral courage of his father, who 'hated cruelty above all things'. It was the custom to 'billet cocks' on Shrove Tuesday. 'The dastardly game was like the modern "Aunt Sally", only that instead of a wooden effigy . . ., a live cock was tied to a post by its leg with a string, a piece of cloth being bound round the bone lest the string should break the foot off in the fluttering efforts of the unfortunate bird to escape the blows of the billets thrown at him.' A post near Mr. Helmore's garden gate in Maidenhead Lane was chosen one year for this sport. 'The brave man went out among a set of villains, with a knife severed the string, and before they had time to recover from their amazement, brought in the poor bird under his arm and fastened the garden gate. An attack was made upon the garden and yard gates, and Tom, his eldest son, was sent over the fence to fetch the constables. An attempt to summon the minister for theft was made without avail and billeting cocks has never since been attempted.' Helmore faced subtler opposition when he preached against theatrical amuse-ments. As a result he was subjected to stage satire, probably from Charles Mathews, but he bound the lampoon 'as a garland round his brow'.

Frederick Helmore's mother was renowned for her labours amongst the needy. 'Her charming presence and sweet optimism cheered many a drooping spirit and by her careful watchfulness and wise treatment, patients of whom the doctors had despaired, were nursed back to life and health.' One incident reveals the spiritual power of Olive Helmore. There was a woman at Luddington who was blind, deaf and dumb and who had lost the use of her limbs. 'This poor,helpless mortal showed evident signs of joy at the approach of Mrs. Helmore. As soon as her foot touched the stair which led to her bedroom, her face lighted up and during the visit showed appreciation of the kind presence of her visitor, who while she clasped the poor lifeless hand in her own gentle grasp, offered up fervent prayers for the soul of the helpless one.'

Exeunt Omnes

The theatre project ensured that Charles Mathews was seen frequently in Stratford and performed there occasionally. At one entertainment in the Town Hall, he selected the weekly market as the prosaic highlight of the town's life:

> There were pigs and donkies, pork and veal,
> And lots of tempting mutton . . .
> With geese and niceties,
> To suit the greatest glutton,
> And Lord! There were such pretty girls,
> I could not get away, sirs.
> And this was all at Stratford-on-Avon,
> On a market day, sirs.

The song is that of a travelling performer, adapting his material to local topography. Such characteristic patter can be heard from the North Country comedian, Woolmer, in his 'Yorkshire Neddy's Ramble in search of a Wife'.

> I've travelled thro' Alveston, Clifford and Tiddington, Charlecote and Snitterfield, Newbold and Eatington; But now I'm thinking marriage is surely a lottery. Yes, icod after being in so many places and not be able to get a wife was surely provoking enough, but however thinks I bad luck now, better luck another time, soa I set off again. Singing Ritum, titum . . . I went to the Red Lion, then to the White Lion, Cross Keys, Horseshoe, Duke of Wellington, George and Dragon, Dog, Green Man, Horse and Jockey, till at last I wandered to the Thatch, but just as I was going down a Lane nearly opposite, I meets a very pretty modest looking lass, so I goes to her and says I, 'pray my Love be so good as to tell me where I am?' 'Oh,you're quite at home, Sir,' says she, 'or very near it. This is Hell Lane.' 'Dom it! I'm in for it again', says I so I turned on my heel and began singing, Ritum, titum, &c.

The fullest account of a dramatic performance in this era comes from James Saunders, who cryptically recorded the shortcomings of a travelling company in 1823. The venue was the old Tythe Barn[1] in Hell Lane, rented from Baldwin the butcher for 30s a week. The company's poor potential was further reduced by animosity between the proprietor, Davenport, and Melmoth, his leading actor. Davenport was a Scot, whom Saunders considered 'utterly unfit to open his mouth before a Southern audience'. Melmoth possessed some talent, but 'lost himself by eternal drinking and smoking tobacco'. He had a violent temper and had knocked down old Macready while playing at Bristol. At Stratford he made two malicious stage thrusts at a colleague after a minor disagreement.

Nor was the rest of the company reassuring. Mr. Evans 'did not possess a single merit' and was 'old, ill-formed, insignificant and imperfect'; Mrs. Gunning was 'a drunken old stager who had seen better days'; Mr. Cleaver, 'a little duck-legged makeweight, without memory or any other qualification'; Mr. Shearer, 'short and declamatory . . . mutinous and ill-disposed, dirty in person and of bad principles'. His wife was a sad figure who had once been highly talented and 'acquired much applause both in this country and America. In the latter she married Captain Thompson by whom she had two girls . . . who have appeared in childish characters here. Her second marriage now degraded her in the eyes of her family and the consequent penury and discomfort preyed on her spirits and acting'. The only real talent was Mr. Whyte who possessed a pleasing singing voice. He appeared for a few nights before graduating to a superior company at Worcester. Davenport had hoped that Mr. Rowland Green, a local hatter and amateur actor, would play Othello, but he declined. His talents must have been solicited in the hope of boosting the box-office.

The season was disastrous. 'Bad success soured all parties – the treasury was empty and the company seperated, disgusted with each other and their want of patronage . . . Exeunt Omnes.'

A Superseded Idea

The 'Tramway' to Moreton opened amidst great celebrations on 5 September 1826. A band preceded a party of dignitaries in five covered carriages, who were followed down the line by the vital commodities of coal, timber and lime in 21 trucks adapted from farm usage. The powerful horses and the ease with which the axles revolved were much admired.

Another new trade made its mark on the records when Thomas Lark, 'the driver of a Rail Road waggon' was charged with assaulting Joseph Hirons. The world's first recorded railway fatality occurred at Alderminster on 21 May 1830, when a child was run over.

The *Warwick Advertiser* hoped that the railway might prove a blessing to the poor, by bringing cheaper fuel – a thought expressed also by a local poet:

> To see our iron railway we are quite content.
> For what we've saved on coaling will surely pay the rent.

The tramway played a considerable role in the trade of the area for three decades, conveying 15,000 tons of coal annually by 1845. The grand design of a link to London was never fulfilled, although a connection to Paddington was later made at Moreton. The advent of steam soon ensured that the enterprise was a 'superseded idea'.

Crime and Incendiarism

Sentence of death was recorded twice more for crimes committed at Stratford. In 1826 James Johnson and Giles Collins were reprieved after stealing two horses. Two years later, John Windsor, William Slater and William Vale were condemned for burgling the shop of Gibbs the watchmaker. A month later they were conveyed aboard the hulk, *Retribution*, at Sheerness, prior to transportation for life.

Stratford's proximity to the industrial workshops of Birmingham produced a flood of counterfeit coinage. In 1826, Elizabeth Seagrave was charged with passing a dud half-crown. Crying bitterly, she threw herself on the Court's mercy, pleading for her three fatherless children. Despite this, she got twelve months hard labour, with the obligation to find two sureties in £20 for her good behaviour on release. She was probably an habitual offender, for, on the same day, Ann Brotherton, who had many such convictions and was described as going through England like a pestilence, received the same sentence. She was arrested in the *Red Lion*, when £4 8s 6d in counterfeit silver was found in the petticoats of the child on her knee.

On occasions the lawlessness of the times and the driving force of poverty combined to produce a rural terrorism which struck at the wealthy and exploitative. The disaffected resorted to the incendiarism which became known as the 'Swing Riots' and England appeared to be on the verge of revolution.

The first manifestation of revolutionary incendiarism at Stratford (and one of the first in England) occurred at 11 p.m. on 8 March 1826, when two ricks were discovered ablaze in the yard of Mr. Gardiner of the *Red Horse*. Strenuous efforts by the populace saved the nearby buildings. Next day a rick in John Baldwin's farmyard at Hare's Lane, Alveston, was burnt and three days later, a rick at Billesley Hall, three miles from Stratford. Public alarm was increased by anonymous letters threatening further visitations. A reward of £300 for the conviction of the 'diabolical incendiaries' was offered, but no information was forthcoming as ricks and farm buildings continued to blaze. The conspiracy was skilled and closed. On 27 December 1827, the Mayor received a letter advising him that the engines should be prepared for action. The watch was alerted, but the combustibles were already in place and exploded in another rick at Baldwin's farm on New Year's Eve. When the alarm was raised, the Stratfordians 'with their usual activity on such occasions', rushed over with tarpaulins and buckets. Within minutes, over 1,000 people had congregated. When the engines arrived, a human chain passed the buckets 500 yards from the river and the fire was extinguished before it reached the farm buildings. Five days later, Mr. Baldwin received a letter threatening that the 'Firelighter' would act again within four days. The *Warwick Advertiser* also received a letter, signed 'Peter Schlemihl':

> 'There are more things in heaven and earth, Horatio,
> Than are dreamt of in your philosophy.'
>
> Shakespeare.

> Sir, – There is a man, who has actually invented a composition which will set as hard as granite; and what is most remarkable, it will ignite at the slightest contact of fire; it is capable of being formed into balls of any size, and will bear the force of a gun or cannon, to discharge it against any solid substance; and will penetrate equally the same as any other shot. I shot it against (says the inventor) a solid oak with a common fowling piece, and it has answered in every particular.

The outbreaks caused concern in Whitehall. On 14 January 1828 Lord Lansdowne, the Home Secretary, promised a royal pardon and a reward of £100 to anyone turning King's evidence. Such inducements had no effect. In May a rick-yard in the Alcester Road was fired; in January 1829, £400 reward was offered after an outbreak at Binton and two weeks later 'a most alarming fire' was discovered in the stack-yard of Mr. Richard Salmon at Tiddington. A horseman was dispatched to Stratford, post-horses were put to the engines and galloped over in a few minutes. The flames were uncontrollable and spread to the house and farm buildings. The desperate shouting and rushing about of several hundred people provided a 'heart-rending scene of devastation, terror and anxiety'. Several gentlemen, prepared for the chase after the hunt ball, joined the lines of fire-fighters in their hunting pink. Some rode off on their hunters to fetch buckets and tarpaulins. Even the octogenarian vicar of Stratford was seen on the line.

A police officer from Bow Street arrived in Stratford to investigate, but enjoyed no more success than the local vigilantes. Only the rising prosperity of the early 1830s brought a temporary lull to the outbreaks.

The 'Milk and Water' and the 'Bran and Chaff'

The Shakespeare Club was founded in 1824 on the initiative of Mr. Britton, a London publisher. The founder members were some 15 Stratfordians, 'humble in rank, but enthusiastic in their admiration of the Immortal Bard'. Captain Saunders fastidiously loathed the club, regarding it as dominated by those who, 'utterly devoid of the taste, liberality, and the multitudinous variety of attainments necessary to plan or conduct such an undertaking, appeared only emulous of turning the tide of Pecuniary expenditure, each into his own line of trade or influence'. The Club song tended to endorse this view!

> . . .Were the Avon's sweet Bard from the grave to arise,
> No doubt but Old Stratford he'd view with surprize:
> The Bancroft I fancy he scarcely would know,
> With its basins and wharves and black diamond show.
> A bumper I claim, and I am not afraid
> But you'll join me in drinking-success unto trade!

Saunders attended one of the earliest annual dinners of the Club, 'formed to do honour as they call it, to their Immortal Bard'. Two hundred and seventeen members and visitors sat down at three – 'an unfashionable hour truly, but necessarily so to allow for the early introduction of pipes and tobacco which, they imagine (tho the immortal Bard says nothing about it), give a great intellectuality. The system began to work in about an hour after the general muster which consisted of the parish squire – 2 bourgeois squirets – 4 Aldermen – 7 Capital Burgesses – the rest Tradesmen, players, Chelsea pensioners . . . About this period the conversation became gradually metamorphised when the whole assembly were found to consist of and call each other "gentlemen"'. When the Mayor rose to propose the toast of St George and the King, 'Mr. Vice-President began to stare – and protested that he long thought the patron saint of England had been dead – when an Intellectual explained the toast meant his Immortal Health and the King's mortal!'

Despite Saunders' low opinion the Club organised a considerable Festival, scrupulously modelled on Garrick's, in 1827. At dawn the Stratfordians were roused by bands of musicians and the firing of cannon. Despite the obligatory gloomy weather, the roads to Stratford were thronged and by 11 a vast crowd had gathered. Not all were drawn by literary enthusiasm: 'the light-fingered gentry' had mustered in force. One man lost £30, but the Committee had had the foresight to engage police-officers from Birmingham. Ten suspicious characters were arrested soon after their arrival and the rest departed rapidly. Booths were erected in the main streets. Amongst the attractions for non-Bardolators were the Somersetshire giantess and fairy, and Boardman the celebrated dwarf. Crowds clustered around ballad singers, purchasing their eulogies of Shakespeare. 'The doleful ditty of the lame and blind' and the shrill voices of the showmen filled the air.

The formalities began with the Shakespearean procession postponed from 1769. At New Place, Mr.Bond, the actor, recited the obligatory Ode, composed by Mr. Searle of Covent Garden, and gave the day its focus by laying the foundation stone of the Theatre in Chapel Lane. The procession arrived at Holy Trinity to confused expectations. An extraordinary proposal was abroad that Hamlet's gravediggers would be standing in the sanctuary, resting on their spades, as if they had just completed 'their melancholy task of committing "the sweetest bard who ever sang" to the "jaws of the ponderous and silent tomb"'. Sprites and fairies would peer fearfully from behind pillars and a character dressed as Hamlet would speak an oration. Word had it that this amazing idea had been vetoed by the vicar: a judgement in which the local press concurred. 'With all our veneration for the matchless Bard of Avon, we say better had he never been born than that our altars and our temples of religion should become the scene of such profanation.' In the event nothing more spectacular took place than a musical rendering of Shakespeare's laconic epitaph.

That evening Garrick's pattern was continued with a grand firework display at the *White Lion*. The Masquerade Ball was held nearby in a special and 'brilliantly illuminated' pavilion. Memories of 1769 located it well away from the river. Once again 'few characters were taken and these but indifferently sustained'.

For members of the Shakespeare Club, there was a formal dinner at the Town Hall. Speech followed speech and toast followed toast. When obvious subjects like 'The Royal Family', 'The Immortal Memory' and 'The Mayor and Corporation' were exhausted, the company raised its glasses to each other. The evening ended with an unexpected tribute to 'The Revd.

Mr. Jones, the late Chaplain to the Corporation', which finally exhausted members' ingenuity and drinking capacity. The only jarring note was struck by the eminent radical divine, Dr. Wade of Warwick, who used the occasion to attack the draconian game laws. 'Now these are strange modes of inducing the County Gentry to visit us at our next Jubilee', fumed the Tory *Warwickshire Chronicle*.

The Royal Shakespearean Theatre opened on 12 December with an address from Mr. Searle and performances of *As You Like It* and *Catherine and Petruchio*. The decor and style of the building were much admired. Two years later, the theatre received the endorsement of the greatest theatrical figures of the age when Edmund Kean played Richard III and Shylock, and W.C. Macready played Hamlet.

The unanimity of the Shakespeare Club was soon disturbed by a breakaway faction, known as the 'True Blues', or more familiarly the 'Bran and Chaff', which met at the *Golden Lion* and organised a rival celebration on the Birthday. This Club's greatest asset was its permanent President, Mr. Robbins of Warwick, whose qualities at the convivial table were regarded as unsurpassed. More than once he presided for 12 hours without leaving the room.

The original club, nicknamed 'The Milk and Water,' also had its characters. John Warner of Charlecote always dressed in woollen cord breeches and blue stockings. On taking his seat, he untied a handkerchief and, with an appetite reinforced by a three-mile walk, devoured a huge snack – 'more than enough for any other four men in the room.' Once he had settled down to his pipe, the Chairman would often ask him for a recitation, which 'after a little affected modesty on the part of the rural poet, was invariably complied with . . .':

> Every field and pleasant lea,
> And every drooping willow tree
> Growing by a stream of water;
> And every farmer's pretty daughter,
> And the loving swain who sought her;
> Every fat cow for slaughter,
> The butcher, lucky man, who bought her.

At one time, this noted character had 'affected the cunning man' and done good business as a diviner, but tiring of this wizardry, he gave his mysterious books away. His fame, however, had spread and people continued to walk long distances to consult him about the whereabouts of their lost property.

The influence of the Shakespeare Club was recognised by Mary Hornby's daughter, Sarah Raisin, who succeeded her mother as guardian of the sacred relics and promoted her inheritance in singular style:

> Mister Chareman i make bold to solicit the Patromy of the Shakespeare Club – to my shewing the jenuine relks of the bard collected by my respected Mother – and leave to make a nue showband and print cards with your tittle.

Poor Mary Hornby, like many purveyors of fantasy, became deluded and was removed to a madhouse. She died in 1829, aged 63, a week after her return.

The Shakespeare Clubs joined forces in 1830 for a three-day Birthday Festival. The usual elements were present – dinners, a pavilion (this time in the Rother Market), illuminated buildings, a masquerade and pyrotechnics. A number of noted actors walked in the procession, including the wonder of the day, Master Grossmith, 'the Reading Roscius', as Prince Arthur; young Charles Kean, son of the great Edmund, riding as St George and very fatigued by the heavy armour, and Charles Booth, who delivered an address at the Birthplace. Later Kean played Richard III with 'great energy and merit': it was the first time that a Shakespeare play had formed part of the celebrations. Stratford's old friend, the former Prince Regent, helped matters along by conferring the coveted title, of 'Royal', on the original Shakespeare Club, but the event was marred for the fastidious Saunders by the persistent failure of the Stratfordians to observe the niceties of rank. 'Three bourgeois squirets' designated themselves 'Esquires' and the theatre manager had advertised for a 'Gentleman' to build a show booth.

A figure whose name would describe an age visited Stratford in August, when the Duchess of Kent toured the Birthplace with her 11-year-old daughter, Princess Victoria.[2] The widows Hornby and Court had realised what was now dawning on the world: the Birthplace was a gilt-edged property, said to be worth £2,000. Another glimpse of its heyday under free enterprise comes with the visit of the American humourist, Nathaniel Willis, in 1833. Lacking relics, Mrs. Court had made a box of mulberry wood the pride of her collection: 'I had such a time about that box, sir. Two young gemmum were here the other day – just run up, while the coach was changing to see the house. As soon as they were gone I misses the box. Off scuds my son to the *Red Horse* and there they sat on the top looking as innocent as maybe. "Stop the coach", says my son. "What do you want?" says the driver. "My mother's mulberry box! – One of them 'ere young men's got it in his pocket." And true enough, sir, one of 'em had the impenence to take it out of his own pocket and fling it into my son's face: and you know the coach driver never stop a minnut for nothing or he'd a smarted for it.'

24. Flowers' Brewery at the height of its prosperity, as pictured in the Illustrated Midland News.

'Citizen of the World'

Another American visitor was Edward Fordham Flower, who signed Mrs. Court's book as 'Citizen of the World'. This man who was to become Stratford's most eminent Victorian was born in Hertfordshire in 1806, the son of Richard Flower, a radical pamphleteer, agriculturist and Unitarian, who took a gloomy view of prospects in England and, with a group of friends, founded a settlement in Southern Illinois when Edward was twelve. The boy shared the rigours of life in the wilderness, which were increased by the proximity of the Mason-Dixon line. The settlers pursued the practical implications of their radical views and participated in the 'Freedom Trail' for escaped slaves, often clashing with their Southern neighbours.

When Edward was 19, he visited England, and finding much to attract him, decided to remain, marrying Selina Graves of Barford in 1827. Soon after he settled in Stratford, buying a house in Payton Street and going into business with James Cox as a timber merchant on the wharves behind the *One Elm*. He possessed great personal strength and courage. Once he slew a bull with a pick-axe while rescuing a man from drowning.

In 1831 the business was divided when Flower opened a brewery on the site for which Cox provided the cooperage. Cox also possessed great public spirit, energy and integrity. An Independent by denomination, his theology clashed with that of the Reverend Thomas Helmore and he was expelled with eight others. They formed a Baptist congregation, for which Cox built an elegant chapel in Payton Street. In 1832 he began a 'Ragged School' in Sheep Street with 40 scholars.

Sanitation and Disease

Stratford was changing slowly. Unambitious residential suburbs were spreading along College Street and Warwick Road and the rise in economic activity which the canal and tramway had engendered spawned awful little slums between the Guild Pits and the canal. In 1830, the alley linking Bridge Street with the Guild Pits was expanded into a highway named Union Street.

In 1831 after the Mayor, James Pritchard, received recommendations from the Privy Council, he called a meeting to form a Board of Health. After surveying the town, the Board issued directives to abate or remove nuisances and to ventilate the cottages of the poor. Compared with the comments of the Inspector of Health two decades later, its conclusions seem complacent, but they constitute a start in clearing the filth of the centuries. Stratford was considered to be 'in a very clean and wholesome condition . . . the poorer part of the population, in almost all cases, enjoy ample accommodation and a free circulation of air in their dwellings'.

The Board of Health played a vital role in the cholera scare of 1832. A General Inspector of Nuisances was appointed to close cesspools, clear offal from slaughterhouses and scour open ditches and drains. Old men from the Workhouse questioned travellers entering the town about possible contact with the disease. Thus Stratford was preserved from the epidemic, whereas Shottery, 'one of the dampest, dirtiest and poorest villages in Warwickshire', with a population of less than 100, suffered some 20 cases of cholera and nearly 40 of diarrhoea, resulting in six deaths.

Other efforts were being made to improve the lot of the poor. Thrift was encouraged by the establishment of a savings bank in Chapel Street, for those 'whose pecuniary conditions in life are narrow and humble'. The 'Labourers' Friends Society' was founded to let allotments to the poor, 'for their moral and pecuniary benefit'. Tenants were sometimes more deserving than green-fingered: those culpable of drunkenness, dishonesty, or Sabbath-breaking were deprived of their gardens.

FOOTNOTES
[1]   'I thought Stratford was a larger place', wrote Charles Mathews, 'and that there was a theatre. So there
       is, but it is a barn and holds twenty eight!'
[2]   It had been suggested that the young princess might attend "Avonbank", an exclusive school for young
       ladies with fees of £140 per year, situated at the end of the church path. It had moved to Stratford in
       1824 and was run by Miss Maria Byerley and her three sisters, great-nieces of Josiah Wedgwood. The
       best-known of its pupils was Elizabeth Stevenson (Mrs. Gaskell), who despite this exclusive background
       became one of the acutest recorders of the social abuses of her age.

CHAPTER 13

'The Interests of the People'

'Let them endeavour to atone for their past conduct . . . by vying with the Reformers in studying the interests of the People'

Warwick Advertiser, 1836.

The 1832 Election

During the era of Reform, the Stratfordians broke the constraints of their apathy. Because the ancient borough did not return members to Parliament, it was not dominated by a patrician political dynasty and the political enthusiasm of its inhabitants was uninhibited and unprecedented. In April 1831 Sir Gray Skipwith, the Recorder of Stratford and a moderate reformer who lived at Alveston House, was elected a county member. The inhabitants were personally and politically delighted and the Corporation requested him to give the people 'the pleasure' of escorting him into the town. On 13 May, a huge crowd, accompanied by a band, greeted his carriage at the boundary of the borough. At the Town Hall it took some time to obtain silence, but when all was quiet, the Mayor declared the inhabitants 'fully satisfied . . . that we are trusting our interests to the care of a gentleman well worthy of our entire confidence'. Sir Gray's reply was a model of moderation. 'Many excellent men' he knew admitted the need for some reform, but thought that the bill went too far. 'They think it will make the House of Commons too democratic and thereby incur the danger of a revolution. I have no fear of that kind. I have too high an opinion of the strong sense of Englishmen'.

One who lacked this high opinion was the vicar, James Davenport, who signed a county petition against the Reform Bill: the only Stratfordian to do so. In September a packed meeting at the Town Hall sent a petition to the Lords which declared that 'a full, fair and free representation of the People, is not only their just right, but absolutely necessary, for the Peace and Prosperity of the Country'.

The great day of Reform finally arrived on 9 June 1832. In December, the borough franchise of 99 electors had its first experience of local ballotting, in a three-cornered contest for two places. Committee rooms were established for the Tory candidate, Mr. Evelyn John Shirley and for the Whigs, Sir Gray Skipwith and Sir George Phillips. The unfranchised took a Hogarthian view of the proceedings. While there was no interference at either of the polling booths, it was popularly believed that an election represented an extension of the 5 November frivolities. On the first morning of the three-day poll, disorderly groups roamed the town. By two o'clock, the constables were powerless to disperse a huge crowd which had assembled in Ely Street. Mischief was in the air: George Cope rushed from his house in Windsor Street brandishing a poker, shouting, 'Damn my eyes if I don't murder somebody with this before I have done with it'. At four o'clock the mob, now exceeding 500 and armed with bludgeons and staves, marched to the Tory headquarters at the *White Lion* and smashed the windows with pitching broken from the street. The constables tried to arrest the ringleaders but were forced to retreat. Leaving the *White Lion,* the mob performed the same service for the *George and Dragon* up the street. A party of gentlemen rode to Coventry for the military, while the mob created great disturbance all round Stratford. At the *Shakespeare,* when the constables grouped to bar their entry, George Cope raised his poker at a special constable and threatened to split his skull. When the military arrived at ten p.m., the Riot Act was read, several rioters taken into custody and the mob dispersed. Constable John Ashfield spotted Frederick Lewis in the *Bricklayers' Arms* with a bludgeon concealed under his coat. When he tried to take it from him he was knocked to the ground. At the Quarter-Sessions, Lewis, Cope and nine others were gaoled for riotous behaviour.

Despite such lively scenes, Stratfordians were generally tolerant. The *Warwick Advertiser,* commenting on a dinner at the *Golden Lion,* commended Stratford for its 'peculiar happiness . . . of being so little disturbed by political divisions that on all these festive occasions . . . old and young, grave and gay, Whig and Tory, collect together almost to a man'.

The Tories were accommodating themselves to a reformed world. Mere resistance to change had no future. Locally they had inveighed against the radicals and their political unions. Now they sought to emulate them. On 9 May 1835 the inaugural meeting of the Conservative Association for the southern division of the county was held at Warwick. The cry of 'The Church in Danger' ensured strong clerical backing. There were 17 clergymen amongst the 'nobility, gentry and farmers' in the audience, including the vicar of Stratford, Dr. Davenport, now 85, who seconded one of the resolutions to establish the Association. The Chairman, Mr. E. J. Shirley of Ettington Park declared himself sure that every one who had any feeling of loyalty in his heart, love to the King, attachment to the constitution and, above all, love to the Protestant religion (of which everyone present was a member) would enroll his name. The main threat to the nation was its infiltration by Roman Catholics, particularly of the radical Irish variety! His remarks brought loud cheers and it was decided to incorporate the aims of the Association in a Loyal Address, signed by as many citizens as possible. The *Warwick Advertiser* considered it unlikely that the new Association would succeed, but it changed its tune as the patrician power of organised Toryism became apparent. In a subsequent by-election Mr. Shirley enjoyed the support of almost all the clergy, who, on the Sunday before the election, 'devoted the usual and useful length of their moral and instructive sermons for the purpose of canvassing their parishioners'.

The South Warwickshire Reform Association was formed on 20 September 1836, but proved ineffectual at divisional level. The Conservative ascendency over the semi-feudal world surrounding Stratford ensured that it would be 30 years before there was another election.

'The Demon of Party Spirit'

By 1833 the Corporation debt had risen to £5,500, causing conflict between the contemporary ideals of economy and progress. A recent Parliamentary Act enabled the provision of street lighting with the consent of two-thirds of the ratepayers. At a public meeting, the principle of economy prevailed. A poll was demanded which revealed that although most voters – 127 to 114 – desired public lighting, the majority was insufficient. That year the ratepayers of Old Stratford resolved to light their streets, so the fringes of the town were lit and the centre was not. Nevertheless the volition engendered by the campaign ensured that some of its supporters rapidly raised the capital to start a gas-works company. In September 1834 the gasworks in Chapel Lane were set in action to illuminate transparencies at the Town Hall, including one of Shakespeare bearing the inscription:

> All the world will be in love with night,
> And pay no worship to the gaudy sun.

Next day the Committee dined at the *Falcon.* The dinner was cooked by gas and 'for cleanliness, cheapness and saving of trouble nothing could surpass it'. Soon most shops and many private houses had installed it and the new wonder had encouraged the provision of street lighting.

The self-appointing oligarchies which had controlled the boroughs for centuries were terminated by the Corporation Act of 1835. At Stratford, the first chance for the 304 ratepayers to choose their own representatives resulted in the re-election of most of the old councillors. A letter to the *Warwick Advertiser*, signed 'Justice', alleged that 'threats were made, promises were held out . . . They took advantage of the poor, ignorant newly-made burgesses, and defrauded them of their votes by all sorts of false pretences'.

It is a measure of the urge for change that the old tradition of holding meetings in camera was causing outrage. Even worse, the borough had established a four-man police force 'to strut about the streets, insinuating that the people are becoming thieves and pickpockets . . . yet they know well that three years ago the people rid themselves of a night-watch, put on by the same party, which watch is not a tenth part as odious as these Peel's police are become; and they are annoying the inhabitants with a code of by-laws, so ridiculous as to excite one universal feeling of contempt'.

These by-laws provoked great outrage. There were 34 of them, covering over 300 subjects, many related to the Board of Health. The first 33 were generally ignored, especially by the councillors, 'yet our one-eyed police, acting under their directions of course, have not been able to discover but one infringement'. It was the 34th, forbidding the Sunday opening of shops, which drew the fire. This, the only free day for working people, was the only time when many could shop. Over 60 stores opened on Sunday mornings, some openly, others when the backdoor was knocked. Great resentment was caused when five shopkeepers were prosecuted. 'It is only those who are honest enough to open their fronts that commit sin, just as if God could not see them up their back yards! Oh! What a nation of hypocrites we are becoming!' One case was dismissed; four were convicted, but refused to pay the fines, although that of Henry Baldwin the butcher was later paid anonymously. The goods of the others were ordered to be sequestrated. They demanded a public sale of their property, but it was refused, 'such was the magistrate's dread of public opinion'. A valuer was employed, but no-one would buy the goods, so he was obliged to have them himself. George Compton, the ironmonger, had nothing he wanted, so 'our *liberal* Mayor' (Mr. David Rice, the surgeon) committed him to prison for 14 days' hard labour. The police hired a gig at the *Shakespeare Hotel* ('the headquarters of the Tories') to take him to Warwick, but when he learned why it was required, the proprietor, Mr. Leyton, ordered its return.

'Justice' considered that the by-laws had caused 'the demon of party spirit' to take root in Stratford. This was much in evidence in October 1836, when four councillors (one-third of the total) came up for re-election. The factions were associated with public houses: the Tories at the *Falcon* and the Liberals at the *Golden Lion*. The Liberals were first into action, having selected their candidates two months before. The Tory four were supported by a handbill signed by 26 'leading men', although they were so pushed for friends after the Sabbath affair that not all were voters. In an attempt to gain popularity, they dropped one of their candidates and added the popular Liberal, Mr. Charles Lucy, to their list, canvassing for 'Mr. Lucy and party'! They also put a dissenter on their list, although they were half-hearted in their support for him. They justified the 'foolish and vexatious bye-laws' and the 'useless and odious police force' by the extraordinary claim that the Reform Act had obligated their establishment. Joseph Price was paid six shillings to canvass on the Sunday before the election; presumably the righteousness of the cause justified Sabbath-breaking.

The tenuous position of employees under the open voting system is revealed in an affidavit from Matthew Hirons. Mr. Timothy Smith, junior, the son of his employer, went to see him and said, '"Matthew, Mr. Horton and me shall want your vote again this year." I said I had promised my vote to the Golden Lion Party. He said *"Damn that – we must and will have it."* On

Saturday evening last he again tried to persuade me not to vote, saying that if I did vote, it would be the worse for me'. He voted as he intended on his way home from work. Soon the son arrived and ordered him to go to his father to be paid off. Mr. Smith, senior, told him he was a great fool for voting against their instructions. At the *Golden Lion* a spontaneous subscription raised a pound as a small compensation for his loss of earnings. Doubtless he found a new situation with a wealthy Liberal.

The election was a triumph for the Liberals. Charles Lucy topped the poll with 254 votes and their three other candidates, including Edward Flower, were not far behind. For the Tories it was a disaster. Their best candidate secured a mere 48 votes and poor William Bolton, the only councillor to seek re-election, secured an unenviable record in the borough annals by achieving just one vote – perhaps his own!

Public opinion had prevailed. The next council meeting resolved to open all meetings to the public and to instruct the police to take no further action on the by-laws. The correspondent of the *Warwick Advertiser* was jubilantly free in his advice to the vanquished, urging the Tories to 'learn wisdom' from their defeat; 'and instead of trying to further incense the people of this town against their party – weak as it is in number, in influence and wealth – let them endeavour to atone for their past conduct and rashness, by vieing with the Reformers in studying the interests of the people at large, and not sacrifice the public good to please and promote the interest of the few; but should they let the present opportunity slip, their power is gone for ever – the people now know their strength, and never will again be Tory slaves'.

The Tories took this advice and learned to look beyond the days of oligarchy. Their performance improved in the following year when five vacancies occurred. A contemporary account gives an insight into the polarised nature of local politics. There were 386 local voters: 70 were Tories, 100 Whigs: there were 197 working men[1] and 19 'in the middle class' who would ally with the working men. Ten of the 16 councillors were Whigs or Tories, but there were no working men, although it was freely pointed out that to be proportionally represented, they should have had nine – so they ran four candidates. Three were elected and the fourth exerted himself to prevent his election; 'so that this was a contest between the Whigs and the Tories against the working men; and although they made use of all their influence, still the working men beat the combined parties'.

The newly-elected reformers turned their attention to a notorious abuse – the ancient grammar school. There were seldom more than 15 pupils, but the master was paid the handsome salary of £145 per year, which included £30 in lieu of the house, which was considered insufficiently grand for his habitation. It was said that the salary was sufficient to provide education for all the children in Stratford. After one of the martyrs of Sunday opening, Mr. Joseph Brandis, tabled a motion to examine the structure of the school, the issue was raised in Parliament. The result was a further expansion of the fee-paying curriculum to suit middle-class aspirations.

Victoria Regina

On 24 May 1837, the Princess's birthday, the Royal Victoria Spa was opened at Bishopton, which had long been known to possess a spring whose water was 'very beneficial in various complaints'. The Pump Room was the first building in the area to be built in what became known as 'Victorian Gothic'. There would be thousands of buildings all over the world named after Victoria, but this obscure spa was probably the first.

Within a month of the opening of the Spa, Victoria ascended the throne. A committee was formed in Stratford to plan the local Coronation celebrations. Collections were considerably boosted when the young Queen drove through the town on her way to Ragley Hall. The poor of the district were invited to apply for dinner tickets. The quantity of victuals was gargantuan:

3,304 lbs of beef; 60 legs of mutton; 620 huge loaves; 340 large plum puddings; 2,260 eggs; 2,214 quarts of best ale and 1,500 of table beer. The happy day dawned fine and clear on 26 June 1838. The town was filled with tables and decorated with flags, banners and flowers. Triumphal arches were erected in the principal streets. A band preceded a procession of the clergy and 'respectable inhabitants', followed by 1,000 children from the denominational schools, each wearing a medal and singing 'God save the Queen' as they paraded the streets, before 3,150 people sat down to dinner.

Church Militant

A camp meeting of Primitive Methodists was held in 1832 and a stable at Shakespeare's Birthplace became the first chapel. Each June members of this sect processed round the town, singing hymns. On Clopton Road, orators ascended waggons and held forth, before the processions returned to town.

Religious revivalism brought a number of odd sects in its wake. One had Stratford roots. The Catholic Apostolic Church, founded through the influence of Edward Irving, numbered one Taplin amongst its chief adherents. This humble Stratford shoemaker nominated the 12 new apostles who would usher in the second coming.

One who was profoundly affected by the Catholic revival in the Anglican Church was that talented musician Thomas Helmore, son of the Independent minister. Influenced by the interest in the worship of antiquity which the Oxford Movement inspired, he joined the Church of England. His father was not distressed but told him, 'If your conscience bids you go, you will be wrong to stay'. He formed a choir of 60 singers at Holy Trinity, largely from the singers at his father's meeting who were mainly Anglicans who had joined through their love of music. Soon it was said that this choir was as fine as those of the great cathedrals. It was regarded as a matter of particular pride that its members were 'respectable resident tradesmen of the town and their children'. After Tom Helmore left to study for the priesthood at Oxford, he was succeeded by Edward Adams, who conducted the choir with 'great spirit and care'.

Holy Trinity Church was in another of its spells of disrepair and an appeal was launched for its restoration, which was begun in 1835. Despite the energetic efforts of Dr. Conolly to raise funds, there was a shortfall, which placed the churchwardens in a dilemma. They were legally obliged to maintain the building in good repair, but the only way they could make up the deficit was through the imposition of a church-rate, which would be generally unpopular and an issue of principle to dissenters. As was feared, many refused to pay and in July 1837, four dissenters were summoned, which gave them ample opportunity to air their grievances. Mr. James Cox put the basic argument when he objected to being compelled to support a church that he did not use. He paid a voluntary contribution to his own place of worship. The members of the Church of England were wealthy enough to support their own services. Compulsory payments were contrary to all true principles of religion.

Mr. Brandis stated that, as religious objections were no use, he would state a legal one. He refused to pay because the rate was unequally levied. Over half the rate-payers were never called on to contribute. All the legal authorities laid down that all property must be equally assessed.

After a long consultation the magistrates decided that the rate must be paid. The dissenting four declared that they would pay nothing, and 11 days later their goods were sequestrated. Official memories of the Sunday opening fiasco ensured that the property was sold in Warwick.

The anti-raters had a great success on 6 April 1838, when a crowded vestry meeting, at which all ratepayers were entitled to vote, met to consider a Church-rate. An amendment to adjourn the meeting without a rate was carried by a considerable majority; an attempt to convene a poll on the issue failed because the meeting was closed, so the rate was deferred.

The issue was revived in August at one of the largest vestry meetings ever held in the parish church. A rate of twopence in the pound for the borough and one penny for the parish was moved, but the ancient vicar refused to put an amendment calling for the adjournment of the issue for one year. The only question, he said, was whether they should have a rate or not. After great confusion a show of hands resulted in 105 votes for the rate and 103 against. The

25. Bridge Street market. From a sketch of the 1880s.

opponents demanded a poll, which started immediately at the Town Hall and continued until two evenings later. It was conducted with great spirit and good humour and resulted in a victory for the pro-raters by 410 votes to 310. The anti-raters were swift to deny anything other than a tactical victory for the church party. There was multiple voting according to rateable value and those overdue with their poor rates were prohibited from voting. In fact 224 people had voted for the rate and 294 against: the other 582 electors were 'afraid to vote, or their poor rates were not paid'. The correspondent of the *Warwick Advertiser* considered that if they had voted, about 500 would have polled against the rate. Amongst the successful minority, 62 people, mostly living outside the borough, polled 248 votes. 'The only supporters the Church had in this contest were the interested parties, the time-servers and the slaves'.

The church-rate issue subsided with the completion of the restoration at Holy Trinity, an event commemorated with a service chanted by the newly-ordained Thomas Helmore. The growing reverence for church buildings and a romantic neo-medievalism was considered to be reflected in the Gothic style adopted. Helmore pursued a distinguished musical career. He founded the Motet Society, which did much to revive interest in older forms of Church music, and he composed such hymns as 'O come, O come, Emmanuel'.

On 16 August 1841 Dr. Davenport died at the age of ninety-two. He was vicar of Stratford for 54 years and of neighbouring Weston for sixty-seven. His career stretched back to a confident Anglican ascendency and he had striven to slow its passing. Through his longevity, he had become an institution. Virtually every inhabitant turned out to watch the passing of his *cortège* and business ceased for the day.

A missionary for a new religious view from afar appeared in 1843. Elder James White, a Mormon, hired Brandis's Assembly Room for a meeting, but only raised 2d at the collection. After this he lectured the handful willing to listen at a labourer's house in Wood Street. On a cold February day he baptised three converts in the Avon. A curious crowd followed these frozen and sodden 'ducks of delusion' through the town. One developed a serious illness and Elder White was stoned by a hostile mob and escorted from Stratford by the police. 'Oh *Sheam*, hide your faces in Disgrace, blush for humanity', he wrote in an outraged letter, adding justly, if ungrammatically, 'you have brought a Disgrace on your Town and on the *Authoritys* of the same, boast no more of your liberty in *worshiping* God according to the dictates of your *Conscianc*'.

The church-rate issue resurfaced during the next incumbency. John Greves, a young radical lawyer, denied the validity of the rate in 1844. After lengthy litigation, he obtained a protection order from process in the Birmingham Bankruptcy Court. Another 22 people refused payment on the grounds that he was not paying and this effectively blocked payment for some time.

The social and political divide between Church and Chapel was reflected also in educational issues. Governmental support for denominational education upset nonconformists, who, generally lacking wealthy backers, were obliged to rely on small voluntary subscriptions. In 1845 Thomas Mason, a staunch supporter of the Church of England's National School, presented a site in Alcester Road for a new building. Another rich Anglican, William Woods Weston, donated the bulk of the costs, which made the scheme eligible for a topping-up grant from the Treasury. At the annual meeting of the British Schools, such intervention was denounced as 'unconstitutional, expensive, unnecessary and dangerous to liberty, to education and religion'.

The Bitter Pangs of Hunger

In 1837 a trade recession combined with agricultural depression to ensure the re-emergence of the wild talk and action of the 1820s: a situation aggravated by the Poor Law Amendment Act of 1834, which severely curtailed outdoor relief for the able-bodied and gave the under-employed the choice between destitution and the workhouse. The need for more spacious premises thus engendered led the 'Union' to move to a new site in Arden Street where those unable to support themselves lived under a regime of increasing severity. A Stratfordian signing himself 'A Lover of Justice' wrote an open letter to local farmers in 1838, appealing to them to increase wages to a level which would keep their labourers out of the Workhouse and enable them to fight 'the bitter pangs of hunger'. The first sentence reveals the religious basis of contemporary radicalism with a quotation from the Epistle of St James: 'Behold, the hire of the labourers who have reaped your fields, which you have kept back by *fraud*, crieth: and the cries of them which have reaped are entered into the ears of the Lord of Sabaoth'.

Another correspondent revealed the miserable standards suffered by the labourer in an anonymous letter to the Chairman of the Union. 'Is nine shillings a week enough to maintain a labourer, his wife and three children?' It provided a penny per person per meal with threepence over. 'Now, Sir, let any individual go and lay out his money in the provision market, then picture to yourself, what has he gotten to sustain life. This takes the whole income! If we are to spend the whole in this luxurious manner, where is the rent to come from? Where the firing? Where the clothing? Not from the Board, I presume.'

A problem created by the Act was its idiosyncratic local operation, which ensured an unevenness of provision based on the interpretation of individual Guardians. Another correspondent to the Chairman of the Union invoked religion in the cause of radicalism. 'It behoves you to enquire minutely of each respective Guardian whether each able-bodied labourer is in constant work, and if not to render him some little assistance. His demand and right of a living out of the soil is as great as that of the most potent aristocrat in the realm. That BEING who has caused such a fecundity in the human species, has likewise produced every requisite for the . . . labourer, but which is unfortunately witheld by man's inhumanity to man.'

Others took a more sanguine view of the plight of the poor, considering moral reform the imperative. In 1837, Mr. Chapman of Birmingham lectured at the Town Hall on 'the object, means and success of Temperance Societies'. 'O! my friends', he told his audience, 'if I could but persuade all my working friends to learn and keep sober, then I should live in hopes of seeing you better off; but as long as you swallow the intoxicating drink, so long you will be subject to poverty, and all that can be done to relieve you of your present degraded situation will be in vain'.

The *sequela* of abject impoverishment, whatever its cause, was once again desperation. Incendiarists' fires were smouldering anew. The most mysterious was at Radbrook House, the property of Mr. Ralph Smith, in an enclave of Gloucestershire which bordered on Old Stratford. On the morning of 20 October 1841, a boy at work saw a man running from the yard. Soon after a fire occurred in a cow-shed, which was soon brought under control. Mr. Smith and some of his neighbours galloped off in search of the suspicious character, but found no trace of him. In the afternoon, a fire broke out in a barn and raged with great fury: after the bells of the Guild Chapel rang the alarm, the Stratford fire-engine was heaved up the Shipston Road to play ineffectually upon the flames. Hundreds poured out from Stratford to assist or to watch the spectacle. After great destruction, the fire was suppressed. Such was the sensation that scores of people remained on the premises all night. They were not disappointed. Next morning another fire broke out in a calf-pen. The engines were again sent for, but no sooner was this fire extinguished than smoke was seen pouring from an oat-rick which could not be saved. That evening a clover-rick started burning and an hour later, a large heap of straw burst into flames, destroying a nearby copse. On Saturday afternoon, the engines arrived too late to prevent the stables being reduced to ashes. On the Sunday, an engine arrived from the Birmingham Fire Office to play on the smouldering debris. 'The highest praise' was accorded those Stratfordians who had fought each outbreak.

The episode struck great terror through the neighbourhood. While the perpetrator clearly possessed good local knowledge, it was felt that the capacity to use combustibles so skilfully would be beyond a common labourer. All the servants had been in Mr. Smith's employ for lengthy periods and they were completely trusted. Mr. Smith was not a magistrate or a Guardian and was not involved in politics. Indeed he enjoyed local esteem. The affair was a great mystery, which deepened two weeks later. The Birmingham fire-engine, which had remained in case of further outbreaks, was finally ordered home. Within hours of its departure, two ricks were destroyed. A large body of police was left to guard the farm-buildings, yet in the morning, flames billowed from the house itself, which would have been totally consumed but for the efforts of the fire-fighters. Four servants were arrested and questioned, but were released for lack of evidence. Amazed panic spread and it is hardly surprising that rumour identified Mr. Smith as the incendiarist. The rumours were officially denied, but produced lamentable effects. Mr. Smith was confined to his house at Clifford and dared not return to Radbrook. His brother at Barford was driven insane by the reports and had to be placed under restraint. The Radbrook mystery was never solved. It provided several weeks of local sensation and force to the arguments of those who considered that men driven desperate would seek desperate remedies.

The foundations of a public welfare system and the means to resist the worst deprivations of poverty came with the formation of medical and benefit clubs. In 1843 a penny club was established which provided 122 poor children with an annual nine shillings-worth of clothing. The Medical Club covered over 2,500 local people against the 'overwhelming embarrassments' caused by sickness. Those of better means made up the shortfall by supporting an annual Charity Ball, which also supported the Victoria and Becher Benefit Clubs. The 'Victoria' paid a shilling benefit for each weekly halfpenny collected. The low subscription suited the lowest paid, those with large families and the elderly. Better-off workers could insure through the 'Becher', for an annuity in old age, or for death, sickness or accident. The 'Victoria' had 372 members, the 'Becher' 206 members. Every year, preceded by bands, they paraded through Stratford before adjourning for tea at the Town Hall.

'Taylor's Boot-Jack'

In 1842, Stratfordians were outraged or amused by the revival of an ancient form of punishment. The magistrates sentenced a man to sit in the stocks in Bridge Street for being drunk and disorderly. When asked by a passer-by what he thought about it, he replied: 'I beamt the first mon as ever were in the stocks, so I don't care a fardin about it' – a sentiment expressed by his townsman two and a half centuries before in *Richard II:*

> . . . like silly beggers,
> Who, sitting in the stocks refuge their shame -
> That many others must sit there.

Two weeks later three others suffered similarly for the same offence, which led to protests against this 'barbarous exhibition'. Some concession was made to enlightened opinion: when the wind was in the north offenders were transferred under the Town Hall. In the following May a woman from Knowle was set in the stocks for having been, as the local expression deemed, 'disguised in liquor'. A year later a well-known character, John Cowley, endured what he called, after the police superintendent, 'Taylor's boot-jack'. The propensity for tippling ran through his family. His mother and brothers habitually drank 'more than would allow of their keeping an upright position'. Cowley could not be certain whether he could resist the allure of a jug of ale in the future. His caution was justified. Six weeks later he was sent to the House of Correction for being drunk and disorderly. The stocks continued in sporadic use until 19 July 1865.

'A Most Unmanly and Unfeeling Spirit'

Social legislation was becoming more intercessory as Government was seen increasingly as a means of redressing the moral balance. An Act of Parliament enables Margaret Morris to emerge from the shadows of history and represent a Victorian type, the seduced and abandoned female. This respectable-looking young woman was a housemaid with the Reverend Mr. Parker, who ran a small private school in Ely Street. She fell in love with the assistant teacher, Orlando Cooper, who also lived at the school. He paid her great attention and repeatedly promised to marry her. In what was described as 'an unguarded moment', he took advantage of 'her attachment and confidence'. Someone told on the lovers: when Mr. Parker discovered them in the girl's bedroom, he dismissed them both. After Margaret revealed she was pregnant, Cooper deserted her, but fortunately she came from a loving family and her parents stood by her. On 19 October 1844, she gave birth to a girl.

There was some redress available to Margaret. The recent Act enabled her to bring what was bluntly called a 'Bastardy' suit. On 22 November, the case was heard and the fact that it was the first of its kind in Stratford ensured an overflowing courtroom. Public sympathy was with her, particularly as the defendant, 'as if lost to all sense of shame and and decency, endeavoured, in a very improper manner, to annoy his unfortunate victim'. His conduct was observed by the magistrate and brought a timely rebuke. Cooper's lawyer attempted to denigrate Margaret's character, causing her much distress. The line of questioning appeared to have been suggested by 'a most unmanly and unfeeling spirit' on the part of her seducer, who was much amused by its effects. After a short consultation, the Bench made its first maintenance order: four shillings a week for the first six weeks from confinement and two shillings subsequently.

Despite the gallant feelings aroused by such a case, there was little practical protection for women in service. A young governess, 'highly connected', left in charge of the children, disciplined one by sending her to her room. When the parents returned she was subjected to a volley of abuse and thrust out of the house with no means to find lodgings. She was taken in by a lawyer, who obtained the small amount of money due to her on the following day. The correspondent of the *Warwick Advertiser* was disgusted by the affair. 'That a young lady . . . should be driven forth, at a moment's notice, without a shelter for the night! Such cases as these, we trust, are few, for the credit-sake of masters and mistresses.'

Happy as may be

The earliest descriptions of the Mop date from this era. One year tended to be much like any other, with imperceptible changes occurring through fashion or technology. Thoughts of poverty and recession receded as young people who had completed a hiring spent their gratuities. A correspondent noted a country lad and his sweetheart: 'He does not mean to be stingy today – he will treat his lass and buy her a new gown into the bargain. It's a treat to see how they go rolling along; he holds up his elbow sharply by his side, she thrusts her arm through his up to the elbow and away they go as happy as may be'.

In front of the inns there were ox and pig roasts. For many years the noted expert in the craft, Billy Ball, had his pitch outside the *Garrick*. 'Armed with knife and fork and steel . . . he stands in front of the steaming carcase, fencing at the fire, radiant with the heat thereof, and brilliant in his blue attire'. For those who preferred daintier meals there were stalls selling gingerbread and Banbury cakes, presided over by 'decidedly unclean and untidy persons', who also invited the public to partake of questionable looking fish at a halfpenny a slice. 'As an additional inducement to buy, on the top of each piece was a pickled onion, attractively displayed, and few persons could resist the bait'.

The Rother Market was filled with amazing shows, with such novelties as 'the wonderful pig, the cunning pony, the fat girl, the giant, the dwarf, serpents, crocodiles, monsters of the deep, and a host of peep shows'. The ladies of Holloway's 'Acting Show' impressed one observer, 'with their red cheeks and spangled dresses, and then the men too in their grotesque attire. First a dance, then some fun, then a general shouting from the foot-lights, the clown taking his stand, whip in hand, at the top of the steps: "Now gentlemen! Forward! Forward! Forward! Remember this is positively the last night of the sublime tragedy of *Blue Beard* in five acts, concluding with the screaming farce of *A Frog in a Consumption on the top of a Hay Stack*, never before performed before a British public! Forward, gentlemen! Forward!" (a crack of the whip). "Stand away there, you little boys, let the ladies pass. If any young lady is wanting a beau, let her pull out her threepence and come and see Holloway's show. Most select company within. We are now going to commence. Be in time! Be in time! The star actors are just going in. Forward, I say! This way to the preserved seats". (Exit Blue Beard attended by wives, clowns, pantaloons and attendants).'

CHAPTER 14

'A Spick and Span New Villa'

'A Spick and Span New Villa, standing in its own grounds'.
Critic of the restored Birthplace, c. 1850.

Railway Mania

Less than two decades after the canal and horse-railroad had placed Stratford at the hub of a communications network, the town was again becoming a backwater. Steam was the threat. The great trunk lines had swept away the coaching and posting traffic with calamitous effects for Stratford. Attitudes to travel were changing rapidly. 'Nobody', it was said, 'cared to settle in a town that could not be got out of, even for a day, without considerable difficulty and inconvenience.'

Railway fever was in the air. In the closing weeks of 1845, the press was filled with flotations of railway shares. Several schemes were proposed for Stratford and the timescale for applications was short. On the last weekend in November, representatives of the companies rushed into the town to deposit notice of Parliamentary enabling Bills with the Clerk of the Peace. All the posthorses in the area were requisitioned and the rattle of carriages continued into the night. During 1846 enabling legislation was obtained by the Oxford, Worcester and Wolverhampton Company for a link to its line at Honeybourne, but progress was minimal.

Improving energy was beginning to affect other areas of town life. With the growth of the adult education movement, the Royal Shakespearean Theatre was converted in 1844 for secular enlightenment. The stage and pit were removed, the decorations obliterated and the building converted into one large hall. Only the boxes and gallery remained to show the original purpose. Classrooms and a kitchen were constructed in the basement and the building was formally reopened with a dramatic reading by Charles Kemble. 'The Royal Shakespearean Rooms' never had much vitality; one critic considered it a place where 'niggers and serenaders, itinerant lecturers and travelling showmen display themselves'. Later the Rooms housed the county court and witnessed 'forensic displays equal in grotesqueness to anything produced upon the mimic stage'.

The urge for improvement soon extended to the Birthplace. We get a last glimpse of Mrs. Court maintaining its traditions when an American visitor got her to lay down a mattress, so that he could sleep in the room where Shakespeare was born. In 1846 she died and the property was put up for auction. Wild rumours circulated: it was said that the American showman, Phineas T. Barnum, wanted to transport it brick by brick across the Atlantic. As long as the Birthplace had remained a ramshackle but available shrine, concern about its status was not profound: the moment an interloper tried to secure it, national pride was at stake. Thus a Shakespeare's Birthplace Committee was formed in 1847 and soon enjoyed the patronage of the Queen and Prince Albert. Many and various were its fund-raising activities: Jenny Lind sang and Charles Dickens organised theatricals. In Islington, Sarah Martineau and a friend agreed that the one raising the most money would 'have the honour of sending it to Charles Dickens with a letter which we hoped would provoke a reply'. It did. Sarah's future was more closely bound with Stratford than she knew. In 1852 she married the brewery heir, Charles Flower.

The first act of the Committee was to buy four cottages on the western side of the Birthplace, which gave them possession of part of John Shakespeare's property. The sale of the rest occurred in London on 16 September 1847, amidst scenes of great excitement, marred only by the temerity of a moustachioed American who called upon the auctioneer to prove that Shakespeare was born there. Such presumption was dismissed as an attempt to soften the market for his own bid and the house was knocked down to the United Committees of Stratford and London for £3,000.

Now that possession of this considerable block of property had been achieved, the Committee had to decide what to do with it: one engaging suggestion was that it should be converted to an almshouse for 'decayed dramatists of approved character'. A local architect, Alderman Edward Gibbs, was appointed and recommended that the western property should house a small museum where all that could authentically be connected with Shakespeare could be collected. The former *Swan and Maidenhead* presented greater problems. It was resolved to

26. Henley Street and the Birthplace, with photographers plying their trade.

restore the frontage, but no-one knew how this decaying pile of bricks had appeared in Shakespeare's day. Folk-memories that a large gable had once existed were confirmed by a sketch of eight decades before. In the absence of anything better, the building was 'restored' to conform to that impression. The original massive beams interfered with the architect's 'fanciful composition', so they were pulled down. Shakespeare's house must stand alone, so those of his neighbours were demolished. The Age decreed a picturesque garden, so down came the barns, outhouses, piggeries and brewhouse, reminders of the working life which was the property's *raison d'etre*.

The restored Birthplace was described by a critic as 'a spick and span new Villa, standing in its own grounds'. The flow of visitors was undiminished by the new order. 2,207 visitors crossed the narrow threshold in 1851, including 444 Americans.

'About the best Beer brewed in England'

At first Edward Flower's brewery did not go particularly well, paying little more than the household expenses. The Flowers often talked of emigrating and would have gone to Australia had the sale of the business paid their fares and left them with £500 when they landed. Charles Edward Flower, born in 1830, was compelled to leave school and go into the business when he was fifteen. He began at the copper side under his father's direction, 'but as we only brewed about 82 quarters about three times a week, I had plenty of time for office work and kept the Cash and Cask books and frequently did some of the travelling'. In 1846, he was left in charge of the workforce of seven while his father was in America. The price of barley kept rising so the brewers had a meeting and agreed to raise the price of ales. 'I was very glad of the rise at the time as I knew we were losing money, but it was a very bad step and injured the trade and we soon had to come down again to the old prices.' In hot weather the brew was in the early hours, 'for then it took much longer to get through an eight quarter brewing with the old plant than it did to get through any quantity after better refrigerators were invented'.

Yet Edward Flower was a man who would be cited as an exemplar of 'self-help' by its proponent, Samuel Smiles. The 'hungry forties' over, the family discovered the truth of Dr. Johnson's opinion that their chosen trade could make a man as rich as Croesus. In 1852 the brewery was rebuilt on three times its former scale. Technical innovation ('Flow-

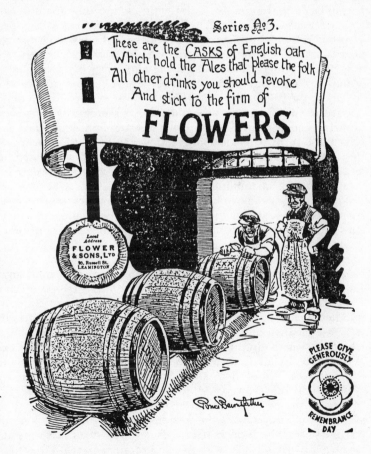

27. *An advertisement for 'the best beer brewed in England' by Bruce Bairnsfather.*

ers' was the first brewery to introduce coolers) helped produce what *Punch* described as 'about the best beer brewed in England'. A dominance of the local trade was established by steady purchase, although houses like the *Queen's Head, Oddfellows* and *Windmill* long maintained their independence and home brews.

The Problems of the Centuries

In 1897 an old man recalled the state of Stratford before its transformation by Victorian energy. The streets were filled with rubbish and scarcely paved even in the High Street. 'The scavenging was done by two old men . . . One cart and horse did the work of the whole borough. There were no underground sewers. The drains discharged at any low spot . . .'.

The transformation began in 1848, when growing concern for public health was increased by a national cholera epidemic. The means to improvement was created by the recent Public Health of Towns Act, whose application could be secured where the mortality rate exceeded 23 per thousand. The Medical Officer, Dr. Thomson, demonstrated that Stratford's mean annual death rate of 23.47 was one of the highest in England for a town of its size. Something had to be done. In October, a large public meeting unanimously demanded an enquiry by the General Board of Health. The Inspector appointed, Mr. George Clark, made his first visit in December. His report, published in May 1849, revealed the Augean deposits accumulated in generations of ignorance, malpractice and neglect. The connection between public parsimony and private squalor was evident. He had never before visited a place where the link between 'damp and dirt and sickness and increased expenditure has been so clearly established'.

One of 'the filthiest and least healthy quarters' was the Guild Pits. Many were the complaints about the offensive muckpits and piggeries lining its town side. Behind were badly-drained, crowded courts with flooded cellars, whose privies leaked into open cesspools, into which refuse was thrown. Water poured down to flood the road and the residents complained that meat would not keep. The slums on the other side abounded in nuisances. Shakespeare Street and Victoria Terrace had the highest rate of zymotic disease in the town, clearly linked to the damp and filth abounding there.

There was no house drainage in the town and few water-closets. The cesspools were emptied by purchasers of the manure, who mixed it with lime and carted it onto the land. Water was supplied by pumps and rain-butts: pump-water was considered too hard for washing. Those living near the canal used its water, which, although very dirty, was softer than that of the river, which was little used.

In wet weather the unmetalled roads were deep in mud and scarcely passable for vehicles. Each householder paved as he chose in front of his house. Many favoured a cheap flagstone, known locally as 'petrified kidneys', which contained clay and split easily, forming muddy puddles. Seventy pounds was paid annually to clean up after the markets, but the side streets were not cleaned at all. A small section of the streets was inadequately watered in summer. The town was badly lit. Because the gas company charged exorbitant prices, the few street-lamps were lit for limited periods and gas was rare in private households. The Inspector expressed regret that the Act did not enable the Board of Health to establish its own gasworks.

Public nuisances were depressingly numerous. The seven slaughter-houses were inadequately drained and surrounded by discarded blood and offal. Eight annual cattle fairs polluted the streets with the excrement of a thousand livestock. The graveyards were in a terrible state. The Independents placed their dead in vaults at the chapel – 'a most injurious practice'. Most burials were in the cramped parish churchyard. The vicar considered that during a severe epidemic it would be difficult to find plots without encroaching on new graves.

The Inspector's proposals were no less important for their predictability. Cattle-fairs should be established on the outskirts of the town; nuisances should be removed and a decent water supply and sewerage and drainage system provided. The cost of full implementation was estimated as a 9d to 1s rate to pay off capital borrowing over 30 years, which could be set against the reduction in out-door relief resulting from the improvement in public health.

An early start was made on implementing the report. The Board of Guardians appointed an Inspector of Nuisances, Mr. John Tasker, who worked assiduously to reduce pollution, but was handicapped by his restricted powers. Concern was increased in September by another national cholera epidemic, which produced an isolated case in Stratford. The authorities took their usual precautions, but the vicar followed a more transcendental path, declaring 3 October a day of general humiliation and prayer. Shops closed and business ceased for the day. At a crowded service at Holy Trinity, he took his text from the psalmist: 'For thou dost deliver a humble people; but the haughty eyes thou dost bring down'. Nor did the Dissenting Churches allow 'this terrible affliction from the Omnipotent' to pass unobserved.

The Report became a local political issue. Although Stratford was one of the first boroughs to ask for the Act to be applied, its name was inadvertently omitted from the enabling statute, leaving implementation to local initiative rather than governmental decree. There were differences between those who wanted full implementation and the 'Economists' who were cautious about costs. The parties coalesced around public houses: the *Falcon* was broadly in favour of increased spending, while the *Seven Stars* (popularly known as 'The Star Chamber') supported the Economists.

Memories were short. Greater sanitary consciousness and cheaper food after the repeal of the Corn Laws led to a sharp fall in the death rate. Public opinion, which had supported an extensive programme of public works, now faltered, but swung again in favour of action after a torrential rainstorm proved the existing system inadequate. In Rother Street, over 3,000 gallons of water poured into the cellars of the *Fleece*, floating the beer barrels and causing great loss to the owner.

In the autumn of 1850, a local Board of Health was established, dominated by a progressive majority. According to the *Warwick Advertiser*, public opinion had swung again: 'There are few persons in the town who do not cry out against the fallaciousness of this measure'. Nevertheless, sappers and miners of the Royal Engineers started to survey the lines of drains and sewers, using the tower of the Guild Chapel as a vantage point, much to the consternation of the older inhabitants, who mused on the old theme of 'They will never let any of our old things be'.

In spite of sniping criticism, the Board followed an energetic path. Edward Gibbs was appointed as the first Borough Surveyor and also as Inspector of Nuisances and began the obligatory registration of common-lodging houses and slaughter houses. After the borough rate rose to a shilling in the pound, a member of the Board, Mr. Tombs, presented it with a petition signed by 290 of the 400 ratepayers, demanding the repudiation of the Act. Dr. Thomson, the chairman, told him that the Board could not repudiate its function. The Act had been applied on the request of the Stratfordians, including some of the petitioners. Mr. Charles Lucy had the last word and expressed a fine spirit of philanthropy: 'I shall participate in none of the advantages, but it will be for the benefit of the poor. I shall advocate it'. At the same meeting the Board extended its powers to town planning, granting permission to build six houses in College Lane.

The Economists called a public meeting on the issue a week later. This time Dr. Thomson was uninhibited by the constraints of chairmanship. In recent years, he calculated, 133 people had died through the town's insanitary state. 'Are these poor creatures to be allowed to die because the remedy is attended with some expense?' The Economists were elected on a programme of retrenchment. 'What was the first expense they occurred, an expense never before contracted – why to vote £40 towards the Hunt ball! Who was the proposer of this outlay? Why the financial reformer, Mr. Tombs.'

Dr. Thomson's scathing remarks ensured that the motion was lost overwhelmingly. Opponents of the scheme maintained their campaign, but the reformers were not to be deflected. The Board turned its energies to paving-stone, selecting blue weather as the most suitable and seeking advice on its powers to enforce adequate paving. Two months later it was vetting plans for two new streets – Bull Street and College Street. The Economists were driven into a flurry of fury, when the plans for piped water were published, including a reservoir, to be paid for by a general rate of 9/2d.

The last pipe of the sewerage scheme was laid on 26 February 1859. It comprised six miles of sewers and 51 ventilators. Outsiders began to comment favourably on the town. The *Athenaeum* reported that the streets had been made 'to gleam so bright and smell so sweet'. The writer had not wandered far. Most streets remained unpaved; the new sanitation was barely adequate; wretched housing would remain the lot of many and there would be no cemetery for 30 years. Yet the Board's achievements were great. It had transformed Stratford in a decade, setting expectations which changed the scope of local government.

The Great Catholic Truths

In 1848 the Reverend Henry Harding, who was born at Baraset House at Alveston, became vicar. As a priest in Staffordshire, he was the first in the area 'to take up and try to enforce the great catholic truths which had been revived a few years before'. At Stratford he found ample scope for such revival. 'Church life was at its lowest ebb . . . the Blessed Sacrament was celebrated only four times a year.' Almost immediately he introduced daily services.

One problem he inherited was that of church rates, which had not been collected since Mr. Greves' clever prevarication. Judgement was obtained in the Consistory Court that the bankruptcy suit did not exempt him or others from payment. The vestry resolved to enforce payment and costs, but Greves was told by the churchwardens that they had no wish to injure him, implying that they merely required him to acknowledge the validity of the rate. This he did at the next vestry, while maintaining his personal opposition to the principle. Nevertheless, Mr. Lane, the legal advisor to the parish, recommended that proceedings must be taken, or any future rate could be invalid. This may have been the case, but, given the labyrinth of ecclesiastical law, it was tactically a mistake. Greves won an appeal in the Court of Arches on the grounds that he had never been charged with contempt. In victory, he mocked the churchwardens: 'this petty, insignificant impotency of those barking poodles is to be pitied and not feared'. Yet the action against him, in the perverse spirit of contemporary justice, had enabled the imposition of another rate.

The next incumbent, the Reverend George Granville, took a conciliatory line, expressing his personal opposition to church rates, while asserting that it was the churchwardens' duty to collect them. This satisfied the honour of all parties and the rate continued to be collected until its abolition in 1868.

The sectarian spirit was nowhere more apparent than at a public meeting in November 1850, called to protest against 'Papal Aggression' – the restoration of the English Hierarchy by Pope Pius IX. A Loyal Address condemned 'the Bishop of Rome', considering that his action had been encouraged by 'the many Romish errors' creeping into the Established Church, 'which represent greater dangers to our Protestant faith than any interference of the Pope of Rome'. A tactical amendment from the Dissenters deplored any attempt to restrict religious freedom. After many speeches, accompanied by groans and hisses from several factions, the original motion was overwhelmingly carried. Further opposition to 'the aggressions of Romanism' was expressed in a sermon by the Baptist minister, the Reverend M. T. Bumpus. Although there was no Roman Catholic Church in Stratford at this time, there were strong feelings in his congregation. James Cox, junior, son of the Chapel's founder, had converted to Rome the year before. This genial, liberal-minded man was to do much to enhance the reputation of his Church.

Such altercations obscure the fact that this was the last epoch of general religious confidence before doubt and pluralism undermined the fabric of institutionalised devotions. This world on the brink of change is revealed in the 1851 census, when the numbers attending Sunday services were uniquely recorded. The method of assessment was vague and of variable accuracy, but if the techniques of analysis employed by Horace Mann, the national enumerator, are followed, some indication of the state of religion in contemporary Stratford is obtained.

The Dissenters provided seats for 1,748 worshippers, of which 948 were in free sittings. The Anglicans provided 2,113 seats, but only 648 were free. There were around 3,870 sittings available in the churches of the town. The population of the borough and its contingent areas was estimated at 5,000.

Mann reckoned that, excluding those under ten, the sick and those on essential work, 70 per cent of the population could attend a place of worship on any Sunday. In Stratford this represented 3,500 people. Adding the 1,044 dissenters who attended chapel to the 1,926 at Anglican worship and estimating 40 Roman Catholics worshipping outside the town, there were some 2,320 local worshippers that Sunday – some 66 per cent of the eligible population, as against Mann's estimated national average of 58 per cent. By modern standards the total is very high, but the returns must have shocked local churchmen. Only 43 per cent of the active population attended services of the Established Church in a town which did not possess strong traditions of dissent and less than 60 per cent of all worshippers were Anglicans. Around one in three Stratfordians had not attended worship that Sunday, and a high proportion of these were probably as remote from the churches as those heathen in far-off lands for whom the missionary societies collected. No-one looking around the streets at service times could doubt who constituted most of the absentees: those known as 'the submerged one-tenth.' A poetic wit wrote of one of Stratford's worst slums, situated off Ely Street:

> The sound of the church-going bell,
> The Russell-Court folks never heard
> Never sighed at the sound of a knell,
> Or smiled when the Sabbath appeared.

When such people were asked why they did not go to church they gave several reasons: it was too far to walk, the services were too long and the free seats no good. Thus land was purchased to build a church in the Guild Pits, where the adjacent population consisted of 'that class of persons whom it is eminently desirable to draw within the fold of the Church'.

The project did not escape the attention of the Reverend Alfred Dayman, to whom it represented 'Heresy and Sin'. He had been an Anglican curate, but had been obliged to resign because of Romish tendencies in his preaching. Now he was in Stratford as a Roman Catholic priest. A site for a church was acquired in the Warwick Road, but costs were too high and for several years it was used as a burial ground. In 1852, 'The Firs', a mansion in Rother Street, was converted into the chapel of Notre Dame de la Salette, in 'pious association' with the Alpine shrine where in 1846 two children saw a vision of the Virgin. 'Boldly we see before us her banner', waxed Mr. Dayman, 'who, terrible as an army in array, has alone destroyed all heresies . . . we fear nothing and hope for all things.' Such language provoked its reactions. *The Times* considered the mission an 'impudent imposture'. At the consecration of the new Anglican church of St James, the preacher, the Reverend P. Claughton, declared that there was, 'even but a few yards from where we now meet, the so-called shrine of an idolatrous, because creature worship'.

The Catholic mission was not a success. Dayman's reckless controversialism provoked disunity amongst his congregation, who resented the trouble he caused with their Protestant neighbours. After a period of ill-health, he left, leaving most of the effects of the chapel, presbytery and school, which were his property, for auction. The sale aroused great curiosity. Fascination with this exotic foreign religion filled even the most Protestant breast. Many of the applications to view were from local clergymen. Dayman's richly embroidered vestments were bought by local Roman Catholics, who hoped to open a new church soon.

Fierce partisanship also characterised relations between the parties of the Church of England. The clergy of 'High' Holy Trinity ignored services for the Church Missionary Society at the 'Low' Guild Chapel. Low churchmen were shocked by the increasing ritualism at the parish church, which was beautified in 1854 by the eminent architect, William Butterfield. At the service of reconsecration, Sarah Flower was amazed by the changes. 'A procession of white surpliced choristers came in and took their seats each side of the tower – the pulpit having been removed to the side . . . Mr. Twells, the sub-vicar, intoned the service, and in a sermon explained the use of the alterations, saying they were as far away as ever from the Romish Church.' Such modest innovations as candles, flowers and a cross on the altar were condemned by the Archidiaconal visitation in 1860. Yet those who tried to break the droning monotony of Anglican worship met disapproval. The Reverend Julian Young, Vicar of Ilmington, was celebrated locally for his intonation, but Sarah Flower recorded that, at Holy Trinity, 'all the good people thought him quite sacrilegious to be so dramatic'.

The religiosity of contemporary bourgeois life is revealed by Alice Diehl, who as a young girl was invited to stay with her godmother at Alveston.[1] 'I was eager to go. My godmother, Miss Marks, was enshrined in my memory as the image of some beautiful woman-saint in a niche. To be with her, to breath the air she breathed, to hear her speak – it seemed too good to be true.'

Miss Marks lived at Alveston Cottage with Miss Holbeach, 'an upright, vigorous old lady, who wore very high caps . . . Butler, housekeeper, maid, as well as coachman, had grown grey in the service of their respected mistress . . . "You and I are the only young people in the house", said Alice one evening to the second housemaid as she was brushing her hair.' Next day she was told 'not to talk to Ann'. The household was 'all rule – rigid rule. The change from the absolute freedom allowed by my grandfather was tremendous. I was literally then a wild weed, unkempt . . . At Alveston Cottage everything moved like clockwork. The bell rang for prayers . . . The bell rang for breakfast. Then my morning was parcelled out. So much piano practice, so much reading with my godmother, a quarter of an hour in the garden sandwiched in. Dressing for luncheon . . . at which there were consultations between the ladies as to the exact quantity I was to consume . . .' Alice wrote to her mother that Miss Holbeach was 'Betsy Trotwood. . . to the life. And my mother had given permission to both ladies to read my letters before they were sent on!'

Shortly after her arrival, Alice's godmother began to give her religious instruction. 'These hours in her own room, alone with her, were like fleeting visits to heaven. Seated in her chair among her exquisitely-arranged *impedimenta*, She spoke of God to me, with a light in her sweet, faded brown eyes which seemed to make her transparent features luminous. She spoke of law, order in life being dear to God: that we could not love Him who loved us so dearly if we did not love what He loved. The words of such a fervent lover of God set me on fire with a longing to do right. I remember that a great revulsion of feeling ensued; instead of liking freedom and license, I conceived so intense a desire to live by rule that it has never really ceased since.'

Such fervour linked childish pranks with Man's first disobedience. 'Although I became obedient, heart and soul, to the noble women who were trying to "train me for God", as my godmother termed it, they tempted me more than they knew.' Alice was allowed to pick up windfalls in the orchard, but could never eat of the 'forbidden fruit . . . raspberries in abundance, gooseberries, a most tempting bed of Alpine strawberries, ripening pears and ruddy apples from the trees'.

Much of Alice's day was spent in visiting the daughters of the local squirearchy. She developed a 'violent admiration' for Augusta Woodmass, a girl of her own age who sat in the front pew of Alveston's 'pretty, very ritualistic church'. 'She was slim, with a long graceful neck. Her round face had a warm colour on her cheeks – a colour which came and went as she spoke, when we were introduced afterwards by our elders. Quick, bright, slightly scornful dark eyes were her greatest attraction . . . Her father, a squire, had married the daughter of Lord Erskine and Mrs. Woodmass was slowly dying of consumption.' Alice never saw Mrs. Woodmass. When she visited, Augusta presided at the table, 'with a dignity and self-possession strange in one so young. We became very intimate; for she was a girl who had thought, felt and reasoned upon what she had read as well as upon her own personal observation of men and things. I parted from her, after two months' frequent companionship, with pain. We corresponded frequently afterwards. Two very touching letters I well remember. One recorded her mother's death. The other, a year later, was dated from either Torquay or Bournemouth. I knew she was ill and taken here and there according to the advice of various lung specialists, but that letter was a blow. "I am dying", she wrote – her handwriting was still clear and firm. "You will know that I don't mind – especially as I am allowed to receive Holy Communion. Fancy, what a privilege for anyone as young as I am!" Then after much affectionate reference to our talks together, she ended with, "Remember, when you hear that I am gone, I am quite happy to go". Softened though the news was by herself in that unselfish consideration for others which was one of the beautiful traits of a wonderful young creature, I felt her loss, and missed her letters severely. . .'

Overseas Perspectives

With the growth of Empire, Stratfordians were developing overseas perspectives. Australia was increasingly seen as a land of opportunity for the enterprising, rather than a place of transportation for the villainous. As early as 1828, William Court, a relative of the Birthplace family, embarked upon this great adventure. Twenty-four years later, not realising that the Birthplace had been sold, he addressed a letter to a cousin there: 'You can tell the people of Stratford that if they wish to better their condition Australia is the place . . . there is not another country in the world like it. Doctors have little or nothing to do . . . There is plenty of employment of all sorts . . . and the man of forty or fifty will do well'.

The glories and anxieties of war were brought home again by the Crimean campaign. The Mayor called a meeting to support the Patriotic Fund, 'for the relief of the widows and orphans of those gallant soldiers, sailors and marines, who may fall while bravely fighting the battles of their country'. The ladies did their bit by forwarding large quantities of flannel shirts and other necessities. Dr. Thomson invented a machine to lift the wounded while their wounds were dressed and their bedding changed. One was presented to Florence Nightingale's hospital at Scutari, from where Lieutenant William Flower, youngest son of the brewer, was invalided home after suffering severe frostbite. He later pursued a distinguished medical career.

A letter received in Stratford said nothing of such horrors. 'The Russians have made several strong sorties', wrote Sergeant H. Madew of the 97th Regiment from his camp near Sebastopol in August 1855, 'but have been gallantly repulsed. We are in so strong a position that no army in the world could dislodge us; and we are creeping every day nearer and nearer to the town – we are that near we can hear the enemy conversing quite plain. Sometimes we amuse ourselves by throwing bottles loaded with powder, with a fuse inserted in the mouth, which causes great sport. Our batteries', he added, 'are now playing on the town.'

During the 1850s, the celebration of 5 November became a focus of patriotic fervour. In 1850, during the 'Papal Aggression', His Holiness was burnt in effigy. In 1855 there was a grand procession, a firework display and the public burning of a 'stupendous dummy figure of the Great Russian Autocrat, Alexander the Second'. In 1857, the Indian mutiny illuminated the proceedings. A torchlight procession of boats floated down the Avon, accompanied by the town band, before a huge effigy of 'that Prince of Monsters, Nena Sahib' was burnt at the stake.

Yet overseas involvements also brought a sense of burden. Days of humiliation and prayer marked the progress of the Crimean War. Collections were held for the dependents of servicemen, or 'to promote the religious welfare of our troops in the East'. In 1857, a day of humiliation remembered the victims of the Indian Mutiny. At Holy Trinity, the preacher took his text from the Book of Daniel: 'To the Lord our God belong mercies and forgiveness, though we have rebelled against Him; neither have we obeyed the voice of the Lord our God, to walk in His laws, which He set before us by His servants the prophets'.

Religious concern for events overseas was used to raise interest in what were considered abuses at home. In 1850, meetings were held on successive evenings on 'American and English Slavery'. The first introduced 'two men of colour': Mr. John Williams spoke of life on the cotton plantations and his escape from slavery and Mr. Benjamin Benson, of the Narranganset tribe, described the life of the American Indians, the means to evangelise them and the destruction wrought among them by the 'fire-waters'. This last point set the theme on the following evening when members of the Stratford Temperance Society spoke about 'English Slavery'.

One whose service overseas was motivated by Christian dedication was the Reverend Holloway Helmore, second son of the Independent minister. In 1839, aged 19, he went to Africa with the London Missionary Society. In 1857, he was feted during a brief return to Stratford, preaching to overflowing congregations at the Rother Street Chapel. At a public breakfast in his honour, he made a memorable speech: 'I know not where I am going. Having come from the wilds of Africa, I can hardly be able to give an opinion on such matters, but I assure my friends that when I return to Africa I will frequently look back to this pleasant meeting. I trust the recollection of it will enable me to do the work of my Redeemer with greater energy and zeal'.

He never saw Stratford again. He was sent in 1859, at the request of Dr. Livingstone, to establish a mission amongst the Makolo people on the Zambesi. His party traversed an arid and unexplored region for three desperate months. Helmore, his wife and two babies died, poisoned, according to one account, by the Makolo king. Their two surviving children were returned to Stratford.

Borough Police

Although dire poverty was the lot of many Stratfordians, a slow improvement in living standards was obliterating the wild lawlessness of earlier years. The last incendiarist was Charles Robinson, aged 20, who set fire to a haystack in Old Stratford in 1853 and was transported for 15 years. The last local man to receive such a sentence was Joseph Randle of Billesley, who was transported for life in 1855, for raping Mary Lifley of Clifford Chambers at Stratford. Twenty years earlier, both offenders would have been hanged.

Despite the reduction in the crime rate, problems remained. Stratford was frequently invaded by gangs of tramps, who threatened to smash windows unless given bread. The problem was increased by their clear desire to be sent to gaol. At the Workhouse, they often refused to do their allotted tasks in the hope of gaining the security of a prison sentence, which parodoxically deterred the magistrates from giving one. In 1853, George Bradfield, aged about 60, was charged with begging in the streets with his wife. He said they were reduced through misfortune: he was not a professional beggar. After the Mayor imprisoned him for ten days, the wife, possessing no means of support, asked to go with him. When this was refused, she thrust her fist through a window and was granted her wish with six weeks hard labour.

Irish itinerants made seasonal appearances. At harvest-time in 1852, a small number employed by Mr. Bruce of Tiddington slept in his hayloft. One night, one of the men asked for a light at the house, saying that his wife was ill. Soon after, he was heard at the pump.

Next morning, he announced that his wife had given birth to a fine boy and he had 'well washed him'. The woman was given clothing and next day she was on the road with the baby in her arms, begging from passers-by.

Most notorious of the local rogues were the brothers Wilkins, George and William, who amassed scores of convictions for poaching, drunkenness, vagrancy and other offences. In 1860, they appeared at the Quarter Sessions charged with larceny. The Chairman said that Stratford was tired of them and imprisoned them for a year. Yet crime was being dealt with in a less exemplary style. The brothers' extensive catalogue of felony had amassed only 25 months' previous imprisonment between them. Similarly, between 1850 and 1863, Philip Taylor was convicted of indecent exposure three times, assault twice and resisting arrest, yet his sentences totalled under two years.

This more liberal approach was seen at the Michaelmas Sessions in 1864, when George Haines, aged 25, pleaded guilty to stealing a joint of beef. His career stretched back to less enlightened days. When only 13, he had been sentenced to 14 years' imprisonment for horse stealing at Gloucester. He was sent to Gibraltar, but was sent back to England on parole. He lived at Emscote, where he joined the church choir and later found work in Stratford. He was dismissed by his employer and from the choir at Charlecote, after a policeman called to ask if he was 'a ticket-of-leave', and stole the meat to feed his starving family. His story was confirmed by the vicar of Emscote, who vouched for his good character. The Deputy Chairman said that, in consideration of the circumstances, including the two months he had already spent in custody, he would only sentence him to 14 days. 'Let us hope that after his discharge he may meet with more encouragement to persevere in the better course of which he has shown himself capable and that he may no longer be unnecessarily hunted about by the police. We may reasonably call upon Stratford Police to temper their zeal with more discretion.'

Some mixed morality with sensation. In 1856, the Reverend Thomas Bumpus preached a special sermon to a packed Baptist Chapel, on 'the life and untimely end of William Palmer', the mass-murderer who had been hanged a week before. The chapel was packed to overflowing. There was growing recognition of the relationship between crime and lack of spiritual vision. Great attention was paid by local philanthropists to the welfare of the 'navvies' working on the drainage works. Since they were unwilling to attend church in their working clothes, the vicar held services for them in the Guild Hall and evening classes in basic literacy and numeracy were supported by all denominations. At a tea-party for the navvies and their wives, the organiser, Henry Perrott, stated that their objective was to establish a permanent night school, where working men could receive 'such improvement, moral and spiritual, as may tend to raise their position in the social and religious scale'. The loquacious Baptist Thomas Bumpus spoke of the alienation of the working-classes from the churches, which would only be increased by condescending philanthropy. 'We must approach them in the spirit of Him, who, while he could hurl his censures at the proud and self-righteous Pharisees, . . . was the impersonation of tenderness and compassion . . . when stooping to relieve the wants of the necessitous'.

Such material and spiritual improvement would represent the apotheosis of England: all that she required to 'crown her with a glory such as the world has never seen . . . are goodliness, righteousness and sobriety of life among her people. Were these secured, then no man of intelligence . . . could regard her decay as possible'.

FOOTNOTE
[1]   Which was pronounced locally, she reveals, as 'Awston'.

CHAPTER 15

'A New Era'

'Far-seeing men are preparing for a new era in the annals of the ancient borough.'
Stratford-upon-Avon Herald, 1861.

Revival of the Railway

The hopes of the railway boom proved illusory. In 1852 the Stratford-upon-Avon Railway Company (S.R.C.) was formed with capital of £100,000, but its scheme for a railway to Leamington through Charlecote collapsed through technical difficulties and the opposition of landowners. Stratford's other hope for a railway was also barren, the financial difficulties of the Oxford, Worcester and Wolverhampton Company (O.W. & W.R.) preventing the construction of a branch line. The Company had taken over the horse tramway in 1847, six years later opening Stratford's first primitive passenger service in adapted trucks, which conveyed the moderately-reckless to mainline connections at Moreton. An account of this odd journey appeared in *London Society in 1864*:

> Attached to the carriage in front was a platform, on which the sagacious horse leaped to prevent being tripped up as we descended at a rattling good speed. The inspectors of the Board of Trade not having found this tramway, the occurence, or non-occurence, of accidents was left chiefly to the goodness of Providence.

Down inclines, the guard applied his brake 'as tightly as he could; we all to the best of our individual capacities held on to our seats, and . . . thus managed to avoid being pitched off head-foremost. When the carriage came to a standstill, the horse dismounted and drew us along as before'. On approaching a tunnel, 'the driver was kind enough to suggest that such of the outside passengers as thought it likely they would have any further use for their brains, should duck their heads as low as possible, and carry their hats in their hands'. The Royal Society for the Prevention of Cruelty to Animals took a less frivolous view of life on the Tramway, bringing an action against the horse contractor, Joseph Haynes, for 'cruelly ill-treating and torturing his animals'. He was fined £20.

During the fierce winter of 1855, a tram got embedded in the snow; with the canal and river frozen, Stratford's commerce was cut off. Coal was beyond the pockets of the poor and the emergency soup kitchen could hardly cope with the demand. Something had to be done. After intensive lobbying, the S.R.C. was re-formed to construct a nine-mile line to the Birmingham and Oxford Railway at Hatton. The great engineer Isambard Kingdom Brunel was engaged as advisor and the Bill was passed with the stipulation that the line should be constructed on the mixed gauge of which he was a proponent. At the banquet to mark the cutting of the first sod, the vicar declared that railways were a means to improve man's social and moral condition: 'no missionary effort yet made has done so much as they will do for the Christianisation of the world'.

The O.W. & W.R. decided that it too had a role to play in this mechanical mission to South

Warwickshire. By June 1859, its works from Honeybourne had reached the confluence of the Avon and Stour below Stratford and excited Stratfordians crowded the river banks to watch the locomotives shunting. The navvies worked at a frenetic pace, and a month after the laying of the foundation stone for the Avon bridge, the railway was opened. A long train, drawn by two gaily decorated engines, the 'William Shakespeare' and the 'Ben Jonson', conveyed three bands and a merry crowd of guests and the town turned out to cheer. Three months later the S.R.C. distributed hundreds of free tickets for its first train out of Stratford. One problem remained. The two branches terminated in direct line half a mile apart. In 1861 rivalry was suppressed and they were joined. In the ensuing years, an elaborate system of branch lines grew to link Stratford with the world.[1]

Now Stratfordians could take the 7.05 morning train on the Hatton line and arrive at Paddington at 10.30 for a Third Class return fare of 8/6d. The effects of rapid transportation were not to everyone's taste. The American writer Harriet Beecher Stowe had warned that the railway might destroy Stratford's 'air of respectable, stand-still repose'. Soon the Flowers' summer calm was disturbed by 'a wretched little steamer' taking trippers up the river and The *Stratford-upon-Avon Herald*[2] was complaining about 'holiday-keepers' thronging the town:

> The principal amusements of the majority . . . were eating and drinking – the latter excessively in many cases – smoking, wandering through the churchyard and taking away the flowers which decorate the tombs, or stripping the chestnut trees in Bree's Lane of their splendid blossoms. Some exhibited in a limited degree a taste for the fine arts, by inquiring at the shops where photographs were exhibited if 'loiknesses' were taken there.

Yet the number of visitors to the Birthplace was also increasing. By 1862 some 6,000 were arriving each year. The wealth thus engendered enabled the Trust to acquire Nash's House and the site of New Place in 1864, and Anne Hathaway's Cottage in 1892.

The arrival of the railway caused property values to rise sharply and led to a demand for 'improvements' which caused the final destruction of the old Middle Row in Bridge Street in 1863, under the direction of Robert Hobbes, son of the diarist. 'If Mr. Hobbes were not one of the most respected and agreeable men in Stratford', declared the outraged scholar, James Halliwell, 'he ought, in penance, to be made to stand in front of the market house, looking at the waste he has created and have his ears well lugged for his pains.'

The End of a Dynasty

At Holy Trinity the Kite family had held the sextonship since the Restoration, except for a brief interregnum in 1829 when Thomas Kemp was appointed, but he died two weeks later after drinking a bottle of gin, so tradition asserted itself and another Thomas Kite became sexton. He maintained the family role of escorting visitors over the Church, while recounting extravagant and apochryphal stories. The aged Sir Walter Scott was led round by his daughter; Lord Byron, Queen Adelaide, Ralph Waldo Emerson, Nathaniel Hawthorne and such noted actors as Edwin Booth, Edmund Kean and W. C. Macready were amongst those submitting to his singular tour. Visitors could be as odd as the sexton: Mrs. Beecher Stowe and her brother obtained special permission to receive Communion over Shakespeare's grave.

All this was highly lucrative. Mrs. Beecher Stowe opined that Tom had a higher income than the vicar. In 1832, it was rumoured that he was negotiating to sell Shakespeare's skull to a phrenological society in London. Equally hazardous for the bones of the Bard were his dealings with Delia Bacon, an American lady of independent means who believed that the works bearing Shakespeare's name were written by her namesake. She was drawn to Stratford, said Nathaniel Hawthorne, 'by the magnetism of those rich secrets which she supposed to have been hidden by Bacon, or Raleigh, or I know not who, in Shakespeare's grave . . . She took a humble lodging and began to haunt the church like a ghost.'

Miss Bacon must have bribed Kite for the key to the church, for one night she gained entry and groped her way up the aisle to Shakespeare's grave. 'If the divine poet really wrote the inscription, and cared as much about the quiet of his bones as its deprecatory earnestness would imply, it was time for those crumbling relics to bestir themselves under her sacrilegious feet.' She made no attempt to disturb them, although she satisfied herself that she could lift the tombstone:

> Had she been subject to superstisious terrors, it is impossible to conceive of a situation that could better entitle her to feel them, for, if Shakespeare's ghost would rise at any provocation, it must have shown itself then; but it is my severe belief, that, if his figure had appeared within the scope of her dark-lantern . . . , she would have met him fearlessly and controverted his claims to the authorship of the plays to his very face.

Charles Flower always doubted the validity of Hawthorne's story, but what is without doubt is that Delia Bacon fell in love with Stratford and would have given anything to live there permanently. 'She liked the old slumberous town, and awarded the only praise that ever I knew her bestow on Shakespeare . . . that he knew how to choose a suitable retirement for a person of shy but genial temperament.'

She gradually became a recluse, remaining in her room for days. It was only with great difficulty that her landlady, Mrs. Baldwin, persuaded her to eat. When a contribution that she sent to *The Times* was returned, she tried to commit suicide and the Baldwins had to stay with her all night. Next morning they called in the doctor: the windows were boarded up to prevent her throwing herself out and she was watched night and day. She devised all sorts of subterfuges to deceive her custodians: before her worst attacks, she read and recited from the Bible and engaged in edifying conversation, but afterwards relapsed into violent and abusive language. When the Baldwins could cope no longer, she was removed to a private asylum in Henley-in-Arden. In the spring of 1858, a nephew in the U.S. Navy came to take her back to America, where she died soon afterwards.

The end of the Kite dynasty came two years later. It was the sexton's duty to attend services. One morning Thomas Kite remained in his seat after the congregation had departed. It was discovered that he was in a drunken stupor and the vicar was summoned. When he arrived, the sexton was still snoring. The vestry decided, despite a petition on Kite's behalf, to dispense with the institution the Kite family had become.

A Doge Indeed

In 1853, Charles Flower attended the Birthday lunch of the Shakespeare Club, which was 'very dull, long and stupid'. The 'Bran and Chaff' had folded up in the 1840s and the original Club met at the *Golden Lion*, under the presidency of its proprietor, Henry Hartley, a professional comedian.

The Flowers were great hosts, entertaining a wonderful variety of people. During 1857, they heard W. M. Thackeray lecture at Leamington. Afterwards his agent, Mr. Boddy, stayed at 'The Hill', the new family mansion on the Warwick Road. A fellow-guest was the famous revolutionary, Felice Orsini, in England to purchase grenades. Sarah Flower found him very melancholy. One morning he told her of his children and how sad it would be for them if he died. On a visit to the Birthplace, he expunged the name of the Emperor Louis Napoleon from the visitors' book and substituted his own. Later, the papers carried a story, for which Sarah supposed Mr. Boddy responsible, that while at The Hill, Orsini had indulged in early morning target practice. Subsequently he made a bloody and abortive attempt to assassinate the French Emperor with the grenades and was guillotined. Sarah remembered how sorrowful he had been.

The penchant of the Flowers for interesting people and their strong Liberalism led to friendship with the rising Radical, Joseph Chamberlain. The two families acted together a playlet, *Fair Rosamund*, which Charles had written. In 1858 the Chamberlains attended a lively Christmas party at 'The Hill', when 86 guests danced till 3 a.m. In the New Year, the families attended the Infirmary Ball together. At that year's Shakespeare Dinner, the comic actor, Harries Tilbury, suggested a Grand Festival in 1864 to celebrate the tercentenary of Shakespeare's birth. The suggestion engendered enthusiasm and a committee was formed under the chairmanship of Edward Flower.

Sarah Flower's enthusiasms ranged over such causes as lunatic asylums, life-boats and the 'underground railway' for escaped slaves. Charles also busied himself, forming a local rifle corps – 'It is thought necessary to do so throughout England', wrote Sarah, 'in case of French invasion'. On 23 June 1860 the detachment took part in a royal review in Hyde Park. Later that year Charles bought 'Avonbank', a property on the river by the church. With characteristic sensibility, Sarah was glad their new home was amongst neighbours, 'for as people grow older I am convinced they are more dependent upon cheerful society and it is wholesome to have the common friction of life'.

28. *'Avonbank', home of Charles and Sarah Flower.*

The rebuilding of 'Avonbank' was delayed for six years by a recession in the brewery which caused great family tension: the sons and their wives received 'a great scolding' from the father about the state of the business. Sarah thought this unfair: Charles and Edgar had been working hard to improve things. Harder times meant the curtailment of pleasures. The sons sold their hunters and Charles gave up, 'with a great pang', a musketry training course. The mother made everyone so anxious and depressed that Charles and Sarah agreed that he should pull out of the business as soon as he honourably could, but 'the dear father seemed so sorry that nothing was said'. Her conclusion reveals the inner resource of this splendid family: 'These miserable times have been the drawbacks of our very happy life; and perhaps they have made us more particular and considerate for others. I was always so very fond of the father; he had such a fine generous spirit and was so very miserable when anything upset the harmony of the family'.

Soon after, Edward Flower retired, but the parents continued to be obsessive about the business and the sons and their wives were admirably patient. Such difficulties never restricted Sarah's philanthropy. She held a party on Boxing Day for the children of the brewery workers and began a charitable infant school.

As well as recession, there were other developments to darken Victorian confidence. The critical spirit made an impact at the Flowers' table in 1861: 'The publication of *Essays and Reviews* was now an engrossing subject – Mr. Granville [the vicar] said one night at dinner with us he did not like people's minds being disturbed by such books, he had signed the petition against it, but he had never read the book!' Later the Flowers entertained the widow and sons of Professor Baden-Powell, a contributor to this milestone of Victorian religion. The youngest was the future hero of Mafeking. Momentous events across the Atlantic made their mark. In 1862 a ball at the Town Hall raised funds for the Lancashire cotton workers made destitute by the American Civil War. The Flowers entertained Mr. Moncuse Conway, a Southern abolitionist. Four years later their first guest at 'Avonbank' was Mr. Lloyd Garrison, a Southern abolitionist, 'who had lived to see the emancipation of the slaves – the work of his life – effected'.

1862 saw the last night of the Royal Shakespearean Rooms: an address expressed the hope that the management might reopen in a new building. This was not to be and the theatre stood empty for seven years.

In 1863, Edward Flower became Mayor for the fourth time, throwing a gargantuan party at the Town Hall. Plans for the Tercentenary celebration were not meeting universal approval. The Committee was breaking tradition by making the event more Shakespeare than Jubilee and many townspeople were upset by the omission of a procession. Thus an independent committee was formed to organise its own festival. An old boy of the Grammar School, Mr. Ginnett, a circus proprietor, offered to provide any number of bipeds and quadrupeds for the occasion. The 'swells' of the official committee were not happy with this development, 'surmising that it would not greatly increase the grandeur of their ceremony'.

Others dissented for opposite reasons. William Kerr of Long Marston wrote an outraged letter to *The Revival* denouncing the Festival and declaring himself 'anxious to set on foot a counteracting influence to have the gospel preached and tracts distributed'. His opinion of the town was not high. He regarded his efforts as 'simply an evangelising in a dark and benighted and almost, I might say, idolatrous place as it regards Shakespeare'.

29. *Edward Fordham Flower, Mayor of Stratford, 'looking like a Doge of Venice when a Doge was a Doge indeed'.*

The official preparations were on the grand scale. A huge pavilion, modelled on John o'Groat's House, was constructed on Charles Flower's land in Southern Lane and extra railway-sidings were built to accommodate the rush of visitors. Efforts to engage leading theatrical talents led to complications. When Charles Fecther, the French actor, was asked to play his celebrated Hamlet, there were protests that the leading English actor, Samuel Phelps, had been snubbed. Phelps said he would not come if Fecther was there and Fecther withdrew because he said that some of the Committee had put it about that he had manipulated the choice of his Hamlet. Fortunately some other notable actors like Edward Compton agreed to appear. There were also problems with the ladies. Stella Colas, the beautiful French actress, agreed to play Juliet. The celebrated Helen Faucit, then 47, was asked to appear as Rosalind, but declined because her husband, Sir Theodore Martin, wanted her to play Juliet.

The Festival began with a huge Birthday dinner in the Pavilion, at which Mr. Flower presided, looking like 'a Doge of Venice when the Doge was a Doge indeed'. On the Sunday, an annual Shakespeare sermon was inaugurated by Archbishop Trench of Dublin. His delivery was bad: 'those a little way off could only catch the word – Shakespeare – which rather shocked them'.

The three-week theatrical season opened with *Romeo and Juliet*, which was much enjoyed, although Mlle. Colas' performance was not highly regarded. 'She is beautiful and fascinating, but we are afraid she is not Shakespeare's Juliet', said the *Herald*, adding gallantly; 'We feel like brutes as we write it.'

Other sensibilities were prickled. When the Reverend M. C. Tompson of Alderminster tried to drive his gig down Church Street, he was stopped by a police constable on traffic duty. Failing to see why his right of way should be impeded, he struck out with his whip, for which assault he was fined. More hardened lawbreakers appeared at a special court, which dealt with more than twenty pickpockets.

Charles Dickens made the journey, enjoyed himself and wrote about it in *All the Year Round*. At the Birthplace he was disconcerted by two huge policemen blowing their noses 'like thunder in two sheets of red calico', but he found the production of *Twelfth Night* enchanting.

The alternative festival began on 2 May. Mr. Ginnett had erected a huge pavilion behind the *Unicorn*, from whence the long-awaited pageant emerged and paraded the streets to great approval. The *Herald* got the right phrase: 'If it was relatively, it was not absolutely magnificent.' Next day the parade was repeated by popular demand, completing its journey at Wombwell's Menagerie in the Rother Market.

The official festival had other attractions: for the erudite, there was a lecture in German by Professor Max Muller; an exhibition of Shakespearean paintings at the Town Hall proved popular, as did a fancy dress ball in the Pavilion. *The Messiah* was performed to great approval, but one intended highlight – a flight by Mr. Coxwell in his famous balloon – was a fiasco. Vast crowds gathered, but the balloon failed to ascend. On enquiry it was found that much of the gas had gone to light the Pavilion. The *Herald* excruciatingly described the situation as 'gasly'.

The theatricals closed with an abridged version of *Much Ado* and the trial scene from *The Merchant*, with the popular favourite, Mrs. Vezin, who was greeted with delirious applause whenever she appeared as Beatrice and Portia. At the close, there were hearty cheers for Mr. Flower, which he acknowledged with a little speech.

A last event remained. The Evangelicals opposed to the Festival had obtained the celebrated Baptist preacher, the Reverend Charles Spurgeon, although he was unavailable until it was all over, so the visitors departed, unaware of the moral danger which had surrounded them. Stratfordians did not, however, escape the wrath. On 7 June, he addressed 2,000 people at an open-air meeting.

The Tercentenary celebration had proved that the railway would augment local support by bringing thousands of visitors to a Shakespeare season. It was not long before the mind of Charles Flower turned towards a permanent implementation of his father's idea. Yet despite the success of the Festival, it had lost money. The deficit was borne by Edward Flower and members of the Royal Shakespearean Club. This temporarily dampened enthusiasm and the last annual meeting of the Club was held the following year. It was not until 23 April 1874, that 12 gentlemen, ten of them borough councillors, dined together at the *Red Horse* to revive the Club tradition.

Despite his spectacular success, Edward Flower was relieved to retire as Mayor and 'get clear of town squabbles'. He had used his casting vote to support the amalgamation of the borough police with the county force. This was long overdue. Stratford Police had a strength of four for a population of 3,672. They were badly equipped and, in addition to their other duties, acted as assistant relieving officers for the casual poor. Nevertheless, local patriotism was stirred and the Mayor endured a brief unpopularity.

Obscenity, Filth and Vulgarity

A number of low houses existed in Stratford and generally caused little stir. A brothel was cannily situated in Bull Street between the jurisdictions of the Borough and County Police.

30. The banquet in the Shakespeare Commemorative Pavilion. The Earl of Carlisle proposes 'The memory of Shakespeare'.

31. The exhibition of Shakespearean pictures and relics, held in the Town Hall.

The Madam of this unrefined establishment was Emma Day, who had walked the local streets for years, sustaining her workshy husband, Stephen Day, with her immoral earnings. In 1858, the Days were found guilty of keeping a disorderly house, but they had the satisfaction of hinting that the police superintendent was a regular customer! Perhaps Fanny Harris and Hannah Woodford were prostitutes at this brothel. One evening they lured John Hawkes up a court off West Street. Hoping to satisfy his predilections, he climbed into a loft where one girl blew out the candle and the other robbed him of £50.

During 1869, a commotion at the *Ship* beerhouse on Waterside caused the police superintend-ent to seek entry. At first the landlady refused to open the door. When he got inside he found a man in bed in one room and a woman in another, but there was female clothing scattered about the man's room. The *Ship* was a notorious haunt of bad characters. Many went straight there on release from gaol and it was well situated to attract bargees and railwaymen from the wharves opposite. When Emma Bradley brought a paternity suit against Charles Beckett, it was rejected because she had been seen in the *Ship*.

Despite frequent exhortations to moral behaviour, a steady flow of young men made court appearances and were charged the going rate to support the infant reminders of their indiscretions. Other babies were abandoned by their mothers: in the first four months of 1858 three newborn babies were found drowned in the canal. Some little bundles arrived at the Workhouse where the Guardians performed the Bumble-like task of naming them. One foundling was named Mary Whitfield, 'after several amusing suggestions', having been discovered in Whitfield hovel. Charlotte Sumner, a maidservant, was brought to trial for murder after the severed head of her newborn baby was found in a closet. She found compassion in a jury which ignored the judge's directions and found her guilty only of concealment of birth, accepting her plea that she had severed the head while trying to cut the umbilical cord.

Victorian morality had what was considered a pragmatic basis. A local doctor, J.J.Nason, considered it vital in youth to keep the sexual organs in a state of quiescence:

> The habit of continence, early established, will make the practice of it in after years a comparatively easy thing; whereas the early and unrestrained indulgence of the passions will bring about such nervous irritation and constitutional unrest- not to mention great instability of purpose and diminished powers of self-control – as will lead the unhappy sufferer to seek relief in unlawful and perilous expedients, which will, like dram-drinking, not only feed the disease they were intended to remove, but also in themselves become the parent of other ills far more difficult to bear than the salutary rule of self-restraint.

The Mop attracted the attention of moralists. The hiring system was a potential means to procure girls for prostitution – although there is no evidence that this occurred at Stratford, where girls plying for hire were generally accompanied by their formidable mothers. Critics of the fair claimed that, once hiring had been accomplished, the rest of the day was spent in 'immoral amusements which bring degradation upon many a young female and sorrow to many an honest parent'.

In the 1860s a new class of Mop itinerant, the travelling photographer, became 'as plentiful as blackberries in Autumn.' The *Herald* reporter was amused to see 'a yokel making a present of his likeness to his cherry-cheeked companion, his head resembling a swede-turnip, with a gash for a mouth as though cut at random with a dull hatchet'. Outside one 'studio' was a *carte de visite* of the Emperor Napoleon III. The reporter wondered what had induced 'his Imperial Majesty to honour such an establishment with a sitting'. However, as the proprietor resembled 'a decayed prizefighter, we refrained from putting impertinent questions'. In Wood Street, a large crowd gathered around two men, who claimed to be miners and crouched dejectedly on the ground. A large crude oil painting showed a coal pit in which they claimed to have been injured. One man sang a mining song in a monotone, while beating time with his pick on a lump of coal. Every few minutes his companion held forth in 'a whining, hypocritical tone . . . "Only one good leg between the two on us". The sympathy of bystanders was evoked 'for pennies fell at times nearly as thick as hailstones in a storm. In less than an hour the men's pockets were literally gorged with coppers, yet they continued to appeal to . . . the gullible British public with good effect'.

Such exhibitions of 'obscenity, filth and vulgarity' gave impetus to those who sought to abolish the Mop. In 1859 a public meeting at the Town Hall unanimously resolved to establish a 'Servants Amelioration Society' to keep employment registers. At the next Mop a registry was opened in the Corn Exchange which achieved some success, but the *Herald* considered that the alternative to the hiring system was 'fruitless journeys from farmhouse to farmhouse' and doubted the motives of those who sought to take from the poor man 'the last remaining holiday which grasping avarice has left him'. The movement to abolish the Mop could not compete with its popular following. Dr. Collis, vicar from 1868, organised a petition for its abolition signed by 154 people, including 21 clergy. When it was presented to the Borough Council, next business was moved immediately.

Sexual impropriety bothered Dr. Collis on more occasions than Mop night. The churchyard was a favoured trysting place and there were sometimes as many as 150 young people hanging about there. This gave rise to the sort of scandals which a Victorian vicar was unwilling to discuss publicly, but an example was made of Phoebe Hughes, 'an intelligent looking lass', who was fined 1/- with 9/6d costs for loitering.

Love could lead to violence. In 1870 a fight occurred on the river meadows between two aspirants to the favour of a 'blooming young lass in violent curls'. After three unequal rounds, the spectators cheered when 'O.B. gave in and P.O.B. was declared the winner'. The *Herald* reporter, who clearly hoped to see blood, considered that if the 'loser estimated the prize by the amount of punishment he endured for her sake, he placed it at a very low figure'.

Shotteryites

Fighting was a major pastime at Shottery, that curious hamlet, whose poverty ensured that it remained part of a disappearing rural England. After the *Shakespeare Tavern* closed, the young men of the village would form a ring and wrestle for each others' belts. One night Police Inspector Joseph James entered the ring with Sergeant Glenn and announced that wrestling was forbidden. Some of the crowd formed another ring a short distance away; when the Inspector warned of the consequences of persisting, William Wooten thrust his fist into his face and yelled: 'Damned if we don't wrestle for them'. Inspector James tried to arrest him, but the crowd pulled him free. William Smith and Shadrack Best threw their caps into a third ring and the two officers, despite the hostile crowd, arrested them. The mob rescued Smith, but the Inspector pursued him into the village and recaptured him. 'Will you let the bugger take me?' shouted Smith to his pals. 'No! No!' was the response. The Inspector hung on to Smith until he was knocked unconscious. At the Petty Sessions, seven Shotteryites were fined 10 shillings each and imprisoned for 28 days; six others received six months hard labour at the Assizes. Shadrack Best, who had gone quietly, was bound over.

Traditional means to censure offenders against the moral code caused more problems. In 1869, after an 'indignation meeting', the effigy of a married woman who had committed adultery was paraded round the village. The local constable had given permission for the rite to continue over three nights. On the third evening 150 people massed across the road and three men were arrested. The magistrates expressed their sympathy with the moral atmosphere prevailing at Shottery, but could not overlook the offence. Fines and costs on each defendant totalled 15s 6d. An old Shotteryite wrote indignantly to the *Herald* recalling 'well and gratefully the days when a good old English gentleman occupied the Hall. His name was Thomas More, Esq. He was what is called an "eccentric"; perhaps this means Catholic as he was accustomed to go to Wooton on Saturdays to meet a priest. That don't matter; he was just, and noble and kind-hearted. He paid a labouring man a good day's wage for a good day's work. He cheerfully assisted in every case of real distress in the village; and instead of instructing the parish constable – there were no police in those days – to keep his eye upon the poor villagers, with a view to fining them and grinding them down to a state of grovelling pauperdom, he shut his eyes to any temporary obstruction of the highway . . . In those days the quiet villagers . . . "boiled over" but once a year, and that was when keeping up their ancient "wake"; and if it occasionally happened that any person found himself next morning in the Sheep-street "lock-up", it generally turned out that the delinquent was nearer to his own house than Shottery.'

The new occupant of Shottery Hall, Admiral Douglas Curry, had apparently complained about the ritual. At the Petty Sessions, the villagers got their revenge when a number of them testified against his three sons, who were each fined one pound with costs for vandalising a hedge. Admiral Curry considered that the main problem of his adopted village was its lack of spiritual and educational facilities. A church school for 80 children was held in the cramped dissenting chapel. Occasional services in a tithe barn were well attended, demonstrating, in the view of the vicar, 'the universal desire' for worship. If a school and a church were provided, a curate could serve the impoverished population of around 450 and the outlying hamlets of Drayton and Dodwell with their 100 souls. 'A mighty interest', declared the *Herald*, 'has sprung up recently with regard to the once benighted hamlet, formerly famous for its Summer amusements of boxing and wrestling matches, and its bouts of juggling, jumping in bags, racing for gownpieces, etc.'. In 1870, Shottery School was opened in a converted tithe barn and soon after the handsome little church of St Andrew, largely endowed by the Currys, was consecrated. Yet old ways died hard. When an outbreak of typhoid occurred, medical opinion was ignored and Mr. Cloves, the Shottery pumpmaker, was widely quoted. 'Cloves', said the *Herald*, 'had given an opinion', and the view of the Medical Officer of Health sank 'into insignificance beside the livid light of the newly discovered genius of our town'.

The Demon Drink

Another area where the hand of morality descended on the poor was drink. Again the code was rigid because its abuse was widespread. The police court had its weekly crop of the drunk and disorderly, especially during the 'Irish Season' when itinerant labourers arrived for the harvest. Some amused the court, like the drunk given a discharge after stating that he had mistaken the outside of his house in Shakespeare Street for the inside; or that regular attender, Jack Kemp, a self-styled 'Cervantic Rabelaisian', who referred to press reports of his court appearances as his 'notices'. He would address the bench in doggerel – 'This cursed spite. I hope that I shall live to set it right.'

More frequently the archetypal Victorian drunkard emerges, with the abject poverty and violence suffered by his family a corollary to his condition. Two such cases, nearly thirty years apart, may represent the *genre*. In 1867, Sergeant Cross saw William Baily, 'a small octavo specimen', of Russell Court, fighting drunk and beating his decrepit old wife. He was riled because his 'old woman's grandchildren' had lied to him. The bench jailed him for seven days and found some cash for his wife, who had suffered many years of abuse.

In 1895, John Wesson of Ely Street appeared for neglecting his wife and children. 'Were any novelist', said *The Birmingham Globe*, 'to picture a young Englishman as consuming a comfortable meal within sight of his starving wife and children, without offering them a single scrap, most readers would pronounce the incident impossible . . . He used, after getting drunk, to stagger home and send out for food with the remainder of his wages. On this being placed on the table, down he sat and consumed every morsel, giving no heed to the supplications of his hungry wife and little ones for a share, however small. They were always in a state of semi- starvation, as he made a point of spending nearly all his earnings on himself. Occasionally he varied this . . . torture by taking himself off and leaving the poor creatures to the tender mercies of the relieving officer . . . And for all of this atrocious work, the inhuman brute received a fortnight's imprisonment!'

Such cases fuelled the Temperance Movement. Its national power led to the introduction of licensing hours in 1872. Nightly at 11 (ten on Sundays), local pubs echoed to the new cry of 'Gentlemen out, turn out!' To compete with the pubs, temperance meetings were jolly affairs. The Band of Hope met weekly at the Primitive Methodist schoolroom for stirring orations, or to sing campaigning songs:

> We know the cause in which we've joined
> Is worthy of all zeal
> God grant that all who join our ranks
> The growing fire may feel.

Temperance audiences were regaled with horrific tales of vile deeds committed under the influence. The vicar opened meetings of the Church Temperance Society by reading such improving tales as 'Bob the Telegraph Boy'. Occasionally a reformed drunk testified. Jack Kemp became such a one, devoting his colourful talents to temperance platforms. His reformation came too late to prevent him ending his days in the workhouse, but he used this as a salutary illustration. A flourishing 'Junior Abstainers Union' sought to avert such tragedies in the formative years. At the licensing sessions protests were made about parents sending children to fetch jugs of ale, which they would sip as they ran home, and publicans were condemned for giving sweets to children to encourage such errands.

At one temperance meeting the speaker, Archdeacon Robert Wilberforce, estimated that intemperance caused nine-tenths of pauperism, crime and misery, pouring scorn on those who related social evils to bad conditions. 'Put a pig in a drawing room', he thundered, 'and see if the drawing room will convert the pig or the pig the drawing room.'

Others took a broader view. 'We must remember', wrote Mr. Henry Fisher to the *Herald*, 'that there is a very close connection between the physical and moral condition of being – between our outward circumstance and our inward character. Domestic purity, social refinement, religious sensibility, cannot flourish in foul recesses, upon which the day scarcely looks, or where the balmy, life-giving air can hardly penetrate.' Mr. Fisher's reflections were prompted by a survey he had conducted of local housing. He was horrified to find one family of ten living in a small, dingy house with only one upper room. 'Only imagine the effect upon the morals . . .'

Stratford was a whited sepulchre whose attractive main streets concealed desperate poverty. William Greener of Rother Street found the cleanliness and happiness of the inhabitants 'but an outer dress. A vast amount of real misery and poverty lurk beneath'. In 1866, Greener bought five cottages, which he considered unfit for stables. They measured ten feet square with one room over the other and a wretched little outhouse. In one lived seven people. When told to move, they implored his wife 'to use her influence with me to let them stand, for if driven from there they could not find shelter . . .'.

The Mayor opined that some property owners in Stratford had 'hard hearts and no consciences' – an opinion rendered less effective by the fact that the worst slums were Corporation property. The Council owned nearly all the available development land and charged a prohibitive fee, which went to Henry Hunt, the Town Clerk, for each sub-lease.

Greener's scheme to develop his property as model artisan's dwellings was thus precluded and he launched an attack in the *Herald*: 'The poorer classes in Stratford want, and that urgently, dwellings. The Corporation have plenty of sites, money is ready to build; but . . . the "legal gentleman's coach" stops the way. Notwithstanding the Act reforming Corporations swept away all right on the part of town clerks to make out deeds with a view to prospective benefit to themselves . . ., we have an example in 1868 of the same injustice . . .'. His campaign was effective. The Council leased him land in Arden and Mansell Streets for £35 a year.'

Russell Court, situated in a dark, narrow passage off Ely Street, whose defective ventilation permeated the air with the smell of burnt frying pans, was regarded as the worst slum in Stratford. Its ramshackle cottages housed appalling squalor. Some possessed only one room upstairs and the small, stuffy landing was used for sleeping. Such overcrowding brought frequent quarrels between neighbours. 'This classic region', wrote the *Herald*, 'hath a Vesuvionic quality: it slumbereth for a time, a thin cloud of smoke only denoting its existence, but after a while the volcano bursts forth, the "lava" – in the shape of particularly strong expletives – literally swamping all vestiges of humane and kindly feeling.'

One Sunday morning, Mrs. Mary Cooper went to collect milk from a neighbour. They chatted for a while and Mrs. Caroline Boyce, who was nearby, thought they were 'brass-nailing' her and let fly a volley of abuse. As Mrs. Cooper went home, Mrs. Boyce attacked her, pulling her hair with one hand and bashing her with the other until she was pulled away. At the Police Court, she was bound over for six months, the neighbours turning out to testify, mostly for Mrs. Cooper. The magistrates instructed the police to keep a special watch on Russell Court and announced that they would, if necessary, bind all its inhabitants.

Stratford's back alleys housed residual ignorance and superstition. In 1867, residents of another slum, Emms Court, off Sheep Street, believed they had been bewitched by an elderly neighbour, Jane Ward, and had abused her for some time. One evening, while two women were haranguing the poor old woman

32. Emms Court, one of Stratford's worst slums.

at her door, John Davis, a maltster, rushed at her and struck her in the face, causing a deep cut which bled profusely, and shouted, 'There you old witch, I can do anything with you now.' When arrested, he exclaimed, 'Serve her right. She can do no more for me now. I have drawn first blood.' A good character reference from his employer, Mr. Flower, ensured that he received eighteen months' hard labour rather than penal servitude.

FOOTNOTES
[1]   In 1864, the first turf of the East and West Junction Railway was cut by Lady Palmerston, the Prime Minister's wife. The line was opened in 1873 and extended to join the Redditch and Evesham Railway in 1879. The S.R.C. was absorbed by the Great Western Railway in 1883 and a Stratford-Henley-Birmingham line opened in 1908. The canal was bought by the G.W.R. in 1863: trade effectively ceased in 1875. The Tramway closed in 1881. One waggon remains, standing on a section of flanged rail on the Tramway Bridge.
[2]   Founded in 1860 by Edward Adams, who saw that educational advances would make newspapers 'a necessary adjunct to every breakfast table'. Another paper, the *Stratford-upon-Avon Chronicle*, was founded in 1861 and survived for two decades.

CHAPTER 16

'We are Nobodies'

'It is true, we are nobodies, but we have waited 300 years for the somebodies to do something and they have not done it.'

Charles Flower, Mayor of Stratford, 1879.

Elections

Contests in General Elections were rare until the franchise was further extended. For 28 years after 1837, Tories were returned unopposed for South Warwickshire. In 1865, Lord Duncan put up for the Liberals, favouring the abolition of church rates and a modest extension of the electorate. The Tories, Sir Charles Mordaunt and Mr. Wise, opposed both measures.

An election was a novelty to many people, who were astonished at the rushing about of placard-covered vehicles. Perhaps it was this unfamiliarity which ensured that 'scarcely a black eye was given all day'. The *Herald* had declared that the election of Lord Duncan would reflect honour upon any constituency, but the local electorate narrowly failed to so distinguish itself and the Liberals drank to 'Better luck next time' at the *Red Horse* while congratulating themselves on having done so well. The Conservatives dined at the *Shakespeare* and made pleasant speeches on the way the day was won. Both agents spoke highly of the conduct of their opponents. Next morning, 'pale faces spoke of the excitement of the previous day. But a friendly glass pledged to neighbours soon restored the healthy tint . . . and opponents of Friday jingled glasses on Saturday to the toast, "May difference of opinion never destroy friendship." '.

Edward Flower had stood for the Liberals at Coventry and lost by 59 votes. The family helped strenuously and in gratitude he gave Sarah £350 to furnish her new house. After 1873, he lived mainly in London. One of his great causes was the abolition of bearing reins for horses and he wrote a widely-read pamphlet on it.

After extending the franchise and abolishing church rates, the Tories, like true politicians, returned to the polls in 1868 to recommend the programme they had previously opposed. This time Mr. Wise put up with Mr. John Hardy in the Conservative interest and the Liberals fielded Lord Hyde and Sir Robert Hamilton of Alveston.

Election morning was quiet. The only disturbance came from a few small and very dirty boys, who sported blue Liberal favours and cheered all those voting. With the arrival of some Grammar School boys and a few non-voting shop assistants, blazing with orange Tory rosettes, groaning and howling started. This brought out some 'unwashed hobble-de-hoys and roughs of a maturer age' who chased the Tory supporters off the streets and then amused themselves by groaning or cheering each voter as he made his declaration. Anyone who interfered with them became a marked man and some people were roughly handled. That evening the mob, which had considerably increased in numbers and noise, paraded the streets. At the Tory committee rooms in the *Shakespeare*, someone rashly made a provocative gesture out of a window which led to an assault on the building and several windows were broken. The police, who had shown great forbearance, were soon on the spot and arrested four ringleaders who were bound over by the magistrates. This time *bonhomie* did not prevail, the Liberals accusing their opponents of intimidating the electors. Despite winning a majority in Stratford, they lost the division: the *Herald* considered this reflected the influence of 'the old maids of Leamington, duly organised to do battle with the Pope'.

This was the last election with a carnival atmosphere. The introduction of the secret ballot in 1872 made elections less public affairs, but not everyone approved of this reform. Years later the *Herald* published 'The Lament of an Old Voter', which revealed the attraction of the old ways for those with a vote:

> 'Tis true that tracts and bills galore are now before me set,
> And lots of talk to keep us straight – but how can I forget?
> For oh! There are so many things recall the past to me;
> Plum puddings hot, prime roast beef, with plenty of gravee . . .
> They tell me to be happy now, the gayest of the gay,
> But little will they think of me after the polling day.

'Church Influence'

The Catholics of Stratford achieved their first great objective in 1865 when their school reopened for local children, 'whatever their denomination', with a wider curriculum than the other denominational schools. Apart from small statutory grants, the school was dependent on voluntary aid, mainly drawn from the twopence halfpenny parents paid weekly. In 1878, the 23 children moved to the former premises of the workhouse school, which were 'comfortable, well lighted and well furnished'.

In 1866, the second great objective was achieved with the dedication of St Gregory's Church on the Warwick Road by Bishop Ullathorne of Birmingham – a handsome little building created largely through the generosity of James Cox, junior and based on designs by the celebrated architect, Augustus Pugin. The Bishop had clearly had enough of idiosyncratic behaviour amongst local Catholics and placed the church under the charge of the Benedictine Order.

In 1870, Forster's Education Act sanctioned the building of schools out of public funds, but only where existing schools were not providing enough places. Implementation of the measure was opposed by local Anglicans, whose ascendency over Stratford's education was threatened and by many ratepayers, who feared the expense. Some indication of the fierce denominational flavour of education is found in the log book of the British School. When the master, Henry Cordingley, went to ascertain why two brothers were leaving his school, the parents told him that their elder brother was going to the Church of England night school and he had been told he would not be allowed to continue unless his younger brothers went to the National School. 'So much for Church influence', Cordingley concluded cryptically. He also had a problem with his pupil-teachers,[1] who found it difficult to enforce discipline.

Log books had to be kept in all schools receiving government grants, so that they could be examined by the school inspectors on their annual visits. Payment was by pupil numbers and results, so all the schools were zealous in their efforts to recruit youngsters. The pressure to achieve results made the Inspector's visit an awesome affair and the *Herald* would carry an account of it.

As late as 1862 an attempt to introduce congregational chanting of psalms at Holy Trinity was scoffed at because of the number of illiterates in the congregation. Now literacy levels were rising, but, apart from those who received the modest advancement provided by the pupil-teacher scheme, the restricted curriculum and strong stress on obedience and discipline ensured that education enabled children to fulfill their allotted roles more efficiently, rather than providing a route through the class-system. The Grammar School, which was later to be a means for working-class boys to gain an academic education, was little more than a superior elementary school. In 1869 it contained 52 boys (five of whom boarded) with an average age of nine. It was not until 1880 that a discretionary scholarship was used to admit a boy from a local elementary school.

In 1881, an educational census revealed that 248 children in Stratford, out of a total of 1,512, were at private schools. There were a number of these and, if the evidence from one of them is indicative, standards were very low. Cambridge House occupied what is now Hall's Croft as a school for young ladies. Details of conditions there emerge in a legal action brought in 1877 against an aggrieved parent who refused to pay the fees. His daughter complained that there was no light in her bedroom and the food was coarse. She had thick bread with very little butter for breakfast. There was no fire except on Sundays and bath nights. Dinner was frequently inedible: when one of the girls could not cut a baked pudding, she was told to eat it with her fingers.

The best-known school in Stratford for over thirty years was Trinity College, founded in 1872 by Dr. Collis, the vicar, at a large house in Church Street. When he came to Stratford, Sarah Flower heard that he was a broad churchman, but this betokened his liberal views rather than his doctrinal position, for he continued the process of 'raising' the sacramental life of the church begun by the Reverend Henry Harding. This led to controversy in an age when religion was still a matter of household discussion. In 1870 his Advent sermons, devoted to Church Order, divided opinion in the parish – it was only three decades since the latitudinarian days of Dr. Davenport. The controversy formed the 'staple conversation at the genteel dinner table, penetrated the murky atmosphere of the hotel smoking room and reigned predominant at the scandal-provoking tea table'. Some alleged that the sermons pointed towards 'priest-worship' and the Reverend J. Scott James, the Congregational minister, launched a series of lectures attacking ritualism, which won the approval of many local Anglicans.

Dr. Collis's abilities as a controversialist were not restricted to matters liturgical. Within a month of his arrival, he gained national publicity with a campaign against elaborate funerals. The rituals of interment could impoverish: 'a vulgar, vicious idea prevails', declared the *Daily Telegraph* in his support, 'that a certain amount of display is a token of respect to the dead, and that proper economy would indicate want of grief; and many a poor widow has been compelled to spend upon stupid, senseless, ugly trappings, fit only for savages, money that would go far to support herself and her children . . . Why four horses to a hearse when two are enough? Why those hideous plumes? Why "mourning" carriages? Why scarves and headbands? Why those theatrical supernumeraries called mutes?'

Dr. Collis set out his practical schemes in a letter to *The Guardian*, announcing that to 'Christianise' and 'cheapen' funerals and 'to emancipate the poor and the respectable gentry of limited means from the miserable thralldom of public opinion under which they groan, and to abolish that stringent *undertakers' ritual* which they seem powerless to shake off', the clergy of Stratford had procured a hand hearse, bier and violet pall, which could easily be managed by two bearers. These were hired out for a fee of 3s 6d – 'probably less than half the cost of the cheapest funeral'. In future the clergy would decline 'gloves, scarves or hat-bands from the friends of deceased parishioners'; they would adhere strictly to the rubric instructing them to meet the coffin at the entrance to the churchyard and they would never attend the elaborate and costly wakes which were a feature of contemporary funerals. Letters of support came from all over the country and Dr. Collis formed the 'National Burial Reform Committee', which was instrumental in changing attitudes.

In 1872, Dr. Collis, together with members of the Corporation and some young ladies, placed flowers on Shakespeare's grave on the Birthday. Although he did not repeat this ceremony, it was remembered and revived two decades later to become one of the town's cherished traditions.

It was the Catholic neo-medievalism of Dr. Collis which inspired a grand plan to reproduce at Stratford its collegiate establishment of the 15th century. He liked to think of himself, the priest-chaplain and the four curates as representing the old College, with its warden, sub-warden and four canons. He was thus a controversial figure at a time when 'The Protestant Religion' was a regular after-dinner toast. 'But for the ill-fated sacrilege of Henry VIII', he wrote to *The Gospeller*, and the 'culpable negligence' of those who had demolished the College, there would have been ample revenues for the work of the church in Stratford.

Part of the scheme was Trinity College, which opened with 22 pupils. Dr. Collis gathered a group of able teachers and soon the school was attended by boys from all over the country. The school boasted 19 admissions to the universities and scholarships to such schools as Westminster, Marlborough and Charterhouse. Emphasis was placed on the boys' backgrounds, as this attracted enrolment, although he did not believe in exclusivity, never tiring of relating how he owed his own education to Thomas Arnold, whose custom it was at Rugby to accept one boy in ten without fees. He hoped to institute something similar at Trinity College.

Dr. Collis's catholic vision extended to a lay order doing good works. A parochial organisation was founded in 1870 for the care of the sick poor and a small house was acquired in West Street. A woman of 'culture, high principle and wide experience' was needed as a nurse. Such a one was found in Emily Minet, the daughter of a Madeira wine shipper, who had trained with Florence Nightingale and shared the Christian ideals of Dr. Collis. She rapidly built a team of helpers into a Nursing Institute. By 1872, the team had paid over 2,500 visits to the homes of the poor: these were, in the words of the Vicar, 'not casual, haphazard visits, aimless and resultless . . . Our devoted women not merely help the poor directly, but they *teach* them to help themselves'.

Emily Minet and her ladies organised outdoor relief for the poor, appealing each Christmas for money, clothing and food. On Christmas Day, 'each cottage small' boasted a portion of 'good old English roast beef'. In bad weather casual labour, on which many poor families depended, was impossible and a soup kitchen at the Town Hall alleviated need. The seasonal unemployment rate could reach 20 per cent, yet, Christmas once over, the needs of the poor could have low priority. The soup kitchen was suspended during a severe frost in 1871 because it interfered with arrangements for the Hunt Ball.

In 1875 £3,000 was raised to start a Nursing Home for women and children, which did much to alleviate suffering and reduce the mortality rate. It was of great benefit during a scarletina epidemic in 1887. Scarlet fever was a much feared and often fatal disease. Seven years earlier, Sarah Flower had recorded the death of her little niece, Violet, from it although she saw this as a disguised blessing. 'We never considered her like other children and probably much trouble and suffering had been saved for her – poor child.'

The epidemic of 1887 began in March, when seven families were infected. By June this had risen to 19, so Miss Minet opened a temporary fever hospital at Copham's Hill Farm. The schools closed early for the summer holidays and did not open again until mid-September. The last reported case was in December. By then 99 families had been infected, but thanks to the ministrations of the nursing team, there were no fatalities.

Such was the public respect for Emily Minet that a public subscription was opened for her in 1891. She died, exhausted by her efforts for the poor, a few weeks later. At her funeral the streets were lined by hundreds who had benefited from her dedication: along the route to the cemetery every house had its blinds drawn. 'Her whole energies', said Dr. Collis's successor, 'were devoted to the . . . mitigation of the miseries of the poor.' A memorial window was erected in Holy Trinity and the Childrens' Recovery Hospital remains a monument to her work.

Dr. Collis's time as vicar was marked by an odd controversy. The Reverend William Connor, the priest-chaplain at the Guild Chapel, became an adherent of Irvingism, that strange adventist sect which had some roots in Stratford. Dr. Collis worked hard at diocesan level to secure his resignation, which proved a traumatic process. Connor was a well-liked figure and those who knew little of theological niceties used his predicament to play the traditional game of 'Bash the Vicar': scurrilous leaflets were circulated and protest meetings held, but the vicar held firm to his orthodox viewpoint.

Despite such militancy, Dr. Collis was a man of great personal charity. On the night of his death in 1879, his old dissenting antagonist, Dr. James, called to pay his respects. On learning of his presence at the door, the dying vicar said, 'Give him my dearest love, and tell him I have learned to regard him as a companion in arms for Christ, and doubt not that we shall meet in Heaven.' After his death, plans for the endowment of Trinity College collapsed. Without his *charisma* numbers fell to 65 in 1893, when the school mainly prepared boys for entry to the Civil Service. Yet exclusivity remained. There was 'soreness amongst boys and parents' after an astute local innkeeper got his son accepted by giving his address, without the name of the inn.

Joseph Arch

Miss Minet's stress on self-help was finding echoes elsewhere. In 1872 Joseph Arch, 'a splendid hedger' in the employ of Mr. Angell James at Bridgetown, formed the Warwickshire Agricultural Labourers Union, the first such body. Arch,[2] a Primitive Methodist preacher, was a fine orator and a familiar figure in Stratford, addressing meetings in the Rother Market during the farm labourers' strike of 1872. Stratford magistrates showed sympathy for the strikers, dismissing a case against two labourers for absenting themselves from work after hearing that their weekly wages were only 12 shillings.

Stratford's drapers' assistants were also organising themselves. In 1873 a meeting at the Town Hall demanded an early closing day and the adoption of Bank Holidays. The shopkeepers were agreeable provided that all did it, but Fred Winter refused to close his shop, describing the proposal as 'senseless'. There was strong public sympathy for the shop assistants. James Cox, junior proposed a boycott of Winter's business: 'If the ladies will only help us, it can be done'. After the intervention of Dr. Collis in the dispute, Winter agreed to close at five on Wednesdays, rather than the usual seven p.m.

Others were faring better with leisure time. A Saturday half-holiday was becoming general and football the passion of the masses. The first recorded local match took place on 11 April 1873, when Stratford played Birmingham. From the time it was announced it was the all-absorbing topic for local fans. The Stratford team, although beaten, played well.

Everything Conspired to Make the Occasion Happy

The Royal Shakespeare Rooms reopened in 1868, only to close forever in 1872. In 1869, the Flowers saw a 'very badly acted' production of *'The Lady of Lyons'* there. 'Charles and I', wrote Sarah, 'both felt sorry that Edgar and Isabelle took Rosalie and Agnes for the first time – we should like them to have a high respect even veneration for their *first* play.' The entry provides a key to the vision of Charles Flower. He desired a theatre in Stratford devoted to Shakespeare's work and imbued the project with a moral imperative. After the losses of 1864, he cannot have conceived that such a theatre would be profitable, but he saw it as edifying the neighbourhood. He was aided by the constant support of a loving and remarkable wife. 'How happy we are', she had written on their 16th wedding anniversary.

At least things were improving in the brewery. The workforce was now 130 men and 45 clerks and travellers. Next year a great new brewery was opened on the Birmingham Road. 'Many of the improvements in the manufacture of beer', wrote *The Illustrated London News*, 'which are now in use throughout the country, owe their origin to members of this firm.' By 1872, Charles Flower was worth £30,000 annually. This financial stability enabled him to proceed with his great project.

In 1874, the Shakespeare Memorial Association opened a public subscription to build a theatre complete with library, art gallery and, if possible, Charles Flower's dream of an acting school. To boost donations, anyone subscribing £100 or more was made a governor, and, optimistically but worthily, it was announced that any surplus would be used to assist 'poor and deserving members of the acting profession'.

Charles Flower set the pattern for the appeal. He gave £1,000 and donated the two-acre site on the Bancroft where Garrick's Pavilion had stood, but the response was disappointing: only £1,000 was raised outside Stratford. Most of the money came from the Flower family and, it may be surmised, through the freemasons of the *Heart of England* Lodge, to which Charles Flower belonged. In November 1875 advertisements asked for designs for the theatre. Free-standing theatres were rare and the site magnificent. The design accepted, that of Dodgshun and Unsworth of Westminster, was bold, not concealing the fly tower, but making it a conspicuous part of a building which appeared like one of Ludwig II's castles done in Tudor style, with curious turrets and gables, all faintly reminiscent, in an odd Victorian way, of Shakespeare's *Globe*.

Work was slow because of trouble with the foundations – the Mere Pool stream ran into the river across the site – but on the Birthday in 1877, 500 freemasons processed to the Bancroft. Sarah Flower found the gentlemen nervous about their speeches, 'except my dear Husband who knew his well, and his delivery was the best of any, short and concise and good'. Although only 45, she was crippled with rheumatism and went in a bath chair, sitting next to old Mr. Hobbes, that 'fine, bumping boy' of 1800.[3] She found the speeches fairly good, except that of poor Mr. Creswick, who suffered the Victorian orator's disgrace of reading his. Charles Flower spoke of plans for the theatre and his hope of establishing a drama school: a daring idea in 1877. After Lord Leigh the provincial Grand Master had laid the foundation stone with full masonic ritual, the company adjourned to a tent in New Place Gardens for a 'cold collation', which looked good, but proved inadequate and great dissatisfaction ensued. The Flowers compensated the chief guests with a noisy dinner in the evening.

The theatre project did not curtail the Flowers' activities as philanthropic employers. Every year all the men, with their wives and children, were conveyed by steamer to Luddington for food and games. Early in 1879, the eminent churchman, Dean Stanley, was the first to sign his name in the visitors' book of a new Brewery Club for the workforce.

The official opening of the new theatre came on the Birthday in 1879; an event which most London critics either greeted with derision or ignored. 'Can it be imagined that the poet who sought in London the sphere for his intellectual life, stands in need of a Memorial which takes the shape of an addition to the list of petty provincial theatres?' asked one journalist, although others were more sympathetic. Charles Flower replied in caustic terms. 'It is true', he said. 'We are nobodies, but we have waited three hundred years for the somebodies to do something and they have not done it.' The theatre, at least, matched the taste of the age. Oscar Wilde regarded it as 'a beautiful building, one of the loveliest erected in England for many years'.

The opening production was *Much Ado about Nothing*. Helen Faucit, now 67, was persuaded to come out of retirement to play Beatrice. Sarah Flower specially decorated her dressing room. This led to complications: her Benedick, Barry Sullivan, demanded the same treatment or he would walk out. 'You, my dear', said Charles Flower placidly to his wife, 'must send across silver candlesticks, vases of flowers, and a lace pincushion for Mr. Sullivan.' The Flowers must have wondered what their theatre would involve. On a first night of driving rain, a capacity audience of 800 saw a performance which won general approval. 'Everything', wrote Helen Faucit, 'conspired to make the occasion happy.' It was a triumph for Charles Flower in his Mayoral year.

The first season ran for a week. Next year Barry Sullivan returned for a three-week festival of Shakespearean and other plays. This set the pattern for several years. Various actor-

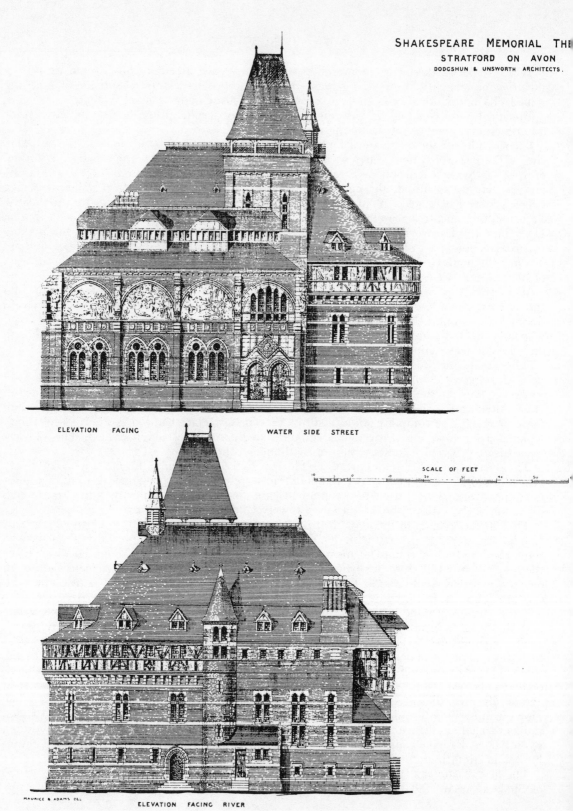

ELEVATION FACING   WATER SIDE STREET

SCALE OF FEET

ELEVATION FACING RIVER

MAURICE & ADAMS DEL.

33. The original architects' drawings for the Shakespeare Memorial Theatre, 1876. Note the variations from the actual building, on which there is less decorative effect.

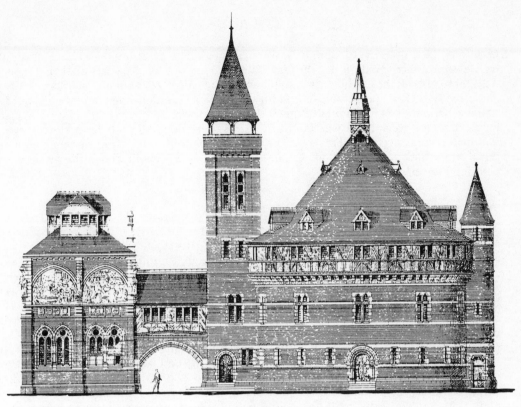

ELEVATION FACING THE GARDEN

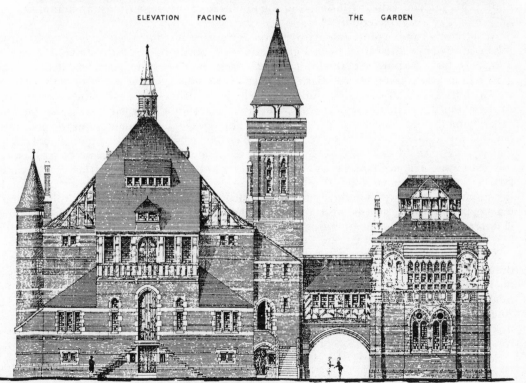

NORTH ELEVATION

managers, notably Edward Compton, were engaged. The theatre did good business during the festivals and was then 'dark' for the rest of the year, except for the occasional visiting company. The highlight of the early years came when the adulated young American actress Mary Anderson, who had spent two triumphant years on the London stage, announced her intention to make her debut as Rosalind at Stratford, before returning to America. There was a scramble for tickets and every hotel was jammed. Prices were doubled and the performance received national critical acclaim. To commemorate her perfomance, Miss Anderson donated two terracotta panels depicting Comedy and Tragedy, which stand above the circle entrance to Charles Flower's theatre.

The School Board

An event of considerable local importance occurred in 1879 when the borough was expanded to include Shottery, Old Town, New Town and Alveston. The division of the town into electoral wards diminished oligarchical power, although public house parties, like a new one at the *One Elm*, which claimed to represent ratepayers, continued to exercise influence.

In 1879, a new vicar was appointed. The Reverend George Arbuthnot was a priest whose High Churchmanship and militancy made him a natural successor to Dr. Collis. He was a fine and fearless preacher: although he was accused of many things, no-one ever called him dull. As an embattled and impetuous defender of what he regarded as revealed truth, he was respected and feared, but never loved. He was no stranger to controversy. In his previous incumbency at Arundel, he got into a wrangle with the Catholic Duke of Norfolk over the custody of the family chapel. Amongst his first acts at Stratford were the restoration of the surpliced choir, the donation of the offertory to the memorial fund for the great apostle of the Oxford Movement, Edward Pusey, and the abolition of private sittings; an action he justified on grounds of religious equality.

Arbuthnot's campaigning talents were soon exercised in educational controversy. Enforced school attendance after 1878 placed great strain on Stratford's exclusively voluntary system. Two years later the powers of the Education Department were stiffened to enable it to withdraw grants from inadequate schools. Sarah Flower's little school was an early casualty. Her grant was withdrawn because it had a stone floor, which she believed kept the air fresh; 'so different to the close, dirty smell that a quantity must occasion on a boarded floor'. She had the sad task of announcing the closure to the parents. 'There was much lamentation, the poor mothers begging me to go on with it – they could not pay the larger fees of the other schools and they had always liked Miss Barwood. I felt sorry, for it has been a great source of pleasure and interest to me. The needlework was distributed by lottery among the mothers and I managed for every mother to have something to take away . . .'. At a party for the children on her lawn, her niece and nephew, Rita and Fordham, helped dress the figure of Mrs. Jumbo sitting on a tea box, from which sweets were dispensed. Fordham gave a magic lantern show and the children sang. Sarah presented a delighted Miss Barwood with a tea set. When they had all left, she was sad that her 'happy little school' was no more.

Next year the Department refused further grants to the British School because of its unsatisfactory premises. A closure date was announced and, since the voluntary societies could no longer provide sufficient school places, Stratford was legally obliged to elect a School Board. The first election, in 1881, resulted in its domination by the 'Church Party'. Local Anglicans feared that a proposed new Board School with heavy government subsidy would threaten the status of their own National School. The main factor in the election, however, was the fear that the provision of a Board School would be a costly burden on the rates.

As a temporary measure, the British School was reopened as the Board School, but the Department insisted that a new building for at least 400 children would have to be constructed.

Shakespeare
MEMORIAL THEATRE,
STRATFORD-ON-AVON.

INAUGURAL FESTIVAL
ON
SHAKESPEARE'S BIRTHDAY, WEDNESDAY, APRIL 23, 1879,
AND FOLLOWING DAYS.

WEDNESDAY EVENING, APRIL 23rd,
MUCH ADO ABOUT NOTHING

On this occasion, the Council have the honour to announce that Mrs. THEODORE MARTIN (HELEN FAUCIT) has most kindly consented to appear.

Benedick	Mr. BARRY SULLIVAN
Don Pedro	Mr. LUIGI LABLACHE
Don John	Mr. HERBERT JENNER
Claudio	Mr. EDWARD COMPTON
Leonato	Mr. RYDER
Balthazar	Mr. W. H. CUMMINGS

Who will Sing, "Sigh no more, Ladies."

Dogberry	Mr. W. H. STEPHENS
Verges	Mr. FRANK BARSBY
Beatrice	Mrs. THEODORE MARTIN (HELEN FAUCIT)
Hero	Miss WALLIS
Ursula	Miss HUDSPETH
Margaret	Miss GOLIEN

Previous to the Performance, A DEDICATORY ADDRESS, written by Dr. WESTLAND MARSTON, will be recited by Miss KATE FIELD.

THURSDAY EVENING, APRIL 24th,
HAMLET

Hamlet	Mr. BARRY SULLIVAN
Claudius	Mr. HERBERT JENNER
Polonius	Mr. W. H. STEPHENS
Laertes	Mr. EDWARD COMPTON
Horatio	Mr. LUIGI LABLACHE
Ghost	Mr. RYDER
First Gravedigger	Mr. FRANK BARSBY
Gertrude	Mrs. CHARLES CALVERT
Ophelia	Miss WALLIS
Actress	Miss EMMERSON

FRIDAY EVENING, APRIL 25th,
A CONCERT

The Music of which is associated with the Works of Shakespeare.

Madame ARABELLA GODDARD, Mrs. OSGOOD, Miss KATE FIELD, Madame ANTOINETTE STERLING, Mr. W. SHAKESPEARE, Mr. W. H. CUMMINGS, and Mr. SANTLEY. The LONDON CONCERT GLEE UNION, under the direction of Mr. FRED WALKER.
Conductor .... SIR JULIUS BENEDICT.

SATURDAY AFTERNOON, APRIL 26th,
HAMLET
Will be repeated.

Hamlet	Mr. BARRY SULLIVAN
Claudius	Mr. HERBERT JENNER
Polonius	Mr. W. H. STEPHENS
Laertes	Mr. EDWARD COMPTON
Horatio	Mr. LUIGI LABLACHE
Ghost	Mr. RYDER
First Gravedigger	Mr. FRANK BARSBY
Gertrude	Mrs. CHARLES CALVERT
Ophelia	Miss WALLIS
Actress	Miss EMMERSON

MONDAY AFTERNOON, APRIL 28th,
Mr. SAMUEL BRANDRAM will Recite
"THE TEMPEST."

The Songs incidental to the Play will be sung by Miss de FONBLANQUE.

On MONDAY EVENING, APRIL 28th, and THURSDAY EVENING, MAY 1st,
MUCH ADO ABOUT NOTHING

Benedick	Mr. BARRY SULLIVAN
Don Pedro	Mr. LUIGI LABLACHE
Don John	Mr. HERBERT JENNER
Claudio	Mr. EDWARD COMPTON
Leonato	Mr. RYDER
Balthazar	Mr. W. H. CUMMINGS

Who will Sing, "Sigh no more, Ladies."

Dogberry	Mr. W. H. STEPHENS
Verges	Mr. FRANK BARSBY
Beatrice	Miss WALLIS
Hero	Miss EMMERSON
Ursula	Miss HUDSPETH
Margaret	Miss GOLIEN

On TUESDAY EVENING, APRIL 29th, and FRIDAY EVENING, MAY 2nd,
HAMLET

Hamlet	Mr. BARRY SULLIVAN
Claudius	Mr. HERBERT JENNER
Polonius	Mr. W. H. STEPHENS
Laertes	Mr. EDWARD COMPTON
Horatio	Mr. LUIGI LABLACHE
Ghost	Mr. RYDER
First Gravedigger	Mr. FRANK BARSBY
Gertrude	Mrs. CHARLES CALVERT
Ophelia	Miss WALLIS
Actress	Miss EMMERSON

On WEDNESDAY EVENING APRIL 30th, and SATURDAY AFTERNOON, MAY 3rd,
AS YOU LIKE IT

Jaques	Mr. BARRY SULLIVAN
Duke	Mr. ALLERTON
Banished Duke	Mr. LUIGI LABLACHE
Orlando	Mr. EDWARD COMPTON
Adam	Mr. RYDER
Touchstone	Mr. FRANK BARSBY
Amiens	Mr. W. H. CUMMINGS

Who will Sing, "Blow, blow, thou Wintry Wind."

Rosalind	Miss WALLIS
Audry	Miss HUDSPETH
Celia	Miss EMMERSON
Phœbe	Miss GOLIEN

Return Tickets at Reduced Fares.—SPECIAL TRAINS after the Performances to Leamington Every Evening; to Birmingham on 23rd and 24th; and to Worcester on 25th and 28th, stopping at intermediate stations.

For further particulars see Official Programmes, to be had Price 6d. on application to the Festival Ticket Office, New Place, Stratford-on-Avon.

All the Evening Performances will begin at 7 o'clock; doors open at 6·15 p.m. Those in the Afternoon begin at 3 o'clock; doors open at 2·15 p.m.

PRICES OF ADMISSION (for Seats Numbered and Reserved).

WEDNESDAY, April 23rd, 20s., 10s., & 5s. THURSDAY, April 24th, 20s., 10s., 5s., & 2s.6d. REMAINDER OF FESTIVAL, 10s., 5s., & 2s.6d.

Remittances for Tickets can be sent by Post, addressed to Mr. H. DOWNING, New Place, Stratford-on-Avon, and the best available places will be selected by the Strangers' Committee.

34. Playbill for the inaugural festival at the Memorial Theatre, 1879.

THE SCHOOL BOARD MEETING
TO-NIGHT.

FELLOW BURGESSES,

The School Board was originated last March by the Education Department to see that our Children received proper education, but the individual members of it were elected by us Burgesses to see that such education was given at the least possible expense.

At present school room is not provided for the number of children the Department have fixed, and the School Board will have to provide for the deficiency at our expense unless the offers which have been made to the Board to find it, free of charge to the ratepayers, are accepted.

It is estimated that Schools built by School Boards cost about £10 for every child, while we know that the Managers of the National Schools have built for 175 children at less than £4 10 per child, or less than half the money which the Ratepayers must have paid if the Managers had not built.

The School Board has told us that there are 1265 children educated at the various Schools, of which 791 go to the National Schools and 192 to the Board School.

The Reports of the National Schools show that to educate their 791 children the Managers have to collect about £160.

For the School Board a Rate of 3½d in the £, which brings in more than £350, has just been collected.

A comparison of these figures shows that every child educated in the National Schools costs the subscribers 4s., while in the Board School each child costs the Ratepayers £1 16s. 6d.

If the Board had to educate all the 1,265 children it would cost us annually over £2,300, or a 2s. rate, in addition to a very heavy rate for building Schools.

21st November, 1881.

A BURGESS.

35. Notice advertising a School Board meeting, 1881.

The Church party countered this by offering to extend the National School, but the Department threatened to use its powers to dismiss the Board, unless it undertook to build an adequate new school. At the 5th of November supper, Alderman Robert Gibbs proposed the toast of 'Success to the Stratford School Board', although his speech made clear his educational perspectives: 'If we are to have "hewers of wood and drawers of water", it seems almost a mistake to give them a classical education, because, if we do, they think they are good for something better'.

A public meeting was held at the Town Hall. Leaflets were circulating, containing spurious claims about the cost of the new building. The blood of the ratepayers was up as only the blood of ratepayers can be. The few dissenting speakers at the meeting were shouted down. Steam was let off, but nothing achieved against the inexorable demands of the Department. The Board School was opened in 1883 in Broad Street and continues in use today.

The School Board elections presented the riotous with a new opportunity for uproarious assemblies. At a turbulent meeting of candidates at the Town Hall in March 1884, two-thirds of the packed audience were under voting age. They were very disorderly, but impartial, cheering and hissing indiscriminately. When they got bored with this, they started to throw chairs about. The Church party again won the majority, demonstrating an impressive power to turn out its vote: there was little difference between its highest and lowest candidates. Educational issues were polarising the town on denominational lines, the headstrong vicar even using his influence to prevent dissenting ministers from visiting patients in the hospital. An Anglican lady rejected the opportunity of moving into lodgings which overlooked the Methodist church and, when a Nonconformist lady engaged a maidservant from an outlying village, the family was visited by their vicar, who tried to prevent her taking the situation. A leading Congregationalist, Fred Winter, complained that he frequently heard of cases of distress, 'where all kinds of assistance are refused because the parents happen to send their children to the Board School'. The lodging-house keeper Caroline Cook believed in keeping in with the Church party. 'There's no pickings from Chapel', was her adage. When little George Hewins was asked by the vicar why the church Sunday School was so well attended, his hand shot up: 'Please, sir, cos of the Clothing Club!'

The advent of compulsory education brought difficulties to poor families which had trouble finding the required 2d per child per week – and most families had more than one child. 'Very few of the labouring population are in a position to pay', declared a correspondent to the *Herald* during the disastrous summer of 1888. He knew of cases where the week's earnings were less than five shillings 'and to ask for school fees out of that miserable sum is sheer cruelty'. Survival was an uphill task on the standard wage of 13s per week. Clothing alone cost a married labourer with four children around 3s 11d a week; rent was two shillings; school fees, eightpence; coal, 1s 10d; candles, threepence; food was 5s 1d and the total had reached thirteen shillings. Those with gardens grew vegetables and some people kept a pig, their only regular source of meat. Other items were 'pinched out'. Prudent fathers paid sixpence a week into the Benefit Club; work lost in bad weather cost an average of sixpence a day. Then there was the replacement of household items and rent and rates. Where the money came from was a mystery – although some wives found work to enhance the family budget. Items like church collections, postage, books, newspapers, beer and tobacco passed into the realm of luxury.

In theory, help could be obtained from the Guardians of the Poor, but this entailed a means test which could reduce the applicant to pauperdom. In any case, the Guardians rejected virtually every application for help with school fees, including one from a woman whose husband had been unemployed for three weeks and who had no money and little food.

Child labour was often a necessity. The father of 11-year-old Florence White was fined 1s after she went 'leazing'[4] at harvest-time. Many children ran errands before school and were kept by the tradesmen until the last minute, when they rushed off dirty and tired. On Tuesdays children were sent by their parents to queue at the soup kitchen. Father Fazakerley complained that a tenth of the pupils were absent from the Catholic School on that day. At the National School, recalled George Hewins, 'once you'd paid they didn't care if you didn't go in again till next Monday. If it was raining, or the steeplechases, or peapicking, a lot of us *didn't*. The School Attendance Officer, he never troubled once your money was paid in. And plenty o' kiddies spent a penny or ha'penny of it on jibber and jumbles[5] afore they got to school. They had a good swipe o' the cane: the teacher told tham to bring another ha'penny quick! "The older the boy the greater the ass!" he shouted'. Parents charged with the non-payment of fees often protested that their children had spent the money on the way to school. Sometimes this was an attempt to conceal poverty, but the Vicar had a different view: 'Nothing', he said, 'can be more distressing than to hear a parent confess that his or her children will not go to school . . . Of course this is a confession that the child rules the house and not the parent'. The solution was simple. 'Scores of instances are before our magistrates in the course of a year in which the pitiable spectacle is presented of children setting at defiance the authority of their parents. Kindness to such youngsters is thrown away, and if persisted in will result in their ruin. A good flogging is the best way of reaching the feelings of an obstinate child.'

The school leaving age was 13, but those reaching the necessary standards could leave before then. Most left as soon as possible. Either their earnings were needed, or they went into the world to reduce the family budget. Only two out of 36 from the boys intake of 1884 stayed on after they could leave, probably becoming pupil teachers. When the School of Art[6] offered 12 reduced-fee scholarships to pupils in local elementary schools, there were no takers. The *Herald* fumed about lack of ambition, but lack of money was a more likely cause.

Outside the classroom, the main activity for boys of the National School was drill. They stomped around the vicar's field in companies of four, to the barked orders of a former sergeant-major, holding staves for rifles. This was regarded as important character training, making 'the lads smart at their work, as well as fine in their appearance, and it will tell on the future by making them grow up stalwart and healthy men'.

Yet schooldays could be a sojourn before the cares of the world; a time when relationships were untainted by the necessity for survival. Real affection could exist between teacher and pupils. When Miss Lydia Neall ceased teaching at the Girls' National School to get married, her pupils presented her with an engraved clock. Many shed floods of tears, which did not stop even when the vicar assured them that they could call on her in her new home.

The Grammar School was improving under a new headmaster, the Reverend R. de Courcy Laffan, who introduced new courses and revolutionary innovations such as organised games. On his appointment in 1885, the school had less than 40 pupils, but when he departed to become Headmaster of Cheltenham College a decade later, there were over 100.

The Choir School, so-called because the vicar subsidised the fees of the choirboys, was founded in 1881. It was a 'commercial' school, providing education to fit a boy for a career in business, thus placing great stress on mathematics. The schoolroom was on the vicar's property at 'The Firs' and the boys played in his field at times when the National boys were not drilling there. Boarders lodged with the headmaster, John Priest, at his house in Guild Street. Not all choirboys got full benefit from this education. The vicar expelled ruthlessly anyone who fooled about during services. In 1890, he fell out with Priest. The schoolroom was closed and the choirboys given scholarships at the Grammar School. Priest transferred his renamed 'Commercial School' to premises in Greenhill Street. The vicar's antipathy erupted at the diocesan religious examination, for which the rural dean had instructed Priest to take his boys to the National School. When they arrived, the door was locked. After repeated knocking, a teacher appeared at the window and refused admission. Priest demanded to see the vicar. When that formidable figure appeared, he too refused entrance. Priest retreated but at least had the satisfaction of reading the *Herald's* description of his adversary as 'self-willed and intractable'.

FOOTNOTES

[1]   The pupil-teachers were employed as assistants for five years after the school-leaving age. In return for their help, they were instructed by the master out of school hours.

[2]   In 1885 he became M.P. for North-West Norfolk and, in 1893, the first working man to serve in a British cabinet.

[3]   See p. 111

[4]   Gathering the corn left on the ground after harvesting.

[5]   Sweets.

[6]   Later the Technical College.

CHAPTER 17

'No Hope of Escape'

'There is no hope of escape . . . except by emigration to foreign lands'
                                      Local clergyman on paupers, 1870.

The Door of the Workhouse

For those of the poor who lost the unequal struggle for survival the door of the Workhouse beckoned. A visitor in 1875 considered it 'as unlike the Workhouse of 50 years ago as can be. It would literally astonish anyone not having watched the gradual but slow change'. The institution, variously known to inmates as 'The Home of Rest', '50, Arden Street' and 'The Grubber', was now run on strict utilitarian lines. 'Classification is most methodical; the sick and infirm are watched with tender solicitude in the Infirmary; the children receive instruction at the hands of a duly qualified schoolmistress or master, and undergo periodic examination by a Government Inspector; they have their play-ground and their "day-room", and the whole of the inmates are provided with the loving instructions and wise admonitions of the Chaplain, who, three or four times a week, conducts religious services in the Chapel.' Such an uncritical visitor felt no irony in that a favoured hymn for the paupers was 'Thy Will be Done'. 'People are admitted', said the chairman of the Board of Guardians, 'to maintain an existence, nothing more.'

The dreary hours at the Workhouse were unrelieved by a 'single ray of sunshine', actual or metaphoric. The door was open for the old and infirm and they were encouraged to go into the garden, but they preferred to sit round the fireplace. Younger inmates were not allowed out – the women were regarded as 'fallen'. The children suffered the same fate. There were around 35 of them, aged between four and fourteen. The girls wore long pinafores with STRATFORD-UPON-AVON WORKHOUSE emblazoned on them in big red letters. The only time they saw outside the walls of the House was when they went for a walk twice a week in a long crocodile. No toys were provided. When the older children sought positions in service, they were usually greatly disadvantaged because of their shyness and dullness. Attempts were made, notably by the Reverend George Arbuthnot, to school the children locally, but the argument that they would be persecuted or corrupted by the other children prevailed until 1891, when they began to trot off each morning to the National School. Sadly, they had a hard time, with the town children shouting 'Workus brats' after them. In the same year horizons were expanded further, with the opening of an Industrial Home in College Street, training girls for domestic service. From 1897, the workhouse boys were allowed to mix freely with other children. 'The change', it was felt, 'will undoubtedly do them good, besides making them happy.'

Dickensian scandals rippled periodically through the Workhouse, particularly after meetings of the Board were opened to the press in 1870. Mary Berry, a young pauper

182

To the Worshipful the Mayor of Stratford-on-Avon.

We, the undersigned Burgesses of Stratford-on-Avon, considering the amount of distress now existing in this Borough and its immediate Neighbourhood owing to the scarcity of Work, request your Worship to call a

PUBLIC MEETING

To consider the advisability of Opening a

SOUP KITCHEN.

ROB. GIBBS.
W. G. COLBOURNE.
R. M. BIRD.
H. W. NEWTON.
JAS. COX.
JOHN MORGAN.
J. J. KEMP.
ALFD. RIDER.
J. G. REYNOLDS.
W. H. EATON.
W. S. HOYLES.
THOS. WOMACK.
W. J. NORRIS.
EDWARD FOX.

RICH. HAWKES.
CHAS. GIBBS.
J. FARMER.
FRED WINTER.
W. B. EAVES.
JOHN PARKER.
THOMAS C. NEW.
CHARLES WYE.
THOS. J. OLNEY.
ROBERT GUY.
C. THOMAS.
D. DRINKWATER.
H. SELLERS.

I, the undersigned, in accordance with the above requisition, do hereby convene a MEETING of the INHABITANTS of the Town and Neighbourhood in the UPPER ROOM OF THE TOWN HALL, TO-MORROW, January 19th, 1888, at Three o'clock in the Afternoon.

ARTHUR HODGSON,

Mayor.

January 18th, 1888.

HERALD PRINTING WORKS, STRATFORD-ON-AVON.

36. Notice calling for a soup kitchen to be established to relieve the sufferings of the poor, 1888.

mother, died of pleurisy in dank surroundings, attended only by her child. To conceal his negligence, the Master omitted to register her death. The matter was raised on the Board and the Master, tramp wardsmen and surgeon resigned. The next Master left in 1876 after the schoolmistress complained of his cruelty to the children. She went two years later after similar accusations against her. In 1890 Emma Rawlings, the pregnant wife of a farm-labourer, was brought from Hatton Rock, suffering from severe burns. At the Recovery Hospital, her wounds were dressed, but she was not admitted. There followed a further jolting ride to the Workhouse, where the Master turned her away because she didn't have an admission order. She was taken to the house of the Receiving Officer, who refused an admittance note because she lived outside the district, but later relented. She died a few days later. Great was the local outrage; the inquest jury censured the Master for 'disgraceful neglect' and he was obliged to resign.

The Guardians generally did little about abuses until they were too conspicuous to ignore. Their visits were always prearranged and even when they tried to be conscientious, they got little help from the officials. Once they were upbraided by a government inspector for 'wasting time' discussing the deaths of two old men two months before.

Many would do anything rather than endure the Workhouse, which of course was one of the objects of its constitution. In 1899, a Guardian, the Reverend Oswald Mordaunt, successfully proposed the abolition of outdoor relief for the able-bodied. Mr. Fred Winter passionately opposed this, declaring that 'anyone advocating such a system must have a heart of stone'. It was their duty to do all they could to relieve the sufferings of the less fortunate, 'not to rack our brains to find new hardships to put upon them . . . "Offering the house" is a very easy, off-hand way of getting rid of a poor applicant, but think what that involves. The house must be broken up, the little furniture, which has been got together bit by bit at much sacrifice, must be sold, the children separated from their natural guardians and handed over to officials . . . some gentlemen, by their actions, seem to think there can be no love amongst the poor for their offspring . . .' He concluded with the lines of Thomas Hood – ' "Rattle his bones over the stones, He's just a pauper whom nobody owns" '

The 'one real day of happiness' came at Christmas, to which the inmates looked forward for weeks. Roast beef, plum pudding, ale, tobacco for the men and snuff for the women; all were plentiful and a Christmas tree was hung with presents for the children. The dining hall, usually chilly and bare, was festooned with decorations. Such was the public interest in this annual respite for the paupers that the *Herald* always carried an account of it. The conviviality of the occasion was diminished for many paupers in 1896 when ale was banned at the Christmas dinner, through the influence of a temperance lobby led by the vicar, who claimed that no teetotaller had ever been admitted to Stratford Workhouse. Some inmates, through judicious exchange, had been obtaining more than their ration and their resultant boisterousness had upset several Guardians. In compensation for the loss of ale, the vicar provided tea and tobacco. One old man, when asked for a song at the Christmas dinner, said he could not sing on cold water. The 'beer question' was to be an annual topic at Board meetings.

An occasional social evening also broke the monotony of Workhouse life. At one a pauper child, Nellie Allibone, recited a long and difficult poem called 'Robert of Sicily'. Such songs as 'How did You Leave the Pigs?' and 'The Farmer's Boy' appealed to the old country folk. Just before the National Anthem, Mrs. Frisby, an aged inmate, sang spontaneously, in a clear voice, 'Far Away', which deeply moved the other old residents.

The workhouse abounded in ancient characters with memories of bygone days. Many were living history, like John Adams, who enlisted in the 37th Foot Regiment at Stratford in 1846 when he was 17 and served through the Indian Mutiny, entering Lucknow with the relief army of General Havelock. Others had fought in the Crimea, one at Balaclava. The longevity of the residents was a byword and folk pointed to the Workhouse. as demonstrating that plain fare was healthiest. Doyen of them all was William Stanley, known as 'The Duke' because of his strong resemblance to the Duke of Wellington. He had been variously a farm labourer, timber sawyer and carrier. He celebrated his 100th birthday in 1904, sitting up in bed with a mug of stout in one hand and a briar-pipe in the other. Seemingly indestructible, he died in his 102nd year. Another resident celebrated for her longevity was Lucy Freeman. As a child she was declared 'imbecile' and sent to the old Workhouse in Henley Street. She was wonderfully active until her 80th year, working in the Workhouse laundry. For months before the Mop she saved her pennies to buy toys for the Workhouse children. The number of little paupers she had nursed totalled hundreds. When visitors asked to see her she performed the dainty dancing steps of another era for them. She spent her last years in the Infirmary. Her death at 90 in 1911 was unexpected: she was about to eat her lunch, 'when she fell back into that gentle sleep from which there is no awakening'.

The Union ministered also to passing vagrants, who slept in casual wards. Some were walking the country looking for work, but others were called 'professional mouchers' and spent their lives in aimless wandering from one workhouse to the next. In bad weather the wards were full, but most travellers preferred to sleep rough during hot spells. On arrival, they were searched and any money found was taken for Union funds, so most hid their cash and tobacco outside and collected it on their departure. They were asked their name, age, occupation, where they had spent the previous night and where they intended going. Seven-eighths of the men called themselves labourers; the remainder were usually looking for work and represented a wide variety of trades. Most of the women described themselves as 'field-women' or 'charwomen'.

The questioning over, the tramps were given eight ounces of coarse bread and sent to take a bath. Contrary to popular belief, they really enjoyed this. Undressing was an elaborate ritual: tramps seldom wore shirts and preferred 'toe-rags' to socks. They did not use buttons, but held their clothes together with string. By special request, clothing could be 'stoved' (fumigated) overnight. After bathing they went to their hammocks of coconut matting. They were woken at daybreak and breakfasted on bread and oatmeal. They then performed an obligatory task, perhaps joining the residents in oakum-picking, or sawing wood, breaking stone, or working four at a time at the pump. The tramp wards were also full of characters. Some appeared to have known better times and some visitors speculated romantically on the human tragedies which had reduced their circumstances. It was, however, an unwritten rule that privacy should be respected, so the intriguing stories, if any, were never related. For the 'mouchers' tramping was a way of life that lasted till death. One spring Emma Messenger, aged 67, died in a hedge on the Warwick Road. Walking on two sticks, she had taken three days to cover the 12 miles from Shipston, sleeping in hedge-bottoms, with no choice but to creep on. Whole families tramped around. It was common to see tiny children patching their shoes beside the road as they accompanied their parents in pursuit of casual work. In the summer of 1898 William and Mary Fisher, 'habitual tramps', were evicted from their lodgings in Leamington and walked with their four eldest children to Stratford Workhouse, where one had been born four years before. Harriet, aged 18 months, was pushed in a battered pram. On arrival she was taken ill and the parents asked for a nurse. The assistant matron felt the child's pulse and said she seemed very ill, but nothing could be done until the Head Nurse came on duty. Next morning the family walked the eight miles to Alcester Workhouse, in the company of Margaret Glover, a 'mouching' widow. On arrival the baby was very ill. The nurse gave her two spoonfuls of brandy as she lay in the lap of

Mrs. Glover and was about to give her a third when the poor child died. The Inquest heard that she was emaciated, with a large, neglected sore behind her ear and an empty stomach. The Fishers were sentenced to six months hard labour for child neglect, the jury expressing concern about the indifference shown at Stratford Workhouse. The lesson was learnt: next year a child who had tramped from Worcester with bad legs was sent to the Infirmary and the case reported to the Society for the Prevention of Cruelty to Children. In 1902, the Guardians resolved to deprive tramps of the control of their children and to send them to an industrial home until they were sixteen.

Travellers who could afford the modest fees and who preferred greater freedom used the common lodging houses. If a policeman met 'a superior sort o' travelling man looking for a bed he might direct them to Caroline Cook's on Waterside'.[1] Rougher customers were pointed over the bridge to Mr. Hoare's behind the *Shoulder of Mutton*. George Hewins remembered characters like Sam the Pig Poker:

> 'Sam, Sam dirty old man', we hollered after him, 'Washed 'is face in the frying pan!' He was a beggar, pea-picker, scrap iron, rags, bones, anything. Tramps in those days had to earn a living. One of them had a Russian bear, twice as tall as me, a great fat thing. We kept well back when we saw that bear! He came every year. . . they knowed the places where they'd done well- and slept at the *Shoulder o' Mutton*, in the stable. He was a regular Russian tramp, with baggy trousers and ribbons hanging down. He'd got no musical instrument, just talked to the bear in his way and it danced! Then he went round with his hat for the money. The bear grunted and pulled on his chain and we ran off. We'd heard tell that bear ate a little girl called Laura Edkins, once upon a time.[1]

Once, after the police broke up a drunken brawl there, cries of 'Murder!' were heard next morning. Mr. Hoare was beating up his wife. Four inmates later appeared in court. When Hoare was called, he was too drunk to testify. Mrs. Hoare appeared with two black eyes and said firmly, 'I shall not prosecute, gentlemen. No one saw him assault me, so you cannot do anything'.

Complaints were frequent about 'lazy and dirty-looking fellows' prowling the streets, begging for 'a bit o' bread' in cringing tones. They were very offensive and threatening with women, always calling when the men were out. Some tried crude confidence tricks. Once when Police Superintendent Simmonds answered his door while off-duty, he was handed a charitable subscription list by Samuel Bond, a professional beggar. The vicar was down for 2s 6d, but his name was mis-spelt. 'You have come to the wrong door', said the policeman, as he escorted him round to the police station. Others used the safer means of the Royal Mail. Stratfordians frequently received pleading missives from such unfortunates as Jose, the Spanish prisoner, who needed financial assistance to recover a million francs left at a French railway station. The money would, of course, be shared with anyone aiding him. Then there were the local 'slaves of the lamp-posts' who gathered at Bridgefoot and upset ladies with their foul language. Yet even the poorest possessed the consolations afforded by man's best friend. 'Persons who have to study for a livelihood', observed the *Herald*, 'as well as the idle and dissolute, all keep a cur of some sort.' The streets swarmed with mongrels of 'every degree of ugliness and filthiness. From the costly carpets and fancy goods exhibited at the draper's shop door, down to the humble hamper of celery at the greengrocer, nothing escapes their indelicate attention.'

Yet there was an alternative to pauperdom. 'There is no hope of escape', wrote a local clergyman, 'for a reckless and degraded peasantry except by emigration to foreign lands or manufacturing districts, which will take away the strong, the healthy and the brave and leave us the cripple, the drunkard and the beggar.' Societies to encourage emigration wrote to the *Herald*. The agent for the Tasmanian Government lectured on 'this charming colony and the opening it presents for intending Emigrants'. During the agricultural slump of the 1870s, the Warwickshire Union of Agricultural Labourers helped its members to emigrate to places as distant as Brazil, Canada and Queensland. The Board of Guardians started to send paupers overseas, in 1870 providing £6 for Ben. Whiston to go to Canada. There was self-interest in this; he had been gaoled for misbehaviour in the Workhouse. Canada was a popular destination and Workhouse children were sent to farm-colonies there. The fate of those sent to locations nearer home roused some concern. The *Herald* considered that it would be 'a great deal more merciful' to keep lads in the Workhouse for life than to apprentice them to Grimsby fishermen: an opinion not echoed by at least some of the lads at Grimsby. 'I am not apprenticed now', wrote Joseph Dyde in 1888 from the Fisherlad's Institute, 'for my master failed and gave me my papers. I am earning 12s a week in a trawler. All the other lads from the Union are getting on very well. H. Burden was down at Iceland seventeen weeks last year, and was frozen in the ice six weeks. Frank Pratt is out of his time, and has gone down to Scotland for eight weeks and I am tired of fishing. Me and Burden are going to Hull to engage ourselves on a steamship . . . as engineers stewards, and are going to America.'

The urge of Stratfordians to spread over the globe led to rare adventure. After the *Swan* was demolished, the landlord John Williams became a Major in the U.S. Army, serving on the frontier. William Monk was sergeant-major in Garibaldi's British Legion, marching under 'a hot broiling sun and nothing to eat but ship's biscuit – and water could not be obtained for love nor money'. Others, like Private George Turvey of Russell Court took the 'Queen's Shilling': he served on the expedition to relieve Gordon at Khartoum. The Mop was a fruitful place for the recruiting sergeant. In his gaily bedecked cap, he mingled with those plying for hire in search of impetuous youths.

A Quiet Thoroughfare

Despite the altercations of the desperate, to the casual visitor Stratford was a sleepy place. For the townsman of moderate outlook and respectable habits life was uneventful. Where some saw teeming alleys and dire poverty, others observed picturesque streets. To the editor of the *Herald*, the greatest hazards were those dangerous innovations, bicycles and velocipedes, which added to the existing perils of perambulators. Miss F. D. Rowley, daughter of the police inspector, remembered Sheep Street in the 1870s as a quiet thoroughfare, except on market days, when breeders like Mr. Wynn of Ryon Hill showed their horses in the street. It was a great delight for little Miss Rowley to watch these 'beautiful creatures charging along the roadway while their red-faced, shiny-pated owner, with coat tails flying, vigorously rattled his whip stock inside his top hat to make them show off their paces'. This custom was, astonishingly, curtailed by prudery. In 1892, after the police had received a number of complaints about 'indecent exhibitions', George Rathbone, a groom, was summoned for exposing a stallion to show in the High Street. Although the case was dismissed, costs were awarded against the defendant, which effectively stopped the practice.

Miss Rowley recalled that the streets were metalled with stone sand, which had 'a lovely ochre tint and the deflected light from it on a sunny day had a wonderful effect on the appearance of the old houses. But oh, the clouds of dust that resulted on a windy one! The tarmac stopped all that, but it also brought to an end the little colony of swallows who made their homes in the arched window heads of the old Town Hall. 'Often when the road was dry and dusty in the early Spring, Harris the day man (a kindly soul and very fond of animals) would come round to say "swallows have come Sir, and the road is dry, shall I throw some water down?" And then passers-by had the unusual sight of a policeman swilling the roadway with water to provide "mud-pies" for the swallows. On Summer mornings the smell of sweet, newly-made bread from old Mr. Tustain's spotless little shop pervaded the street. In the evening, tradesmen took their horses and ponies for a "freshener" in the cool of the flowing river . . . What a flurry of hooves and splashing took them scampering up Southern Lane to their well-earned rest in the quiet fields.'

TO THE ELECTORS, 1885.

The issue is between Mr. Gladstone and Lord Salisbury.

Elliott & Fry, Phot.

THE RIGHT HON. W. E. GLADSTONE.

Mr. GLADSTONE has done more for the people than any other living statesman.

He is the great Leader of public opinion; and concedes full liberty of conscience to all.

He is for Progress, Sound Finance, and Firm Government.

He has secured for Two Million New Voters their title to vote; and believes in admitting to Parliament every duly elected Member.

He defends Free Trade, by which every BUYER is advantaged and healthy competition fostered.

H would sweep away those laws that tie up and prevent free trade in Land.

VOTE FOR COMPTON,
THE LIBERAL CANDIDATE.

PRINTED AND PUBLISHED BY W. B. WHITTINGHAM & CO., 91, GRACECHURCH STREET, LONDON, AND "THE CHARTERHOUSE PRESS," 44, CHARTERHOUSE SQUARE, E.C.

[REGISTERED.

37. The Liberals exploited the prestige of their leader in the 1885 election.

THE
PLAIN TRUTH
ABOUT
LORD WILLIAM COMPTON AND THE CHURCH.

Some Conservatives are trying to prevent you from voting for Lord William Compton by holding him up before you as an enemy to the Church and to Religion.

They call him a Liberationist, which they interpret to mean one who would destroy the Church.

This is untrue: he is **NOT** a Liberationist. He is a **CHURCHMAN.**

He has no desire "to drive away from your Village the Clergyman." Lord William Compton is a **LIBERAL** Churchman, and desires that the Clergy should always deal fairly and justly by all of you, treating those who agree with them and those who differ from them in a spirit of Christian tolerance.

Lord William Compton is a **TRUE FRIEND** to the Church because he is a true friend to religion as the gospel of fairness and justice.

Read what he said himself about the Church in his Stratford Speech:—

"I, as a Churchman, and as one who is fond of his Church, have seen with regret the efforts which have been made to drag into party strife the question of the Church. I feel that it is something degrading to our Church that it should now be dragged before the country, because I am as certain as I stand here that it will be impossible for the next Liberal Government to Disestablish or Disendow the English Church. . . . If any one tries to bring forward the question in the New Parliament I shall be found voting against him."

Printed by G. Boyden, 29, High Street, Stratford-on-Avon. Published by S. Mawer, 13, Guild Street, Stratford-on-Avon.

38. This poster was intended to counter a smear campaign during the 1885 election.

Sheep Street had its characters, like 'Old Nance', whose 'honesty, sobriety and good name never seemed in question, yet who was a 'perfect example of the good-humoured slattern. To see her racing for a "ring-side seat" at anything promising entertainment – (weddings, funerals, elections – anything which drew a crowd . . .) – was a sight to behold. She wore a marvellous bonnet with roses and feathers on top and long strings flying behind her, but how on earth she kept the thing on her head, perched as it was, nearly on the back of it, was a mystery!'

There were great survivors like John Walker, the driver of the 'Shakespeare bus', a sturdy, elderly man with bowed shoulders, a russet face, grizzled hair and side whiskers. 'In his cut-away coat, breeches and low-crowned bowler hat, he was a typical figure of the last days of the coaching period.'

Home Rule

A Nonconformist Association was formed in 1885. At its inaugural meeting Alderman Newton, the Chairman, said that probably every member was prepared to work for the Liberal Party. The vicar tried to resist the converse identification of the Church with the Tories, declining an invitation to speak at the annual dinner of the Conservative Working Men's Club, because 'I consider that a clergyman's presence at a political meeting is a great mistake.' He was certain that 'those who take an active part in politics greatly diminish their influence with their people'.

The vicar's scruples were not shared by the Priest-Chaplain, the Reverend Frank Smith, a low-church Irish Tory, who attended the dinner instead. His speech caused great offence to many, the *Herald* declaring that the toast of 'Church and State' always provided the chance for 'some enthusiastic churchman to have a go at his dissenting fellow countryman'.

The election of 1885 was the first in which farm-workers were enfranchised, which, together with boundary changes, gave the Liberals their best chance for years. The opening shot of the campaign came when a Mr. Walter upset local Conservatives by advising voters to wear Tory colours, ride to the poll in Tory carriages and vote Liberal! In return the Liberals accused the ladies of the Primrose League of canvassing the poor with extravagant promises.

The Liberals possessed an attractive candidate in Lord William Compton of Compton Wynyates. A radical philanthropist, he had assisted in the work of the East End settlement at Toynbee Hall. His support for free education meant that the Tories claimed he was a Communist. The combination of patrician aristocrat and enfranchised labourer proved a success: Lord William's eve-of-poll meeting was the largest ever seen in Stratford. At the declaration a large excited crowd heard that he had won by 4,639 votes to 3,738. Sarah Flower, who had worked hard for the Liberals, thought how happy Lord William and his young wife looked on the Town Hall steps.

The reforming fears and hopes engendered by Gladstone's Third Ministry emerge at two meetings held shortly after the election. A branch of the Church Defence Movement was formed to oppose disestablishment and the M.P. upbraided republican elements within the local Liberal Association, but the great question was whether the Irish Home Rule Bill would bring down the Government. The crisis emerged in the Liberal Association during May 1886. Most of the leading members opposed the Bill, including the President, R. N. Phillips, the philanthropic owner of Welcombe House, a Lancashire industrialist who was a founder of the Anti-Corn Law League, and his son-in-law, Sir George Trevelyan, the President of the Board of Trade. Public feeling, observed the *Herald*, had rarely run so high. A week later it reported the Government's defeat and a dissolution. Lord William Compton had voted with his leader.

It was inevitable that the Flowers, closely associated with the leading Liberal Unionist Joseph Chamberlain, would split with their party on this issue, as did another frequent guest at 'Avonbank', the great Liberal statesman, John Bright, whose daughter had married a stepson of Dr. Collis. 'He loves to sit in the Palm House with a cigar and a cup of coffee', wrote Sarah Flower, 'to be surrounded by us all . . . and it is a delight to listen to him.'

Despite their opposition to his policies, the Flowers felt no animosity to Lord William Compton. Edgar described him from a Unionist platform as 'a man who, above most others, has a high sense of duty, one who has so unselfishly worked in the slums of the East End of London and elsewhere for the improvement and alleviation of suffering among his poorer neighbours'. The Conservative, Frederick Townsend of Honington Hall, was less inspiring. He was even introduced at a Tory meeting as 'no orator, but one of those great and worthy and silent workers'. Lord William fought hard to keep the seat, facing the main issue head-on. 'You have to decide', he told the voters, 'whether we shall grant self-government to Ireland with proper safeguards or whether we shall continue to misgovern that country with the help of coercive and repressive measures.' His campaign had its lighter moments. This attractive man sang well and enlivened his meetings with renditions of 'Upon the Danube River'. The delighted audience would call for an encore and he would respond with 'The Midshipmite', before leading them in the National Anthem and cheers for 'The Grand Old Man'. Yet the forces against him were too great. On polling day, Townsend gained the verdict.by 489 votes. The announcement was greeted by cheering and groans.

Lord William was soon found a safe seat at Barnsley. On the deaths of his elder brother and father, he went into the Lords as the Marquis of Northampton and held Cabinet Office in several administrations. He continued his interest in Stratford, where he was frequently seen on public platforms supporting liberal causes. The vicar fought a good election, freely expounding what Church and State should be doing. 'It is all very well', he declared, 'to take an interest in the labourer at election time when his vote is required, but Christ's law requires an interest at all times.' There were cottages in Stratford which were 'a disgrace to the civilisation of this nineteenth century'. A severe winter had revealed the wretchedness in which many of their poor neighbours lived. They had done well to institute soup kitchens and other relieving agencies, but were these just palliatives? Arbuthnot's answer was less radical than his analysis: shut some of the public houses and start a crusade against drink and immorality. A few months later the vicar returned to this subject:

> The proper remedy is to increase the wages, not to dole out charity in Winter. Do not ask an employer to give charity to men willing to work instead of a fair wage. Do not tempt a man to sooth his conscience by subscribing a few shillings when he ought to be spending some pounds. Such "relief", so called, cannot succeed in the long run. As well try to turn our river aside with a few barrow loads of earth.

His social programme was now well-considered. Why not use the money subscribed for the soup kitchen to provide work? The streets needed cleaning; a recreation ground was to be laid out – why not put the men to work on these? Instead of giving away food to paupers, why not prevent people reaching that stage by subsidising the price of bread? 'The payment of a sum of money – be it ever so small – saves the loss of self-respect, which so many unconsciously suffer by accepting year after year a dole of charity. My heart bleeds at this season', he concluded with undoubted sincerity, 'for the wants of many of my people.'

Blood and Fire

During the Home Rule election, the attention of Stratfordians was diverted by a contingent of Salvationists who commenced an onslaught against 'sin and the devil'. They made a big impact. In the Magistrates' Court the clerk interrupted proceedings to complain about being woken up by vibrant hymn singing at five a.m. Whoever this was was freelance; the Salvation Army issued a denial that anyone had been authorised to conduct its services in Stratford. The enthusiasts were but presagers of the real thing. In September an official group arrived. The *Herald* was hostile: 'To see half-a-dozen slatternly girls, with perhaps a similar number of unkempt boys, trying to preserve military order, and to hear them howling questionable hymns during their progress through the streets, gives rise to feelings the reverse of favourable.'

Despite, or because of, such publicity, the Army was attracting crowds of two or three hundred to its Sunday meetings in the Rother Market. Complaints rolled in about its street corner meetings. 'I live in close proximity to the Parish Church', wrote one aggrieved citizen, 'and acting on an old adage, "the nearer to church the further from God", I suppose the "Army" consider the inhabitants of this particular quarter fit subjects.' Amongst the renditions in the half-hour serenade to tambourine accompaniment was 'You won't be right until you're saved, Mary Ann' and words sung to the tune of 'Annie Lisle':

> Death is coming, surely coming,
> And the Judgment Day,
> Hasten sinner to your Saviour,
> Seek the narrow way.

An Army orator declared West Street the most spiritually destitute in Stratford. 'The result of this destitution', complained a resident, 'is that the band blares under our windows and the "soldiers" make the air hideous for about an hour on Sunday morning.'

The Army was undaunted by criticism. In October 1887 Emma Booth, daughter of the renowned 'General', visited Stratford. The Sunday started with 'knee drill' and meetings were held all day. Next evening she presented the local corps with its 'Blood and Fire' flag, while singers yelled to a tambourine accompaniment. By 1890 the Army was sufficiently established for a special railway excursion to be laid on for Mrs. Booth's 'Promoted to Glory' service. In 1906, the great 'General' himself paid a visit and the *Herald's* response demonstrates the respect which the sect had gained, describing him as 'a man who has done more for the relief and raising of the submerged tenth than any man in England'. He visited again in 1911 at the age of eighty-two.

There was one in Stratford whose enthusiasm matched that of the Salvationists. Inevitably the vicar weighed forth on the Army. Parishioners should not admit Salvationists to their houses. Courteously but firmly, they should refuse to buy 'War Cry' and they should never be lured into argument. A Birmingham paper found it difficult to detect much charity in this approach, but it was rather that George Arbuthnot was uncompromising about what he saw as Truth. On the Board of Guardians, he collaborated freely in common causes, notably with the Catholic priest, Father O'Brien, in efforts to get children boarded out. When this was rejected, he said he would boycott meetings of the Board until a more humane approach was adopted. He could be equally aggressive about fellow churchmen. When the wealthy landowner, the Reverend Oswald Mordaunt, declaimed on the virtues of thrift, George Arbuthnot asked cryptically, 'Who can be thrifty on ten shillings a week?' He had the sense and courage to see that there was no future for a church rooted in past privilege. In a sermon on 'Liberty, Equality and Fraternity', he attacked those who regarded the secret ballot as 'unmanly and un-English', commenting perceptively that such epithets usually came from those who 'would like to control the consciences and votes of those over whom they suppose they have control or influence!' Yet his pronouncements could border on absurdity. 'One of our greatest national sins', he told the congregation at Holy Trinity, 'is the sin of drunkenness; it is possible, to my mind, probable, that the influenza is sent to us as a punishment for it.' It was small wonder that Henry Labouchere, M.P., editor of the radical paper, *Truth*, declared that he received 'a hundred complaints against the Vicar of Stratford to one against any other cleric'. The churchwardens of Holy Trinity would earn his deep gratitude if they organised a 'Society for the Suppression of the Vicar'.

George Arbuthnot's great cause, for which his fervour bordered on the fanatical, was Temperance. He saw a division between his work with the Church of England Temperance Society ('which works upon individuals and devotes itself . . . to the spiritual life') and the

Temperance League, which he founded with ministers of other denominations to campaign for laws restricting the sale of drink and whose local objective was clear: 'We have too many pubs in Stratford-on-Avon'. Local option in licensing, with no compensation for the publican whose licence was not renewed was demanded. Hence the licensed victuallers formed an association in 1891 and announced that they would campaign against any Parliamentary candidate who stood against their interests.

Another area for denominational co-operation was 'the great work of moral purification'. The vehicle for this was the local branch of the Vigilance Association, formed for 'the repression of vice and public immorality'. At its inaugural meeting the treasurer, Mr. Milton Chesterton, suggested to young men the importance of refusing to listen to indecent conversation. The vicar, for once, waxed mellow and compared favourably Stratford's morals with those of Birmingham. The Congregational minister, the Reverend James Pugh, was unable to concur and was prepared to give, privately, details to support his case. Doubtless he was thinking of the prostitutes who still frequented the town. The centre of vice had shifted to Meer Street, where there were several houses of 'ill-fame'. One was kept by Sarah Adams, a woman in her twenties; her 'husband', John Timms, had turned out to be already married and had been imprisoned for bigamy. After his release, the couple continued to live together. It was when he was in hospital for a spell that the house became a brothel. During Christmas week in 1891 the police noted the names of visitors. When proceedings were brought, the superintendent requested the bench's discretion about this list; many were in 'respectable positions' and several were married. Sarah Adams expressed her regret and said it would never have happened had 'the master' been home. As always it was the poor that got the blame: she received a month's imprisonment. When the Mayor suggested that there were other brothels in Meer Street, the superintendent said it was difficult to prove. In his youth, George Hewins visited a pretty whore called Poll there. Once when he knocked on the door she shouted: 'You'll 'ave to wait! I got somebody's give me sixpence – and you lads come 'ere wi' cocks like men for twopence!'

Yet sexual ignorance was still the prerogative of many. Annie Woodall, a maidservant in College Street, woke a fellow servant early one morning to tell her that she had had an awful fright. She had given birth to a baby which was found to be dead. She had fainted and not regained consciousness until after the birth. When asked why she did not call for help, she replied that she had no idea of her condition. The child appeared weak, but there were no external marks of injury. The Inquest attributed death to lack of attention at birth.

With the Swallows

'With the swallows', wrote a Stratfordian in the 1890s, 'come our American visitors. They are now to be seen, with Baedeker in hand, making notes and sometimes taking "snap shots" of the buildings.' The ever-improving trans-Atlantic crossing was revealing the American style of tourism: 'Although their visits are generally marked by express speed, they manage to leave some cash behind.'

The most distinguished visitor was the least inspiring. The Flowers were hosts to President and Mrs. Ulysses S. Grant in 1877. The famous general was 'very *un*interested in everything he saw', in contrast to his former protagonist, the Confederate leader Jefferson Davies, who showed great enthusiasm. The writer Oliver Wendell Holmes expected Shakespeare's image to be ever before local youngsters and was disappointed when he asked some boys fishing in the Avon about the poet. 'Boys turn around and look up with plentiful lack of intelligence in their countenances. "Don't you know who or what he was?" Boys look at each other, but confess ignorance. Let us try the universal stimulant of the human faculties. "Here are some pennies for the boy who will tell me what Mr. Shakespeare was." The biggest boy finds his

39. Inauguration of the American Fountain, erected to mark the Golden Jubilee of Queen Victoria, 1887.

tongue at last! "He was a writer – he wrote plays." That was as much as I could get out of the youngling.'

Others had the reverse criticism. As the number of tourists increased so did the mercenary interest of the local lads. Visitors were accosted by urchins clamouring, 'Tell you all about Shakespeare for a penny'. An American journal, *Youth's Companion*, caught the rhythm of local speech.

'William Shykespeare, the gryte poet', they are almost humming in chorus, 'was born at Stratford-on-

Avon in 1564 – the 'ouse in which he dwelt may still be seen – 'is father in the gryte poet's boyhood was 'igh Bailiff of the plyce – one who shykes a spear is the meaning of 'is nyme', and so on, in an even monotone, undisturbed and tranquil, almost like a distant sound of bees.

That is about all the stranger can understand. The rest is lost in faint, incoherent mumblings, only an occasional word being at all intelligible. The boys do not look at any one in particular. One gazes vacantly across the street, another at his shoes, still another at the sky, but all unite in telling the one weird tale. For it, of course, they expect to be tipped.

If the visitor ventured a question, the monologue stopped in full flow and started again at the beginning. 'There is never a laugh in its delivery, not even a smile. It is just a self-imposed duty – a ceremony bequeathed by one generation of Stratford boys to the next.'

As always the Stratfordians could be as put upon as they put upon others. In 1887, to commemorate the Queen's Golden Jubilee, a wealthy Philadelphian, George W. Childs, presented a clock-tower, the American Fountain, which stands in Rother Street. Soon after its unveiling by the celebrated actor, Henry Irving, a charming young man presented himself in the town, claiming to be Mr. Childs' nephew, come to inspect his uncle's gift. He was entertained by several local worthies, relieving them of substantial 'loans' before departing. The young man, Ernest Rolfe, was caught after trying a similar trick on Joseph Chamberlain. He had made a habit of this sort of thing and got ten years' imprisonment.

The vicar upset those Americans who could not understand his devotion to the *living* church, rather than museums of Shakespeareana. *The New York Tribune* was particularly scathing.

Mr. Arbuthnot is fond of ecclesiastical processions; he likes to array himself in full canonicals and to walk up and down. Other people do not care nearly so much for this imposing pageant as they do for the relics of the Bard. Who is this arrogant cleric, that he may please his taste for ridiculous high-church ceremonials, to outrage the feelings of intellectual people throughout the world?

The last word was with the vicar on this one. Mrs. de Courcy Laffan, a minor romantic novelist who was married to the headmaster of the Grammar School, had revived the pleasing little ceremony of senior boys laying flowers on Shakespeare's tomb on the Birthday. In 1899 the vicar invited 'great and small' to do the same and stood on the chancel steps to receive their floral tributes.

FOOTNOTE
[1]   *The Dillen*, edited by Angela Hewins.

CHAPTER 18

'No Thieves and No Burglars'

'There are no thieves and no burglars . . . I think we might fairly consider ourselves in the position of being well managed'.

Mr. C. Holton, 1897.

'Send me a Fast Bowler to play Laertes' (legendary telegram sent by F. R. Benson to his agent)

In the year Charles Flower opened his theatre, Francis Robert Benson won the Oxford University mile. All sport he loved but his greatest passion was the drama. After Oxford he appeared with Henry Irving and then, to extend his range, with a touring company. When it went broke, he got the cash to take it over from his wealthy father and the Benson Company was born. Those he engaged frequently shared his fanaticism for sport and his ability to mould a team, both theatrical and sporting, made him a great actor-manager. As an athlete and aesthete, he helped make the theatre respectable. He was born for the uncommercial theatre at Stratford, conceived in a private dream he was to share. He formed a desire to act there and, in the spring of 1885, arranged for Charles and Sarah Flower to see his company perform at Leamington.

The night was a disaster. The play was *Macbeth*, notoriously the stage's unluckiest – and with good reason since it contains such potential for accident. Everything went wrong and the Flowers left before the end, but they had seen the nucleus of 'good shows' and the Benson Company was engaged to play the following season. Years later Benson's wife, Constance, recalled sitting by Anne Hathaway's Cottage, 'little more than boy and girl . . . planning our lives and our work, in which Stratford, we hoped, would play a big part'.

On Easter Monday in 1886 'F.R.B.' opened the first of his many Stratford seasons as Hamlet. The evening was a great success and favourable comparisons were made with Henry Irving. It was, however, his Birthday performance as Richard III which most intrigued – 'infinitely more subtle and kingly', said one critic, 'than Barry Sullivan's'. The enchantment was reciprocated: Benson wrote to his fiancée, enthusing about the town and the Flowers, who conducted their theatre with 'personal love and reverence'. By the standards of the day, the scenery was simple and the stage hands were all locals on a week's secondment. Stratfordians also performed as 'supers', playing walk-on parts. Whenever they appeared on stage, their friends in the gallery shouted their names.

Next year, the Bensonians returned. The noted comic actor, George Weir, was not happy with his padding and made a depressed Falstaff in the *Merry Wives*. The irrepressible Benson played Dr. Caius, merely, thought his wife, to participate in the comic sword fight. The audience loved it, shaking off their 'customary frigidity' and applauding wildly.

In the season of 1888, Mrs. Benson made her Stratford debut. A painstaking but not brilliant actress, her Juliet was not a great success, but her Titania was. In a very Bensonian *Dream*, 50 tiny local children scattered over the stage as fairies with little wings fluttering on

196

their backs; a fight was staged between a spider and a wasp and Benson, as Oberon, descended to bribe an Indian boy with bull's eyes.

Stratford then had a two-year break from Benson. Charles Flower was keen to bring a scholarly approach to his theatre and to explore the range of the Shakespearean canon, so Oswald Tearle revived *Henry VI, Part I*. Benson followed this pioneering approach on his return, when another obscure play, *Timon of Athens*, was chosen for the Birthday production. Constance Benson was not pleased, preferring to dance in the masque in Act I than to play a speaking part. She remembered throwing off her exotic costume and spending a pleasant hour on the river. Her opinion that 'no one could possibly be interested in Timon' was generally shared by the audience.

Ten days later the man to whom Benson always referred reverentially as 'The Founder' died after collapsing at a meeting of the newly-formed county council. Some months previously he and Sarah had chosen the plot in the cemetery where he was laid. Like Wren, his monument may be seen in what he created. His brother Edgar became Chairman of the Theatre governors, but decisions were often taken by Sarah.

When the Bensonians returned for the season of 1893, their leader was suffering from typhoid, which had been misdiagnosed as influenza. He was rushed to bed in a delirium and remained there for several weeks. Lyall Swete learnt most of the part of Petruchio in a day for the Birthday production and improvised the rest. A young and very large Australian, later to be famous in musical comedy, Oscar Asche, made his debut that season. It had been intended that the Birthday performance should be *Coriolanus*, but this had been rendered impossible by Benson's illness. The governors were loath to let a year go by without introducing a new play, so it was arran-

---

ER 25/3/32/10

MEMORIAL THEATRE,
STRATFORD-ON-AVON.

THE ANNUAL SERIES OF

DRAMATIC PERFORMANCES

FOR 1886, WILL COMMENCE ON

EASTER MONDAY, APRIL 26,

And will be continued

FOR ONE WEEK ONLY!

Under the direction of

MR. F. R. BENSON.

THE COMPANY INCLUDES

MESSIEURS

F. R. BENSON	G. R. WEIR
T. J MERRIDEW	W. MOLLISON
THALBERG	HERBERT ROSS
H. ATHOL FORDE	H. HOLMES
OSWALD YORKE	S. PHILLIPS
H. MURRAY-INNES	O. STUART
A. RITCHIE	H JALLAND
MISS W. BEADNELL	MISS ETHEL JOHNSON
MISS TAIGI KEENE	MISS MAY PROTHEROE
MISS C. FETHERSTONHAUGH	

Monday, April 26, 'HAMLET'
Tuesday   „   27, 'THE RIVALS'
Wednesday „   28, 'OTHELLO'
Thursday   „   29, 'RICHARD III.'
Friday   „   30, 'RICHARD III.'
Sat. (afternoon) May 1, 'RICHARD III.'
Sat. (evening) „   1, 'PRIEST OR PAINTER'
and a Comedietta

Richard III. will be played strictly from the Text of Shakespeare.

PRICES OF ADMISSION:— Orchestra and Balcony Stalls, 4s.; Circle, 3s.; Pit, 2s.; Gallery, 1s.
Morning Performance only, children under twelve years of age half-price.
Places for Stalls and Circle can be secured at the Memorial Library, between 10 and 4, on and after Monday, April 19th.

Afternoon... Doors open at 2.0; Curtain, 2.30
Evening ... „   7.0;   „   7.30

RAILWAY ARRANGEMENTS.
Special Trains after the Performances will run as follows:—

MIDLAND—

G.W.R.—

---

40. *Advertisement for the Benson company's first Stratford season, 1886. Miss Fetherstonhaugh, who later became Mrs. Benson, did not appear because of her mother's illness. Note the Shakespearean text used, purged of Colly Cibber's alterations.*

ged that the company should return to act it in August. The weather was glorious. Many rehearsals were in the Theatre grounds, or in the garden of the *Black Swan*: from that summer always the *Dirty Duck*. The townspeople gave the actors a magnificent welcome and Constance reflected that there was 'no other theatre in the world where the actor may work in such perfect conditions'.

Memory was to exaggerate the extent of Bensonian athletic activity at Stratford. So busy were they rehearsing for the cramped season that they had little time for diversions. Occasionally they would squeeze in a game of hockey against local opposition, with Benson on the right wing and the enormous bulk of Oscar Asche filling the goal.

In 1894 the new play was *Henry IV, Part Two*. Benson stocked Shallow's farm with live sheep, fowl and pigeons, which maintained a cacophony of sound. The most remarkable performance was from Constance as Doll Tearsheet. Many people tried to dissuade her from playing such a role, but she had her own reasons: 'I had watched a living "Doll Tearsheet" in Manchester, and was most anxious to turn my copy to account. The Press were good enough to say many complimentary things of my performance, but several clergymen preached against me . . . though not one of them owned to having come more than once to the performance. Nowadays no one would be shocked', she recalled 30 years later, but then 'it was thought highly immoral to "make vice attractive".'

Here is the essence of Victorian morality – that a sense of retributive justice should always manifest itself. We should not judge too sardonically: the social effects of vice were probably clearer to a clergyman than a theatre audience; in any case, Benson himself was primed in Victorian values, bowdlerising his way through Shakespeare's works.

In 1895, it was time for another change and a future theatrical knight, Philip Ben Greet, presented a season, introducing to Stratford the actor Frank Rodney, who for a few brief springs was a Festival favourite. This was the Bensonians' last break from Stratford for 20 years. 'Pa' Benson had built the prestige of the theatre. By the late 1890s scores of people were travelling from London for the season, necessitating a ballot for tickets. In 1898 the season was extended to two weeks: that year Benson mounted the most extravagant of his productions, *Antony and Cleopatra*, with himself and Constance in the title roles. Since it was too elaborate to tour, most of the huge outlay was non-returnable. Halliwell Hobbes made his Festival debut as Varrius. He was a Stratfordian; a great-grandson of that Robert and Betsy who were such avid playgoers a century before. The following season another monumental drama was staged: *Hamlet* in its entirety, played at a snail's pace over an afternoon and evening. That season, Benson was a phenomenon of energy, playing nine other parts, including Henry V, Richard III, Macbeth, Richard II, Malvolio and Orlando. His unfailing enthusiasm and genteel spirit of adventure suited Stratford well, although there were already complaints that Stratfordians did not attend Festivals as assiduously as they might. If upbraided with this, there was a ready reply: with the exception of the revival play, they had seen the Bensonian repertory over and over again, with the same actors filling the same parts and Benson in most, if not all, the title roles. This criticism was inapplicable in 1900, when Benson, busy in London after a disastrous fire had destroyed most of the company's properties, sent down a scratch company led by John Coleman, an old actor from an earlier age. Despite the misgivings of Sarah Flower, a bizarre, bowdlerised *Pericles* was presented, which lived long in memory as the worst production ever seen at Stratford.

Even less could the criticism of repetition be applied to the Festival of 1901. After a first week of six revived comedies (four of them Shakespearean) the company embarked on a long-remembered 'Week of Kings', when eight of Shakespeare's History plays – half of them new to the repertory – were presented in sequence. Thus a different play could be seen every evening for a fortnight. Constance recalled the hectic schedule:

Most of the Company had four or five new parts to study, and with the entire day given up to rehearsing and the night to acting, and constant matinees, there was little leisure for study. The agony of nervousness we all went through that week beggars description. When there was a short period of "rest" between the rehearsal and the night's performance, many of the company were to be seen lying in boats among the rushes, trying to memorize their parts. Some would roam the fields, declaiming to the startled sheep. You seldom met a member of the Company . . . who was not carrying a Shakespeare.

One delighted by the theatre, 'made, not to make money, but pleasure', was W.B. Yeats, who eulogised that the Bensons spoke verse, 'not indeed perfectly, but less imperfectly than any other players upon our stage'.

The Festival of 1902 brought one of the theatre's great moments. The *doyenne* of the stage, Ellen Terry, came to play Queen Katherine in *Henry VIII*, fulfilling a promise made 20 years before – that one day she would act under Benson's management. Prices were doubled and the seats sold out weeks before. 'Those of us who can look over the vista of the years and note the swell . . . of the enthusiasm which greets our Shakespeare festival', wrote a local theatre buff, 'will find it hard to recall one in which that enthusiasm has been so wide and deep and real.' When Miss Terry entered she received a prolonged standing ovation, but it was not she who was to be most remembered on that amazing evening. It was public knowledge that Frank Rodney, one of those fine middle-part actors who are the mainstay of any classical company, had cancer of the tongue. The shocked Benson, knowing he would never act again even if he survived an operation the following week, offered him any part in the repertory and he chose Buckingham in this *Henry VIII*. A deathly hush descended as he spoke his final, terrible, majestic lines in Act 2:

> All good people
> Pray for me! I must now forsake ye; the last hour
> Of my long weary life has come upon me. Farewell;
> And when you would say something that is sad,
> Speak of how I fell. I have done; and God forgive me!

At the end of the scene, the audience shouted for him, but he did not return. He had taken his exit from the stage and, a few weeks later, from life. The Bensonians gave a fine processional cross in his memory to Holy Trinity, which is still carried in services.

Benson also brought drama from the beginning of life to this production. Always a stickler for accurate effects, he engaged a baby from Waterside as the tiny Princess Elizabeth. The infant screamed the house down and had to be taken off.

Despite thus taking third place in the evening, Ellen Terry was enchanted by Stratford and made a graceful little speech at the final curtain.

> This really is a beautiful little theatre and you must all be proud and happy that you have built it with the splendid motive of honouring Shakespeare in his own town. It really is the nearest approach to a national theatre in England.

Charles Flower's vision, scorned by the sophisticate a quarter-century before, had become part of the theatrical firmament.

Science wins New Victories

The progress which brought the growing number of visitors was affecting Stratfordians. In 1885 the Flowers installed electricity at 'Avonbank'. Five years later Charles Flower, sitting in his Palm House, spoke into a phonograph with Sir Arthur Hodgson of Clopton House. Isabella, his niece, sang, but this was less satisfactory and 'her voice was not immortalised'.

Even quack medicine was becoming technological. In 1888, Mr. Retallack demonstrated his 'curative electrical appliances' at premises rented in Ely Street. Imposing testimonials were advertised to support the 'greatest remedy of the age'. Such was the demand that he extended his stay. Mr. Days, a railway-guard, may represent the grateful sufferers:

I don't know how to thank you sufficiently for the marked benefit I have received from your electric belt, as for years I have suffered from Lumbago and Indigestion, which your belt has taken away; neither am I now troubled with the wind, which previous to wearing your creative band was most unpleasant. Increased strength and energy has now returned to me, and the pain and weakness gone. I shall do my best to add to the fame of your wonderful appliances, which have done me more good than anything and everything I have tried.

Innovation was escalating. 'The truth of the famous remark made to Horatio', said the *Herald* sagely in 1896, 'becomes clearer every year as science wins more victories.' That year the extraordinary noise of two motor cars was heard a quarter-mile away. When they parked, they were surrounded by inquisitive crowds, who were repelled by the stink of oil, but impressed by the steering and speeds of up to 20 m.p.h.. Many were sceptical. Motor cars might have their uses, but they would have to be improved drastically before they could replace the horse.

Such doubters were confounded three years later when 20 vehicles from the London Automobile Club passed through. Their ugliness, lack of comfort and smell were much remarked upon, but their 'oscillating properties' were considered 'fearful and wonderful'. One driver claimed to have covered two miles in as many minutes, a feat, it was conceded, no horse could emulate. To curb such excesses the County Council introduced a speed limit of 12 m.p.h., but it was honoured only in the breach. Those predicting dire consequences nodded sagely in 1899, when Warwickshire's first road casualty occurred at Edge Hill, but the internal combustion engine was not to be denied. Soon 40 cars an hour were monitored on the Birmingham Road and roadside trees and gardens were white with dust. There were those who hired cars in Birmingham and Coventry and drove to Stratford, imbibing freely *en route*. Concern was expressed about the way they terrified the public with their recklessness.

Yet horseless carriages were becoming a public utility. There were complaints about the Stratford and Shipston steam omnibus blocking Clopton Bridge while it took on water and passengers. By 1903, a network of motorbus services was connecting Stratford with the neighbourhood.

Other wonders appeared. In 1896 a charity show at the Town Hall demonstrated

The marvellous KINEMATOGRAPH PICTURES

or

ANIMATED PHOTOGRAPHS.

As produced in London at the various places of Entertainment.

The Sensation of the Day! Every incident is depicted on the screen, in all its detail, with absolute fidelity.

No-one was impressed. The frames slipped and many were defective. For 'life absolutely reproduced', Stratfordians waited a year for Fred Ginnet's Circus which showed the Fitzsimmons-Corbett fight for the World Heavyweight title, Queen Victoria's Jubilee procession and other topical scenes on 'the most perfect machine on the Road'. Soon Chipperfields' were filming local scenes to show to packed houses at the Mop. In 1903 the Birthday procession from the previous April was screened and an excited audience identified its fellow townsfolk.

The *Herald* wisely saw that technical innovation was not an unmixed blessing. It was not pleasant to contemplate, it declared in reporting experiments with airships in 1903, 'the dropping of explosives among a sleeping army in the field, and it is to be hoped that the Powers will agree among themselves that such a way of destroying life shall be prohibited in civilised warfare'.

New ideas were also under discussion. The Methodist minister, the Reverend J. J. Ellis, declared himself a Socialist. His ideology was a curious mixture of the homespun and the theoretical. Society, he considered, was founded on clothing. Socialism would abolish fustian, corduroy and moleskin and dress the people in broadcloth – it was widely believed that fabrics other than wool were bad for the skin – equality would ensue through a modest programme consisting of manhood suffrage; free, compulsory, non-sectarian education; adequate housing and worker share-holding. The railways might be nationalised with adequate compensation. Land nationalisation was also desirable, based on the slogan, 'The Land for the People, the People for the Land'. Industrial disputes would be settled by arbitration. The keystone to the vision was 'the gradual evolution of the people through the influence of moral education into a christian brotherhood'. Attempts were made to work out the practicalities of such ideas. In 1896 a Co-operative Society was founded in Stratford and a movement set afoot to found a free library.

New and fervent voices were emerging. The *Herald*, which had once dubbed Joseph Arch 'the Warwickshire Agitator', came to regard him as a quaint, homely figure, whose Trade Unionism was of the 'jog-trot, solid, responsible order'. The 'Red Van' of the 'English Land Restoration League' travelled the area, proclaiming the 'abolition of landlordism'. Local idealists like the Quaker, H.P. Bullard, or Bolton King, the Liberal activist, who had organised an unsuccessful farmworkers co-operative, orated from its platform, as well as more militant outsiders like Dr. Edward Aveling and his common-law wife Eleanor, daughter of Karl Marx. He was a familiar figure in Stratford, writing a column of London tittle-tattle for the *Herald* under the pseudonym of Alec Nelson and reviewing the Festival season for the London papers. 'Discontent is your duty', Mrs. Aveling told her audiences. 'The workers of England are poor not because they are idle, but because they are robbed.'

The appearance of Eleanor Marx on campaigning platforms betokens the stirring of activity among another aspirant group. In 1887, at a meeting in the Town Hall, the Reverend de Courcy Laffan, headmaster of the Grammar School, proposed the extension of the franchise to duly qualified women. He was supported by Charles Flower, who suggested petitioning the local M.P. The large and influential audience, not surprisingly, consisted chiefly of ladies.

'Ladies' were still accorded a special role in the scheme of things and their behaviour was expected to be decorous. In 1890, Mrs. de Courcy Laffan anonymously reviewed a play which had been performed in aid of the Parochial Clothing Club in the *Evesham Journal*. She expressed shock that, during the performance, one of the ladies gracefully drooped her head on a man's shoulder. 'No doubt', she remonstrated unctuously, 'those who selected this piece for charity were guided by the old Jesuit maxim that the end justifies the means. Yet it is impossible not to regret seeing such questionable matter set before the public under the direct patronage of the clergy.' She was reaping the whirlwind. Not only was the clergyman in question the explosive vicar, but the lady was his cousin! He fired off a furious letter, which provoked a reply from Mr. Laffan, breaking his wife's *incognito*. George Arbuthnot's response illustrates the attitude of the genteel classes to the 'fairer sex'.

> I find then, that my opponent is a lady, and I can only take my hat off and stand aside. I do not fight with women, nor will I notice anything which Mrs. Laffan may chose to write against me, if she will append her name to it. As long as women write as women they have the privilege of attacking men without producing a reply.

Life was not simple for those caught in the cross-fire of such disputes. The vicar had sounded off with a few choice remarks about the Laffan affair in the parish magazine. As a result Mr. Laffan obliged the printer, John Morgan, to withdraw his sons from the Grammar School. He had little choice but to send them to the Commercial School of Mr. Priest, the vicar's sworn enemy, so he lost the contract to print the magazine.

Ironically, Mrs. Laffan soon mended her breach with the vicar. Two years later she told an approving meeting at the Town Hall that he supported votes for women qualified by property. In 1893, a local branch of the Women's Liberal and Radical Union was formed and an advance was made towards suffrage when women became eligible to be Guardians of the

Poor. Mrs. Rachel Lowe, a widow from Ettington, was elected in April and proved an energetic and humane Guardian.

There was modest progress for women elsewhere. Lady cyclists pedalled energetically through the countryside and fashion reflected this activism. The 'New She' was fetchingly dressed in gaiters, knickerbockers, surtout and hat. New expressions horrified traditionalists. 'A few words of slang from a pretty woman's lips', fumed a columnist in the *Herald*, 'tend to obscure her charm and to cause a refined man's lips to curl with contempt. Such is the vulgar abuse of the word "awful". "Thanks awfully", "an awful nice man" . . .' The new slang made its appearance at the Theatre. A dancer arriving half an hour late for rehearsal pouted coquettishly when upbraided by her manager: 'And was ums angry with its Popsy Wopsy den?'.

But it was the growing possibilities of employment that was doing most to expand female perspectives. It was becoming difficult to find servants. The long-resisted aim of those who wanted to abolish Mop-hiring was being achieved by the simple lack of servants to hire. Many women were finding jobs in public services like the G.P.O. and the demand for shorthand typists always exceeded the supply. The rise of a new middle-class was reflected in the ribbon developments creeping out of Stratford. Many were acquiring servants for the first time and older wealth considered that this contributed to the problem.

> The *quid pro quo* principle is so much lost sight of by the mistress that the obligation which should be mutual is one-sided, hence, 'our servant' quickly degenerates into a 'slavey'. . . She receives neither common courtesy nor consideration from her 'missus', has a time of it also with the children who know no better . . . and soon she looks about her for relief and freedom from an intolerable strain, often as it happens to fall from the frying pan into the fire.

Vulgar women caused other outrages. In 1897, a nurse, Elizabeth Brandish, faced committal proceedings on a charge of murdering her illegitimate baby. A large crowd, consisting mainly of women, gathered outside the Town Hall. When the doors opened they were allowed in first and chattered and laughed as if they were going to an entertainment rather than a grim judicial procedure. Since there were few men present, the order to remove hats when the Court went into session was greeted with giggles. There was a happier ending to this sad case. At the Assizes, Nurse Brandish was discharged after a juror, George Enston, a local Guardian of the Poor who was opposed to capital punishment, persistently blocked the verdict.

Stratford's first divorce occurred in 1897. When Henry Edwards, the billposter and town crier, came home after three months in hospital, he discovered that his wife Ethel had been drinking a great deal and seeing a lot of William Smart, a local butcher. The neighbours had monitored the affair. Three of them told the court that they had seen two figures silhouetted on the bedroom blinds and that Smart had left the next morning.

The servant problem was exacerbated during the celebrations of the 60th year of the Queen's reign in the summer of 1897. The *Herald* warned that those girls who had saved a little money, or who had a good home to go to would cease working until the national festivities were over. At Stratford the festivities included a Shakespearean procession; a water pageant; races and tea for 2,000 children; illuminations and a performance at the theatre of 'that screaming farce', *My Turn Next*.

From his pulpit the vicar gave thanks for the peace and prosperity which the reign had brought, but even on occasions of national rejoicing he could not resist controversy. The church, he declared, had also prospered during Victoria's reign, 'but I cannot admit that its wonderful progress has been so much due to the influence of her Majesty, who has failed to grasp the true meaning of the Catholic faith'. The storm was predictable and perhaps even calculated. One correspondent was grieved that 'even upon so graceful and generous and patriotic an occasion . . . your Vicar could not repress his aggressive and defiant spirit'. Another protester regretted that Stratford was the 'only place in the Empire where a growl was heard on the day of the Queen's Jubilee'. The vicar considered such criticism the inevitable lot of those who did their duty as social reformers, who were in contact with 'abuses which some persons preferred remaining in ignorance of'.

Despite such altercations, assessments of the reign were generally optimistic. 'The duties of the Bench', opined its chairman, John Smallwood, 'are light and becoming lighter. People are becoming better and I think the schoolmaster has not been abroad to no purpose.' At the 5th November Supper, Mr. C. Holton favourably contrasted Stratford with its state in his youth.

> It says something for the improvement in morals of the town that it is only necessary to pull down your blinds to shut up shop. There are no thieves and no burglars. The town could bear comparison with any town of its size. It is well lighted; it has a good trade, for I hardly ever see a shop to let, and it is impossible to get good houses. I think we might fairly consider ourselves to be in the happy position of being well managed.

Big Shows

Improved transport was bringing 'big shows' – and 3,000 visitors – to the Mop, where gradual change reflected innovation. In the 1890s the waxworks were gradually melting away, living prodigies received scant support and the 'sonorous and unmusical' barrel organ was becoming a rarity. Steam and electric motors were taking over from manual and animal traction. The most popular attraction was the switchback railway – even clerics were seen on its 'giddy whirl', although the vicar's attitude to the pleasures of the Mop was unchanging. In a sermon preached from Jeremiah 22.1, he attacked the heavy drinking which occurred on Mop day and regretted that many considered indecency a 'subject of merriment and laugh at an indecent picture or a dirty exhibition'. The issue for all decent Christian people was 'How can this be avoided? Fathers and elder brothers, you don't want your daughters and your sisters to see sights which should make honest girls blush. I ask you then, in whatever walk of life you are, to say boldly and insistently, "It shall not be." Go and see for yourself, especially after nightfall, and if a low fellow makes a coarse joke, just silence him forcibly: knock him down if necessary. You may technically be breaking the law, but public opinion will be on your side. . . Sin winked at, even if not indulged in, is bound sooner or later to bring its punishment, and the state of Jerusalem at the present day and the condition of the Jewish nation, are startling examples for us that the prophetic warning of Jeremiah has indeed been fulfilled.' Some wondered what would happen if they followed this course and found they had 'caught a Tartar'. Others felt that the vicar was contradicting his latest campaign, to abolish corporal punishment in elementary schools.

It was not just 'What the Butler saw' and strip shows which interested those concerned with public morals at the Mop. At the turn of the century, a new sort of confidence trickster appeared. The popular illustrator Phil May once started to sketch a clever gentleman who appeared to be wrapping up sovereigns and half-crowns and selling them for two shillings. The 'sharp' saw what he was doing and announced breathlessly: 'If that there celebrited portrit painter with the tight breeches on will 'and up the picter to the equal celebrited benefactor to 'oomanity wot is giving away quids for coppers will reward 'im accordingly.' Phil, with a twinkle in his eye, handed up the drawing. The conjuror was delighted, pinning it to his cart. He screwed up three sovereigns, three half-sovereigns and several half-crowns in a piece of paper and handed it to the artist. 'You'll be president of the bloomin' Ryal Academy some dye, young man', he promised. 'Here catch!' 'A bargain's a bargain', said Phil. When he opened the packet and found two pennies and a halfpenny, he declared it the most entertaining commission he had ever had.

The Mop was celebrated for its roasts, even ·then becoming a rarity. Some Stratfordians were celebrated ox-roasters, travelling the length of the kingdom for special events. Spits were established outside pubs. At the *Horse and Jockey* in Wood Street, George Luckett, self-proclaimed champion roaster of the world, presided. He had roasted for such celebrities as the Marquis of Bute and Lord Derby. His claim to ascendency was challenged by 'Judy' Hewins who roasted at the *Prince of Wales* in Rother Street for more than half a century. Mop days in his company were a delight to his grandson, George, who stuffed his pockets with stale crusts and caught the dripping and ate it while he was carving. Other roasts were at the *Garrick*, under the supervision of another famous roaster, 'Panham' Worrall; the *Seven Stars*, *White Swan* and *Plymouth Arms*.

Other, more transitory, shows occurred. One summer Sequah, the 'Indian medicine man', paraded the streets in an exotic gilt caravan with a band on its roof to promote his remarkable remedies, 'Sequah Oil' and 'Prairie Flower'. Later a small crowd gathered in the field behind the *Unicorn* to witness his curative miracles. He commenced by extracting teeth free of charge. So skilled was he that the sufferers were frequently unaware that the teeth had gone. He then made a 'temperate little speech' about the diseases which he specialised in curing and the nature of his medicines. The first patient, George Clarke, aged 57, of 53, Shakespeare Street, had suffered long with chronic rheumatism and had to crawl upstairs. He was accompanied into the caravan by several witnesses. Lying on a couch, he had Sequah Oil rubbed vigorously over his knees and thighs. After ten minutes, he could bend his legs freely and soon, to the delight of the crowd, he was dancing a jig to the music of the band.

The crowd grew over the next three evenings as further cures were performed. Some 30 people climbed the platform to have their teeth pulled and those cured of rheumatics testified to the efficacy of the remedy: one former sufferer, old Mr. Norris, had walked the five miles to Wellesbourne and back. The most remarkable cure was on the last night. William Unitt, aged 17, of 6, New Street, had suffered from chronic rheumatism since he was two and was wheeled to see Sequah in his bath chair. On the couch he suffered excruciating pain, but after being rubbed with the oil for 25 minutes, he pulled his father round in the chair to loud cheers. Many expressed scepticism about the cures, but could provide no explanation. Sequah's medicine was certainly lucrative: his annual profits were £45,000.

Most spectacular of the exotic visitors was Lord George Sanger's Circus, 'the oldest, richest, largest and most sumptious establishment in the World', whose huge tent was erected in a field off Cherry Street. 'IDIASA, the Queen of the Eastern Star! The beautiful woman of Egypt!' was followed by equestrian displays, animal acts, acrobats and trapeze artists. The *grande finale* often struck a topical note, like the war in Sudan, in which 250 horses, a battery of camels with huge cannons firing on their backs and the Field Artillery appeared simultaneously in the arena. Five hundred locals participated as the Mahdist army. In 1901, after troubles in China, the 'latest and greatest' novelty was 'Real Chinese Boxers' who had been at the siege of the British Legation in Peking. One year a football match was staged, with a massive cup for a prize, between the captain of Stratford Rovers F.C. and Sanger's 'centre-forward elephant'.

The School Board

After the first School Board elections, the denominations, realising that there was little gain in such raucous affairs, established a *modus vivendi* in which the Church of England filled four of the seven seats; the Nonconformists, two and the Catholics, one. The arrangement was uneasy. The Nonconformists suspected that the Anglicans were in league with the Catholics to underfund the Board School and thus make their denominational schools appear more attractive. The inevitable conflict came in 1896 when the Anglican majority refused to endorse the appointment of a Unitarian, Miss Gold, as a teacher. A national storm ensued. The Board, said the *Herald*, had made itself notorious from Land's End to John o'Groats. Joseph

Chamberlain expressed sorrow that such bigotry still existed, while at Stratford there was a stormy public meeting.

The Anglican majority, undaunted by such protests, decided that the Apostles' Creed should be taught in the Board School to those children whose parents did not object. Who these were was to be ascertained by asking the children. 'Among people who are not priest-ridden', wrote a protester, 'to ask babies whether they or their parents object to the Apostles' Creed is sheer imbecility.' To Nonconformists this was an objectionable form of religious teaching in a maintained school. Even so, they considered it in their interest to maintain the pact at the next School Board election in 1899, fearing that their representation might be obliterated.

Mr. Francis Talbot, a Unitarian, was not bound by any such caution and his nomination ensured a contest. The fact that public personalities not usually associated with elections, like Father Thomas, the Catholic priest, and the controversial vicar, were standing served to increase excitement. The degree of decline in institutional religion was an uncertain factor: a high proportion of voters went to neither church nor chapel and their influence might prove decisive.

Numerous canvassers pounded the doorsteps. The Anglican clergy, unlike their Nonconformist equivalents, campaigned hard. On polling day, carriages, mostly Anglican, ferried voters to the polls and there was a high turn-out. The issue was complicated by a complex voting system which enabled the elector to distribute seven votes as he chose. Father Thomas was expected to do well. Most of his little flock would give him all their votes and he could expect to pick up Anglican votes for not being a Nonconformist and *vice-versa!*

A large crowd waited outside the Town Hall to hear the declaration. The news that John Smallwood, a Nonconformist, had topped the poll with 1,542 votes was greeted by huge cheers, as were the names which followed: Father Thomas got 1,447 votes and the other Nonconformist, John Henson, 1,229. The biggest cheer came for Francis Talbot's 1,289 votes. The vicar's name, 20 votes behind, provoked loud hooting, mingled with cheers, which was repeated for the other three Church candidates, including Mr. Ashwin, who failed to get elected. When Mr. Smallwood tried to say a few words, the cheering crowd surged forward and the candidates fled for home. The crowd continued its frivolities by knocking a policeman unconscious before dispersing.

There were agonised post-mortems in church circles. The vicar had instructed his supporters to plump for him, rather than distributing their votes, so he appeared to have few friends outside the inner circle of churchmanship. The regular cry of defeated candidates was raised: that scores of people had failed to deliver votes they had promised. The *Herald* was not surprised. If an elector would not promise a vote, canvassers assumed that he intended to support the opposition.

> This suspicion finds its way to the committee room, and if he be a poor man the order goes forth that he must in future be struck off the charity list; or if the elector be in a good position, patronage from his business must be withdrawn. This is a very common thing, and to prevent this kind of intimidation being exerted, canvassing should be an offence, disqualifying the candidate resorting to it.

The elation of Nonconformists was great. The Reverend J.J. Pugh, the former Methodist minister, wrote to congratulate 'lovers of civil and religious liberty' on the splendid result.

> All parties are now represented as in justice should be the case in a community holding diverse opinions. The day of "family government" is over. No clerical corner or party preserve should be in possession in Stratford again.

In fact the Anglicans maintained control of the School Board through their alliance with Father Thomas. Yet Mr. Pugh was basically right. The election reflected the decline of the church's hegemony over social policy. Doubtless the vicar would have gone down with all guns firing, but the necessity to do so was removed in 1902, when the powers of the Board were

The Entries in these Columns should be copied from the "Child's School Book," which, admission...is to be given to the Teacher, who will keep it, &c."

Admission Number	Date of Admission and Deposit of "Child's School Book." Day / Of M'th / 18 (Yr)	NAME OF CHILD. SURNAME.	CHRISTIAN.	RESIDING AT Enter Number of the House and Street (if any.)	At (Place.)	WAS BORN On the (Day)	Of (M'th)	18 (Yr)	As Certified by the Registrar of the District of
313	7 1 84	Winchester	Robert Thomas	Henley St	Wellington	6	10	75	
314	" " "	Keithman	Charles	Wood St	Son A	27	4	74	
315	" " "	Keithman	Walter	"	"	10	1	76	
316	21 " "	Pickering	Frederick Chas	Canal Side	Warfield milthqued	6	12	72	
317	" 5 "	Ward	Samuel	Burial Pl	Son A	10	3	77	
318	" " "	Parsons	Harry	Rother St	"	20	12	77	
319	" " "	Hodge	Albert	47 College Lane	"	3	10	77	
320	" " "	Hine	Frederick	College Lane	"	22	11	77	
321	" " "	Harris	Hazel William	5 Holloм St	Stourbridge	4	10	77	
322	" " "	Warrington	Frank	24 Gd Wm St		6	2	77	
323	" " "	Taplin	Albert	6 Sheep St	Birmingham	15	4	77	
324	" " "	Wilson	Henry	Henley St	"	9	6	77	
325	" " "	Cook	Albert	Birmingham Rd	"	31	3	77	
326	" " "	White	George	Meer St	"	1	1	77	
327	" " "	Hughes	John E.	18 Bull St	"	22	10	77	
328	" " "	Hartwale	Albert	Mansell St	Shipston	22	12	77	
329	28 " "	Sara	Henry	Wood St	Son A	6	10	69	
330	" " "	Green	Albert	Alcester Rd	Son A	28	10	71	
331	" " "	Harris	Frank	Clopton Lane	"	20	5	77	
332	18 2 "	Hiam	Arthur Ed.	Burial Lane	"	16	5	77	
333	" " "	Jelleyman	Frank	Shipston Rd	Son A	7	4	77	
334	19 " "	Thomas	William Hy	Mansell St	"	3	6	74	
335	" " "	Thomas	Albert	"	"	31	5	76	
336	18 " "	Hiam	George	Burial Lane	Son A	6	4	75	
337	25 " "	Carwood	Henry	Sanctus St	Brampton	19	11	73	
338	" " "	"	Arthur	"	Clare Suffolk	24	3	75	
339	" " "	"	Charles	"	Newton Bucks	10	3	76	
340	17 3 "	Walton	Bernard David	Ely St	Stratford	17	1	76	
341	" " "	Hall	William	Narrow Lane		23	1	76	
342	31 " "	Brookes	Frederick	Bancroft Hall Shipston Rd	Loxley	20	5	74	
343	21 4 "	Howell	Jesse	Sanctus St	Barton	7	4	72	
344	" " "	Hewins	Robert Wallis	"	Son A	22	4	72	
345	" " "	"	Thomas	"	"	31	8	73	
346	28 " "	Phillips	James	5 Gd Wm St	Lichfield	17	12	72	
347	12 5 "	Nesfall	George	30 Bull St	Blandford	27	11	76	
348	13 " "	"	Walter Edward	"	"	23	2	75	

41. *The Leaving Register for the Church of England National School, 1884.*

Name of School	No. of Attendances made in the Year	Standard passed in such Standard	Age at passing in such Standard	In what Class at Admission	Successive Standards passed in this School (I., II., &c.)	In what Class at Withdrawal	Date of Leaving — Day	Of 18 (M'th)	(Y'r)	Copy of last Entry	Parent Name	Occupation	Whether exemption claimed
al. Sch	I			3	II III IV V	1	6	5	87		David	Cordwainer	
d. Sch	–	–	–	2		2	27	2	84		Charles	dyer	
"	–	–	–	4		4	27	2	84		"		
nesti Sch	132	IV	10	1		1	21	3	84		Charles	Labourer	
Inf. Sch	0		"	5	I II III IV V	1	12	6	89		William	Labourer	
"			"	5	I II III IV V	1	3	3	90		Joseph		
"			"	5	I II III IV V VI	1	1	8	90		George	mechanic	
"			"	5		5	21	3	84		Thomas	Bricklayer	
"			"	5		5	16	5	84		William	pigon weigher	
"			"	5	I II III IV V	1	13	9	89		Edwin	Gardener	
"			"	5	I II III IV V	1	31	1	90		Joseph	clockmaker	
"			"	5	I II III IV	1	27	1	88		William	clerk	
"			"	5		5	19	9	84		William	Stoneman	
"			"	5		5	20	6	84		George	malster	
"			"	5	I II III IV V	1	8	3	89		John	drainer	
"			"	5	I II III IV V	1	12	9	90		John	Bailiff	
d. Sch	IV	13	1			1	20	6	84		Elijah	chemist	
at. Sch	III	3			II	2	27	6	84		William	Labourer	
Inf. Sch	0			5	I II III IV V	1	25	1	89		Thos Rich'd	shoemaster	
at. Sch	0			5	I II III IV V	1	18	10	89		Samuel	Builder	
Inf. Sch	–	–	–	5	I	4	14	5	86		Thomas	Ironmonger	
at. Sch	III	3			IV V VI	1	25	2	87		Harry	Engine turner	
"	I	4			II III IV V	1	3	8	88		"		
al. Sch.	II	3			III IV V	1	25	2	87		Samuel	Builder	
ndle Sch	–	–	–	3			20	6	84		Thomas	Surveyor Royal Engineers	
"	–	–	–	4			20	6	84		"	"	
"	–	–	–	5			20	6	84		"	"	
at. Sch	I	4			II III IV V	2	8	9	89		George	Labourer	
"	I	4			II III IV V		16	3	88		Thomas	ditcher	
octon h Sch	II	3			III	3	16	10	85		James	Carter	
d. Sch	III	2			IV	2	20	3	85		Thomas	Horse Keeper	
Private	0	2			IV	2	24	4	85		Robert	Fruiterer	
"	0	3			III	3	24	4	85		"	"	
Inf. Sch	IV	1					30	5	84		William	Printer	
oindon	0	5				5	13	2	85		George	
"	II	3				3	13	2	85		"	"

transferred to the newly-formed Warwickshire Education Committee. Not that this reform was hailed by Nonconformists, for it enabled denominational schools to receive extended subsidies from the rates. A passive resistance movement developed which had its effects in Stratford. In 1904, nine men were summoned for non-payment of rates, including H. H. Bullard, the auctioneer and Fred Winter, the draper. There would have been more, but 'some friends, so called' had paid some of the debts. In court, J. E. Asquith of Rother Street declared that they had deducted the portion of their rates which would go to denominational education. There should, he said, be no taxation without representation and no doctrinal tests should be applied to those whose wages were paid by the state. It was decided to sequester the goods of the resisters to the value of the debt. Two weeks later goods to the value of £4 18s 9d were auctioned amidst great hilarity, the proceedings closing with a hymn, 'Dare to be a Daniel'. Honour was satisfied and the denominational issue in education gradually faded.

CHAPTER 19

War on all Fronts

At 29 Windsor Street lived Mr. James Barnhurst, who in 1881 had participated in the disastrous defeat at Majuba Hill in the first Boer War. This would have been a forgotten colonial episode, but the discovery of mineral wealth in the Transvaal ensured an influx of fortune-hunters, including several Stratfordians. A further war appeared inevitable and was much in the air during 1899. On 1 October, the vicar courageously inveighed against the government for its aggressive policies towards the Boer republics. Two weeks later, when war was declared, he changed his tune, considering it everyone's duty to rally round the flag. On a visit to the National Schools, he asked the girls about the meaning of words like 'Patriotism' and 'Britannia' and was readily answered. They were faced, he said, with a sad and possibly long war and all must take every opportunity to express their patriotism and their readiness, if necessary, to fight and die for their country. The 240 girls sang 'God Save the Queen' and 'Rule Britannia' before a like performance occurred for the 260 boys. At the Mayor's Ball, the centrepiece of the dinner was a boar's head, inscribed 'Straight from Majuba'. The patriotic surge was reflected in babies' names, which included such future embarrassments as 'Dundonald' and 'Redvers'. Others felt unease about the War. The Bullard brothers, antique dealers and auctioneers, were outspoken in condemning its injustice: a stand which would cost them dear.

In November the first 14 local reservists were called up. Employers held 'smokers' at which patriotic songs were sung and each conscript presented with a pipe and a tobacco pouch. A crowd of 2,000 saw them off at the station, shouting 'Good old Warwicks', 'Give it to 'em boys' and 'Don't forget old Kruger' while weeping women said farewell to husbands and sons. One soldier, Private Frank Huckfield, proudly displayed a medal he had won at the Battle of Omdurman in the previous year.

Several employers announced that they would keep jobs for men called up and pay their wives five shillings a week during their absence. Not all dependants were so fortunate. One soldier had been sending his grandmother a small weekly allowance, but after he embarked for the Cape, she was destitute. As the soldier was not her son, she was ineligible for help from the fund started by the Mayor and the vicar to relieve conscripts' families. Her case was taken up by Mr. Wyatt of 38 Sheep Street: 'Having known the lad since he could walk, I can say that he is equal to a son in every respect. She brought him up, fed, clothed and sheltered him, and I know her one great grief is this, that she thinks she will never see him again'.

The combination of slack censorship and increased literacy ensured that letters from the front gave a full and frequently contrasting view of events. After a series of British disasters, Private Wilfred Rickatson wrote that he would not go through the Modder River Battle again for £1,000. 'We had to lie flat on our backs for thirteen hours, and the least move you ran the risk of getting shot. If a dust storm had not come on when it did we should have had to retire, and God knows what would have happened then . . . although we are at the scene of the operations, you people in England know more of what is going on than we do, as we have the order to take a certain position no matter what it may cost, and no matter how many lives are lost, it has to be done. If they think you are hanging back you get court-marshalled for cowardice . . . I would not like you to hear that I was a coward before the enemy. I think there are only two other Stratford chaps in our battalion out here . . .'.

Private Turvey of the 2nd Royal Warwicks wrote from Zoutpan's Drift in February, declaring himself 'a little wild to get at the Boers, for we had a go at them last Wednesday and made terrible havoc among them. We charged and charged them with the bayonets till hardly one was left . . . You ought to see the field after a fight. It would make your blood run cold. Next morning our bayonets were rusty with blood . . . My heart ached for some of them, especially when it was for me to stab one, but it is either you or him, and you have to take a true aim. But it is our duty, and when we have been at it for a bit it seems more like sport'.

At the outbreak of war, C. A. Savage, son of the Secretary of the Birthplace Trust, slipped out of the Transvaal, where he had been mining with his brother. From Durban, he wrote a view of events which found frequent echoes away from the front: 'If there is any spur wanted to urge the young men of Stratford to become Volunteers, surely it is enough to think that someday the call may sound and they may have the honour of fighting under the Union Jack for the honour and glory of our Queen and Country'.

On 31 January the Stratford Troop of Yeomanry, whose section commander was Lieutenant Richard Fordham Flower, embarked for the Cape in a company commanded by Major Orr-Ewing, nicknamed 'The Weasel'. Local ladies were busy knitting woollies for them, but apprehension was lessened with the surrender of the Boer commander, Cronje. It seemed that the war would soon be over. On 30 February, news of the relief of Ladysmith brought unbounded joy. The bells rang, flags were hoisted and schoolchildren marched through the streets wearing red, white and blue ribbons. The *Herald* magnanimously declared Cronje 'a valiant and accomplished foe, and now that he has surrendered in the presence of overwhelming odds, the last thing that the British people will be disposed to do is to crow over him in his downfall'.

Such generous feelings were not shared by all. That night a mob gathered outside the Conservative Club in Rother Street and marched through the streets, bawling patriotic ditties and visiting the premises of 'pro-Boers'. In Sheep Street, Mr. Wyatt's shop window was splintered by a heavy stone and coal was thrown through his bedroom window. The mob yelled for him to come out before moving on to the antique shop of the 'conchy' Bullard brothers in Chapel Street, where hisses and groans were given. Rumours had been circulating that the Bullards hoped that the British Army would be annihilated and that they had flown a Boer flag, which had been removed on the advice of the police. The mob, now some 200 strong, battered down the door of the shop. The Bullard brothers and their young lodger were met by a hail of missiles. An appeal to a nearby policeman proved fruitless, so the three, with great bravado, drove the rioters out. Several of the crowd were hurt in the *mêlée*, one quite severely. After a semblance of order was restored, Mr. W. P. Bullard started, with amazing *sang-froid*, to explain his views to the crowd. Surprisingly he got a hearing, until someone shouted, 'Don't listen to his soft soap' and a stone was hurled through his window. Shortly after midnight, the mob moved off to attack the houses of other 'pro-Boers'. Vicious rumours had been circulating about a local resident, Mr. Flint. His sons were said to be helping the Boers and he was alleged to have expressed hopes of a Boer victory. In fact his one son in South Africa had taken no part in the War. Mr. Flint's repudiation of such 'odious insinuations' did not save his windows from destruction.

It was common knowledge that the mob would rendezvous next evening to continue its destruction. The police should have taken decisive action, but did too little too late. The superior courage of the Bullards, in dispersing the mob, rankled the malignant. Reinforced by local roughs, they went straight to Chapel Street, where a mere half dozen policemen waited. Such a feeble force was no deterrent. The gas lamp opposite the shop was extinguished and the front windows were smashed to loud cheers. The Bullard children, asleep in the front bedroom, were endangered by falling debris. The mob dragged furniture from the shop window and set it alight. George Hewins saw frightened faces at the upstairs window and flames reflected in the glass. He felt sorry for the Bullards: 'They hadn't done me no harm.' The bombardment continued for over two hours. A bystander, Mr. T. R. Ellerker, found it remarkable that none of the crowd appeared the worse for drink. He discovered later that the pubs were very quiet that night. Around midnight Councillor E. Deer managed to quieten the mob by calling for three cheers for the Queen and for the soldiers at the front, before persuading them to disperse. Part of the crowd, however, smashed into Bullard's workshop on the Banbury Road and their auction rooms in Guild Street.

Next evening the 500 rioters were heavily outnumbered by spectators hoping to see more fun. Some rushes at the 'kopjes of the pro-Boers' were easily checked by the large police-force drafted into Stratford. Bullard's shop was so boarded up it looked like a 'minature Ladysmith'. The disappointed mob trekked towards Tiddington, where a prominent resident had come under its suspicion. They were met by policemen with drawn truncheons and fled back to Stratford. Numerous names were taken during the evening and, after four men were arrested, the town was quiet. Two weeks later, the news of the fall of Bloemfontein brought a noisy crowd onto the streets, but no damage was done. That week came the news that the Stratford Yeomanry had been ordered to the front.

Soon after, Henry Bullard announced his intention to claim compensation for the riot damage. Many people communicated their sympathy, but most did so secretly, for fear of reprisals. Edward Fox, son of a local printer, wrote an arrogant letter to the *Herald*, which implied that he had been a ringleader in the riots and concluded pompously that England was 'too free for those who are not loyal to her'. Mr. Wyatt replied scathingly that his idea of patriotism was 'something higher than terrifying helpless women and young children, and coming to demonstrate and destroy in the darkness . . . Patriotism to my mind consists in deeds not words, and as Mr. Fox and his sympathisers seem so brimful of it there is a splendid opportunity for them to show it by joining some branch of the military service, and so taking the risks of their ideal . . . instead of enjoying the luxury of a feather bed and home comforts while others do the hard and dangerous work, and they the talking and shouting.'

The ripples created by the riots went a long way. 'Who would think', asked *The New York Herald*, 'that dear, sleepy old Stratford-on-Avon could get so excited as to break windows and smash warehouses?'. The Home Secretary was questioned in Parliament about Mr. Bullard's claim that the riots had been engineered by respectable Stratfordians. Enquiries were promised. The theme was taken up by the vicar in one of his most splendid sermons. 'I for one', he declared, 'rather admire a man who is not afraid to give vent to views which he knows are unpopular . . . I am annoyed at the indifference with which many regard what has occurred . . . It has been publicly stated that men occupying good positions were in the crowd encouraging them to violence.' He called for an official enquiry. 'If Stratford with its population of 8,000 can produce an uncontrollable mob, what could Birmingham do if they were similarly stirred?'

When the four 'ringleaders' appeared in Court, one was re-categorised as drunk and disorderly, while two half-drunk creatures were imprisoned for a month. One more prominent individual received the same at the Quarter Sessions and a subscription was opened for him in the town. Stratfordians were in no doubt as to why the real ringleaders had escaped punishment: 'It was their cloth as saved 'em.'

Further trouble was averted on the night Stratford heard of the relief of Mafeking. An official celebration was organised, with a torchlight procession and firework display. A year later a hero of the siege arrived with *Wombwell's* Menagerie: 'GENERAL SNYMAN, THE WONDERFUL

MAFEKING BELL-RINGING APE . . . This intelligent ape was trained by one of Baden-Powell's troopers to ring the town bell directly the Boers commenced firing, thereby warning the inhabitants to seek the bomb-proof shelters'.

In South Africa, the Stratford Yeomanry was faring badly. 'I have not undressed', wrote a trooper, 'except to bathe, since we left Warwick . . . We have not had anyone die yet, but some have been very bad. The water is as thick and red as a sheep dip, but we have it boiled first . . . I went to town yesterday . . . but could not get drunk, as the hotel is kicked inside out and all the stuff gone.' A few days later, the troop received its baptism of fire. While taking an important position, Major Orr-Ewing and a trooper were killed and six soldiers wounded. Yet deaths on the battlefield were low compared to fatalities from enteric fever. At Bloemfontein, Private Wynne of the 2nd Warwicks got weary of conveying corpses for burial and applied for a transfer. 'I think I caught cold at Springfields', he wrote, 'where we stayed for a fortnight, and where it rained the whole time. We had one blanket, no canvass, and woke up in the morning sometimes in several inches of water. I would not tell you this, only I see by the papers how well Tommy is treated.'

War weariness was setting in. 'I wish to goodness it was all over', wrote Sergeant Charles Luckett of Wood Street, serving with the 5th Dragoon Guards. 'Everyone here is heartily sick of what we are doing. It seems rot. We must have nearly 6 to 1 against the Boers now, and they keep going on, dropping down our people, and killing and taking lots of prisoners, and then getting off again.' Drummer E.J. Dimock of Scholar's Lane described the horror of hit-and-run raids: 'I saw the effects of one of the Boer shells. It took one man's left breast off, a hind leg of a horse, then burst in the ground, and struck one man in the head, and broke a pony's leg, so that it had to be shot'.

The flow of disillusion from the front led to protests by a local landowner, the Marquis of Hertford. 'Many of the men fighting our battles', replied the *Herald*, 'are now in rags and tatters, covered with vermin, are without boots, and have scarcely the common necessities of life; one can quite understand that the rank and file might imagine that they were not sharing equally in the comforts sent from England for their special benefit. Starving men are always suspicious.'

The Stratford Yeomanry were in trouble again. In July, Lieutenant Flower fell mortally wounded at Hammond's Kraal. As he lay on the ground, he shook hands with all his troopers, wishing them goodbye and saying 'I did my duty, didn't I now? Tell my mother how I died.' He then ordered them to return to the firing line. He was put in an ambulance and died before he reached the field hospital. 'You cannot crack him up too much', wrote a trooper. 'He was so faithful to his men. He always got us food and bread, and if any of the men wanted money at any time he had only to ask him . . . We buried him under a large tree at midnight, and many were the tears that were shed. The grave was covered with stones, and it has been fenced round and a nice cross erected by Sergeant-Major Smart. The grave has been photographed and we all hope to get a copy.'

Another death shocked Stratford in January. Almost everyone heard of the Queen's passing soon after the news arrived at the telegraph office. Her reign was so long and her image so stamped on the age that most people felt as if they had lost a close relative. Fred Winter, the draper, did not miss the opportunity: 'I am fully prepared with a large stock of NEW MOURNING CLOTHES', he advertised.

After Victoria's death, interest in the far-off war waned. In February, a further contingent of the Stratford Yeomanry embarked, which included Edward Fox, perhaps called to action by disparaging remarks about his role in the Ladysmith riots. He proved a point by his absence, for violence flared again in Stratford that summer, during a by-election caused by the death of Colonel Victor Milward, M.P. The Liberals had wisely decided not to test local passions during the General Election in 1900, but now they had little choice. Their candidate was the radical idealist, Bolton King, whose enduring object was 'to carry the principles of Christianity into political and social life'. In ordinary times he would have been a splendid choice, but these were not ordinary times. His adoption meeting at the Corn Exchange was turned into a farce by the same well-dressed cameraderie that had orchestrated the riots. Speeches were interrupted by the inebriate singing of patriotic songs, chairs were overturned and fighting broke out. When it appeared that the platform might be stormed, most of those sitting on it fled. At his adoption meeting on the following evening, the Tory candidate, Philip Foster of Ingon Grange, appealed for tolerance. He had previously fought a Liberal stronghold in the North. 'They . . . treated me fairly and I do not want it to be said, now the boot is on the other leg, that here, where we have, or hope to have, a Conservative majority, that the fight had not been fairly conducted.'

This generous appeal went unheeded. Two more Liberal meetings at the Corn Exchange were broken up. For the eve-of-poll rally, the seats were arranged to reduce confrontation and 40 stewards imported from Studley. The first speaker, a Welsh M.P., William Jones, did not get very far before he was interrupted by shouts of 'Get your hair cut', 'You're no Englishman' and 'Go home'. "I do not reason with beer', he retorted, 'I reason with men.' Fighting broke out and a number of people were knocked about. One speaker, Mr. A. M. Scott, foolishly tangled with the mob and was dragged into the street, knocked down and trampled in the gutter. He received a severe gash under his left eye and fainted while being helped into a shop. The police arrested a man who had kicked him, but also took Mr. Scott's name, as it was alleged he had struck the first blow.

Outside, a large excited crowd had assembled. Every few minutes someone was ejected from the hall. When Mr. and Mrs. Bolton King arrived, the struggle was so fierce that they were not noticed until they mounted the platform. The police ejected a number of brawlers, but the Liberals complained that these included some of the stewards who were trying to keep order. When William Jones, M.P., threatened to report the matter to the Home Secretary, Superintendent Lambourne replied that the police had no power to interfere unless there was a breach of the peace. This was the cue for Mr. Scott to reappear, covered in mud, his face streaming with blood, to demand if his condition was not sufficient evidence. The Liberal chairman accused the superintendent of siding with the mob. 'You must not accuse me, Mr. Bowen', he replied. 'I do my duty honestly and fearlessly'. When Mr. Scott tried to speak again he was greeted with shouts of 'Traitor'. 'I am no traitor', he retorted. 'The traitors are the men who sent our soldiers to one of the greatest campaigns in which England has ever been engaged without first providing them with the proper means of defending themselves'. Mr. Bolton King tried to address a few words to the orderly part of the audience, but he could hardly be heard. The last speaker, Miss Marshall of the Women's Liberal League, at least got a good-humoured response: the crowd sang 'I'll be your Sweetheart'. As Mrs. Bolton King left, coarse expressions were flung at her. Given the prevailing hysteria and the non-resident 'out-vote', which was overwhelmingly Tory, her husband probably did better than he expected, losing by 2,977 votes to 4,755. During the election, he had learned that he beat his wife; farmed 2,000 acres, but employed no local labour; and that anyone voting Liberal would have to pay a shilling towards his election expenses. For the second time in a year, questions were asked in Parliament about disturbances in Stratford.

In South Africa, the Yeomanry was involved in the internment of the Boer population in a bid to end the guerrilla war, impounding livestock, burning down farmhouses and removing women and children to special camps. Trooper Bullock of Warwick Road thought these distasteful tasks to be, on balance, preferable to allowing them to starve on the veldt. The soldiers, he revealed, had only received £3 of their pay in five months – and prices were four times higher than at home. The Boers could hit quickly and viciously. In one attack, Trooper Hancock was hit by a bullet and fell, his horse on top of him. As he lay semi-conscious, the

Boers took his rifle, bandolier, tobacco and a letter. One was about to shoot him, but was prevented by a comrade. Curiously, his letter was forwarded to his sister at Wilmcote by a released English prisoner, with a note that it had been taken from the body of an English soldier. Meanwhile Edward Fox was discovering the realities of war. After he and seven comrades were captured, the Boers took their rifles, bandoliers and valuables, leaving them to stagger back to base clutching the tops of their breeches. Suffering from nervous exhaustion, he was discharged and shipped home.

Yet the war was dragging its way towards a close. In June 1902, the news of peace brought great rejoicing in Stratford. Signals were fired on the railways and flags hung from every window. Drapers displayed red, white and blue material and nearly everyone wore patriotic colours. The *Herald* was suitably statesmanlike: 'Every generation', it considered, 'has to be reminded of the horrors of the battlefield . . . while the generations now living survive, England will not easily tread the path which leads to bloodshed and carnage'.

The Stratford mob, which had enjoyed the war, had another flourish to offer. Eight weeks after the peace the militant anti-ritualist, John Kensit, arrived in Stratford with his team of preachers, doubtless attracted by the scathing national press that the vicar inspired. Stratford did not take kindly to this. It was all very well for townspeople to criticise George Arbuthnot, but motivated outsiders were another matter. Hostile demonstrations erupted during a meeting at the *Fountain*, although the crowd did not generally consist of 'conspicuous attenders at any particular place of worship'. In the evening over 2,000 people gathered outside Kensit's meeting at the Corn Exchange, imprisoning those within until one a.m.

The Real and Living Hummer

In 1890 the popular novelist, Marie Corelli, on a visit to Stratford, made the obligatory call at 'Avonbank'. The Priest-Chaplain, the Reverend Frank Smith, was one of her multitudes of admirers and recommended her novel *Ardath* to the Flowers. Sarah found it most disagreeable and wondered why people did not protest about the harm such books could do, especially to the young.

Nine years later, the unwitting recipient of this criticism rented 'Hall's Croft' and came to live in Stratford, probably believing that her literary talents would ensure a sympathetic reception in Shakespeare's town. She was at the peak of her popularity through such multi-editioned best-sellers as *Barabbas* and *The Sorrows of Satan*. She certainly aroused curiosity, eschewing photographs in an attempt to build an image of herself equitable with one of her romantic heroines. The material was unpromising. She was in her mid-forties, plump and short, but she hinted she was thirty and dressed as if she were sixteen. An additional handicap was that she was illegitimate: the daughter of Charles Mackay, a journalist and writer of popular songs, who had brought her up, so she skilfully romanticised her origins – a task in which she was assisted by her companion and admirer, Bertha Vyver, a Belgian aristocrat who exercised a subtle influence while Marie ostensibly dominated things.

Marie's residence at Stratford got off to an unfortunate start. Opposite 'Hall's Croft' was a private girls' school run by the formidable Mrs. Cameron Stuart. All day Old Town resonated with the lasses' chatter and the flat tinkle of piano practice. Miss Corelli sent over a curt note requesting silence, as she was working on *Boy*, her latest masterpiece. Mrs. Cameron Stuart's rejoinder was correct but negative and a furious Marie rented 'Avoncroft' further down the street, where in June she played the *grande dame* in Stratford for the first time. The celebrated French actress, Sarah Bernhardt, came to the Theatre to act her famed version of *Hamlet* in French prose, supported by the Benson company. It sold out weeks before amidst great excitement. Many Stratfordians assembled at the station to greet her and the newest resident was well to the fore. The fulsome description in the *Herald* was the first of the many which would eventually rebound on the authoress: 'Miss Corelli was charmingly attired in cream lisse, trimmed with Venetian guipire lace and wore a gold and white toque trimmed with black tips and osprey'. When the special train arrived, she stepped forward and greeted Madame Bernhardt in French, handing her a magnificent bouquet, tied with the tri-coloured ribbons of the two nations. Years later 'the divine Sarah' recalled this pilgrimage as 'one of my heart's memories'.

Marie's desire for social ascendency in Stratford was temporarily sealed a week later when she gave a garden party for the Whitefriars' Club, a literary circle of which Winston Churchill was chairman and Henry Irving a member. To impress the town with such connections, she invited appropriate locals. On her own terms, her generosity could be great. During her first Christmas in Stratford she entertained the children from the Catholic school around a huge Christmas tree and the *Herald* reported that 500 'ragged and hungry' Birmingham youngsters fed with 'the most evident gusto' at her expense. Later she took 250 Board School children on a railway excursion to Ragley and freely presented trophies to the town's clubs and societies. As President of the choral society she secured the great contralto, Clara Butt, to sing at the annual concert. Small wonder that, at the Theatre, bouquets were thrust into her chubby hands and the house rose to cheer her.

In 1901 Marie Corelli moved to 'Mason Croft', a Georgian mansion in Church Street which she refurbished in idiosyncratic style. Her celebrity attracted crowds to the pavement opposite. While publicly deprecating such attention, she tacitly encouraged it by her flamboyance. On Shakespeare's Birthday she produced an enormous wreath, gathered in Dante's garden in Florence; she and Bertha were pulled around Stratford in a miniature chaise by two Shetland ponies named Puck and Ariel. Cabdrivers pointed out her house as Stratford's prime attraction. Even the Americans, as *Punch* wittily observed, were diverted:

> The Yankee streaming to the Shrine
> Of our Immortal Mummer,
> Forgets the dead and doubtful 'Swan'
> And concentrates his worship on
> The real and living Hummer.

Marie's interest in Stratford led to a genuine desire for its conservation. Many of her ideas were sound, but her efforts were often marred by egocentricity and tactlessness. Nevertheless, her first campaign was a great success. When Sir Theodore Martin proposed to erect a large memorial to his wife, the actress, Helen Faucit, opposite Shakespeare's monument in Holy Trinity, Marie wrote a letter of protest to the *Morning Post*, which engendered considerable support, but her triumph was due to assiduous research. When Sir Arthur Hodgson, the High Steward of the Borough, applied for a faculty to remove two monuments to make room for the Faucit memorial, she secured the opposition of the descendants of those commemorated, ensuring that Sir Theodore had to be content with donating a handsome stone pulpit.

After a brief and cautious honeymoon, relations between Stratford and Marie were beginning to sour. She was soon at war with Dr. Earnshaw Hewer, her next-door neighbour, accusing him and his wife of spying on her over the fence. On the other side, the boys of Trinity College kicked balls and threw missiles into her garden, despite the efforts of Mr. Beckwith, the harassed headmaster, to restrain them: the greater the fury of Marie, the more provocative the boys became. According to the childhood memories of Ursula Bloom, a boy named Skinner nearly blew himself up in attempting to bombard Miss Corelli's new winter garden with a starting cannon bought from Mr. Sleath's shop in the High Street.

Storm clouds were gathering elsewhere. Marie's relations with the Bensons were soon delicate. She was irritated when refused entry to a dress rehearsal, upset when the Bensons pleaded pressure of work and turned down an invitation to lunch and mortified when Mrs. Benson's messenger delivered the note at the servants' entrance. During Benson's absence from the Festival of 1900 she vented her feelings in reviews for the London papers, praising copiously John Coleman's ludicrous *Pericles* and pouring her wrath on some of the other actors, one of whom, Corbett Thalborg, brought a successful libel action against her.

In the summer of 1901, Marie entered the parade of decorated boats which closed the annual regatta. A punt was elaborately decked out as a basket of flowers, glee singers hired and she and Bertha donned their most colourful apparel. As they were preparing for their triumph, news arrived that Oscar Asche, holidaying in Stratford, had entered an exotic float, with his glamorous wife, Lily Brayton, basking as Cleopatra on a tiger-skin, hauled by a chorus of Hebrew slaves. The infuriated Marie could not bear to be runner-up and sent a curt note to the committee that her entry was for display only. Ironically her effort was thought the best, but she blamed the Boat Club for what she considered a humiliation, 'forgetting' an offer to present a Coronation Cup and mischievously citing an alleged conversation with Sir Arthur Hodgson: 'Too good for the likes of them, my dear lady. Too good for them!'

Among the children Marie took on her float was little Ursula Bloom, aged six, herself to be a prolific novelist. She was the daughter of the Reverend Harvey Bloom, a scholarly eccentric who was rector of nearby Whitchurch. Marie was charmed by this bright, pretty child and liked her to play in the garden, dedicating a children's book she wrote, *Christmas Greeting*, 'to my little child-friend, Ursula Bloom'. The *dénouement* came one day when the little girl aked her if she had been divorced. Marie's fury knew no bounds. She surmised, possibly correctly, that the child was repeating a discussion between her parents. Ordering her carriage, she drove to the Rectory and, with the parents absent, questioned the servants in front of the child. Despite this, Harvey Bloom tried to be conciliatory, but to no avail. Marie's blood was up and her determination to make a foe of this clever clergyman was as determined as it was unwise.

Marie's desire to 'lovingly and sacredly guard every old building and the form of all Stratford's old streets' led to her greatest trouble in the town. If she could have had her way, every new building would have been in the style of 'the Master's day'. In this she found common cause with local taste: even the new Boat Club was mock-Tudor. In 1902, she paid to restore the 'Tudor House' in the High Street to what was deemed its original appearance. That year the Mayor, Archibald Flower, presented three dilapidated cottages in Henley Street to the town as a site for a long-awaited free library. The American philanthropist, Andrew Carnegie, agreed to put up the money, but Marie declared herself aghast and carried opposition to the press. These, she declared fancifully, were cottages that Shakespeare had loved as a boy. She enlisted celebrities like Ellen Terry and the poetess Alice Meynell to her cause and even interpreted a polite reply from a secretary to represent the King's support. She established a private press on which she published a journal, the *Avon Star*, which launched wild attacks on those supporting the scheme and reflected her artistic prejudices, even making snide remarks about the humble origins of Ben Jonson, whose *Every Man in His Humour* was a Festival production that year.

Stratford was furious. Marie Corelli became the subject of scurrilous verses, although a contribution called 'The Avon Stir' showed a sneaking admiration for her ability to upset the local establishment;

> Miss Corelli had a notion,
> That she'd cause a great commotion,
> In Stratford by the Avon's gentle flow,
> So she launched a shilling number,
> And the tradesmen woke from slumber,
> And she prodded up the Corporation slow.
> Now the town is by the ears,
> Pa is cross and Ma's in tears,

> For 'twas a nasty thing to do,
> And the language, well 'tis shocking,
> Of those she's been a mocking,
> But we wish she'd tell us something really new.

A wag suggested that postmen in Henley Street, in deference to Miss Corelli's sensibilities, should dress as beefeaters. Andrew Carnegie was less subtle. Although he declared that he regarded the Birthplace as 'more sacred than the Holy Sepulchre', he swore that even if the cottages were as old as Jesus Christ they would come down. The age of the cottages was taken up by Marie's new adversary, Harvey Bloom, who produced a counterblast with a journal called *The Errors of the Avon Star*. Two of the cottages had been rebuilt within living memory, although he conceded that the third was Elizabethan. Miss Corelli was no friend of old buildings, for she had vandalised 'Mason Croft' with her winter garden, which looked like a Strand teashop. Even more humiliating was his defence of Ben Jonson. Of whom can he have been thinking when he declared that the poet's birth in lawful wedlock was 'at least as respectable as many a birth in higher walks of life'?

Another of Marie's eruptions was on the way. It came on 12 June 1903, when the editor of the *Herald*, George Boyden, incautiously published a letter from Fred Winter revealing that before any idea of a library was mooted, she had asked him to find out the price of the properties in Henley Street, in order, it was implied, to donate them herself. The price was too high, 'but', added Mr. Winter, 'it would have been a "Corelli", instead of a "Carnegie" library'.

Marie Corelli's lawyers issued writs for libel against Winter and Boyden (although Boyden's was withdrawn). The case was heard in a Birmingham court packed with spectators from Stratford. Marie's appearance in the box in one of her most flamboyant costumes so flustered her counsel that he asked her (to the delight of the gallery) whether she had lived in Stratford for 43 years and this to a woman who claimed to be no more than 30! When George Boyden was called Marie's counsel asked him to explain the flattering paragraphs about her which regularly appeared in the *Herald*. His answer was devastating. She wrote them herself!

The jury's verdict was for Marie, but damages were a mere farthing, with costs awarded against the respective parties. Stratford was immediately inundated with farthings: the door-steps of Miss Corelli and Mr. Winter were covered in them by passers-by and Marie had a huge cardboard one glued to her door. Fred. Winter started a 'farthing fund' for local charities. In a goodwill gesture, Marie sent £12,000, but sadly the gift was returned because she would only release those letters which showed her in a good light rather than the whole correspondence on the issue.

There is no doubt that, although Marie Corelli behaved absurdly in her dealings with the Stratfordians, many of them could be as difficult as she. Joseph Skipsey, 'the Pitman Poet', at that time quite a celebrated figure, said that the only unhappy time in his life was spent as Custodian of the Birthplace and that Stratford was no place for a poet of 'refined and sensitive nature'. As it happened, Marie gained the last laugh over Stratford. It was discovered that the cottages had once belonged to Thomas Quiney and that an obscure by-law forbade the destruction of any property which had been owned by Shakespeare's family. Threat of further legal action caused a sensible compromise and the library was established in the heavily-restored cottages, blending unobtrusively into the hotch-potch of Henley Street.

Marie, still smarting from imagined slights from the Bensons, rarely attended the Festival season, rather patronising Mrs. Sinclair's Company, popularly known as 'The Blood Tub', the last of those itinerant troupes which had been coming to Stratford for centuries and which were disappearing under the onslaught of the picture-palaces. Each summer their tent was erected for a six-week season in the field down Cherry Street. The Misses Corelli and Vyver sat grandly and incongruously in a specially constructed box, which had, unbeknown to them, been reinforced with orange boxes to support their weight. The theatrical delights available included *The Pirates of the Savannah*, or the 'Tiger-slayer of Mexico', with its 'famous duel of four with revolvers and guns in the true American fashion'; *East Lynne*, described by Ursula Bloom as 'eternally a winner'; the 'wildly exciting' *Under Two Flags* with 'The Marseillaise' played on a cornet by Master Sinclair and *Maria Marten or The Murder in the Red Barn*, advertised as 'Not for Children', which ensured 'a satisfactorily large audience who were privately hoping for something dirty'. As an added attraction, locals were employed as 'supers' and plays adapted so that they bore such titles as *The Lily of Stratford*.

The celebrated actor Henry Irving agreed to play Shylock at the Festival of 1905, but by April he was terminally ill and withdrew. Marie's tastelessness reached new depths as she seized the chance to hit back at the local establishment. In a review she wrote that Irving 'was not to be blamed for putting a wide distance between himself and the historic building on the banks of the Avon'. That summer she imported a Venetian gondola, complete with gondolier. The latter was not a success. In the parlour of the *Dirty Duck*, he developed a taste for Flower's ale and was merry at the helm once too often. He was replaced by a more phlegmatic local who must have felt uncomfortable in his Venetian costume as he paddled Marie and Bertha down the Avon. This gondola was remembered in Stratford long after Marie's other exploits had been forgotten. In 1907 Marie achieved a great social *coup* by persuading a reluctant Mark Twain to visit her. The great and aged writer was whisked about to the greater glory of Marie and later confided that he found her an 'offensive sham'.

Across the fence, another of Marie's wars continued. Trinity College had become the Army School, with the main objective of preparing boys for the military academies, which it did with some success. The change of purpose did not improve relations with Marie Corelli. In 1908 she struck, purchasing the paddock behind Mason's Croft where the boys played games. Although the lease had five years to run and Marie gave blithe assurances that she would not interfere, life under such a landlady would be intolerable. Land was purchased in Maidenhead and the school moved out.

Stratford's fury was boundless: the school was a good source of trade. Marie's windows were broken as the boys took their leave and the townspeople were generally glad for any hurt to this harridan in their midst, but this episode was Marie's last as a local controversialist: as her literary star waned she ceased to be involved in the town's squabbles. She died, a half-forgotten figure, in 1924. Bertha lived on at 'Mason Croft' until her death in 1939. Marie had intended that the house should then become a shrine for artists, dedicated to her memory – it was perhaps a recollection of uneasy relations with the Bensons which led her specifically to exclude actors from the category of artist. Even posthumously her schemes went awry. The will was declared invalid and her property was sold. Today the house is part of the postgraduate English school of Birmingham University, which would have pleased Marie until she fell out with the professors!

CHAPTER 20

'The Sleeping Soul of England'

'It is your privilege and ours . . . to help reawaken the sleeping soul of England'.

F. R. Benson, 1908.

In July 1904, George Arbuthnot held a garden party to celebrate the 25th anniversary of his incumbency. His iconoclasm extended to the occasion: rather than a closed, self-congratulatory event, anyone in the parish was invited to apply for a ticket. Thus 1,200 Stratfordians of all denominations mingled happily together. A wave of affection for this somewhat unlovable man swept the town. His achievements were remembered: his zeal for education, temperance and the sacraments; his provision of free sittings and his creation of a comprehensive parochial organisation. His fear of no man and his attempt, however erratic, to propound a social gospel made him a formidable opponent. After a vagrant was prosecuted for sleeping in a brick kiln, the vicar announced that, if men were brought to court for such trivialities, he would challenge the law by sleeping out himself. The resultant alarm on the bench rendered such action unnecessary.

Arbuthnot's eloquence and zeal would have graced the episcopal bench, but his outspokenness mitigated against such preferment. When in 1908 he was appointed Archdeacon of Coventry, his departure was characteristically controversial. His farewell sermon, a swingeing attack on low church practices at the Guild Chapel, revived a dispute over vicarial jurisdiction almost as old as Stratford which was nearing resolution through growing indifference to such issues. Increased leisure was making the church a place of elderly females. The recreation ground and cheap railway excursions were replacing the sharp moral imperative as a means of Sabbath edification. No cleric after George Arbuthnot would establish his dominance of Stratford's faith and morals.

Matters Politic

The Boer War over, the Liberals began a rapid revival. In June 1905, the Women's Liberal Association's rally at Welcombe, home of Sir George Trevelyan, M.P.,[1] opened with a strident song:

> Liberals all now rise to action,
> Rise to fight the Tory faction!
> Through their ranks now spread distraction,
> Scatter all their bands.

Next month their rising parliamentary star, Winston Churchill, received a rousing reception from a packed Corn Exchange. The *Herald* did not find him an inspiring speaker, but conceded that 'his matter is good, and when he wants to drive home a point he is particularly incisive and bitterly sarcastic'.

The election came in the following January. The amiable Tory, Philip Foster, sought re-

219

election, while the Liberals, pondering what would go down well in a Conservative area, chose Captain Kincaid-Smith, who had participated in the Jamieson Raid and been decorated during the Boer War. National politics reached a rare peak of interest that month: a mood thoroughly reflected in Stratford. Kincaid-Smith canvassed assiduously and generally found a good response, but not from George Hewins, the bricklayer, who heard him declare, to great applause, that only those who worked regularly should get relief during depressions. George was stunned:

> 'Any fool knowed that in the building trade you was never in regular work! None of us was idle – you couldn't afford to be! – it all depended on the weather and if you could find a gaffer to take you on. A gaffer might have forty blokes working for him one week, cos it suited him, three or four the next. How could you *save?* That's what we should a-been doing, Foster the Conservative bloke said, – *saving!* I went to hear him speak too. If we'd been thrifty, he said, saved for a rainy day, we'd a-been alright! Some folks was cheering, waving their hats in the air! Well, I got the last laugh. It happened a gang o' pickpockets from Brummagem came to town that day, and those as was well dressed they stripped them of everything of value: watches, pocket handkerchiefs, money! There was some long faces after the speechifying at those meetings.

Polling Day saw a high turn-out. George was given strict instructions by his wife. ' "They got the money, the jobs. You put your cross in the right place", she said, "and keep that on!", meaning my rosette. I'd been switching from the yellow to the blue and back again, according I couldn't make up my mind.'

That evening hundreds assembled in the rain in the High Street, where the electrical shop projected the results onto a screen as they were received by telephone. The Liberal landslide and the defeat of the Prime Minister, A. J. Balfour, were received with deafening cheers. Excitement increased as rumours spread that the local result was close. Indeed it was! Huge cheers greeted the announcement that Kincaid-Smith had triumphed by 148 votes.

The new member proved a dubious asset to the Liberals. In his first six months in Parliament he opposed vital party policies, while developing an idiosyncratic programme of his own: a form of conscription called 'Universal Military Training'. Lloyd-George described Stratford's representative as 'one of the freaks of the last election . . . more Tory than the Leader of the Opposition'. In his constituency he was admired by some Tories who thought he was a better member than Philip Foster, but the Liberal committee resolved to send him a strong protest, with a warning that the membership would be canvassed for its views. Subsequently an emergency meeting resolved that the executive should find 'a fit Liberal candidate'. Kincaid-Smith, who was present, announced that he would try to elicit the views of the electorate. He was as good as his word, visiting 1,500 households. He did not reveal his conclusions immediately, but it was clear that this affable eccentric felt he had a mandate to act. In Parliament he brought forward his National Training Bill under the Ten Minute Rule. One clause proposed exemption for 'habitual drunkards, persons of weak intellect, and members of both Houses of Parliament'. According to *Punch*, 'a roar of cheers and laughter greeted this happy grouping'.

Meanwhile a new party was manifesting itself. Within a week of a public meeting at the *Fountain*, a 'Socialist and Ethical Society' was formed. In 1908 local branches of the Independent Labour Party and various trades unions chose Mr. Kenneth Holden of Stratford as their parliamentary candidate. The new party had a rough infancy: often its detractors were those it sought to emancipate. One public meeting at the *Fountain* made Mr. J. C. Huckvale – not himself a Socialist – ashamed of some of his townsmen: 'The senseless and witless exclamations of the half-drunken and thriftless part of the crowd, together with the sheer inability to frame the semblance of an intelligent question, would have disgraced a horde of primitive savages.'

In 1907 the Stratford branch of the Women's Suffrage Society was formed, with four members: within a year there were over fifty. Some women proposed to raise the issue of the vote at the Conservative A.G.M., but did not do so after it was hinted that it would be discussed. It wasn't and it was predicted that at his next meeting Philip Foster might face heckling from ardent suffragists.

The local branch represented radical female gentility, holding drawing room meetings and including Lady Trevelyan and the vicar's wife amongst its adherents. Its members impressed by their lucid arguments and careful aspirates. Although they did not endorse the violence of the suffragettes, they confessed to admiring their courage. Men and reporters were barred from their meetings, but the *Herald* infiltrated a correspondent, presumably a woman, into a rally at the Town Hall. She was suitably eulogistic: 'Surely there were among those present those who were entitled to the franchise, and who could exercise it with greater safety and discretion, than nine-tenths of the present electorate. Women's enfranchisement must come, and the ladies of Stratford are helping it on at a pace mere man little dreams of'.

The Liberal government was bringing in fundamental reforms. On 1 January 1909, the lives of old people were transformed by the introduction of old age pensions. On the great day, expectant queues formed long before the post office opened. It was estimated that the measure would reduce the permanent population of the Workhouse by two-thirds and that a projected reform of the Poor Law would do the rest.

April brought the amazing news that Kincaid-Smith had resigned his seat and intended to fight a by-election to test opinion on his Bill. It was clear that such a contest would attract protagonists of the issues of the day. First in the field was Stewart Gray, notorious to many for his inflamatory speeches as leader of hunger marches for the right to work. He offered himself to the Liberals as their candidate, but they referred him to the Socialists, who in the event did not contest the seat. He withdrew to the *Fountain*, where he drew large and frequently tempestuous crowds with his fiery oratory. The Liberals selected a distinguished candidate in the Hon. Joseph Martin, a former Prime Minister of British Columbia, who later sat for St Pancras East.

Others were taking advantage of the by-election. The Free Trade Union and the Suffragists opened campaign offices. The ladies did much to enliven the otherwise predictable proceedings, holding by far the liveliest meetings when Mrs. Pankhurst spoke in the afternoon to women only and in the evening to an open assembly. A joke was circulating that there were two performances that night: one at the theatre, the other at the Corn Exchange and both were called 'Much Ado about Nothing'. Mrs. Pankhurst bristled. 'Let them see what that nothing is. In the play the nothing about which there is much ado is a woman's honour and reputation, and the much ado at this meeting is connected with a struggle for womens' rights and liberties.'

The result of the by-election, given the Government's unpopularity and the circumstances under which the contest occurred, was a foregone conclusion. That amiable parliamentary mute, Philip Foster, swept back with a huge majority. Poor Kincaid-Smith polled a mere 479 votes, but perhaps felt his point had been worth making when war broke out five years later.

Despite the magnitude of their defeat, the Liberals were not disheartened. This was another of those rare periods of electric political interest. Their years in the local political wilderness had conditioned them to defeat, making them more interested in issues than power. They adopted a local squire, Oscar Bowen, to fight Foster in the General Election of January 1910. Reform was still in the air. At the largest Liberal meeting since 1886, a packed audience sang defiance of the landed interest:

> The Land! The Land! 'Twas God gave the Land,
> The Land! The Land! The Land on which we stand!
> Why should we be beggars with our ballots in our hand?
> God gave the land to the People.

On election day, ladies flourished petitions for women's suffrage outside polling stations. Foster was again returned in a record poll with a large majority. A second General Election in December produced an almost identical result. The Liberals fielded a blind candidate, Mr. Walker King, 'a gentleman honourable in every fibre' and were not disheartened by another defeat. Out-voting was to be abolished and the rising generation could be enthused with Liberal ideals. A local branch of the National League of Young Liberals was formed with a membership of 60 young men, but no young women. The branch demonstrated great earnestness, holding meetings on topics like 'Electoral Reform', 'Payment of M.P.s', 'Naval Expenditure' and 'The Insurance Bill'.

Like most M.P.s, Philip Foster was a gentleman of independent means, regarding his service as a duty endowed by his position. When payment of members was introduced, he announced that he would retire at the next election, strongly objecting to being 'a paid representative'. Mr. Ludford Docker of Alveston Leys was selected as prospective Conservative candidate. He had captained Warwickshire at cricket and played for England in Australia. The Liberals selected Mr. John Pascoe as their candidate and Stratford looked set for another exciting contest in 1915.

The Borough Council had settled into another period of lethargy. Most local elections went uncontested and complaints about apathy were frequent. A brief controversy in 1910 brought back memories of stormier days. The son of Thomas Lunn, the town clerk, was appointed as his successor without the post being advertised – indeed it transpired that every town clerk had been appointed in this way since 1818. 'A pretty little hole-in-corner job', fumed the popular magazine *John Bull* and in Stratford a protest meeting was held. Elsewhere there was slow progress. Stratford's first six council dwellings were occupied before Christmas in 1910.

The cause of women's suffrage was gaining ground. Locally it was the Suffragists, with their reasoned arguments, who made an impact, rather than the dreaded Suffragettes, who believed in direct action.

The Suffragists were very persuasive. In the autumn of 1909, a theatrical group sponsored by the National Union of Women's Suffrage Societies, presented two playlets, *A Woman's Influence* and *How the Vote was Won*, to a large and appreciative audience at the Corn Exchange. Edith Craig, the daughter of Ellen Terry, played Mary Bull, a Lancashire lass, quietly but effectively demonstrating the social handicaps inflicted on women. 'The words put into her mouth were words of wisdom', said the *Herald*, always sympathetic to this cause.

The Suffragists intelligently avoided partisanship. In 1911 a Stratford Conservative Women's Suffrage Association was formed. Its members included Lady Willoughby de Broke, wife of the most effectively reactionary peer in Britain. Others actively opposed the movement. In 1912, the local branch of the National League for Opposing Women's Suffrage held a public meeting in the Corn Exchange, with Lady Fairfax-Lucy in the chair. A clash in the old Stratford tradition came on 16 July 1913. Fifty-six suffragists, marching to London, passed through Stratford and were welcomed by local supporters. They laid a wreath on Shakespeare's grave before holding a public meeting at the Fountain. After the first speaker, Miss Hanbury, had welcomed the 'jolly sporting' ladies, unruly spirits in the crowd began a barrage of continuous heckling. The mob surged towards the platform and several ladies were jostled. Arrests were made, but the cacophony was irrepressible. The crowd was clearly organised to prevent the speeches and the meeting was abandoned, but from another platform the formidable Mrs. Despard, a sister of Sir John French, awed the remnant of the crowd into silence.

Archdeacon Arbuthnot took up his pen to express shame and regret that his old parish should disgrace itself 'by the violence shown by some contemptible rascals to ladies, who, whether we agree with their views or not, are peaceable citizens and entitled to that free speech, which, within the rights of the law, is the birthright of every Briton'.

The 'Suffragist Riot' was the last flourish of the mob. A year later events would engage at least some of them on a more deadly business than denying a hearing to a few women.

42. Cover of the 1903 programme for the Benson Company's season.

Indian Summer

Despite the lengthening shadows which darkened the Edwardian era, the image of the age is of an Indian summer. In Stratford this was due at least partially to the Bensons. The Company had become an institution and there was even an Old Bensonian Association. On May Day 1905, like a gathering of former pupils, they remembered old comrades with the first of a group of stained glass windows on the staircase in the theatre lobby. Four dead actors were commemorated, including Frank Rodney.

Yet this very institutionalism was causing muted but mounting criticism. The sameness of the productions and the domination of them by the Bensons was disillusioning a new generation of theatregoers, although the multitudes who loved the Company remained forever faithful. F.R.B. was aware of this feeling and went some way to meet it. Leading actors were engaged, some guesting with the Bensonians, others bringing their own productions. Thus began a 'star' system which lasted over half a century. First to come was the matinée idol, Lewis Waller, who played Othello in 1907 and returned as Henry V in the following year, when Constance Collier acted Juliet and Helen Haye, Mistress Page.

As Benson's dominance diminished, so the affection of the Stratfordians increased. Each April crowds gathered at the station to welcome the Company. The approaches were decorated with flags and banners. One hung across the road bore the appropriate Shakespearean motto: 'To meet you on your way and welcome you' and the railway company placed fog detonators on the line, which exploded as the train approached. Once Constance Benson was shocked when one of the porters, 'meaning to be most appreciative and gracious', said to her, 'We have a lot to thank you and Mr. Benson for, you are making Stratford another Blackpool'.

43. *Lewis Waller as Henry V, which he played at Stratford during the season festival of 1908.*

Another custom was added to the Birthday celebations in 1907, when the King donated a Union Jack to be unfurled at the opening. In the following year it was joined by the flags of the nations, 'to signify the universality of Shakespeare's genius' and after the Austro-Hungarian ambassador unfurled the flags of the dual Empire in 1910, it became customary to invite the representatives of the nations to perform this task.

Benson was developing a quasi-mystical view of Stratford. Influenced by his own romantic spirit and his contact with the Irish revival, he began to regard it as Stratford's destiny to be 'a Temple of the Anglo-Celtic race'. His closing speech at the 1908 Festival expressed the theme. 'It is your privilege and ours', he told the adoring audience, 'in this building to help reawaken the sleeping soul of England.'

That year on the Bancroft, Benson inaugurated a day of 'Old English Sports and Games'. Children danced round the Maypole, skipped, sweated at the tug-of-war and a May-Queen of dark eyes and raven locks was crowned. Later the adults did their bit: 'catch as catch can' and 'pick a back' wrestling, the greasy pole climbed for a leg of mutton, fencing, stick fighting and Morris dancing. On the river there was gondola racing and tilting in boats, while an Elizabethan state barge, full of glee singers, rowed up and down.

In 1909 the Old Bensonian, Matheson Lang, brought his Lyceum Company in *Hamlet*, Constance Collier played Portia and Johnstone Forbes-Robertson presented *The Passing of the Third Floor Back*, preceded by an extract from *Henry VIII*, in which the great actor-manager played Buckingham. 1910 promised to be the grandest Festival yet, lasting four weeks. There were two Hamlets, Mr. Martin Harvey's being given the edge over the production which brought Sir Herbert Beerbohm Tree and Marie Lohr. Constance Benson met Tree at the station and he looked with great interest at the Birthday decorations before asking, 'Is all this kind thought for me?' Benson staged an Old Bensonian matinée in which past favourites performed in extracts from Shakespeare's comedies. The audience was enraptured, calling the Bensons to the curtain before every scene. Ellen Terry returned to play Portia, with her husband, James Carew, as Shylock. She was 63, short-sighted and weak on memory, but the audience was determined to make the occasion an overwhelming success. That night the news arrived that the King had died and the Festival was abandoned. For some time it had been under consideration to revive the Summer Festival. Here was the ideal opportunity, given greater poignancy in that Benson was to match Garrick by becoming a freeman of Stratford. As part of his scheme for cultural revival, he had organised a competition for a new play set in a period before 1800. The winner, probably chosen because it employed the scores of children Benson liked to swarm through his *Dream*, was *The Piper*, a verse drama of Hamelin by Josephine Preston Peabody. It was decided to premier it at the Summer Festival, which now became an annual fixture.

At the Town Hall on 25 July, Benson received his freedom in an oak casket and quoted lines from *The Piper*. 'This day you have constituted me your knight, your friend, your serving man. I hope I may be spared to owe you still my life and service.' He and Constance were drawn through the streets in a decorated carriage, as the townspeople bombarded them with flowers.

The Piper was not a success and lost money when it transferred to London. Never a sound administrator, Benson's resources had been exhausted by the loss of Festival receipts to the celebrity performances, the curtailing of the Spring Festival and the losses of *The Piper*. The Theatre governors and their chairman, Archie Flower, helped with grants and loans, but it was never enough. Thus a syndicate, the Stratford-upon-Avon Players, was formed to run the Company. Benson was paid a generous salary, but one of Archie Flower's provisos was that Constance should no longer pick her parts, but be replaced in certain roles by younger actresses.

The old order, including Constance, survived the Spring Festival of 1911. Fred Terry, forgetful of his lines, but dominant of his part, played Benedick to the Beatrice of his wife, Julia Neilson. Lewis Waller came as Romeo and Oscar Asche played an Othello of primitive passion. Benson was showing great talent as an impresario: the National Theatre Society of Dublin, a manifestation of the Celtic revival he so admired, brought three controversial new plays: *Kathleen ni Houlihan* by W. B. Yeats, *The Rising of the Moon* by Lady Gregory and *Playboy of the Western World* by J. M. Synge.

It was the latter which drew the fire (its presentation in Dublin had led to riots). 'Blasphemous', 'indecent', 'reeking of the pothouse', 'impious', 'disgraceful', were some of the epithets hurled by the departing audience. One man declared that he would have given £20 not to have seen it. The critic of the *Manchester Guardian* had a more balanced view:

> It does not seem to some of the worshippers at Shakespeare's shrine . . . that Synge's play is not the only one that reeks of the pothouse, and that if by some operation the cateract of literary respectability which blinds them could be removed, *Henry IV* and *The Merry Wives of Windsor* and a crowd of scenes and figures in other plays would appear so 'impious', indecent' and 'disgraceful' that, without doubt, they would willingly incur a much larger forfeit of £20 to be spared the pain of seeing them. Antiquity gilds the disreputable; the rags and tatters and profane speech of common humanity become amiable if it is long enough dead.

The Bensons continued their own version of revivalist folk art in the May Day celebrations; subconscious compensation, perhaps, for loss of power at the Theatre. For Constance, even this ostensibly harmless activity had its tensions as she became reluctantly embroiled in disputes about the correct style of Morris dancing – 'stiff' or 'loose' knee. Some mocked such attempts to revive 'the true spirit of Merrie England', but despite, or perhaps because of, the arguments, the Stratfordians loved it. For the first time, a part of the season was truly theirs.

The May Day of 1912 was the most elaborate yet. Scores of children were decked in smocks and print gowns from the Bensonian wardrobe. The procession was led by a white knight on a white horse, followed by a Maypole. Each flowered ribbon was clutched by a girl in white and it was escorted by six girls in smocks – all from Shottery School. Behind came the fantastic figure of Jack o' the Green, a man enclosed in an elaborate frame of evergreens, leading the Stratford schoolchildren, girls first, in white dresses and bonnets. At the Birthplace, the procession halted and these children sang and danced. Next came six sweeps with a master sweep, a hobby horse, a clown, a fiddler and the children of Ilmington, a village whose dance traditions had never died. The May Queen was preceded by six maids with peeled wands and four maids with candles and escorted by four maids of honour. She was riding on a decorated cart pulled by four white oxen from a Shottery farm. There had been concern about how these beasts would take to the hard streets and cheering crowds, but they were led by their carters in smocks and 'treated it calmly', in Ursula Bloom's words, as 'a lot of silly nonsense'. There was more to come: Robin Hood and Maid Marian with six foresters, another clown and fiddler, Barford School with another maypole and Binton School with a tableau about weaving. In front of the Theatre Benson crowned the May Queen. A photograph caught the moment. Benson raises the crown as if he is playing Prince Hal; the little Queen is blandly bemused by the whole odd show; the Maids of Honour gather round, one with an expression that says 'My turn next'. After the crowning, the schools demonstrated the results of weeks of careful rehearsal, performing their elaborate and stately dances.

A few days after this extravagant happiness, Archie Flower, in a painful meeting, told Constance that her future role was to be different. Through pain or tact she did not return that summer and her roles were played by Dorothy Green. Musical Director during 1912 and 1913 was Dr. Ralph Vaughan Williams, who wrestled with Benson's musical philistinism, set his famous arrangement of *Greensleeves* for a production of the *Dream*, lectured on folk song and received an inscribed baton from admiring playgoers.

The Benson legend was irrepressible amidst the audience it had created. In the spring of 1913, Constance returned by popular demand to play leading parts. She was met at the station with bouquets and when she screeched her first off-stage words as Doll Tearsheet, the audience erupted in cheers. That spring saw the Stratford debut of a great actress. Edith Evans played Cressida with William Poel's English Stage Society: she made her last Stratford appearance, under the direction of Peter Hall, nearly 60 years later. Another friend of Fame made a debut that summer: Basil Rathbone, straight from Repton and looking a 'glorious Apollo'. In September, the Stratford-upon-Avon Players toured North America for nine months to mixed receptions amongst audiences for whom the Benson mystique did not create an advance atmosphere of success. Constance, elated by her Stratford reception, was over-demanding, did not go and escaped a savaging from the Chicago critics. Benson's stand-in for the Spring Festival of 1914, Patrick Kirwan, made little impact, but he was not entirely to blame. Oscar Asche withdrew after an accident and Sir Herbert Beerbohm Tree forgot to appear. The *Herald*, getting daring as the Victorian age receded, likened one production to 'an Orgie in Babylon with its clothes on'.

Trit, Trit, Trot

Customs are often noted as they wane. Benson's 'Merrie England' revivalism led to an interest in recording what was disappearing for ever. One very old lady recalled that dancers competed for ribbons in the 1820s. At the end of the day there was a ribbon dance, in which only the winners participated. Susan Rice, from an old Stratford family, remembered that, 50 years before, any boy arriving at the Grammar School on Oak Apple Day without a sprig of oak in his cap would be buffetted by the other boys with cries of 'Ship-shap: no oak in your cap'. Even stranger was a custom recalled by the librarian, Salt Brassington. On May Day, the sweeps paraded the streets, singing, capering and making discordant noises to attract attention. One was decked in traditional foliage as 'Jack in the Green': another, dressed as a clown, collected coppers in a long ladle thrust at passers-by. Formal dances occurred at set points. In the rituals of May Day the sweep possessed a special and forgotten significance and his character was often represented in the children's dances.

One of the last repositories of this declining folk-culture was the playground. May Day songs were particularly well preserved in the Stratford area, partly as a legacy of poverty: they represented a legitimised opportunity for children to beg. A 'Maybrush' of hawthorn was cut from the hedgerow and ribbons, bright-coloured rags and flowers were tied to its branches. The children dressed up in whatever finery and garlands they could get hold of. One held the Maybrush and the others danced round it, chanting the May Day song. Each parish had its own version, which was passed down from child to child. The one most sung at Stratford went:

> Dance around the Maypole,
> Trit, trit, trot,
> See what a Maypole
> We have got.
> Fine and gay,
> Skip away,
> Happy as the new Mayday.
> For God save the King!
> Garlands above.
> Garlands below,
> See what a Maypole
> We can show,
> Fine and gay,
> Skip away,
> Happy as the new Mayday.
> For God save the King!
> Our box it shall stand
> At the shade of your hand,
> Whatever you choose to bestow.
> Gentlemen and ladies
> Don't turn away,
> On the first day of May!

Other, cruder ceremonies went unrecorded. Trades had vulgar initiation ceremonies. Young Bob Jones was sent off by his mother to his first day as an apprentice railway clerk, with instructions to take care of his best suit. When he arrived at work his new colleagues seized him, removed his knickerbockers and smothered his private parts in axle grease. The fury of his mother on his sorry return was considerable.

But traditions were being forgotten as technical innovation stretched horizons. In July 1912, Stratfordians thrilled to their first sight of an aeroplane. A great cheer went up as it appeared over Bordon Hill, circled and landed on the Recreation Ground. The pilot, Monsieur Salmet of the *Daily Mail* flying corps, then flew over the hospital so that the nurses and patients could see his wonder. Before departing he gave a breathtaking exhibition, diving, flying between trees and skimming the river like a bird.

The steps of the May dancers faltered further that October with the opening of the Picture

House in Greenhill Street. Here was a place of dreams, with exotic murals of ladies in gondolas amidst romantic nights in Venice. The Working Men's Club found it difficult to compete with its wonders. Despite splendid facilities attendance was poor. 'The young men', said the *Herald*, 'have succumbed to the fascinations of the picture palace, and the click of the billiard ball, the ping of the bullet, is rarely heard on the club premises.'

How he thought he was going to use it—

—And how he did use it.

44. First World War cartoon by Bruce Bairnsfather.

War and its Aftermath

The *Herald*, which a few years before had expressed its admiration for the Kaiser, had become convinced that England's chief potential enemy lay over the German Ocean. In 1913, it noted that pessimists considered war with Germany inevitable. Yet in July 1914, the paper relegated news of the assassination of the Austrian Archduke below such items as 'The Search for Fertilisers' and 'Municipal Apathy'. Summer wound its usual way. The regulars at the *One Elm* organised an outing to Blackpool; at Hereford regatta the Stratford eight won the West of England Challenge Vase; the G.W.R. announced August Bank Holiday excursions to South Coast resorts and, nearer home, to the Kineton Horticultural Show and a river trip to Cleeve, which included tea.

Amidst this tranquillity war clouds were gathering. The *Herald* took more seriously the Austrian bombardment of Belgrade. To match the hour the Picture House showed *The Hundred Days*, which culminated in a spectacular portrayal of the Battle of Waterloo. On 31 July, a reception was held in the Theatre gardens for the returning Bensonians. F.R.B., back with his own company again (the syndicate had been dissolved), made a balanced speech, recalling that from the same source as

> Come the three corners of the world in arms,
> And we shall shock them. Nought shall make us rue,
> If England to itself do rest but true.

there had come also 'One touch of nature makes the whole world kin.' He concluded amidst applause that the one thought should not preclude the other in the trials that were to come. On 4 August war was declared and there was a special performance of *Henry V* – 'now all the youth of England are on fire' – with Basil Rathbone as the Dauphin. After curtain-fall the company drilled on stage with halberds and spears.

Already food shortages were apparent, popularly blamed on hoarding by unscrupulous middlemen.[2] Some feared that a prolonged war would produce near-starvation. Despite such fears an intense patriotic fervour swept the area. A recruiting station in Sheep Street was swamped with volunteers. Stratford was contributing more men to the war effort than any town in the county three times its size. A Roll of Honour of local recruits was displayed from the Town Hall. A new company of Territorial Rifles had temporary headquarters lent by the vicar in the parish parlour. First commander was the 26-year-old Major Bruce Bairnsfather of Bishopton, an artist who was a noted figure in local theatricals. He would devise a prime image of the War with his cartoon character, 'Old Bill' of 'If you know a better 'ole, go to it' fame.

All activity became subordinate to the war. The Mayor, Councillor Fred Winter, in sentencing a drunk to a month's imprisonment, told him that all Englishmen should be keeping the peace. The Picture House screened the latest war news and appeals to 'The Common Cause': 'Eat no eggs in Easter Week', suggested a headline in the *Herald*, 'but give them to the wounded.' The Town Hall became a hospital with 40 beds filled by wounded Belgian soldiers. The *Herald* was reduced to six pages, an indignity which may have influenced its view that economics precluded a lengthy war. Some considered that the war would be over by Christmas and the troops home in the spring. Political differences ceased: a mass meeting at the *Fountain* was addressed by the Tory and Liberal parliamentary candidates. On 7 October the first Stratfordian died in action when Sergeant J. H. Savage of 24 Henley Street, was struck by shrapnel at the Battle of the Aisne. In December, the recruiting office, desperate for men, announced that the minimum height had been reduced to five feet. Attention turned to the 100 'unwilling and selfish' young men who had not volunteered. One big strong fellow of about 26 caused derision when asked 'Why not enlist?' by replying 'Mother won't let me.' The father of four youths sent them to London to escape the recruiting officer. The *Herald* considered that taxpayers should 'give those enlistable men no peace until they do their duty. Failing that they should give the government no rest until the order is issued for conscription.'

F.R.B. was back in the spring of 1915 with a much-depleted company. Age had prevented him enlisting despite several attempts, but at least he could boost morale as Henry V. Oscar Asche played Shylock and Genevieve Ward, Queen Margaret, to stalls filled with the convalescent blue of the wounded. On the Birthday the flags were absent: a ceremony intended to preach the unity of the nations was inappropriate. More and more wounded were returning from 'the inferno on the continent': a military hospital was opened at Clopton House and the spectacle of those who had lost limbs at the front was becoming sadly familiar. The Mop was a shadow of its former glories. Only two beasts were roasted and there were no excursion trains, but thousands thronged the town, glad of the temporary illusion of relief from war, although the recruiting sergeant mingling with the crowds served as a reminder. The Mop continued through the War, but had to close at 6.30 p.m. because of the war regulations. It is a reflection of the growing gloom that few thought it would ever recover its former jollity.

Early in 1916 came the Zeppelin scare. The news that enemy aircraft had raided unspecified locations in the Midlands was sufficient to send Stratfordians into a panic: some took cover in cellars and shelters on hearing the news that Zeppelins had crossed the east coast. The anti-German propaganda which had prevailed for two years bore inadvertent fruit: saturated with stories of Hunnish atrocities against cultural institutions, Stratfordians believed their town would be a prime target. Word of this penetrated to Berlin where the press waxed indignant at the suggestion, declaring that Germans so venerated Shakespeare that they would do nothing to violate the sanctity of his birthplace. This 'touch of nature' was not reciprocated in Stratford. At the Town Council of 8 February, the Mayor, Archie Flower, said that its priceless historic buildings could cause Germany to pick out Stratford. 'We also have our due complement of women and children and that is another reason for Germany coming against us.' Blackout orders were introduced. 'Until the war is over', said the *New York Evening Mail*, 'Stratfordians shall go to bed with the chickens or spend their evenings in darkness.' Offenders against the Lighting Orders were fined, including a clergyman and the owner of 'Hall's Croft'.

Conscription entailed the establishment of war tribunals, where appeals were heard from those who argued that their work was vital. Generally the response was the same: a short period of grace was given in which the appellant could arrange alternatives – a woman, a boy or a discharged soldier. The emancipation of women was becoming a necessity as more jobs were propelled into the female domain by acute labour shortages. Albert Pearce, a confectioner of Wood Street, was given a respite to sort out his business affairs, but that night, in the back bar of *The Windmill*, a woman gave him the white feather of cowardice. He promptly enlisted in the Durham Light Infantry, temporarily billeted in Stratford, *en route* for Salonika. Such was the need for manpower that he was embarked immediately and did not receive a uniform till he got to Marseilles.

The censors had learned their lesson from the Boer War and news from the front was generalised and sparse. Even letters recounting the stories of deaths, sent to sorrowing relatives by comrades, had a sameness: all died instantly and without pain.

A release for Stratfordians from the horrors of war was provided by the knighting of Frank Benson, with characteristic theatricality, in the Royal Box at Drury Lane Theatre. The news was announced to a delighted Festival audience at the Memorial Theatre and cheers resounded through the house. Next day, cheering crowds waited at the station and sheaves of lilies were presented to Lady Benson and a chaplet of bays to Sir Frank, before the townspeople drew them to the Theatre in an open landau.

After this even Benson deserted Stratford. He and Constance ran a canteen for wounded soldiers in France. After Ben Greet brought a depleted Old Vic Company in the summer of 1916, there were no more Festivals for the duration of the war. Many were the sad reflections on the emptiness of Stratford during these two bitter years. The town was devoid of men under 40 and the lengthening casualty lists, which even rigorous censorship could not suppress, recorded those who would not return. Eventual victory was muted by reflection on the scores of the fallen which the *Herald* had poignantly recorded throughout the War. Four years later, the War Memorial was dedicated at the top of Bridge Street. At a second ceremony in the summer of 1925, Dame Ellen Terry silently unveiled two more windows in the Theatre Gallery to dead Bensonians: one for those lost in the War, who included Benson's son, Eric.

In 1919 Frank Benson returned for a brief April season to re-open the Theatre. Archibald Flower showed the percipience of his uncle, the Founder. He knew how much had changed: the Festival, to survive, must become a national event. In such a scheme there was no longer a place for Benson. Constance thought of the banished Norfolk:

> I am too old to fawn upon nurse,
> Too far in years to be a pupil now.

Benson had tried to weld his theatrical dream to a dream of Stratford. Now both were swept away. The Stratford of May Queens crowned in Edwardian sunlight had vanished, just as the Maypole, a symbol which had stirred Jacobean riots, had been anaesthetised to folk-art. In the post-war era, the internal combustion engine brought trippers in their hordes to destroy the delicate balance of the little town and took Stratfordians to work in the surrounding cities. Rows of 'semis' spread out along the main roads to accommodate newcomers or to rehouse townspeople away from the cramped alleys which had been their homes for generations. The place was going through another of those periods of change which had transformed it over the centuries. Many would dislike this process and the Stratford it produced, but there was little they could do to avert it.

FOOTNOTES

[1]   Father of the historian, G. M. Trevelyan, who was born at Welcombe in 1876.
[2]   In 1918, Marie Corelli was, somewhat unjustly, convicted of hoarding sugar and faced the humiliation of a fine in the Magistrates' Court.

South East Prospect of Stratford upon Avon 1746.

Postscript

The Theatre Gallery and its windows survived the ravages of a great fire on the blustering afternoon of 6 March 1926, which destroyed the auditorium and provoked G. B. Shaw into sending a telegram of congratulation that the old, restricted building had been destroyed. For five years the Festivals were housed at the Picture House, while a new and controversial building designed by Elizabeth Gilbert Scott arose next to the ashes of the old.[1] The new theatre was opened on the Birthday in 1932, but for many the real opening came with an Old Bensonian matinée at Whitsuntide, at which Sir Frank made his last Stratford appearance and was presented with a laurel chaplet simply inscribed 'Pa'. The 'star' system he had reluctantly pioneered was maintained under a succession of directors, but in 1960 Peter Hall launched a new phase in the life of the Stratford Theatre: a permanent company and an additional London home. Just as Archibald Flower had extended the ideal of his uncle, the Founder, so now, under the chairmanship of his son, the Royal Shakespeare Company[2] sought and gained international status. In the process it ceased to be uniquely of Stratford, but such change was a necessity for survival.

The Birthday, too, was becoming more an international than a local institution, attended by more and more representatives of the nations. In the 1930s the presence of the Nazi flag presaged another war which manifested itself in the skies over Stratford.

The borough council ceased to be in the local government changes of 1974 and the town is reduced to the status of a parish, although the Mayor and all his trappings blend with other traditions to give an air of continuity. Around that time Flower's brewery closed, victim of a tendency to bigger units. With its demise went what had been one of Stratford's staple industries over the centuries and also part of the heritage of local initiative which had given the town its character. All that remains is a logo on a beer brewed elsewhere and the concrete slabs which cover the artesian wells of the vanished brewhouse.

FOOTNOTES
[1]   In 1986 a new theatre-in-the-round, *The Swan*, was established in the shell of the old auditorium.
[2]   A title conferred by royal charter.

Select Bibliography

It would have been prohibitive of space and time to have documented every reference in the book. Some are mentioned in footnotes, some in the text. At the end of each reference in this bibliography, a note indicates the chapters to which the material most appertains. Books of general interest do not carry such a reference. I have marked with a * some books which might particularly interest the reader who wants to learn more about the history of Stratford.

Manuscripts

Borough of Stratford, *Accounts of the Chamberlains*: Birthplace Library.
——, *Bridge Book of the Corporation*: Birthplace Library.
——, Council Books of the Corporation: Birthplace Library.
Daniel, George, *The Jubilee*: scrapbook in the British Museum. [9]
Flower, C. E., *Scrapbooks in the Birthplace Library*. [17-19]
*——, Sarah, *Aunt Sarah's Diary*, beginning with her copy of the early reminiscences of C. E. Flower: Birthplace Library. [13-19]
Hill, Joseph, *Joseph Hill, His Book*: Birthplace Library. [10-12]
Hobbes, Robert and Elizabeth (*nee* Ashford), *Diaries and Papers*: Birthplace Library. [10-12]
Hunt, William, *The Hunt and Garrick Correspondence*: Birthplace Library. [9]
Miscellaneous Documents, Borough records in the Birthplace Library; 16 vols. (listed in Halliwell[-Philips]'s *Calendar*.
Morgan, John, manuscript reminiscences in the Birthplace Library. [17-19]
Rowley, Miss F. D., *Stratford-upon-Avon in the Seventies*: typescript reminiscences in the Birthplace Library. [17]
*Saunders, James, *An Account of the Stratford Jubilee*: Birthplace Library. [9]
——, ——, *Jubilee Correspondence*. [9]
——, ——, *Stratford Races and the Theatre*: Birthplace Library. [8-12]
Stratford-upon-Avon parish records, comprising the parish registers, documents concerning charities and other miscellaneous papers.
Wheler, Robert Bell, *An Account of the Jubilee at Stratford on Avon*: Birthplace Library. [9]
——, ——, *Collections on the Stratford Jubilee*: Birthplace Library. [9]
——, ——, *Wheler Papers*: Birthplace Library.

Newspapers

The Stratford-upon-Avon Chronicle, 1861-1886. [14-16]
The Stratford-upon-Avon Herald, 1860-1921. [14-20]
The Warwick Advertiser, 1806-60. [11-14]
The Warwickshire Chronicle, 1826-35. [12-14]

Printed Works

Adderley, H. A., *A History of the Warwickshire Yeomanry Cavalry* (W. H. Smith & Son, Warwick, 1912). [10-11]

Barber, Alexander, *A Church of the Ejectment, Stratford-upon-Avon* (Stratford-on-Avon, 1912). [7-13]

Bearman, Robert, *Education in Stratford-upon-Avon* (Shakespeare's Birthplace Trust, 1976). [10-14]

——, ——, *Stratford-upon-Avon as it was* (Hendon Publishing Co., Nelson, Lancs, 1978). [16-20]

Benson, Constance, *Mainly Players* (Thornton Butterworth, London, 1926). [18-20]

——, Frank, *My Memoirs* (Ernest Bain, London, 1930). [18-20]

Bisset, James, *Bisset's (Anticipated) Joys of the Jubilee, at Stratford-upon-Avon* (Leamington, 1827). [12]

The Black Book of Warwick; ed. Thomas Kemp (Henry C. Cooke & Son, Warwick, 1898). [2]

Bloom, J. Harvey, *Shakespeare's Church* (T. Fisher Unwin, 1902).

——, Ursula, *Rosemary for Stratford-on-Avon* (Robert Hale, London). [19-20]

Boswell, James, *Boswell in Search of a Wife*; ed. Frank Brady and Frederick A. Pottle (London, 1957). [9]

Brinkworth, E. R. C., *Shakespeare and the Bawdy Court of Stratford* (Phillimore, Chichester, 1972). [3-6]

Brown, Ivor, *Shakespeare* (Collins, 1949). [2-5]

——, ——, Ivor and George Feardon, *Amazing Monument: A Short History of the Shakespeare Industry* (London, 1939).

Chambers, E. K., *William Shakespeare, A Study of Facts and Problems*, 2 vols. (Oxford University Press, 1930). [2-6]

Concise Account of Garrick's Jubilee . . . and of the Commemorative Festivals in 1827 and 1830 (Stratford, 1830). [9-13]

Cradock, Joseph, *Literary and Miscellaneous Memoirs*; 4 vols (London, 1830). [9]

*Deelman, Christian, *The Great Shakespeare Jubilee* (Michael Joseph, 1964). [9]

Dodd, James Solas, *Essays and Poems* (Corke, 1770). [9]

*Eccles, Mark, *Shakespeare in Warwickshire* (The University of Wisconsin Press, 1963). [2-6]

England, Martha Winburn, *Garrick and Stratford* (New York, 1962). [9]

——, ——, *Garrick's Jubilee* (Ohio State University Press, 1964). [9]

Fairfax-Lucy, Alice, *Charlecote and the Lucys* (Oxford University Press, 1958). [3]

Forest, H. E., *The Old Houses of Stratford-upon-Avon* (Methuen & Co., 1925).

*Fox, Levi, *The Borough Town of Stratford-upon-Avon* (Stratford, 1953).

*——, ——, *The Heritage of Shakespeare's Birthplace*: Shakespeare Survey 1 (Cambridge, 1948).

Fripp, Edgar, *Master Richard Quiney* (Oxford University Press, 1924). [2-5]

——, ——, *Shakespeare: Man and Artist*, 2 vols. (OUP, 1938). [2-5]

——, ——, *Shakespeare's Haunts near Stratford* (OUP, 1929). [2-5]

——, ——, *Shakespeare's Stratford* (OUP, 1928). [2-6]

The Gild Register, Stratford-upon-Avon; ed. J. Harvey Bloom (Phillimore, Chichester, 1907). [1]

*Greene, Joseph, *The Correspondence of the Rev. Joseph Greene, parson, schoolmaster and antiquary*; ed. Levi Fox (HMSO, London, 1965). [8-10]

Hadfield, C. and Norris, J., *Waterways to Stratford* (David and Charles, 1962). [12-17]

Halliwell, J. O., *A Descriptive Calendar of the Ancient Manuscripts and Records in the Possession of the Corporation of Stratford-upon-Avon* (1863).

——, ——, *An Historical Account of the New Place, Stratford-upon-Avon* (1864).

*Hewins, Angela (ed.), *The Dillen, Memories of a Man of Stratford-upon-Avon* (Elm Tree Books, London, 1981). [18-20]

Ingleby, C. M., *Shakespeare and the Enclosure of the Common Fields at Welcombe* (1885). [5]

Irving, Washington; chapter on Stratford from *The Sketch Book*, ed. Richard Savage and W. Salt Brassington (Shakespeare Quiney Press, 1900). [11]

——, ——; chapter on Stratford from *The Sketch Book*.

Jarvis, J. A. *Correct Detail of the Ceremonies attending the Shakespearean Gala at Stratford-upon-Avon, 1827; Together with some Account of Garrick's Jubilee, 1769* (Stratford, 1827). [9-12]

Joseph, Harriet, *Shakespeare's Son-in-Law: John Hall, Man and Physician* (Hamden Conn., 1964). [6]

Kemp, T. C. and J. C. Trewin, *The Stratford Festival* (London, 1953).

Lee, Sidney, *Stratford-upon-Avon from the Earliest Times to the Death of Shakespeare* (new ed., 1904).

Malone, Edmund, *Original Letters . . . to John Jordan, the Poet*, ed. J. O. Halliwell (privately printed, London, 1864). [10]

*Masters, Brian, *Now Barabbas was a Rotter* (the story of Marie Corelli) (Hamish Hamilton, London, 1978). [19, 20]

Mordaunt, C. and W. R. Verney, *Annals of the Warwickshire Hunt* (Sampson Low, Marston and Co., 1896). [10].

Morley, *The Story of Methodism in Stratford-on-Avon*.

Mullen, Michael, *Theatre at Stratford-upon-Avon*, 2 vols. (Greenwood Press, Westport, Connecticut, 1980).

Savage, Richard and Fripp, Edgar (ed.), *Minutes and Accounts of the Corporation of Stratford-upon-Avon*, Vols. I-X (Publications of the Dugdale Society, 1921-30). [2-6]

*Schoenbaum, S., *William Shakespeare, A Documentary Life* (The Clarendon Press, Oxford in association with The Scolar Press, 1976). [2-6]

Sibice, John and M. Cason, *Independency in Warwickshire* (1855). [7-13]

Simpson, Frank, *New Place: the Only Representation of Shakespeare's House, from an Unpublished Manuscript*, Shakespeare Survey 5, p. 52 (Cambridge, 1952). [8]

*Styles, Philip, 'Account of the History of Stratford' in *The Victoria History of the County of Warwick*, Vol. III, pp. 221-8 (1945).

Terry, Ellen and St John, Christopher, *Ellen Terry's Memoirs* (Ernest Benn, London, 1933). [19-20]

'Topographical Notes', ed. by Rev. J. H. Bloom: reprinted from *The Stratford-upon-Avon Herald* (1903). [1]

*Trewin, J. C., *Benson and the Bensonians* (Barrie and Rockliff, London, 1960). [18-20]

——, ——, *The Story of Stratford-upon-Avon* (Staples Press, 1950).

Vestry Minute Book, Stratford-upon-Avon, 1617-1699, ed. G. Arbuthnot (Bedford Press, 1890). [5-8]

Victor, Benjamin, *The History of the London Theatre, from 1760-1771* (London, 1771). [9]

Ward, Revd. John, Diary of, 1648-79, ed. Charles Severn, 1839, from the original preserved in the Library of the Medical Society of London. [7]

Wellstood, F. C., *Rambles among the Old Records of Stratford-on-Avon*.

——, ——, *Shakespeare Club Papers* (Stratford-upon-Avon, 1920). [12-14]

——, ——, 'Stratford-upon-Avon Papers', reproduced from *The Stratford-upon-Avon Herald* (1915-21).

Wheler, Robert Bell, *History and Antiquities of Stratford-upon-Avon* (Stratford, 1806).

INDEX: Part One, People

Part Two: General